D0494865

Second Amongst Equals

Second Amongst Equals

Chancellors of the Exchequer and the British Economy

Richard Holt

P
PROFILE BOOKS

First published in Great Britain in 2001 by
Profile Books Ltd
58A Hatton Garden
London ECIN 8LX
www.profilebooks.co.uk

10 9 8 7 6 5 4 3 2 1

Designed and typeset in Sabon by MacGuru
info@macguru.org.uk

Printed and bound in Great Britain by
St Edmundsbury Press, Bury St Edmunds

A CIP catalogue record for this book is available from the British Library.

ISBN 1 86197 028 5

Contents

Introduction

IN HIS MEMOIRS, *In Office*, Norman Lamont tells a sad tale. On the afternoon of his resignation from government, following his sacking by John Major from the post of Chancellor of the Exchequer, Lamont went to visit his son at school in Canterbury. As he got out of his car near the school, a mother and her small child passed by. 'Mum,' said the little boy, pointing, 'it's that man who has ruined the country.'

If economics is the dismal science then Chancellors of the Exchequer must be the dismal politicians: the counters of candle-ends, the breakers of bad news. We blame them in part for what's wrong with the country, and for what's wrong with the contents of our wallets. Nor is this just a popular attitude: most Chancellors are denigrated by their ministerial colleagues, and both collectively and individually they have been heavily criticised by economists and pundits for the apparently unsatisfactory state of the British economy.

Why then write a book about Chancellors of the Exchequer and the management by them, over the period from 1945 to 2000, of the British economy? Dismal science, dismal politicians, dismal book too?

Hopefully not: for there are several reasons why the subject ought to provide at least a handful of people with enough to interest them to justify the effort. The central question is a very old one, but none the worse for that. It is the Great Man question. To what extent can we explain the course of historical events in terms of the actions and decisions of a limited number of individuals? A.J.P. Taylor once remarked that the history of modern Europe can be written in terms of just three men: Napoleon, Bismark and Lenin. So does that mean that we can write the economic history of modern Britain in terms of nineteen men, starting with Hugh Dalton in 1945 and ending, for the time being, with Gordon Brown today?

One justly praised book has sought to do almost that. The late Edmund Dell's study *The Chancellors* attributes much of what he perceives to be the poor performance of the British economy since 1945 to the mistakes of the men who held the office of Chancellor. And when Dell lets a particular Chancellor off the hook, it is invariably because he prefers instead to impale whoever was Prime Minister at the time.

The broad question can be split into two. How much influence have Chancellors actually had over the conduct of policy? And how much influence has policy had over the course of events?

The answers to these questions depend in part on what Chancellors have been seeking to influence. At the most basic level there is the question of what are the responsibilities of a Chancellor, and what the job actually entails. Chapters 1 and 2 of this book look at that question, and consider domestic economic management and international economic management respectively.

The big constant is that Chancellors are primarily interested in the performance of the economy *as a whole*, and that they use policy instruments to seek to influence its overall performance. So their objectives are 'macroeconomic'. But if nothing else, Chapters 1 and 2 illustrate the obvious point that within that broad description, the range of issues which Chancellors have sought to address, and the instruments that they have sought to use, have changed greatly through the past half century.

Broadly speaking, there was a general process of accumulation of both aims and means from the time when Hugh Dalton took office in 1945 to the time when Denis Healey stood down exhausted in 1979. The welfare state got underway and needed to be kept an eye on. Planning came within the Chancellor's brief, and in that period never completely left it. The control of government spending and the setting of tax rates grew more important, both in themselves and as the means for controlling the growth of demand in the economy. Monetary policy and exchange-rate policy became more activist and complex, and Chancellors became heavily concerned with negotiating with trade union leaders over pay, social conditions and even the fundamentals of economic management.

Internationally, the management of global finance became once more an important issue, as it had been in the thirties. But instead of occasional grand conferences on particular issues every five or ten years, a time-consuming system of annual conferences evolved, and Chancellors grew ever more conscious of the interconnectedness of the world economy, and their need to influence the decisions of governments abroad. Europe, although always rather *infra dig*, could never be entirely ignored.

From 1976 to 1979 the British Government overloaded itself with problems to tackle, partly because the general lack of cohesion and solidarity that befouled the nation occurred within government too, so that the manner in which government was conducted became part of the problem. Consequently the incoming Conservative administration had an agenda of simplification. And although that has been easier to achieve in theory than in practice, it has clear echoes in the way in which Tony Blair's government has sought to proceed, and particularly the way in which Gordon Brown has acted.

But we all know that you cannot understand a job by listing its responsibilities. Accordingly, Chapters 3 and 4 look at the job of Chancellor from two different perspectives: the kind of person who is needed to do the job, and the way in which he tends to relate to his colleagues, especially the Prime Minister.

To write 'he' is to face up to a striking fact about Chancellors: they have all been men. No woman in Britain has ever been Chancellor, Foreign Secretary or Home Secretary, and although we have had a woman Prime Minister, she got there of her own accord, without any helping hand ever being extended down to her. Whereas Ted Heath, to take just one example, enjoyed the patronage of Harold Macmillan and prospered partly in consequence, Margaret Thatcher clambered over the still-living bodies of Heath and others to get to the top.

To be fair, it is hard to think of many women Cabinet ministers since the end of the Second World War who were Chancellor material: Thatcher herself was one, and so was Barbara Castle in the sixties and seventies. Yet even if there had been more, it is doubtful if any would have been appointed. Margaret Thatcher's one previous Cabinet post was Education Secretary, a job also held by Ellen Wilkinson long ago and by Shirley Williams just before Thatcher. Education means children, and hence a suitable job for a woman. Shirley Williams's previous job was heading the Department of

Prices and Consumer Protection – minister for shopping! – and by no small coincidence, Barbara Castle started her ministerial career in a similar though more junior post, and was told that her ability to understand the housewife's viewpoint made her particularly suitable for the job. Castle ended her career as Secretary of State for Health and Social Security – so minister for sick people and the elderly. Meanwhile the men have looked after the money.

The main quality that Prime Ministers seem to look for in a Chancellor is the ability to out-gun all other ministers without actually being a threat to the Prime Minister himself or herself – which last point might be said to help to explain why women do not get the job. It is of course a bit of a hard combination to find, and most Prime Ministers outlast their Chancellors. The Chancellors themselves are mostly aware of what is wanted of them, and are generally weighed down by it.

Somewhat less highly regarded as a qualification is the characteristic that we outsiders might think was of paramount importance: the possession of a clear understanding of how the economy works and how it can be improved. Where economic philosophy is concerned, Prime Ministers do not normally want their Chancellors to be too fancy. Yet some principles and purposes, however second-hand or unworthy, are needed by any Chancellor, if he is to proceed in any sort of direction. Accordingly, Chapters 5 and 6 look at the Conservative Chancellors as a group, and then at the Labour Chancellors, to see if they did indeed have and apply any economic philosophies.

All of these inquiries end face-to-face with the basic issues with which we started, of what actually happened to the economy from 1945 to 2000, and how much of what happened can be attributed to Britain's Chancellors. Chapter 7 considers these questions. The chapter's subject-matter is a little more technical than the rest of the book, but the answers seem to be that the economy performed better than many people imagine that it did, although not as well as it could have done; and that while the role of government in determining the course of events was quite large, the specific role of macroeconomic policies was quite modest.

This last point is the crux of the matter, implying as it does that Chancellors have not mattered hugely to the recent history of the nation. But it needs to be qualified in certain ways. In the first place, there clearly have been alternative and extreme policies that could have been followed and which would have changed events dramatically. If Reggie Maudling had remained in office in 1964, instead of giving way to Jim Callaghan, it would probably not have mattered much; but if Denis Healey had agreed to adopt the siege-economy policies that half the Cabinet wanted in 1976, the consequences would have been alarming.

Secondly, it is also clear that some Chancellors have affected the work of their governments through other channels than their macro-economic policy instruments. In particular, the control of departmental spending allocations, if it can be exercised, gives a Chancellor great power. Hugh Gaitskell knew it, and infuriated Nye Bevan so much that he stormed out of government; Gordon Brown knows it, but his colleagues swallow their fury and do as they are allowed, or in many cases as they are told.

Thirdly, it may be that the real role of a Chancellor is not so much the setting of a course for the economy, but responding to a crisis whenever it occurs. Certainly, by their crises do we know them, as Chapter 8 recounts. One consequence of this is that a Chancellor's popular reputation can often be a poor judge of his overall qualities and achievements, as Chapter 9 indicates. Mind you, if you look around for a Chancellor who left office popular with the electorate, his colleagues, journalists and academics, then you look in vain. Stafford Cripps was the nearest. And he was an extremely strange man.

That brings us back to the main point: that we probably over-blame our Chancellors. The single largest failure of British economic policy in the past half-century was probably the failure to get fully involved in European integration at the right time – the beginning. Chancellors are partly to blame for this, and for the foot-dragging that we have seen ever since, but so too are others: Prime Ministers especially. And the same is true in other policy areas. Chapter 10 of this book attempts to draw the threads together and assess which of the Chancellors did particularly well or particularly badly. There are no absolute answers to this, but hopefully there are some helpful things that can be said. But helpful to whom? The best advice to a would-be Chancellor is to hold office when the economy is doing well – for which advice, no thanks are expected. The best advice to an historian or commentator is usually that it is too early to draw a firm conclusion on anything, although in Chapter 10 (and indeed throughout the book) a tentative view of Gordon Brown is neverthe-less offered.

What about advice to a Prime Minister about whom to make Chancellor? Margaret Thatcher presumably has a simple answer: 'Don't.' She appointed three Chancellors – Geoffrey Howe, Nigel Lawson and John Major – and the three of them together ended her career. Lawson knocked her off balance by resigning, Howe put her on the floor by also resigning, and Major then stepped over her and took her job. Michael Heseltine added to the drama but did not instigate it. The Chancellors did it. And as a final reason for being in-terested in Chancellors and all that they have done, that will do nicely.

1   Managing the domestic economy

The emergence of the modern Chancellor

Gordon Brown spent the early years of his Chancellorship remodelling, refining, even denuding the job that he assumed in May 1997. He gave away some key powers while appropriating others, abandoned rituals and rewrote, often literally, many of the rules under which the Treasury had grown accustomed to operate. Brown surrendered a key area of power to the Bank of England and, by setting out clear rules for the long-term direction of fiscal (i.e. budgetary) policy, he circumscribed his freedom in that area too. Yet Gordon Brown simultaneously strengthened the Treasury's control over the spending ministries, and over European policy. This shift reflected his belief that as Chancellor he could achieve very little by constantly tickling the macroeconomic pool, and rather more by making strategic decisions and ensuring that both he and everybody else stuck to them.

The job, naturally, had changed before Gordon Brown arrived at the Treasury and will need to change much more if European integration continues apace. The low point for the office, at least since the time of Gladstone, was the Second World War. Hostilities had created an overpowering need for a minister to coordinate the supply of food, fuel and raw materials, and to balance basic military and civilian needs. Juggling priorities between shipbuilding and aircraft production, deciding whether to commit labour to the coal mines or the farms or the armed forces, and deciding by how much more to cut rations before civilian morale was endangered – these were all responsibilities that the Treasury could have taken on, had it been asked. But Churchill, himself an ex-Chancellor (of some notoriety), made no such demands. Deeply suspicious of the Treasury, he instead appointed other ministers to be his domestic 'Overlord' and coordinate economic policies, and left his wartime Chancellors to deal with purely financial matters, usually from outside his War Cabinet.

Since wartime Britain enjoyed near limitless credit from the United States and some Commonwealth governments, immediate financial problems were mostly quite minor (although longer term burdens were certainly building up). Foreign exchange transactions had been suspended, so there were no exchange-rate issues to worry about. And with prices firmly regulated, inflation was under almost direct control. There was no need to delicately adjust interest rates to influence the growth of demand in the economy: the Chancellor merely had to keep taxes high enough to dissuade people from trying to spend money on goods that the economy was temporarily unable to produce. By the heroic standards of the time, Britain's three wartime Chancellors, John Simon, Kingsley Wood and John Anderson, had few major decisions to take, and the post of Chancellor languished well down the Cabinet pecking order.

Labour's Clement Attlee continued Churchill's arrangement when he put together his first peacetime government. The system of having, as the Press put it, a 'financial Chancellor' and an 'economic Chancellor' had seemed to work well during the war. Anyway, Attlee had several colleagues all expecting a senior job. So the new Prime Minister told his first Chancellor of the Exchequer, Hugh Dalton, to concern himself only with managing the nation's finances. Meanwhile, Herbert Morrison as Lord President would coordinate the work of the various economic ministries such as power, labour and trade, to deliver the Government's objectives of full employment and price stability.

Attlee's decision was a major mistake. Morrison and the various ministers whose work he was supposed to coordinate had at their disposal a multitude of controls, rations, directives, allocations and restrictions, applying to almost every aspect of British economic life. This seemed to give them considerable influence over the behaviour of individuals and companies, and hence over the economy at large. But powers that had proved highly effective during the special circumstances of war seemed less effective during the very different conditions of peace. The important difference was not that the objectives had changed, nor that public attitudes had become less accommodating: it was that the new enemy was financial rather than military. Repeated shortages of output and exports manifested themselves in a series of financial crises that threatened to undermine the whole reconstruction process. If the nation could not pay its foreign bills, as often seemed likely in the mid to late forties, then the economy would collapse. All the price controls or import controls or investment controls in the world would not resolve such a situation.

In public, Dalton was confident and ebullient; in private he was anything but. Dalton as Chancellor could see the financial symptoms of the nation's economic plight better than any other minister. Indeed, it was his job to manage those symptoms. What he was not allowed to do was tackle effectively the underlying problem. Nor could he prevent Morrison and the others from making matters worse. Dalton could argue for the use of controls in particular ways to achieve his objectives, but his personal power was distinctly limited. He did not even have complete sway over his own instruments of policy. A cut in spending or a rise in taxes or interest rates to slow the economy down usually needed Cabinet approval. In early 1947 he complained in his diary of the 'easy-going muddle headed irresponsibility' of his colleagues. In a letter to Attlee he wrote, 'I had sooner be out of it all … if all my arguments are to be swept aside like flies.' That summer Dalton told a friend that watching the erosion of the nation's currency reserves was like 'watching a child bleed to death and being unable to stop it.'[1]

As far as the Chancellor was concerned, the basic problem was that Attlee and Morrison were weak. He believed that their power should shift to more able men – perhaps himself, or more likely one of the other two senior members of the Cabinet, Ernie Bevin and Stafford Cripps, or perhaps some combination thereof. The task was to tighten the controls and apply them with more skill than Morrison could muster. Only then would the financial situation of the economy recover.

During 1947 Dalton and Cripps plotted more than once to topple Morrison and Attlee. They failed, largely because Bevin refused to support them. But although Attlee declined to resign, he did accept the thrust of their argument, and accordingly stripped Morrison of his powers and gave them to Cripps, with the new title of Minister for Economic Affairs. Cripps's position was more powerful than Morrison's had been. His reputation was unblemished and his job was to involve more than simply coordinating the work of other ministers. The new system would implement the principle of 'direct economic administration by one leading Minister' that had been articulated earlier in the year in a document, the *Economic Survey*, that Cripps himself had largely written and had presented to the Commons when he was President of the Board of Trade. Under the new regime, the ministers of fuel and power, labour, supply, trade and works would all report directly to Cripps and would, at least in theory, be obliged to do as they were told.

Dalton welcomed Stafford Cripps's appointment. He realised very well that he himself was becoming a spent force and looked forward to a new period of vigorous government, with Cripps as the Cabinet's central figure. What Dalton did not realise was that more was to come. Six weeks later he himself would resign, whereupon his powers would pass to Cripps, to supplement those that the Minister for Economic Affairs had already accumulated. Henceforth there would be one Chancellor in practice as well as in name, and one minister in control of all aspects of economic policy.

Edward Bridges, grandest of all Treasury knights, said that this merger of authorities was the biggest change in the Treasury's role since the First World War. Edwin Plowden, formerly chief of the Treasury's planning staff and another grandee, dubbed Cripps the first modern Chancellor, and Chris Bryant took that phrase as the title of his biography of Cripps. For paradoxically the effect of bringing Morrison's planning system within the Treasury's orbit was to bury it – the very reverse of what Dalton and Cripps had wanted. But although Cripps had initially been keen to use the old wartime planning regulations to achieve his policy goals, he quickly recognised that the tools did not really work. Public irritation with them (irritation that the Conservative opposition quite reasonably inflamed), together with arguments with colleagues over the exercise of the controls, made them less attractive instruments than Cripps had expected. More importantly, growing scepticism over their effectiveness, and suggestions by Treasury officials that they knew of alternative policies that were both easier to operate and more effective, severely undermined Cripps's faith in direct economic controls, and caused him to adopt alternative methods of economic management in their place.

The new system of economic control that the Treasury had to offer was Keynesian demand management. (Not completely new, of course: the pre-war Treasury displayed some Keynesian instincts al-most before Keynes did, and in 1941 the Chancellor, the diminutive and rather skilful Kingsley Wood, introduced a distinctly Keynesian budget, not least because Keynes had just joined the Treasury as an adviser.) Officials at the Treasury argued that, so long as there was careful control over the growth in overall spending ('demand') in the economy (both public and private sector), the Government could abandon most of its direct controls on output, trade and prices. The market mechanism could be given a fairly free rein to distribute re-sources where the individuals concerned saw fit, with the Government worrying only about the behaviour of *total* spending.

Although Cripps had been brought up in Labour's pre-war tradi-tion, his great strengths were his open mind and his willingness to embrace new ideas. Before long, implementing the new Keynesian creed became the central function of the Treasury, and overseeing the policy became the Chancellor's most important task.

In October 1950 Cripps retired early through ill-health. His re-placement, Hugh Gaitskell, also needed to be won over to the new Keynesian creed. But once persuaded, the new Chancellor was a dogged champion. Gaitskell would fight and fight again to build the power of his department, and he was determined to impose the Trea-sury view over the special interests of colleagues. So Gaitskell cheer-fully sponsored the 'bonfire of controls' that Harold Wilson lit at the Board of Trade, and wrestled to himself the critical right to exclude all colleagues save the Prime Minister from the making of economic decisions. In particular, whereas previous Chancellors had been de-pendent on the goodwill of fellow ministers to achieve whatever gov-ernment spending total they preferred, Gaitskell insisted – most notably through his titanic struggle with Bevan over prescription charges – that the overall level of government spending was a matter for him alone to decide.

Rival ministries defeated

Was it an accident that the Treasury espoused an economic doctrine that placed it alone at the centre of the policy-making process, and robbed other departments of many of their key planning functions? Doubtless not. Nor did this state of affairs go unchallenged. When

Winston Churchill regained the premiership in 1951 he was keen enough to remove the remaining direct controls on the economy (although perversely the new Government would be quick to increase the use of import controls). But that did not mean that he necessarily wanted a strong Treasury. Churchill immediately sought to reverse the Treasury's ascendancy and appoint an overlord for what he still anachronistically called the 'home front'.

Perhaps the Prime Minister would not have wanted to do this had he not been forced, through lack of alternatives, to appoint the rather fishy Rab Butler as Chancellor. Whatever the reason, Churchill was disappointed when his candidate as overlord, the ex-Chancellor John Anderson, refused the assignment, realising that the arrangement could only mean trouble. Instead, Churchill had to content himself with asking an elderly but trusted ex-civil servant, Arthur Salter, to take up a junior post in the Treasury, to keep an eye on Butler. (Churchill famously told Butler that Salter was 'the best economist since Jesus Christ' – a view that Butler never entirely shared.)

In addition, Churchill appointed his old adviser and closest friend, the Oxford physicist F. A. Lindemann – Lord Cherwell – to the post of Paymaster General, with Cabinet rank and the right to roam freely across departmental briefs. Cherwell and Butler were old adversaries – back in 1940 when Churchill formed his first government, Cherwell was one of those whom Butler had in mind when he wailed: 'the gangsters will shortly be in complete control'.[2] Now the same thing seemed to be happening again. Many people suspected that Cherwell and not Butler would be the real Chancellor, especially when Cherwell took up residency in 11 Downing Street (accompanied as ever by his loyal factotum Harvey, a former pugilist whom the resolutely unmarried Cherwell had discovered as a young man, waiting tables at Oxford's Randolph Hotel).

Fortunately for Rab Butler, Salter lasted for only a year, during which time he wrote a number of careful memoranda, and Cherwell lasted for just two. The clever professor won most of his Cabinet battles with the feline Butler, but as the creature of a lame-duck Prime Minister with no power base or political future of his own, Cherwell was never able to win the permanent allegiance of other ministers. As a result, the Chancellor remained standing after his rivals were vanquished. Even so, the power of the Treasury and the Chancellor was generally weak in the fifties and early sixties, largely because Harold Macmillan dominated the age and expected his Chancellors to do his bidding. Neither he, nor his fellow Tory Prime Ministers, offered their Chancellors the unconditional support against other ministers that Gaitskell had secured from Attlee; support which modern Chancellors take as their due.

Then in 1964 came Harold Wilson. The new Prime Minister decided to revive the idea of having two economic ministries and, effectively, two competing Chancellors, but with himself as economic overlord above the pair of them. Jim Callaghan became Chancellor, but Wilson gave to George Brown the grand title of 'First Secretary of State' with responsibility for a new Department of Economic Affairs (DEA).

Wilson's motives remain uncertain. To his critics he was paranoid and vain, and simply wanted to set his two closest rivals, George Brown and Jim Callaghan, at one another's throats, with himself, the former economics don, as ringmaster. Yet since his own appointment as party leader, Wilson had largely succeeded in healing the great rift between the Bevanites and the Gaitskellites, and his refusal to prefer either of his rivals over the other can also be seen as an honest attempt to avoid new discontent at the top.

Personality issues aside, Wilson had been persuaded of the legitimacy of the arrangement by Tommy Balogh. A long-time colleague, friend and adviser to Wilson, Balogh combined a sharp mind with a complete lack of judgement and very little sense of decency. Balogh had fled Hungary to Britain in 1931. He had taught at Balliol during the war, where he was awarded a fellowship in 1945, a few months after Wilson received his from University College. His critique of the Treasury, published in 1959, endeared him to the left of the Labour Party and repelled the right. His contemptuous phrase 'whoever is in government, the Whigs are in power' might have been aimed directly at Gaitskell's Frognalites, one of whom, Roy Jenkins, was a former pupil. (Balogh claimed that he needed a shot of brandy to recover from the shock when Jenkins won a First.)[3] Balogh criticised the Treasury's obsession with thwarting the aims of other departments, and complained that the Treasury was staffed with amateurs, as proud of their ignorance of economics as of their knowledge of the classics. He contrasted Treasury insouciance with the grim determination of the Soviet Union's planners to raise their nation's productivity and output and thus overtake the West. He persuaded the Labour Party that, when in government, it would need a ministry of planning to put the economy on the right course and keep the Treasury in its place.

Nobody now doubts that the DEA and the National Plan that it produced were fiascos. Fundamentally the Plan made no allowance for what would happen when the Treasury attempted – as eventually it must – to tackle the overheating of the economy that Labour had inherited from the previous Conservative Government. In July 1966, in the face of mounting problems, Jim Callaghan as Chancellor introduced an emergency package of spending cuts and wage controls. The initiative rode roughshod over the DEA's work. It rendered that department, and its Secretary of State, largely redundant. The next day George Brown resigned in protest (a newsflash interrupted *Coronation Street*), but he later withdrew his resignation when he realised that Wilson would be happy to see the back of him. Brown (who denied that he had offered his resignation, even though his letter had been delivered to the Prime Minister) was now a figure of popular, though affectionate, ridicule. A month later Wilson, as if keen not to deny the nation its amusement, made Brown Foreign Secretary.

The July package brought to a head a set of tensions between rival ministers (Brown versus Callaghan), rival departments (the DEA versus the Treasury), and rival policies (the pursuit of economic growth as prescribed in the National Plan versus the defence of a strong pound). In each case it is hard to be surprised about who won and who lost. The Government duly abandoned the National Plan. It subsequently published a new report, *An Economic Assessment to 1972*. The Government called this a 'planning document', but jesuitically declared that it was not another plan. Then in 1969 Wilson wound up the Department of Economic Affairs. The Treasury and the Chancellor were once more ascendant over all government departments.

Since then there have been no credible attempts to create rival ministries to circumscribe the Treasury's role. After he became Prime Minister Jim Callaghan, who of all people should have known better, briefly thought about splitting the Treasury. He hoped this would ease the workload (and perhaps reduce the power) of his Chancellor, Denis Healey. But Healey said that such a division would create more work. So, instead of creating a separate spending ministry, Callaghan reluctantly accepted Healey's alternative proposal that Joel Barnett, the Chief Secretary, should be accorded Cabinet rank.[4] The arrangement has persisted ever since.

Just before the 1997 election, John Prescott tried to revive the idea of an economics ministry with overall responsibility for the real economy to offset what he saw as the Treasury's preoccupation with financial questions. He too was firmly rebuffed, in this case by Gordon Brown. Tony Blair nevertheless continued the tradition of adapting departmental organisations to the personal rivalries and ambitions of politicians. He made Prescott head of a specially enlarged department covering the environment, transport and regional development issues. That emasculated Prescott's original ambitions, while keeping him literally and figuratively removed from Downing Street. So, while Gordon Brown certainly needed to keep Tony Blair on-side where macroeconomic policy is concerned, he scarcely felt the need to consult the Deputy Prime Minister.

The Budget

Of all the Chancellor's jobs, the one with which he is most popularly identified is the preparation and delivery of the Budget. The convention is that tax changes are always and only announced in a Budget, and then voted on afterwards in a finance bill. From the fifties through until the late seventies, when Chancellors were always messing around with taxes, this meant that Budgets sometimes came more than once a year. Denis Healey once managed four Budgets (or so-called 'mini-Budgets') in a single year. Several years before him, Selwyn Lloyd took special powers, 'the regulator', to vary certain taxes between Budgets, if he chose to do so. Nowadays matters are rather less hectic. Chancellors vary taxes less often: they regard it as a sign of failure if they need more than one Budget in a year. Indeed that only happened in 1979, when the Tories had a quick Budget upon taking office, in 1993 when Norman Lamont changed the time of the Budget from spring until autumn, thereby giving himself two bites in one year, and in 1997 when Labour had a post-election Summer Budget.

This arrangement has the effect of turning the Budget into one of the great set-piece events of the political calendar – which is probably not a good thing. The significance of the Budget as a means by which the Government steers the economy is surely exaggerated. In 1950 Cripps described the Budget as 'the most powerful instrument for influencing economic policy which is available to the Government'. Chancellors and commentators since then, not least the City's moneymaking teenage scribblers, have maintained the myth.[5] Cripps was right to emphasise that macroeconomic demand management is a more effective way of running the economy than the system of direct controls that he was rejecting. But it is wrong to exaggerate the place that the Budget occupies within the overall macro policy scene. The cumulative effect of other events and decisions during the year – changes in interest rates, changes in government spending trends, the scale of debt sales, exchange rate manipulation, perhaps changes to trade policies or wages policy or regional policies – will often be much larger. Indeed, monthly fluctuations in the scale of commercial bank lending to the private sector can inject or deny the economy just as much extra spending power as can an annual Budget.

So it is hard to know how seriously to take the Budget business. The Treasury's purpose is served by exaggerating the import of the event, and much of the ritual that attends the Budget no doubt persists partly for that reason. The Budget is the Government's Easter Passion, and the Chancellor and his senior officials are its high priests. Roy Jenkins records that his first Budget was prepared in an 'heroic post-Gladstonian' atmosphere of secrecy.[6] Only a couple of dozen senior Treasury officials and their secretaries were allowed any part in, or knowledge of, Budget deliberations. An area of the Treasury was marked out with white tape (if only it had been red!) beyond which Budget papers were not allowed to pass. Jenkins himself used to disobey, and take the papers on the train to his home. There he carefully hid them, in a cupboard above the wine cellar, just in case of burglars.

Budget secrecy has some genuine justifications. Naturally it is important to prevent consumers or companies taking advance action, which might undermine the purpose of the Budget measures themselves. But Budget secrecy also has some less commendable aspects. It denies Cabinet colleagues knowledge of what is afoot except in so far as their departments are directly affected. That emphasises their subordinate status. It also deprives them of the opportunity to oppose or leak (the two being closely linked) the Chancellor's plans. Admittedly, all Chancellors canvass the views of a few colleagues and even back-benchers; Nigel Lawson claims that he was among the more assiduous.[7] Nevertheless, the final shape of the Budget is something that usually only the Prime Minister, outside of the Treasury, has a real chance to shape. As a result, a key part of the whole Budget-making process is for the Chancellor to avoid open rebellion when he finally tells Cabinet colleagues the details, mere days or even hours before delivery of the speech.

The plans themselves are formulated over a period of three or four months. They start with a huge range of possible (and in some cases necessary) policy changes. These are gradually boiled down to the small numbers that actually appear in the Budget. For many years, starting in 1982, a key event was a weekend meeting at Chevening, where Treasury ministers and their mandarins absorbed and debated papers on the economy and on the tax and other policy options available to them. Here too, ritual was to the fore: on Saturday night after dinner the Chancellor and one of his ministers traditionally played a game of snooker with the Permanent Secretary and another senior official. The cause of civil service morale was generally taken to require that the ministers be beaten. Nigel Lawson flouted that principle on first becoming Chancellor and Gordon Brown, who doesn't seem to like his officials much, and who hates open debate over policies, has abolished the whole weekend.

The Chancellor takes his final decisions as late as possible. So work on drafting the Chancellor's speech has to start long before the contents of the Budget have been fixed. Until Roy Jenkins, the Budget speech tended to comprise announcements of tax measures but little explanation why they had been chosen. That suited the Treasury's distaste for public discussion of its reasoning. Jenkins made the Budget speech more discursive and expository, which suited him as a politician who was using the Chancellorship to establish himself as the Cabinet's true heavyweight. The consequence was to make for rather long speeches, a fault which Nigel Lawson tried to correct when he became Chancellor two decades later. Either way, modern Chancellors are all keen to include some of their own words in their speech.

While a Budget really has to contain tax changes to justify the name, tax matters are not all that a modern Chancellor concerns himself with when putting together a Budget. Geoffrey Howe used the occasion of his first full Budget to announce the details of the new Conservative Government's Medium Term Financial Strategy – the set of monetary targets that he claimed would henceforth be the centre piece of economic policy. Gordon Brown similarly announced the details of the Labour Government's New Deal in his first full Budget – the scheme that removed young people's entitlement to unemployment benefits and required them instead to accept alternative arrangements such as subsidised employment.

Norman Lamont perhaps went further than any other Chancellor. He made the Budget the occasion for announcing the full details of the Government's spending plans as well as its tax plans, thus bringing together fully for the first time the two branches of budgetary policy. Previously the Budget had been the occasion for announcing only limited changes to spending plans. The change, which necessitated the shift in the timing of the Budget already mentioned, was one of several innovations for which Lamont received insufficient credit. It was to be very short-lived, however: when he took office, Gordon Brown reverted to the old approach of splitting the bulk of the spending announcements away from the tax announcements.

None of which has much effect on the attention that Press and public give to the Budget. In no other major nation does the annual Budget get quite the ceremony that it receives in Britain. Nigel Lawson has written that other finance ministers are jealous of the attention focused on a British Chancellor, not least the display on the steps of Number 11 of the Budget box, held proudly aloft.[8] Usually the Chancellor's wife hovers in the background. On his first outing, the then-unmarried Gordon Brown surrounded himself instead with young apprentices from the Rosyth shipyard in his constituency where his new Budget briefcase had been made. Staff at the *Guardian* were famously unimpressed by the gesture. They airbrushed the apprentices out of the photograph that they printed in the next day's edition.

There are other related Budget rituals, with which Brown is similarly unimpressed but to which the Press remain much attached. These include a photo-call for the Chancellor and his family off-duty at the weekend before the Budget, ideally walking in the country with dogs or failing that in the Chancellor's constituency. A similar event occurs in St James's Park on Budget day itself. On that occasion ducks may be fed, and civil servants generally take the roles of devoted wife and children. These episodes are intended to demonstrate both that the Chancellor is human, despite what he is about to do, and that the Budget has been prepared in an unhurried and rational atmosphere rather than in a frenzy.

Even the dispensation given to Chancellors making their Budget speeches – that they may drink alcohol as they go along – serves in part to emphasise how special the event is. For his first Budget Roy Jenkins disdained the 'bogus prop' of such a drink. In his memoirs he confesses, however, that he had drunk a fair amount of wine at lunchtime. Jenkins then continued with whisky in his office as soon as the event was over – and before recording television and radio broadcasts.[9]

Nigel Lawson drank whisky and soda during his first Budget and white wine spritzers during his next three. Perhaps he recognised the lapse from good taste, for he switched to water for his final two Budgets. An earlier and even more mannered Chancellor, Hugh Dalton, followed a similar journey. During his first three Budget speeches he drank rum and milk that he graciously poured himself from a silver coffee-pot. The affectation attracted much attention, and it was for the purpose of asking Dalton whether or not he was going to do the same during his fourth Budget speech that the journalist John Carvel of the *Star* approached the Chancellor in the Inner Lobby, moments before the Budget speech. As it happened Dalton had decided against his usual tipple. He had just sent his PPS, Douglas Jay, to arrange for a glass of water to be left by the dispatch box instead. Thus in a literally unguarded moment, Dalton spoke to the journalist. The Chancellor left Carvel confused as to what he would be drinking, but very clear about something else – the major tax changes that he was about to make. Thus for once did abstinence lead to indiscretion.

Nigel Lawson has defended the Budget rituals. It is, he says, appropriate that once a year the nation should focus its attention on 'the national economy and the issues involved'[10]. This is a boorish sentiment, and not just because artificial rituals are not the only way of persuading people of the importance of an event. The Budget is only concerned with some of the economic issues facing the nation – those of financial and economic stability. Even under Gordon Brown, other basic determinants of the nation's economic health, such as the rate of product innovation or the quality of primary school education or the competitive strategies being adopted by different industries or a thousand other things, are largely ignored, both by those in the Treasury who put the Budget together, and by those in the Press and the City who subsequently take it apart. Indeed, the public concentration on the event of the Budget may be positively harmful, in distracting attention away from more basic aspects of the health of the economy.

Taxation

For much of the Press and the majority of people, the day of the Budget is not in any case an occasion for contemplating economic policy, however narrowly defined. It is a day for making last-minute purchases of cigarettes and spirits, to avoid the tax increases that typically take effect at midnight. Nigel Lawson's suggestion that on Budget day the nation focuses its collective mind on the state of the economy is akin to suggesting that at Christmas, everybody contemplates religion.

To the consumer, most tax changes are fairly straightforward events, even when their financial consequences are quite large. (The obvious exceptions include changes to the taxation of saving and borrowing, which are inherently complicated.) To the Chancellor and his officials, tax changes are much more complex. The work involved in deciding what the consequences of any changes will be, and whether to make the changes, is invariably very substantial.

Chancellors neglect such work at their peril. In 1964 Jim Callaghan presented a distinctly ill-thought-out Budget within a month of taking office. Callaghan had been telling horror stories about the balance of payments position bequeathed by the Conservatives, and in those circumstances, the overall balance of measures seemed to most outsiders to be distinctly complacent. But just as importantly, the details seemed to have been put together in a hurry – as of course they had been. Callaghan announced that from the following April there would be a new capital tax and a new corporation tax. But he was unable to say at what rates the taxes would apply, or by what rules they would work. It was also clear to everybody that neither the Treasury nor the Inland Revenue had calculated what the economic impact of the taxes would be, nor what revenues they might yield. These failings epitomised the 'remarkably amateurish and ramshackle' manner of government that the Government's top economic adviser, Alec Cairncross, identified.[11] The City observed the botched Budget with some horror. The Treasury's lack of thought contributed to the rapidly emerging crisis in confidence in government policy. That added to the selling pressure in the currency markets, and to the eventual collapse of sterling and of Callaghan's Chancellorship.

What Callaghan did not realise in 1964, presumably because nobody told him, was that Chancellors must spend considerable time taking advice on the detailed implications of tax changes before putting any into practice. The issues that need to be faced are large and various. Trying to figure out how the *existing* system affects the behaviour of individuals and companies is a substantial task. Having to anticipate the full ramifications of any tax *change* is even more difficult. It is not for nothing that the Chancellor is head of the Inland Revenue and of the Customs and Excise as well as head of the Treasury. The consequent range of work for which he is responsible is huge.

Callaghan in 1964 was naïve, both about the scale of correction that was needed, and about the need to think through the details before announcing his tax changes. But his recognition that he had to do something to slow the pace of economic growth was uncontroversial. Callaghan's implementation may have been widely criticised, but his approach was one to which the great bulk of politicians and economists then subscribed.

Indeed it is hard to deny that in the days of demand management, Chancellors were rather too enthusiastic to alter taxes. The history of corporation tax allowances is a case in point. In 1945 Hugh Dalton introduced a system of 'initial allowances', which had the effect of delaying the tax liabilities of firms that invested in new plant and machinery. The Chancellor's aim was to encourage investment and hence the long-term growth of the economy. This was a rare attempt to boost the productive potential of the economy by an administration which on the whole paid too little attention to such matters. But the future of the new allowances was to be anything but stable, and over the next decade short-term demand management policies caused repeated changes in the system of allowances.

Thus in 1949 Stafford Cripps doubled the value of the initial allowances, but in April 1952 Rab Butler, worried by the Korean War boom, suspended them. A year later Butler changed his mind and reintroduced the allowances, but then in 1954 he replaced them with more generous 'investment allowances', which did not simply defer but reduced tax liabilities. The 1955 balance of payments crisis then provoked Butler to reverse his policy yet again, and in that year he withdrew the investment allowances and restored initial allowances. In 1957 the then Chancellor, Peter Thorneycroft, made the initial allowances more generous, and in 1959 his successor Derick Heathcoat Amory got rid of them and went back to investment allowances. Any company that tried to base its investment decisions on these fluctuating tax regimes was almost bound to come a cropper. Rather than having a stabilising effect on the economy, such volatile policies were liable to reduce investment confidence, and impede economic expansion.

Many other examples could be cited, some from the early period and others from more recent years. Often, Chancellors have messed around with taxes for no other reason than to help their governments win elections. For many years the most notorious example was Rab Butler's give-away Budget in the spring of 1955, which he reversed just as soon as the Conservatives had won that summer's general election. Reggie Maudling is generally said to have tried the same trick less than a decade later, although he did seem to believe that economic arguments justified his policy of dashing for growth. Either way the policy failed, so that it was incoming Labour ministers who had to pick up the pieces (which they did only reluctantly and with little skill).

Typically the Chancellors concerned explain away these events as honest errors, committed as a result of unreliable economic information. Harold Macmillan, when he was Chancellor, said that his job was a bit like trying to catch a train using an out-of-date timetable. Denis Healey similarly complained about the information on which he, as Chancellor, had to make tax and other policy decisions. 'Economics,' he declared in his memoirs, 'has acquired a spurious respectability through the use of numbers ... Unfortunately I discovered that the most important numbers were nearly always wrong.'[12] For those reasons and others, Geoffrey Howe decided in 1980 that enough was enough. Howe was the first to say that tinkering with taxes creates instability not stability, and should be eschewed. Other Chancellors since then have professed much the same attitude, although none has entirely lived up to it in practice, causing Gordon Brown to declare afresh that conventional demand management does not work, and that there is to be no more unnecessary fine-tuning.

Howe and Brown and the Chancellors in between all agree: short-term stabilisation measures can make the economy less stable, not more. This is partly because of timing problems, and partly because policies sometimes have perverse results (so that for example a rise in government spending might increase anxieties over interest rates, depress investment and hence reduce, not increase, total demand in the economy). But the Brown version of the doctrine is different to the Howe version. Today's formulation, widely accepted by academic economists as well as by Treasury officials, is less doctrinaire than that which Geoffrey Howe tried to impose in the period of high Monetarism. It is now generally accepted that in moments of crisis (typically, a run on the reserves, or a collapse in consumer or business confidence) it may be necessary to stimulate or dampen demand via tax or spending changes. But dealing with crises apart, it now seems from the econometric evidence that until the early seventies, the overall impact of policy fluctuations on economic stability and growth of the British economy was not especially great, either for good or evil.[13] What policy fluctuations did do was take up an inordinate amount of government time and energy. Furthermore, the 'Barber boom' of 1972–4 (more accurately a 'Heath boom', since Tony Barber, though Chancellor, was mostly under his leader's thumb) and the antics of the subsequent Labour Government surely were damaging. So in general, Chancellors are better off not spending too much of their time trying to stabilise the economy.

The real shift that occurred in the mid and late nineties was towards a more sophisticated view of targets than in the Howe years. The policies adopted by the Tories under Geoffrey Howe concentrated narrowly on trying to stabilise monetary growth and trying to reduce public borrowing, without any cross checks on whether inflation would actually fall, or whether the policies might have side-effects for other parts of the economy. What happened was that personal and especially company finances deteriorated, as did the balance of payments, precipitating a whole variety of crises. So the Howe policies may ironically have made the economy less stable, not more, and Howe's critique of his predecessors can better be applied to him.

In contrast, modern economic management as espoused by Gordon Brown is geared towards finding trajectories for public finances and inflation that do not put undue strains on any part of the economy, and which are sustainable in the long term, while allowing deviations from those trajectories in the shorter term.

Whether or not this way of thinking is right, it has the implication of making for a less obsessive policy regime. That at least reduces some of the work that the Chancellor and his officials have to do (although the amount of work that Gordon Brown *chooses* to do is another matter). It means, for example, less need for continual detailed macroeconomic forecasting, and that part of the Treasury's work has indeed been cut back sharply since 1997. It has not, however, meant an abandonment of tax changes, or tax 'reform' as Chancellors prefer to say. But it is fair to say that even in this area, the exaggerated ambitions of past Chancellors (and the political horrors of such decisions as the poll tax and the levying of VAT on domestic fuel and light) have produced a new caution from New Labour. Gordon Brown introduced a set of rather tough tax rises in his first budget, and has made plenty of tax changes, but in a more planned way than most of his predecessors. He was in any case committed for purely political reasons not to raise income tax, and he has been helped by the tax rises introduced by his predecessors, by the economic boom and even by extraordinarily large revenues from third-generation telephone licences (a perfect New Labour 'privatisation' if ever there was one), all of which reduced his need to go looking for new revenue sources. But in the same circumstances many other Chancellors would either have courted popularity with tax cuts, or would have sought to dampen economic activity with tax rises, or would have tinkered just for the joy of it. Brown has done none of those things.

Nigel Lawson always liked to portray himself as an ardent tax reformer, and was so pleased with himself in the mid eighties for promoting free enterprise through tax cuts that he failed to notice the unsustainable spending boom that he was setting in train. William Keegan called it 'Mr Lawson's Gamble' in his book of that name, and the Lawson boom was about the most irresponsible act of any post-war Chancellor. Lawson had convinced himself that low income tax rates and low taxes on business had stimulated enterprise, investment and output to such a degree that they had raised the underlying growth potential of the economy. Instead they had simply stimulated unsustainable private sector spending.

If Lawson thought that he would go down in history for the brilliance of his policies, then he ought to have known better. Most Chancellors realise that being a good tax reformer does little for your reputation, and they avoid getting too involved in such matters. Selwyn Lloyd, Chancellor from 1960 to 1962, showed little aptitude for macroeconomics but was clear-headed in the way in which he thought about tax issues. He simplified the system, shifted the balance away from direct to indirect taxes, and introduced the regulator.[14] Tony Barber (a former tax lawyer) diligently implemented the tax reforms that Iain Macleod, who died just after taking office, had been planning. Norman Lamont was a creative (if not completely sensible) tax reformer. All did well within their own terms. But none is remembered with much respect.

For a Chancellor, the real route to popularity is via tax cuts, not tax reform. Clearly this is sometimes harder to achieve than at other times. Back in 1945, for example, there was no problem with finding tax revenues. Freed from the burden of waging war but still with restrictive wartime tax rates in place, the Treasury in 1945 had far more revenues flowing in than it needed. In his first Budget in October 1945, Hugh Dalton reduced taxes by £400 million, with most of the reduction coming from income taxes. He cut the standard rate by a shilling and raised personal allowances, taking 2 million people out of the tax net. He also reduced taxes on company profits, but showed his socialist credentials by keeping in place surtax – the additional tax on high personal incomes. 'We cheered rapturously,' said Barbara Castle of Dalton's first tax give-away Budget.

Few Chancellors since then have found it so easy to cut taxes, and when they have, it has often backfired. Beneath the intellectual pretensions of tax reform and an improved supply-side performance, tax cuts to please the voters were the essence of the Lawson boom. Nigel Lawson and Margaret Thatcher alike knew that their political success depended largely on delivering cuts in income tax rates, and that was what they went for, disregarding the possibility that the cuts could not be afforded. Most other governments have been more circumspect, and have instead adopted the approach of announcing large tax cuts, while surreptitiously introducing large tax rises. Since 1979 there have been massive reductions in some income tax rates, but the scale of the tax burden has not fallen, so that taxes have not really been cut at all. A combination of widening the tax base, introducing new taxes, cutting higher rates more than lower rates, and allowing the bands at which rates apply to move upwards, means that it has been possible to conceal repeated tax increases behind the cover of headline tax cuts. All Chancellors have done this, and all shadow Chancellors have expressed great but hypocritical outrage at the calumny involved.

This brings us back to the remark that the management of taxation is a large task for the Chancellor and his officials. The tax system provides considerable work for tax lawyers and tax accountants, and that then feeds back to further work for the Treasury and the two revenue departments, as each side seeks to negate the impact of the tactics and trickeries of the other. This constant battle of wits is in turn an important reason why the Treasury genuinely needs both officials and ministers of a particularly high calibre. But outsiders think that a lot of those involved are too clever by half. Whereas tax lawyers get satisfaction from large pay packets, tax officials, whether in the Treasury, the Inland Revenue or Customs and Excise, rely on more psychological satisfactions. Being loved is not, of course, one of them.

Seeking to control public spending

While it is hard for a Chancellor to win popularity through his tax

measures, it is even harder to win favour through the control of public spending. No other minister has ever tried to steal from the Chancellor the task of controlling government spending. And although
modern Chancellors have a deputy of Cabinet rank to bear much of
the burden of the work and take much of the flak from other ministers, the Chief Secretary's job is to negotiate, not to make policies.
Responsibility for the Government's spending plans still ultimately
resides with the Chancellor. 'No one but the Chancellor,' declares
Denis Healey, 'can set the appropriate level for spending as a
whole.'[15] It is the Chancellor, not the Chief Secretary, who bears the
brunt of any unpopularity, whether with the public or with ministerial and parliamentary colleagues. Nigel Lawson said that 'the Treasury as a department and the Chancellor as an individual are
regarded by most of the rest of government as the enemy' – a sentiment that Denis Healey, as ever, put rather more forcibly.[16]

But how burdensome is the job of controlling government spending? All ministers and civil servants agree that it is an Herculean task
– a judgement that directors of large companies might treat with considerable disdain. Admittedly no private sector company has a
spending budget that begins to compare with that of the state, but
the suspicion is that the difference is not really one of magnitude but
of attitude. Civil servants and ministers alike appear to operate from
the assumption that nobody in government can be forced to cut their
spending, only persuaded to agree. So a good departmental minister
or official is one who successfully thwarts the aims of the Treasury.

There are other genuine reasons why it has always been hard to
exercise control over spending. One is that legislation invariably allows some spending to be determined simply by the number of people or organisations entitled to receive the benefits. Unemployment
benefits are the obvious example. Admittedly it is always possible to
reduce the value of the benefit, change the legislation to restrict its
entitlement, or even abolish it completely. Clearly, such moves tend
to be highly unpopular, and they can seldom be done overnight, so
that the Government struggles along behind, trying to offset what
has already happened, rather than being in control of events.

Another reason is that cuts in spending can be partially self-
defeating. If cuts in military procurement make people redundant,
then spending on unemployment benefits may have to rise. If cuts in

local government spending on housing force more low-income people to rent from the private sector, then payments of housing benefits may have to rise. Indeed, the alleged crisis in welfare spending that so preoccupied ministers in the late years of the last Conservative Government and the early years of the present Labour Government was partly caused by precisely that phenomenon.

Finally, there is a long-run tendency for public sector spending to rise in nominal terms as a proportion of total spending in the UK. This is because the public sector generally has fewer opportunities to cut costs than the private sector. Changing technology and economies of scale mean that it costs less to make a loaf of bread today than it did thirty years ago, and less to make a car. But it costs much the same to teach arithmetic to an eight-year-old child as it ever did. So in relative terms, education has got more expensive. The result is that to prevent government spending from rising as a share of nominal GDP, governments often have to control costs by holding public sector wage increases below private sector wage rises. Either that, or make real cuts in the services provided. Which means that the Chancellor's job is inherently likely to make him unpopular.

It is sometimes alleged that government spending raced out of control during the Attlee government and has never really been brought to heel. Certainly it is true that a major reason why the spending magnitudes today are so enormous is that we have a welfare state, and that much of that system was introduced in the Attlee years (though a lot came before). In his first budget, Hugh Dalton provided funds for industrial development in depressed regions, and he raised spending on education. He even introduced free school milk, and he allowed the Education Minister (Ellen Wilkinson or 'Red Ellen', who marched with the Jarrow miners) to win the argument for raising the school-leaving age to fifteen. Before long, Dalton also found the money for Nye Bevan's National Health Service (NHS).

But none of this was desperately profligate, and for most of the period of the Attlee administration, government spending rose only modestly. The new welfare benefits such as maternity pay, unemployment benefits and most importantly pensions were initially self-financing from national insurance contributions (indeed the national insurance funds slightly subsidised other spending). Ministers such as Bevan agitated for larger rises in spending, and he and others gave successive Chancellors many a headache, but serious problems only really began to emerge in the last years of the Labour Government, when NHS costs started to accelerate, Hugh Gaitskell decided to increase military spending, and (the most important reasons) the costs of food and agricultural subsidies began to reach alarming proportions.

Even that acceleration was modest compared with what subsequently happened under the Tories, when the Treasury was weak and the spending ministers were in the ascendant. The practice of the time was for the Treasury and the spending ministries to make piecemeal spending decisions, line by line, on over 2,000 items covered by the annual Supply estimates and on a growing number of other items not covered by the traditional framework. Having decided how much the Government was going to spend, the Chancellor then had to go away and find the cash. Worse still, if the ministries overspent their allocations during the year, the hapless Chancellor would have to find that cash too. The Chancellor had no right to get his way: spending ministers could and did appeal to Cabinet to settle disputes with the Treasury, and since there were always more spending ministers in Cabinet than Chancellors, the latter's position was inherently weak.

Back in 1950, Gaitskell had forced Attlee to support him in such circumstances; but no Conservative Chancellor could ask Churchill, Eden or especially Prime Minister Macmillan for help and expect to get very far. Particularly burdensome in the early years was Macmillan's own commitment as housing minister to build 300,000 new homes. Spending also increased on the recently nationalised industries, on welfare items and on many other areas of economic policy. Butler made no attempt to fight, and nor in his brief period as Chancellor did Macmillan. In January 1958 Peter Thorneycroft did dig in his heels, got no support from the Prime Minister, and resigned in protest. 'A little local difficulty,' muttered the Prime Minister, and went off on a six-week tour of the Commonwealth. After all, the control of public spending was surely not something with which a gentleman need concern himself.

But there were some who thought that insouciance alone was not enough. Later that year the Select Committee on Estimates published a report that said that there really ought to be a more sensible way of making spending decisions. Treasury officials entirely agreed: they had been thinking of ways to get control over government spending, but had lacked any backing. Now they responded to the Select Committee's report by setting up a committee of their own, packed with Treasury knights under Edwin Plowden, to devise and push through a new set of arrangements for the control of spending.

In June 1961 Selwyn Lloyd presented Parliament with the report of the Plowden Committee. That report is conventionally taken to mark the watershed between the old days, when no serious attempt was made to control public spending, and the modern acceptance that Chancellors and their officials must be allowed the authority they need if there is to be any chance of keeping spending under control.

The Plowden Committee's ideas mostly came, not from Plowden himself but from another official, Otto Clarke, who in consequence was given Treasury responsibility for controlling public spending.[17] In the committee's report, Clarke advanced three general and compelling principles. These were that the total amount of spending should be determined by the likely resources that would be available (rather than the old rule that ministers decided what they wanted to spend and then told the poor Chancellor to find them the cash); that decisions on this required a clear sense of collective responsibility from the Cabinet; and that effective mechanisms should be put in place for implementing the decisions, once they had been made.

Over the next few years the Treasury worked hard to devise the relevant tools and to make its new system work. In 1961 it published its first Public Expenditure Survey Committee (PESC) report, containing spending plans to which all the spending departments had officially agreed, and in 1963 it published the first ever Public Expenditure White Paper. No official or minister today would conceive of trying to run the government without a similar framework.

But there were some deep-seated problems. In particular, Cabinet ministers still refused to help make the system work. The Treasury found it just as hard as it had always done to get the spending decisions it needed, and was even less able to force the departments to abide by the decisions, once they had been made. Worse still, neither Selwyn Lloyd the Chancellor nor Harold Macmillan the Prime Minister saw much need to curb spending anyway. Their main concern in the early sixties was that the economy was not growing fast enough; the last thing they wanted was a crackdown on spending. Even Lloyd was too conservative for Macmillan and lost his job in consequence: his successor Reggie Maudling presented a Budget in 1963 that provided for a sharp increase in planned government spending. Not for the last time, the Tories were proving to be the party of profligacy.

At first it looked as if the 1964 Labour Government might improve matters. Although in opposition Labour leaders had been even more expansionary in their sentiments than Macmillan, their commitment to rational, planned decision-making was also rather higher than that of the Tories. The new Government ring-fenced many existing commitments, and then required departments to bid for extra funds with which to honour manifesto pledges, but all within a clear 4.5 per cent a year limit to the real growth in spending. To enforce the collective responsibility that the Tories had never shown, Harold Wilson set up a committee comprising Jim Callaghan, George Brown and five non-spending ministers, who conducted day-long interrogations of the spending ministers, and who then made the decisions as to which spending bids should go through and which should fall. Looking at these new arrangements, Treasury officials toasted the good sense of their new political masters.

But the success of the new system was short-lived. Although the non-spending ministers were initially happy to participate, they quickly lost interest as the demands of the work became progressively more burdensome, and as the sense of exterior crisis increased. Meanwhile spending ministers rebelled and started to appeal to full Cabinet to have the committee's decisions overturned. Wilson, ever willing to play one minister off against another, colluded in this delinquency.

Callaghan, like Lloyd before him, lacked either the intellectual and verbal firepower, or the Prime Ministerial backing, to be able to control public spending effectively. An acceleration in government spending thus appeared to be inevitable. Furthermore, the control methods that Otto Clarke had advocated in the Plowden report and that had since been implemented turned out to be flawed. The principle was that spending could only occur if the cash was there to be spent. But Clarke had always thought of this in terms of the tax revenues and borrowing receipts that the Treasury would receive over the subsequent five years. Whereas spending by any private sector business was always constrained by the cash it actually had in the bank, or could reasonably be expected to receive almost immediately, civil servants were perfectly happy to spend revenues that they airily assumed they were going to get in a few years' time. So long as the assumptions were sufficiently optimistic, and in those days officials were nothing if not optimistic, spending could rise at almost any rate. The Labour Government's new rules did little to alter that problem.

Secondly, Otto Clarke had couched spending plans in real terms. So if inflation rose sharply, then spending would rise in response. This meant that tax and borrowing receipts had to rise in line, to finance the spending. When inflation was low this did not create problems. But as inflation rose during the sixties, it meant increasing pain for the Government. To control inflation, the Government needed to force wages to rise more slowly than prices. Allowing government spending and tax revenues to rise in line with inflation at a time when the Government was seeking to hold wage increases below the rate of inflation inevitably meant that government spending would grab more and more of the nation's income. The policy made no sense.

Finally there was the simple problem that the 4.5 per cent figure for annual real growth in public spending only made sense if GDP was rising at that rate. But such growth was faster than the economy could bear, even temporarily let alone over the long-term. The 4.5 per cent figure was just part of the hopeless optimism enshrined in George Brown's National Plan. So even without the other problems, the Labour Government's spending plans were bound to create difficulties.

One thing was for sure: the Wilson Cabinet was not going to tackle the problem. But then came the devaluation crisis of 1967, the consequent loss of Wilson's authority within the Government, and the appointment of Roy Jenkins as Chancellor. Spending ministries, traumatised by the near-collapse of the Government, suddenly started to behave. Their ministers kept their heads down. Wilson did not dare to play off Jenkins against other ministers. And for the first time ever, the Treasury made public the spending cuts to which Cabinet members had agreed, thereby committing ministers to adhere to those figures.

Getting a grip

Against the odds, the Labour Government thus ended its days with spending well under control, thanks to an ascendant Chancellor. The Conservative Government elected in 1970 proclaimed its commitment to maintaining this control over public spending. Yet within a couple of years the fundamental lack of a sensible control mechanism began to show through. In practice the system relied entirely on the quality and attitudes of Chancellor and Prime Minister. Ted Heath was too much a creature of Harold Macmillan, and Tony Barber too much a creature of Ted Heath, for the outlook to be very promising. Treasury officials were also horribly complacent: in 1973 Samuel Goldman, the civil servant responsible for spending control, declared loftily that the British system of spending control was 'probably superior to that found anywhere in the world'.[18] Yet inflation was taking off, and so too was government spending. The Chancellor, Tony Barber, took little notice.

Changes since then have improved matters hugely and mean that a modern Chancellor, in conjunction with his squire the Chief Secretary, has more chance than used to be the case of keeping spending under control. Some of the changes have been technical or operational. From 1974 until 1976 the Labour Government hugely exceeded spending plans that were themselves based on quite implausible assumptions about how fast the economy could grow. In those early years the second Wilson government made all its predecessors look like paragons of parsimony, and in 1976 the economy went through a repetition of the crisis of 1967. The details were different, but the need for fundamental action was similar.

So the Chancellor, Denis Healey, approved a new way of managing government spending. In future the actual spending in a given year would be limited to an agreed sum of cash. If higher than expected inflation, or lower than expected economic growth, meant that less could be bought with the cash than had been assumed, then so be it. There would be a contingency reserve, but no more. The Government would run its affairs in the same way as any business or household.

At first the implementation of the new 'cash limits' was only partial. They did not apply across the board, and the spending plans themselves were still based on the flawed principles of Plowden and

Clarke. Nor initially did the 1979 election change matters. Although in November 1979 the Chief Secretary, John Biffen, warned the country to 'prepare itself for three years of unparalleled austerity', a year later the Chancellor had to warn the Prime Minister 'that the expenditure overshoot was continuing to grow'.[19] The legacy of Labour's desperate pre-election measures (large spending programme to bribe the electorate and large indexed public sector pay increases to bribe the unions), plus the recession engineered by Margaret Thatcher and Geoffrey Howe, meant that government spending was still out of control.

But on this matter more than any, Prime Minister and Chancellor saw eye to eye. According to Geoffrey Howe, the need to control spending 'was the issue which brought Margaret and me most closely together'.[20] In 1982 Howe changed the arrangements for planning spending, so that *plans* would be made in cash terms, as well as actual spending being subject to cash limits. And he shifted the planning process to one designed to reduce government spending over the longer term, rather than just keep it constant. The goal proved to be almost impossible to achieve, but at least the tendency for planned spending to spiral upwards was severely reduced.

Other changes have sought to address the deepest problem of all – collective Cabinet responsibility. In 1981 Margaret Thatcher set up an *ad hoc* Committee of the Cabinet to adjudicate on bids for increased expenditure that the spending departments and the Treasury could not resolve bilaterally. The arrangement was a little like that which Harold Wilson introduced in 1964 and which he allowed to fizzle out. But Thatcher meant business. The new committee acquired the moniker 'Star Chamber'. In its early years William Whitelaw presided, with the Chief Secretary acting as prosecutor. The Prime Minister always also appointed three other Cabinet ministers. Nominally independent, these would have received an easy time by the Treasury in the bilateral negotiations, thus making them his ally in Star Chamber discussions. To make that possible, the ministers concerned always headed departments with small budgets, thus enabling the Treasury to treat them generously.

In theory a minister could stand firm in the Star Chamber and ask the full Cabinet to arbitrate. It seldom happened, and the Cabinet usually gave short shrift to such ministers, and told them to return to the Star Chamber for another grilling. To fail to agree in Star Chamber was, in any case, an insult to the system that the Prime Minister had created as well as a challenge to one of her most basic political views. At least during the years of Thatcher's ascendancy, few ministers wanted that on their report cards. Fortunately, William Whitelaw's conciliatory skills helped to make the Star Chamber a success: so too did the fact that ministers were not allowed to bring any officials with them in support. Since Secretaries of State seldom understood the details of spending as well as the Chief Secretary, the Treasury usually got its way. Ministers found attending the Star Chamber an ordeal and preferred to settle bilaterally; partly for that reason, the need to use the system declined after a few years.

Then, in advance of the 1992 election, almost the entire Cabinet got into a funk over the likelihood of losing office. In the autumn of 1991 Norman Lamont, unable to resist pressures for spending rises, gave way and announced large and unsustainable increases in spending. Much to Lamont's dismay, Prime Minister John Major then responded to jibes that this pre-election giveaway would be reversed after the general election by making a public commitment that such a reversal would not take place. So Lamont proposed steps to tighten control over spending, including getting the Cabinet to decide on the overall level of government spending, and then using a revised Star Chamber under his own chairmanship to allocate the funds. This new group, officially a Cabinet committee designated 'EDX', also contained Michael Heseltine and Ken Clarke, who promptly proceeded to run rings round the Chancellor, refusing to discuss the agenda that he set out and talking instead about radical ideas to cut the state pension or to alter the Treasury's tax plans. In October 1992 the Chancellor, irritated by their tactics, stormed out of an EDX meeting and told his staff that he was resigning. Sarah Hogg, principal adviser to the Prime Minister, calmed him down, and in subsequent meetings Heseltine and Clarke behaved themselves, and helped the Chancellor to limp into harbour.[21] But few people now thought that Norman Lamont was up to the job of Chancellor.

This view was never completely fair. Norman Lamont introduced various reforms, including the unified tax-and-spend budget, the first of which Ken Clarke delivered in November 1993. That year, Clarke opted to sharply cut spending plans. When Gordon Brown became

Chancellor he introduced many more reforms, but famously stuck to the most recent spending limits set by Clarke. The new Chancellor told ministers not to make bids for any spending increases until they had sorted out their departmental priorities. Then he told them that their bids had to cover three years, replacing the massive annual PESC review of spending (which took up a large proportion of the time of a large proportion of each department's senior officials) with agreed medium-term spending programmes. He also made it clear that he had plenty of views of his own on what the spending plans should contain, and that wise ministers should fall into line with his own thinking rather than that of their officials. In return for spending allocations, ministers had to make 'public service agreements' with the Treasury, committing themselves to spending their cash in ways of which the Treasury approved. The Chancellor also clarified the separation between current and capital spending and introduced his 'golden rule': that over the cycle the Government would borrow only to fund capital rather than current spending. And with the Prime Minister's backing he replaced EDX with a new Cabinet committee (PSX), under his own chairmanship but advised by business outsiders, to examine the effectiveness of departmental spending.

Although the three-year spending settlements, covering about half of total spending (demand-driven items such as social security spending are still settled annually), were touted as Brown's most significant reform, the really radical step was to end completely the right of spending ministers to challenge their allocations. The only exceptions were John Prescott's super ministry, given special treatment to appease the rumbustious Deputy Prime Minister, and later the social security budget which the Prime Minister took as his personal area of interest after a back-bench rebellion on cuts to single parent benefits.

These arrangements had large implications for both the direction and the style of the 1997–2001 administration. Success depended partly on the willingness of ministers to abase themselves, but more so on the Prime Minister's agreement to go along with the plan, and not countenance any appeals from ministers, over the Chancellor's head. (Andrew Rawnsley tells how David Blunkett once asked for a private meeting with the Prime Minister to appeal against the Chancellor's spending limits: when he arrived at Number 10, the Health Secretary was horrified to find Gordon Brown sitting smugly by

Tony Blair's side. [22] In return the Prime Minister got the opportunity to promote his own favourites and even overrule the Chancellor, something which he did only sparingly, when he felt the need to re-mind Gordon Brown just who was in charge. So the Chancellor's preference for spending on job creation rather than on education, health, housing, defence or transport dominated the first few years of the Labour Government, and Tony Blair allowed his own priorities, education and health, to come second in the queue. It was not a pleasant decision for the Prime Minister to make, since it clearly had adverse consequences for the Government's popular support; and that in turn meant adverse consequences for the relationship between the two men.

In July 2000 the second comprehensive spending review marked a shift away from Brown's priorities towards Blair's. With unemploy-ment low but the Government losing its popularity, this policy ad-justment was no surprise. But there was another change, and one that provoked much criticism from the right-wing Press and the Tory Opposition. Rather than simply reshuffling his spending, Gordon Brown announced plans for a £43 billion increase in government spending in the run up to the 2001 general election.

Prudence, it was said, had been jilted and Brown was no better than past Labour Chancellors (or past Tory ones, it might have been added). But, as has already been said, a combination of earlier tax in-creases (some of them Brown's, some of them Norman Lamont's and Ken Clarke's), a very tight public spending regime, vast windfall rev-enues from the auction of mobile telephone licences, and strong growth with low inflation meant that public finances were in an in-credibly strong state. So long as the economy continued to perform well, the Chancellor could relax policy significantly, and spending would still be fully consistent with his long-asserted rules for the cau-tious management of public finances. In any case, the boost to spend-ing was less than it appeared: the increase was not just spread over three years, but the first year's increase was counted three times and the second year's was counted twice. As a share of national income, public spending was set to increase, but even at the end of Gordon Brown's three-year planning horizon, the share would still be below the legacy of the previous Conservative administration.

The Chancellor had not, as his critics claimed, jilted Prudence, and the worst that could be said was that he had been too restrictive in the previous couple of years, was now being naïve in expecting economic conditions to remain favourable, but was also disingenuous in the way in which he presented his numbers. The real question was what he would do if circumstances deteriorated to the extent that the long-run trajectory of the economy seemed to have changed, requiring policy to adjust or the Treasury's principles of sound economic management to be finessed. Of course that was a hypothetical not a prescient dilemma, but it remained true that Brown had not been tested in adversity in the way that others had been.

Monetary policy

One of the reasons why governments get very worked up about their own spending is that government expenditure tends to rise during recessions. Any attempts at dampening these natural movements can make the recession deeper. Equally, increasing spending during a recession can help to moderate the recession. That at least is the theory, as formulated by Keynes in the thirties and forties. But it all feels very counter-intuitive, like turning a ship's rudder one way to make it go another. And from the fifties to the seventies the practical experience of attempting to stabilise demand by manipulating government spending was just as unhappy as the experience, already recounted, of trying to stabilise demand by manipulating taxes. It is a bit like trying to steer a ship using a rudder connected to the wheel by a Heath Robinson arrangement of cogs, pulleys and rubber bands.

That was one of the reasons why many people greeted Geoffrey Howe's 1980 Budget with relief. This was to be a *Monetarist* government.

The social and economic disarray that had characterised the seventies had provoked a shift in Tory thinking towards a single-minded use of monetary restraint to restrain inflation. Influential commentators such as the journalists Peter Jay of *The Times* and Samuel Brittan of the *Financial Times*, City economists such as Gordon Pepper of Greenwell and the widely quoted (if at that time slightly less widely respected) economic forecasters at the London Business School had all argued that by one means or another, macroeconomic policy should focus only on restraining monetary growth in order to curb inflation, and that the traditional management of demand should be discontinued, along with incomes policies and appeasement of the trade unions.

There is a small and not very interesting controversy whether, in 1979, Monetarism was entirely new to the Treasury. What is certain is that monetary policy more broadly defined was *not* new. Hugh Dalton regarded himself as rather an expert in the field, and from 1945 to 1947 insisted on a 'cheap money' policy of holding down interest rates to allow both businesses and the Government to borrow cheaply. The National Debt Enquiry Committee of 1945 had recommended such a policy, largely due to the influence of Keynes, who feared a post-war slump. Dalton went beyond what the Committee had recommended in his determination to keep interest rates low. He issued gilts at very low rates of interest, but was horrified to find that the financial institutions were uninterested in buying them – not least because they were outraged by Dalton's repeated insistence that an advantage of cheap money was that it penalised the rich (who received less interest on their savings).

Dalton's policy of artificially low interest rates also made it harder for the Treasury to maintain the strong exchange rate to which the Attlee administration was also committed. Despite this, both Stafford Cripps and Hugh Gaitskell stuck with the policy. Then, in 1951, Rab Butler came into office and announced that he was bringing cheap money to an end, and would be allowing interest rates to come closer to their market level. What he really wanted to do was use interest rates to control inflation and support sterling. Butler initially raised short-term interest rates only slightly, from 2 to 2.5 per cent; but by March 1952 bank rate was up to 4 per cent – a giddy figure for the time.

Partly to reduce his reliance on interest rates, Rab Butler also introduced in 1952 a new instrument of monetary policy: hire-purchase controls. He took them away again in 1954, but reintroduced them in 1955 to curb the boom ignited by his over-expansionary 1954 budget. Monetary policy and fiscal policy were now treated almost as interchangeable ways to manage demand in the economy, and for the next quarter-century successive Chancellors periodically adjusted interest rates to speed the economy up a bit or slow it down a bit, just as they periodically adjusted the fiscal balance for the same purpose.

Often the Treasury or the Bank of England also used controls of one sort or another to act directly upon the pace of credit expansion. Indeed, during the sixties the accumulation of controls over the banking system came under increasing criticism for being unfair, ineffective and inefficient. Restrictions such as the lending limits that applied only to clearing banks and finance houses and not to other types of banks, or the cartel that obliged all high-street banks to lend or borrow at identical interest rates, either didn't work because of the huge loopholes, or worked at the heavy expense of some companies versus others.

So in 1971 Tony Barber directed the Bank of England to abandon many of its restrictions on the financial system and introduce new, simpler arrangements, intended to be fairer and to encourage greater competition within the system. Unfortunately the new arrangements proved completely ineffective at restraining the growth of bank lending. The result was an unsustainable spending boom and a sharp rise in the stock of money in the economy. By mid 1972 Barber was desperately hiking interest rates to curb the economic expansion. In November 1973 short-term interest rates hit a staggering 13 per cent. Soon after, Barber reintroduced precisely the sort of credit rationing that he and the Bank had so recently rejected. They followed up rationing with ever more convoluted rules for curbing the expansion of money and credit. These included the supplementary special deposits scheme, generally known by its far more evocative title 'the corset'. As a result, the financial boom started to come under control – but by then wage and price inflation were well entrenched, and escalating.

Denis Healey, taking office in 1974, was in no hurry to sort out the mess. Only after the 1976 sterling crisis did he grudgingly adopt targets for the expansion of money, credit and public borrowing, echoing a similar move by Roy Jenkins in 1968 in the wake of the 1967 sterling crisis. In both cases the Treasury framed the new targets in ways intended to placate the IMF, which was providing the UK with emergency funding. The 1976 targets proved easy to hit, and so neither Healey nor the Bank considered overhauling the methods of monetary and credit control. When Geoffrey Howe took office, he inherited a Byzantine system that, to the eyes of a single-minded Monetarist, seemed completely unsuited to the task of controlling inflation through monetary restraint.

Within months of starting work, Geoffrey Howe declared that from now on, monetary targets would be pre-eminent amongst policy goals. The need to achieve the monetary targets would override all other policy considerations, and indeed make many other policies redundant. There was no longer any point in having incomes policies, and no longer any scope for seeking to manage demand in the economy, in the old Keynesian manner. Demand management and incomes policy were now both dead.

In truth the break with the past was not quite as clear as the Treasury and the Chancellor pretended. The amount of attention paid to monetary trends, and the degree of use made of monetary instruments, had both been rising gradually since Butler's days, and the new regime was the extreme conclusion of those trends. Furthermore, although the Chancellor now paid a lot of attention to measures of the stock of money circulating in the economy, he and his staff still looked at old-fashioned evidence on trends in prices, employment and unemployment and the balance of payments. Furthermore, in practice Geoffrey Howe's actions would prove to be well out of line with his words: he opted to combine lax monetary policy with tight fiscal policy, working within the context of a radical new willingness to brazen out extremely high levels of unemployment. By 1981 it was pretty clear to everybody that over the previous couple of years the pace of inflation had been affected very little by the rate of monetary growth and rather a lot by the recession provoked by the Government's fiscal policy and its exchange rate policy. Howe blinked owlishly, and did not complain.

When Nigel Lawson became Chancellor, he eschewed such pragmatism and determined not to let the facts get in the way of his thinking. He proudly declared that the control of monetary growth would be an essential part of his job. And indeed, Lawson's first three years in office marked the high point of post-war government belief in the efficacy of monetary policy. Yet Lawson could never quite make up his mind about what he meant by 'money', nor about how he could exercise 'control' over monetary growth. So when in September 1986 a currency retreat became a rout and Lawson was forced to borrow from the Bundesbank, the deeply chastened Chancellor did something that he had not done for several years. He instantly and shamelessly abandoned his existing beliefs and adopted new ones instead. So Lawson abandoned Monetarism, and resolved instead to dedicate himself to managing the exchange rate – something that true Monetarists always said was incompatible with their creed.

Sterling's botched entry into the European Exchange Rate Mechanism (ERM) and the trauma of its ignominious exit from that system have since created an opportunity for a resurgent belief in the appropriateness of monetary policy. This has not meant a return to Monetarism. Instead we have an open acceptance that changes to interest rates can stimulate or restrain the growth of demand in the domestic economy, and hence that they can be used, to some degree at least, to control the rate of inflation.

Norman Lamont and Ken Clarke kept monetary policy as their preserve, but Clarke gave the Bank of England more opportunity than before to participate in the public discussion of what should happen to sterling. The results were not entirely helpful, with the monthly meetings between Chancellor and Governor coming to look more like a game of poker than policy-making, with each side engaging in strategic game playing: the notorious 'Ken and Eddie Show'. Famously, Gordon Brown has sought to address this by going much further, and passing to the Bank of England almost all of his monetary responsibilities. This makes him the first post-war Chancellor to have no monetary policy. Indeed, when taken in conjunction with his 'no-change' fiscal policy it is clear that Brown, far more than any predecessor, has opted out of short-term policy-making altogether. Now only the Bank of England has policies for the management of demand in the economy.

An aspect of current monetary policy that is no less important than the transfer of control is the dual emphasis now placed on simplicity and transparency. Under current monetary arrangements it is straightforwardly clear what it is that the Bank of England is trying to achieve. It is clear how it is operating, and fairly clear who makes the decisions. Indeed, perhaps those are the real justifications for putting monetary policy decisions in the hands of the Bank – for it would be ludicrous to expect such straight-dealing from the Treasury.

Debates on the wisdom and impact of conferring near-independence on the Bank of England will never be entirely settled, but so far the large bulk of opinion has been in favour of independence, and initial critics have switched sides (not least the Conservative Opposition). Indeed the Chancellor has mainly been criticised for not going further (although so long as parliamentary sovereignty continues to mean anything, it is not clear how much further he could go). But Gordon Brown's implicit assumption that only interest rates have much effect on the economic cycle and hence on inflation, and that fiscal policy is a poor instrument for demand management, is not obviously correct. It conflicts with Geoffrey Howe's experience, and it may yet haunt this, or some subsequent, Chancellor.

The greatest danger is that at some point Britain will experience the kind of mess that the Americans got themselves into in the eighties. The Federal Reserve pursued a deflationary policy of high interest rates while President and Congress were operating highly expansionary tax and spending policies. The result was a huge current account deficit on the balance of payments, a dollar overvaluation and a tendency for the United States to attract excessive capital inflows. The problem of inconsistent policies took years to undo, and largely robbed George Bush of his second term in office. That should not happen to Gordon Brown, so long as his fiscal policy rules prevent the pursuit of extreme fiscal policies. But if fiscal rectitude is abandoned, by Brown or any subsequent Chancellor, or more simply if the economy falls into a recession which seems to demand fiscal action outside of the boundaries set by Gordon Brown, then the combination of that and Bank of England independence could be very dangerous.

Chancellors and incomes policies

Trust in monetary policy comes and goes: trust in incomes policies seems to have gone for ever, thanks to the sorry history of voluntary and statutory incomes policies in the United Kingdom since the forties and fifties. As governments of both parties gradually gave up their direct controls over prices, they became predictably worried that they would find themselves faced with rapid inflation. Admittedly it was clear that they could and often would use Keynesian demand management (of the monetary or the fiscal kind) to squeeze the economy, thereby slowing spending and reducing output and employment, and hence they hoped inflation. But for three decades from 1945 onwards, the pursuit of full employment seemed to limit the opportunity for sustained use of such policies.

In these circumstances it is not surprising that British governments turned to pay restraint, sometimes voluntary, sometimes statutory, to control inflation. These incomes policies were often nominally the responsibility of another Cabinet minister, whose title varied from humble 'Minister of Labour' to Barbara Castle's rococo designation in the late sixties as 'First Secretary of State and Secretary of State for Employment and Productivity'. In practice, however, the Chancellor was often author and guardian of the policy, not least because all his other policies depended on the success or failure of pay restraint.

Belief in the central importance of incomes policies emerged in the late forties, and became entrenched in the sixties and seventies, when anybody who did not believe in them was dismissed as wild or naïve. Yet this was a view that was very much specific to that period. There had been no direct controls over wages during the Second World War, when the Government controlled almost everything else. Thanks to full employment and a desperate need to raise national output, workers could have demanded large pay rises, if they had chosen to do so. However, a formal incomes policy would have alienated the unions and impeded the national unity that the Churchill government believed was so vital to the war effort. Instead Churchill found jobs for many trade union leaders within his administration, most notably for Ernie Bevin. Churchill treated the trade unionists with genuine respect, and the unions in turn kept inflation down through scrupulous self-restraint over wages.

This approach continued in the immediate reconstruction period, again helped by the prominence of Bevin and others in the Government. When controls over prices started to disappear, however, governments could no longer duck the issue of wage control. In 1948 Cripps successfully negotiated a voluntary incomes policy with the unions, and that worked well until 1950. Then, in October of that year, partly because of the impact of the previous year's devaluation, the incomes policy broke down when the TUC decided to withdraw its cooperation.

Despite that setback neither Clement Attlee nor the new Chancellor, Hugh Gaitskell, even considered introducing a compulsory wages policy. Nor did their Tory successors. Indeed Churchill famously gave his Minister of Labour, Walter Monckton, an explicit instruction to appease the unions over pay. Churchill hoped that by so doing, he could avoid industrial stoppages: his advisers warned him early on that a strike in a key industry such as coal could easily bring the country to a standstill within a week or two, with disastrous economic and financial consequences.

By the late fifties the unions were becoming highly dismissive of the notion of wage restraint. Yet Prime Minister Harold Macmillan reaffirmed his party's firm opposition to statutory controls over pay. Instead he placed great emphasis on the need for the unions to moderate their views and exercise voluntary restraint over wage claims. This proved unrealistic and left the Treasury reliant in practice on Keynesian demand management to constrain inflation. But demand management was already focused on the pursuit of full employment. This basic inconsistency led to a succession of brief policy expansions followed by similar deflations: the notorious 'stop-go' policies of the period.

In April 1961 Macmillan's third Chancellor, Selwyn Lloyd, felt obliged to introduce a Budget that was tight enough to make him the most unpopular Chancellor since the war, yet was nevertheless too lax to satisfy the foreign exchange markets, alarmed by poor balance of payments figures. Meanwhile pay settlements climbed faster and faster. The Government's predicament seemed desperate: Macmillan (a secret funker) seriously considered resignation. The fixed rate of sterling was under pressure from heavy selling and, especially following the revaluation of the increasingly mighty German mark, the Bank of England's reserves were running low. Central bankers elsewhere in Europe refused to extend their already generous help. That presented Lloyd with exactly the same dilemma that has faced countless Chancellors before and since. Eschewing a devaluation and acting on Macmillan's instructions, he opted in July 1961 to squeeze the economy further. Lloyd cut government spending and raised interest rates. He also borrowed heavily from the IMF, and he announced a 'pay pause', forbidding any further pay rises until March the following year.

Of these various initiatives the one which shocked the nation the most and which buried Lloyd's reputation was the pay pause. Few understood its typically Macmillanesque purpose: to reduce the scale of spending cuts, and hence avert a sharp rise in unemployment. Thanks to Macmillan's lack of nerve, the pay pause applied only to the public sector, and Lloyd merely asked the private sector to follow the lead set by government. (He also set up the National Economic Development Council to consider long-term economic policy issues from a tripartite perspective.)

Given Macmillan's fear of a fight, the pay pause scarcely stood a chance. It suffered an early setback when winter came and the electricity workers demanded a pay rise in defiance of the pay pause. Instead of refusing, the Government gave way and agreed to the demand. Yet in February 1962 Selwyn Lloyd published a White Paper on Incomes Policy that explained how the Government now intended to conduct policy. Lloyd asked all negotiators to adhere to a norm or 'guiding light' of 2.5 per cent annual pay increases. Although the details were ever changing, incomes policies became a frequent feature of the policy scene for the next decade and a half.

Frequent but still not popular. Incomes policies set ministers against ministers, governments against unions, and inevitably governments against employers and voters too. In 1964 the incoming Labour Government promised that it would never resort to statutory policies. Instead, George Brown negotiated with the unions and employers for a voluntary policy. But the Treasury did not believe that a voluntary policy would work, and Chancellor Jim Callaghan championed the introduction of a statutory policy. The likelihood of the voluntary policy succeeding was never very great, and in 1969 Harold Wilson and Barbara Castle sealed its fate when they decided to introduce legislation on trade union reform. From that moment forward, there was little point in seeking to impose a serious incomes policy of any sort, voluntary or statutory. Working relations with the unions were to fall apart, and any incomes policy was destined to fail.

By then, Roy Jenkins had become Chancellor. It is possible that he could have resisted the idea that trade union reform should take priority over incomes policy, and clear that he did not. The Treasury came to regard the resultant *In Place of Strife* débâcle as clear evidence that other ministries could not be trusted with economic policy issues – although it was the ex-Chancellor Jim Callaghan, now at the Home Office, who did most amongst ministers to torpedo the policy.

Labour's experience was a lesson to the Conservatives that they chose not to learn. Again they promised not to impose a statutory incomes policy, and again they did – and on top of their own clumsy legislation on trade union reform. Little wonder that Harold Wilson started his second term of office determined not to repeat the same mistake yet again. Instead he got his Chancellor Denis Healey to oversee a voluntary 'Social Contract'. Labour promised to repeal Ted Heath's hated labour reform legislation, raise living standards through tax cuts, hold down interest rates, and raise pensions. In return for all this, the unions promised to hold down pay increases.

But the TUC was unable or (and this was Healey's view) unwilling to keep its side of the bargain. By July 1975 inflation was 26 per cent and wages were rising by 32 per cent a year. The Chancellor concluded that the only option was a statutory incomes policy setting a limit on pay increases of 10 per cent.

Wilson agreed to Healey's demand for a statutory policy only with the disreputable stipulation that any legislation could embody sanctions against employers who conceded too much, but not workers or trade unions who demanded too much. Healey put the resultant plan to the Employment Secretary, Michael Foot, who threatened to resign. Healey quite reasonably ignored him. The Chancellor presented the policy to Cabinet, where typically Jim Callaghan was the only significant member to side with Foot. The Employment Secretary's silliness quickly became apparent when a trade unionist, Jack Jones, the leader of the TGWU, persuaded him to stay in government.

Healey had won, but at great personal cost in terms of his burden of work. For the next eight days the TUC kept Healey in constant negotiation over details, and indeed absorbed much of his time for the next three years. The TUC leadership claimed that they supported Healey's strategy, yet they never stopped complaining. They haggled over anything and everything, forcing Healey to defend his policy against their attempts at attrition. Matters reached a new low in 1976. In his Budget, Healey had made the remarkable promise that he would raise personal allowances if the TUC delivered pay restraint. The unions' response was to turn up for a meeting and then sit in silence, refusing to speak. Eventually in that meeting and many others, Healey won them round to the position that both he and they knew was correct – only to face worse misconduct in 1977 and 1978.

For by then the TUC had lost control over its members, whose growing militancy left the organisation's leaders unable to commit to anything worthwhile: leaders who were themselves rapidly being replaced by lesser men such as Moss Evans and David Basnett, with negligible capacity for seeing, let alone acting upon, the real self-interests of their members. Apart from the consequences for the economy, the implications for the Chancellor were grave. By then, Healey was spending half his working time in interminable negotiations with the unions over pay. He spent perhaps another quarter of his time chairing a Cabinet committee on pay, looking at negotiations in unfeasible detail. The unions had hijacked the Chancellor, leaving him with insufficient time to spend on other policy issues.

The end came in January 1978, when the Prime Minister casually announced in a television interview that the pay norm for the next pay round would be just 5 per cent. Callaghan claimed afterwards that the number just 'popped out' while he was speaking.[23] Certainly he had not agreed it with Healey or other ministers. The TUC professed outrage. They said, perhaps disingenuously, that they might have been able to secure agreement to 10 per cent, but that 5 per cent was so unreasonable that it was now impossible for them to deliver pay restraint of any sort. And indeed over the coming year the unions resisted with unprecedented ferocity the Government's attempt to impose the 5 per cent limit.

For the second time, Jim Callaghan had put an end to a colleague's policy in this area. He helped to end both his own Government's period in office (not bad for a man now Prime Minister) and the use of incomes policies altogether. He had been defeated by the unions whom for so long he had cultivated. It was the last of many insults to his Chancellor Denis Healey who had been successfully running an incomes policy in an atmosphere of emergent class warfare. That achievement testifies to Healey's great powers of intellect and personality; although with hindsight, one wonders whether he might have been better employed preparing for the civil war against the trade unions and the far left that the Labour leadership now desperately needed to wage.

Under the circumstances a Labour defeat in the May 1979 election was both deserved and inevitable. The new Conservative Government came into office feeling somewhat apprehensive, but clear on a few big things. At the absolute centre of its purpose – far more so than its supposed Monetarism – was a refusal to dignify the unions by talking to them: or as it was generally put, there was to be no more beer and sandwiches at Number 10. Linked to that, there would be no more incomes policies. Margaret Thatcher and other ministers seldom met any union leaders.

While commentators viewed this variously as a brave, an arrogant or a foolish decision, it had the undoubted merit of considerably reducing the Chancellor's burden of work. Healey liked to complain that as Chancellor he was required to perform the Labours of Hercules. Geoffrey Howe instead looked forward to a less arduous period in office. Monetary control was clear and simple, and so the same would be true of the Chancellor's job. But Geoffrey Howe had forgotten something. He was about to find himself tested by a problem that had traumatised a quarter of his post-war predecessors, and had haunted the rest: the problem of the exchange rate. Dalton, Cripps, Butler, Callaghan, Barber and Healey had all been whipped by the pound. And Geoffrey Howe was not about to escape unscathed.

2 International policy-making

Exchange rate policies

When Geoffrey Howe became Chancellor he took over a Treasury still haunted by the memory of 1976. In that year officials had denuded the nation's foreign exchange reserves in a futile attempt to stop panic sales of sterling. In June a number of central bankers led by the Dutch Jelle Zijlstra, believing that the markets were over-reacting, had put together a stand-by credit of $5.3 billion. The Federal Reserve contributed $2 billion, but the American Treasury Secretary, William Simon, insisted that the loan was available only until the end of the year: after that, Britain would have to go to the IMF for help. That was not too alarming in itself since Britain, like other industrialised nations, had borrowed from the IMF on earlier occasions. But this time the IMF would only assist if it could dictate economic policy to the British Government. When that indeed was what happened, the British Treasury felt cauterised.

The traumatic experience of 1976 should have taught the Treasury that if you are seeking a stable exchange rate then it is foolish to pursue economic policies that are inconsistent with such stability. However, that was too large a lesson to learn. Instead, officials were now convinced that there was no point in trying to manipulate the value of the currency. Better instead to let sterling take its chances, and to concentrate on achieving financial stability in the domestic economy.

Since Monetarism offered a set of rules purporting to contain the secret of domestic financial stability, the Treasury in 1979 was ready to embrace the Monetarism that Geoffrey Howe and his colleagues espoused. It was a positive relief that the Conservatives said they were intent on being pure Monetarists, taking the doctrine without reservation. In contrast, the scavenger Denis Healey had taken the bits that he liked, put them together with other policies, and ignored the bits that he disliked. For just as the pure Monetarist theory allowed no place for incomes policies, so it allowed no place for an active exchange rate policy. Under the Conservatives, there would be no attempts to manipulate the value of sterling, and hence no sleepless nights for either officials or politicians, whenever the pound refused to do what they wanted. When he delivered his first full Budget, Howe scarcely mentioned the exchange rate. Nor was there much mention of sterling in the text of the newly invented 'Medium Term Financial Strategy' that accompanied the budget.

The new Treasury ministers were so sure that they would not want to manipulate the exchange rate that, within months of taking office, they abolished exchange controls. These controls were the last vestiges of Hugh Dalton's Treasury regime and as such, Geoffrey Howe was glad to see the back of them.

What the Chancellor was soon to learn was that the behaviour of the exchange rate is always an issue, lurking in the macroeconomic policy background, and sometimes pushing itself into the foreground. The election of the Conservative Government was followed by a rapid strengthening in sterling. The currency rose sharply in Howe's first year in office and carried on soaring. Manufacturer after manufacturer found itself unable to compete in the market place at the new exchange rate. Company closures and job losses soared. The Chancellor faced widespread demands to moderate, or even reverse, the rise in the pound.

Much of the rise in the currency in the Tories' first year and a half reflected market expectations of ever-higher interest rates. The Treasury and the Bank were struggling to slow the pace of monetary growth and that seemed likely to demand further interest rate rises. The turning point in market thinking occurred in early 1981 when it became clear that inflation was coming down, even though monetary growth was not. Geoffrey Howe relented and started to let the facts, not the monetary data, guide his thinking. He cut interest rates. Sterling peaked. Within months, the poor Chancellor faced anxieties about the currency descent getting out of control.

Some Chancellors deny that they can influence the exchange rate. That was always Howe's claim, even after he moved away from his initial assumption that the exchange rate did not matter. Other Chancellors seek to use the exchange rate to achieve particular policy aims, as Nigel Lawson did when he tried to use currency stability as a means to achieve stable inflation. More often, Chancellors confine themselves to trying to prevent other policies being toppled by a huge currency shift, or trying to stem such a shift while it is already under way. Whichever it is, the business of watching and trying to manage either the exchange rate itself or the consequence of exchange rate movements always ends up becoming a major element of the Chancellor's job.

Exchange rate policy can also be the most stressful part of the Chancellor's job. The events of 1976 were bad; some previous episodes had been even worse. Much has been written about the damage done by overwork to Stafford Cripps's health. Domestic policy issues were not, however, the main problem. The largest strain on him came from the question that he faced, or refused to face: whether to devalue the exchange rate. This had been fixed in 1945 at a level, $4.03 to the pound, well above what market forces suggested was appropriate.

Problems became acute in 1948 when the American economy went into recession. For countries of the sterling area – essentially the old British Empire – as well as for Britain itself, this meant a large fall in exports. The sterling area countries did everything they could to bolster their reduced inflows of American dollars by selling their remaining sterling reserves to the Bank of England. Although sterling was not fully convertible, the British Government's rules were still sufficiently accommodating to allow another large run on Britain's dollar reserves.

Cripps was strongly averse to devaluation for political reasons. The Chancellor feared that devaluation would undermine Britain's political standing abroad, and would require an unpopular deflation at home, and so he insisted on resisting the market.[1] His advisers, Robert Hall and Edwin Plowden, pointed out that basic economic forces made such a view deeply unrealistic, and argued for a managed devaluation, to bring government policy into line with market reality. Yet the permanent officials at the Treasury and the Bank of England firmly opposed such a step. They never quite managed to set down on paper their economic arguments, but always insisted that they knew best.

In the end the Treasury, the Bank and the Chancellor of the Exchequer lost the fight. After a $300 million outflow between July and mid September 1949, the British Government devalued sterling from a little over four dollars to the pound to well under three. (Cripps himself barely participated in the decision: he was spending time in Switzerland, nursing his damaged health.) Thirty other countries followed. Cripps had to impose a deflationary package to slow the economy and avert the inflation that seemed bound to follow the devaluation.

The experiences of Cripps in 1949 and Healey in 1976 were not unusual. Callaghan, Barber, Lawson, Lamont: they all spent much of their time and a lot of the nation's money defending an indefensible exchange rate. So it is hardly surprising that other Chancellors have tried to avoid such crises, either by highly proactive currency policies, or by not having a policy at all, and letting the currency float.

The strangest policy was that which Rab Butler considered introducing when, soon after taking office, he found himself faced with a large balance of payments problem. Despite the 1949 devaluation, the fundamental weakness of sterling that had so dogged the Attlee government looked set to cause the new Conservative administration trouble. So a small group of clever but naïve Treasury and Bank officials proposed that the Government should abandon any attempts at defending any particular exchange rate, and float sterling instead. And since they feared a consequent run on the pound (and the Bank in particular was very keen that sterling should miraculously float at exactly the dollar-sterling rate that they had found it so difficult to defend), they also proposed that the Chancellor should introduce severely deflationary policies at home.

But the officials feared that these steps would not be enough to avert a currency collapse and so, extraordinarily, they proposed to deny foreign and commonwealth governments access to their own foreign currency reserves, held for them as sterling deposits by the Bank of England. The officials bizarrely believed that such an action would help to strengthen sterling, by making it impossible for the governments concerned to sell the currency – even though making it easier for other governments and individuals to sell sterling (so-called 'convertibility'). And, to add an extra layer of implausibility to the scheme, they proposed that the Government should borrow from the IMF and from the Canadian and American governments, offering the official reserves as security.

The plan, hastily cobbled together and clumsily and quite inappropriately known as Robot, appalled Butler's colleagues and most of his officials. They thought it arrogant, ill-considered and potentially ruinous. The name Robot was an acronym derived from the names of its progenitors, the Treasury officials Leslie Rowan and Otto Clarke, and George Bolton from the Bank of England. The scheme's proper description was the 'Plan for External Action to Save Sterling', but its critics thought it would do the reverse. The idea that sterling could be floated and yet would continue to trade at an over-valued exchange rate was implausible, and offered no solution to the problem of the excessive balance of payments deficit. Equally, the rest of the Cabinet and most of the civil servants who knew of the scheme (very few) rightly doubted whether a currency depreciation, if that occurred, would do anything to improve the trade balance in the short term, given that there was no immediate scope in Britain either to reduce imports or to increase exports. Robot, had it been implemented, would have had the reverse effect to that which was intended, and could easily have caused a terminal currency crisis, with the market value of sterling plunging towards nothing. Ministers feared that to prevent the floating from turning into sinking, they would need to introduce even more draconian policies to curb demand at home than those Butler proposed. Even Butler confided that his plan would probably make the Tories so unpopular that they would be out of government for the next forty years.

Almost every detail of the scheme was cock-eyed. Its advocates presented it to Butler as a scheme for dismantling controls and liberating both sterling and the Government; that description was quite untrue, but Butler fell for their rhetoric. By persuading the Cabinet to reject Robot, Churchill's lieutenant Lord Cherwell scored a great victory over the Chancellor and for common sense. But the fight took up much of the Treasury's time at a critical early stage in Butler's Chancellorship, and Butler never fully recovered from the reversal: he became an easy-going pragmatist, and a mere exponent of what he famously described as 'the art of the possible', rather than a man with authority of his own.

Nigel Lawson adopted the direct opposite exchange-rate policy. His 1986 currency crisis left the traumatised Chancellor clear that he should abandon Monetarism and make currency management the centrepiece of his economic policy. But Lawson knew that Margaret Thatcher deeply opposed the only remotely credible arrangement within which he could fix sterling – the European Exchange Rate Mechanism (ERM). So he decided to adopt a policy in which he and the Bank of England behaved as if sterling was fixed within the ERM, but about which he told nobody, not even (especially not) the Prime Minister.

There is a popular view, spread by Lawson's enemies, that the result was a recession in the UK economy. That was not so: the recession came for different reasons. Nevertheless, keeping the exchange-rate policy secret from the Prime Minister was never a tenable strategy, and on 25 June 1988 for the second time in a few days the Chancellor and his closest ally Geoffrey Howe demanded a meeting with the Prime Minister. The first meeting had been granted 'only with the utmost reluctance and ill-grace', and this second meeting was a final showdown.[2] The two ministers told Margaret Thatcher that unless she agreed to sterling joining the ERM, they would both resign. Momentarily cornered, the Prime Minister agreed, and at the Madrid Summit the following day Margaret Thatcher announced that sterling would certainly join the ERM, just as soon as other nations abolished their exchange controls and as soon as inflation rates converged across Europe. Since exchange controls were due to go in a month's time, and inflation rates were already converging, she was effectively saying that, at last, entry was imminent.

The Prime Minister's revenge was swift. A month later she humiliated Geoffrey Howe by moving him from the Foreign Office to a more junior post. Simultaneously she summoned the opinionated academic Alan Walters back to court to be her personal economic adviser. Walters quickly embarked on the campaign of criticism that would lead to Lawson's resignation a year later.

During the course of that year the Prime Minister and the Chancellor barely talked to one another, making it rather difficult to agree a timetable for sterling's entry into the ERM. But when John Major became Chancellor, the Prime Minister could no longer refuse to talk to her most senior minister. To her annoyance, at their regular private meetings Major repeatedly urged that they deliver on their promise of sterling's entry into the currency system – and made it clear that he would not stop his urgings. They both knew that, as with Wilson and

Jenkins, she could not sack him. Meanwhile the new Foreign Secretary, working in alliance with Major just as Howe had worked with Lawson, added his own weight to the Chancellor's arguments, while never allowing her to see them explicitly colluding. As an ex-Foreign Office official and ex-bag carrier to the arch-Europeanist Edward Heath, Hurd's opinions were never likely to earn Margaret Thatcher's respect, but as the third Foreign Secretary in a little more than a year, he too could neither be snubbed nor sacked.

John Major played his cards with great skill, always tactful and patient, careful to avoid reopening philosophical debates about the wisdom of ERM, taking that argument as won, and focusing instead on the mechanics of entry and the technical question of which precisely would be the best day on which to enter. Meanwhile, the Prime Minister's advisers were now telling her privately that her opposition to implementing a decision that she had already announced was beginning to look silly. At a meeting on 14 June, almost two years to the day since Howe and Lawson had forced Thatcher's hand, the Prime Minister assured Major that she no longer had any real reservations about entry. Major reminded her that his preferred date was 20 July: the Prime Minister said no, but subsequently agreed to an autumn date. She had conceded. At the Tory Party conference in October 1990, Chancellor John Major announced that sterling had become a member of the ERM.

John Major and Douglas Hurd were good departmental men, and the institutional obsession of both the Treasury and the Foreign Office had long been to get sterling into the ERM. The aim of the departments and their ministerial heads was fundamentally the same as Geoffrey Howe's had been when he eschewed having a currency policy: to make life simple. Unfortunately the economics and the politics of the situation soon proved to be much harsher than either Hurd or Major appreciated. The threat of a currency crisis is ever-present, whether under floating or fixed rates. The expression 'fixed exchange rate' only ever means that the monetary authorities have fixed the price at which *they themselves* are willing to trade in the currency markets. It is not a guarantee that others will trade at that price; not even when exchange controls restrict the ability of traders to do business where and how they like. Admittedly, governments and central banks have often persuaded the markets that the official price is a sensible one. Rather often, however, they have failed. Sterling's membership of the ERM was not going to prove easy to maintain.

Entry into the system coincided with the Italian Government's assumption of the European presidency. The Italians decided to mark their period in office by giving new momentum to the Commission's plan to introduce a single European currency. This was a bridge too far for the British Prime Minister. Initially John Major thought he had defused the situation by suggesting a compromise scheme, the 'hard ECU', which would be a *common* currency for Europe, although not necessarily a *single* currency, only to hear Margaret Thatcher shatter the compromise by proclaiming in public that the hard ECU policy would never evolve into a single currency for Europe, and that there never would be a single currency by any means.

Major sat still and kept quiet, as did the rest of the Cabinet, as indeed they did on 30 October when the Prime Minister reported to the Commons on the Rome summit, just ended. Her speech, drafted for her by civil servants, was temperate and diplomatic: she even backtracked on the hard ECU and said that of course it *could* develop into a single European currency, if that was what the people of Europe wanted. But when she took questions, Thatcher ceased to be temperate. She ranted. She denounced the European Commission as anti-democratic. She denounced the idea of a single currency. She denounced the hard ECU as a currency that nobody would want to hold. Still, Major sat on his hands.

Then a day later another worm finally turned: Geoffrey Howe, who had nothing to lose, resigned from the Government. That forced the Prime Minister out of office, to be succeeded by Major, who two years later took a boomerang in the head when sterling's enforced departure from the ERM fatally wounded his own premiership as well as the Chancellorship of Norman Lamont (who had never wanted sterling to join the ERM anyway). It was all very bizarre, and a more powerful argument than any economic theorem for not seeking to manage the exchange rate.

Today we have Gordon Brown who, since he has no control over interest rates and few other policy instruments to wield, effectively has no exchange-rate policy of his own. But still, as always, the exchange rate does not go away. All through 1998 and 1999, manufacturing industry and the Conservative Opposition castigated

Brown for the strength of sterling. Brown denied that he was to blame and at the time he got away with it, largely because the feared economic recession never fully materialised.

But in future, Gordon Brown or his successors may not be so lucky. The public cannot be relied upon to accept ministers' claims that large economic problems are nothing to do with them. The public's response to exchange-rate mismanagement can be very severe; its response to exchange-rate non-management may yet be just as punishing.

Unless the exchange rate has already been abolished, of course. Sterling's entry into the European Monetary Union, if it comes, will mean the end of exchange-rate policies for Britain. The Chancellor will still discuss the appropriate value of the Euro versus other currencies, but only as one of many participants in the debate. Unless a future British Chancellor manages to establish hegemony over other European finance ministers, he or she will have far less power than the President of the European Central Bank. But it is a little hard to imagine that such hegemony will ever come about. For the track record of British Chancellors offering global economic policy leadership has not been a very convincing one, and has been no better in recent than in earlier years.

Reconstructing the world economy

The Chancellor's international responsibilities have never been confined to the exchange rate. All Chancellors must agree with other governments the rules by which they are to manage the world economy. They must break those rules when occasion demands. And they must encourage foreign governments to change their own economic policies, in ways that might be to the UK's advantage.

There is clearly a danger here of delusions of grandeur. Margaret Thatcher's memoirs contain the observation that Chancellors are rather prone to acquiring a taste for attending foreign summits. That, she says, is why they like to move from being Chancellor to becoming Foreign Secretary.[3] No doubt she had Geoffrey Howe in mind, and the comment was surely a criticism. As a generalisation the point is unconvincing: no other Chancellor made the same transition, and at least one has dreaded it. Roy Jenkins initially wanted to become

Foreign Secretary if Labour won the 1970 election. Then, as the election approached, he increasingly feared that the change would mean a move away from the political front line.[4] Even Jim Callaghan had to spend time in purgatory at the Home Office (and then in opposition) before he could aspire to be Foreign Secretary.

Nigel Lawson made a sharper observation: that a Chancellor's inevitable unpopularity amongst ministerial colleagues makes him prone to seek refuge among fellow finance ministers.[5] The remark was not entirely original. A few years earlier Denis Healey had said much the same in his memoirs. Healey described finance ministers as the most 'depressed and unpopular caste' of politicians. He called them 'untouchables' who enjoyed a 'friendly freemasonry, which transcended our economic differences'.[6]

Healey claims that at a meeting of finance ministers in France he taught all the participants to sing a Popular Front version of a French revolutionary song, 'La Carmagnole'. He says that he once stayed up drinking with Helmut Schmidt and friends until four in the morning. Healey says that the American Treasury Secretary, Bill Simon, was 'a good colleague'. He says that Raymond Barre was 'always helpful', that a senior German civil servant, Manfred Lahnstein, became 'a good friend of mine for life'. He calls Bob McNamara from the World Bank a 'good friend'. He says that he developed 'a great respect and liking' for the Japanese officials he met – and so on. In contrast, Healey expresses little affection for any of his Cabinet colleagues – though to be fair, he does at least refrain from the insults that Nigel Lawson, in his memoirs, heaped on former colleagues.

Foreign conferences, meetings and summits surely do provide Chancellors with welcome respite from the unpleasantness and grind of domestic politics and governance. But they are also frustrating events. A great deal of posturing and window-dressing takes place, and the amount of muscle that a British Chancellor can exercise is nowadays so limited. Meetings abroad are also very time-consuming, and were far more so before the introduction of jet aircraft in the early sixties. Indeed, early Chancellors delegated to officials negotiations that a modern minister would probably expect to conduct in person. This was especially true during the Second World War, when substantial work on planning for the post-war world economic order seemed necessary. Indeed, the most famous international economic

conference of all, Bretton Woods, took place in New Hampshire during the war, with no British ministers present.

The British Treasury, perhaps lacking a sense of proportion, had
first started thinking about the shape of the post-war international
monetary order as early as 1940. The American Treasury started
work a year later. In 1943 at Bretton Woods the two Treasuries' representatives, the laconic Maynard Keynes and the belligerent Harry
Dexter White, produced a Joint Statement. They described the rules
of a new international monetary system. They also offered a set of
draft Articles of Association to govern the operations of the International Monetary Fund: the body that they intended would manage
the new global system.

It is not entirely clear whether the British benefited from having
the most celebrated economist of the age, rather than a mere politician, negotiating on their behalf. Keynes seems to have annoyed the
American negotiators more than was entirely necessary. They found
him condescending and too clever by half. But the fact that the eventual deal owed more to the conservative White than to the liberal
Keynes was not primarily a matter of personalities. Nor of course
was it a matter of the merits of the arguments, but a question of
power.

Keynes wanted a system of readily adjustable exchange rates. He
also proposed a large $26 billion fund (or Clearing Union as he de-
scribed it) from which countries in balance of payments difficulties
could borrow. He proposed penalties on countries that ran persistent
balance of payments *surpluses*, and a permissive attitude towards the
use of capital or exchange controls and trade barriers. In contrast
White wanted to make it very difficult for countries to alter their exchange rates. He proposed a much smaller $5 billion fund, and a
prohibition on both exchange controls and trade controls.

The issue on which the Americans were most insistent was money.
The compromise deal hatched out between the two sides provided
for only a modest $8.8 billion for what was to be known as the In-
ternational Monetary Fund. Furthermore, the United States agreed
to contribute only a minority of the cash: $2.75 billion, rather than
the majority $23 billion for which Keynes had asked. But Keynes did
manage to persuade White that under these stringent circumstances
there would be a need for some degree of exchange-rate flexibility.

White also agreed that the removal of exchange controls and import controls should happen gradually, according to pre-agreed plans.

While the deal was very far from perfect, it did at least address explicitly the pre-war international monetary system's main failures. Instead of resorting to competitive interest rate hikes, countries with currency problems would be able to devalue without engendering a collapse in the entire system. To protect themselves from destabilising speculative capital flows, countries could use exchange controls, which they would dismantle gradually through time, when it was safe to do so. Instead of ever-rising tariff wars, there were to be rational agreements on acceptable but temporary trade controls. And instead of a situation in which no government or institution accepted responsibility for the welfare of the world economy, there would be the IMF. The fund would censure governments pursuing internationally destabilising policies, while helping those in distress. Buttressing the IMF would be a sister body, the International Trade Organisation (ITO), to oversee the removal of trade barriers.

These Bretton Woods plans were ready for ratification and then a speedy implementation once the war ended. But when Dalton became Chancellor he faced a crisis that cast doubts on whether the Bretton Woods system would ever come into being. All through the war, Britain had been in huge deficit and had accumulated an external debt that, at £10 billion, was the largest in the history of the world. More than half was owed to the United States under Lend-Lease. The remainder was owed to a variety of nations, again including the United States but also relatively poor Empire nations such as India and Egypt, which had provided Britain with armaments and supplies, without requiring any immediate payment.

Far from being ready to repay this enormous debt, Britain in 1945 was desperately borrowing more. A massive £1.2 billion bill was in prospect for that year, with smaller figures in store for subsequent years. Merely to stabilise the debt within a few years would be an Herculean effort, and paying it off seemed quite impossible. Yet the terms of Lend-Lease said that the moment the war ended, new credits would stop and repayment would need to begin. The prospect was terrifying, especially since if the United States called in its loan, other lenders would feel obliged to do the same. Britain might be unable to buy food, raw materials and essential equipment from abroad. Living standards would immediately fall and probably spiral downwards, and the deprivations of the war might come to seem trivial in comparison.

At first, the Treasury told Dalton not to worry. The fighting in Europe was over, but the war against Japan was still being waged. It would run for many months, perhaps years. During that period the British Government would be able to persuade the Americans that it was not in their interest to bankrupt Britain. After all, Britain was the largest market for American goods and services. The two nations could surely strike some kind of mutually beneficial deal. The Treasury did not even deem it necessary to prepare any contingency planning.

Less than three weeks after Labour came into office, with Attlee still appointing his Cabinet (rather charmingly, he had asked Conservative ministers to remain in place in the meantime), the American Government bombed Hiroshima and Nagasaki. The war came to a sudden end. A week later Truman cancelled Lend-Lease. The new President was no Roosevelt, and was not about to ask Congress to approve an extension to the deal. As had happened at the end of the First World War, American politics were reverting to isolationist-type at a speed that no British civil servant could understand.

Clement Attlee was quite clear that dealing with this was Dalton's task. Dalton turned to Keynes for advice. Keynes argued that it would be perfectly reasonable to ask the Americans for a gift of £1.5 billion, or failing that an interest-free loan, to replace Lend-Lease. Dalton was initially sceptical about how cooperative the Americans would be. Keynes persuaded him. So Dalton eagerly dispatched his adviser to Washington to make the request, in the company of Lord Halifax, the British Ambassador.[7]

Unfortunately Keynes had been more successful at persuading Dalton than he was at persuading Fred Vinson and Will Clayton, respectively American Treasury Secretary and Assistant Treasury Secretary. Once again, the Americans refused to be in awe of Keynes. They were 'frightened by ideas' and impressed by American public opinion, which said that it was time for Britain to stand on its own two feet.[8] This, the American politicians believed, Britain could do: they suspected that the only use that Britain would make of American money would be to finance Labour's new welfare state, an abomination in their eyes. So the Americans said that the most they would do was to lend Britain money, at a commercial rate of interest.

Keynes found himself having to convince ministers in London by telegram and messenger that he himself had earlier been wrong, and that the American position, however unreasonable, was inflexible.

At first, Dalton and the rest of the Cabinet refused to accept this. The Chancellor repeatedly sent messages to the British negotiators, refusing the American terms. Eventually, in late October, Dalton came round to Keynes's pessimistic view. It had, after all, been the Chancellor's own view, before Keynes persuaded him to be more ambitious. Unfortunately several Cabinet members (Manny Shinwell and Nye Bevan in particular) refused to join Dalton in embracing his new realism. The second-hand nature of the negotiations made it easier for colleagues to question the quality of the advice. Dalton was unable to ignore these colleagues, for the reason set out in Chapter 1: in those days the Chancellor could not assume that the Cabinet would accept any recommendation that he might eventually put. Nor, however, did Dalton take matters into his own hands and travel to Washington to negotiate in person. Instead he sent his Permanent Secretary, Edward Bridges, to take control. Only when Bridges told Dalton that Keynes was right, and that the Americans would not give way, did the Chancellor relent and bow to the American terms.

Overseeing the negotiations and the settlement was the most important part of Dalton's job in his first year in office. Indeed, it was almost the most important challenge that he faced in his three years at the Treasury. For Keynes, the burden of trying to achieve the deal was too much. His already poor health had deteriorated, and he died within weeks of returning to London. Dalton, saying that the nation faced a 'financial Dunkirk', presented the deal to Cabinet and to the Commons.[9] Despite opposition from the left of the Labour Party and the right of the Conservative Party ('I nursed a stubborn belief that in certain situations the weak have a power they can exploit if they have the nerve,' says Barbara Castle), both of whom distrusted the Americans, Dalton got it approved.[10]

In the process of getting the deal accepted Dalton had come round to the view that it was not so bad after all. Although the total package was not quite as generous as a straight grant would have been, in pure financial terms it was not very much worse. Indeed it is easy to

understand why the Americans thought the British were being un-
grateful. Keynes had won $3,375 million dollars as a loan and $650
million as a grant. The loan was to be repaid at a modest 2 per cent
interest rate over fifty years. Even then, there was a delay before the
British had to pay the first slug of interest, and provisions for interest
payment holidays later. Remarkably, the American Government
wiped clean all of Britain's Lend-Lease debts. The Canadians added
another $1,500 million loan of their own.

There were two stipulations. Quite reasonably, the Americans insisted that Britain should immediately start implementing the Bretton
Woods agreement. Much less reasonably they also demanded a
change to that agreement. Whereas Keynes had originally agreed that
Britain would restore sterling convertibility after five years, the
Americans now demanded that sterling convertibility be introduced
after just one year.

At first sight 'convertibility' seems a rather technical matter, and
Dalton thought it a small issue compared with the matter of the
overall size and terms of the grant and loan. He was wrong, and the
issue was to emerge as a new challenge to his Chancellorship even
greater than that of the Lend-Lease cancellation from which it had
sprung. Convertibility, once in place, would mean that the Bank of
England would stand ready to buy and sell sterling from and to
foreign central banks. Since those central banks would in turn be
willing to do business with their own residents, such an arrangement
would effectively mean that anybody would be able to buy or sell the
British currency.

The problem was that the British authorities had to commit themselves, not just to trade the British currency, but to do so at a fixed
rate. This commitment meant that if everybody wanted to sell sterling, then the Bank of England would in response have to sell all of
Britain's reserves of gold and foreign currencies to maintain the fixed
rate. Since these reserves were finite, it was a policy that could easily
end in chaos. Anybody thinking of selling sterling would want to sell
sooner rather than later. There was an inevitable risk that the reserves would rapidly run out and that the British Government would
have to change its mind and suspend convertibility. These circumstances almost guaranteed that there would be panic selling. That
was a risk that the Americans were willing for Britain to take. It was

also a risk which Dalton, in 1945, was willing to accept, in return for American cash.

When the time for convertibility came, Dalton found himself facing disaster. Even before the official date of 15 July 1947, foreign central banks had been deluging the Bank of England, insisting on selling their sterling for dollars. Dalton tried to reduce the problem by cutting Britain's overseas commitments, particularly in Germany, but was unable to persuade his senior colleagues, who seemed unable to take in the gravity of the economic predicament. Dalton repeatedly considered resignation. Within six weeks of convertibility the Bank had spent the larger part of the American loan, buying unwanted pounds. The American loan, intended to finance imports of goods from the United States, was being wasted on propping up the pound. When that was gone, the official reserves would go too. On 20 August Dalton called a halt, and suspended convertibility.

Dalton was exhausted, frustrated and humiliated. With no obvious way of buying the imports that Britain needed, he feared that the economy would collapse. 'I saw spectres of mass unemployment, mass starvation, mass imprecation.'[11] The Government hurriedly put in place a set of new import controls and in November the Chancellor introduced a deflationary Budget, including a £200 million increase in taxes. It was a help, but no more than that.

The situation was indeed grave, although probably not as apocalyptic as Dalton supposed, and in any case salvation came quickly, and from the Americans. The Truman administration was at last beginning to realise its earlier mistakes. Britain's problems were replicated across Europe, and American isolationism looked a poor response to Soviet expansionism. So the American Government decided to support capitalist democracy with cash. It made up for under-funding the IMF, and for the convertibility debacle, by providing Europe with $13 billion of Marshall Aid to fund chronic balance of payments problems. When the Korean War came, Japan also received finance for its reconstruction, under the Dawes plan. Suddenly the future seemed workable after all. But it was not to be a future in which Dalton would retain any influence. The occasion of the November 1947 Budget was also the occasion of Dalton's resignation from office.

Looking down on Europe

At Bretton Woods, Keynes had argued for an international monetary system that would meet the needs of every nation. Any lesser system would not last, would not help to prevent another war, and would not therefore serve Britain's long-term interests. A few years later his negotiations to secure the American loan were of a very different nature. Dalton had instructed him simply to secure the best short-term financial deal for Britain. No longer was there any particular sense of commitment to any future stable world monetary order.

Such diminution in ambition was hardly surprising, given the circumstances of the time. The American loan and the terms attached to it, the failure of convertibility, and then the provision of Marshall Aid, all demonstrated how radically the world had changed. Britain's loss of economic might was matched by the awesome rise of American financial power.

Even so, British Chancellors had not completely abandoned all interest in the institutions and health of the international economy. Successive British governments did seek to influence the development of the international system, even if on a distinctly part-time basis. Unfortunately, most Chancellors' perceptions of what objectives to pursue were muddled and misconceived.

For much of the post-war period, Chancellors believed that British economic interests were mainly served by strengthening economic links with the colonies and the Commonwealth, and with the United States. They eschewed the alternative route of placing Britain at the heart of an evolving single unified European economy. With the benefit of hindsight it is clear that this was about the greatest collective mistake that the Chancellors made. During the critical decade of the fifties, the economies of the colonies and the Commonwealth grew much more slowly than those of the continental European countries, as indeed did Britain's domestic economy. The fastest-growing markets were the ones British politicians believed mattered least. The focus of British industry on undemanding colonial and Commonwealth markets also meant that too few firms could match the quality and design standards of European competitors. So belated entry into Europe in 1972, instead of providing easy opportunities, raised challenges that much of British industry could no longer match.

Of course, the early Labour Chancellors could not have known all of this in advance. In the late forties and even in the early fifties, the war-ravaged economies of Europe still looked weak and unstable – although the German currency reform of 1948 was a sign of big things to come.[12] The potential of the colonies and Commonwealth could easily seem to be much greater. Even if the resurgence of Western Europe could have been foreseen, a dispassionate (if rather fatalistic) analysis might still have favoured the old Empire road for Britain, not the new European road. Even in 1945 Britain was already unable to compete head-on with the best European producers, thanks to the British neglect of manufacturing in the thirties.

But British lack of enthusiasm for European integration, and faith in the colonies and Commonwealth, were not the product of any such rational calculations. Such attitudes arose instead mainly from cheap sentimentality. In the forties and fifties few British politicians were willing to think of Britain as just another European nation. Many felt moral obligations and emotional ties to the Empire and Commonwealth nations. Many, most notably Ernie Bevin, who remained as Foreign Secretary through much of the first Labour Government's term of office, also felt that influencing the direction of American foreign policy mattered more than making friends within Europe.[13]

Ernie Bevin was Labour's Winston Churchill: bumptious yet much loved, and deeply inconsistent where Europe was concerned. Bevin was much prone to making grand speeches in favour of the removal of barriers between nations and in favour of the principle of federalism, but when push came to shove he always insisted that Britain should be both an independent agent, and equally close to Europe, the Commonwealth and the United States. Such views made no real sense, which delighted Bevin's officials, who themselves always aspired to face in two directions at once, and who shared Bevin's core belief that Britain was special.

British governments of the period, from Attlee's through to Macmillan's, did not want to become a member of a federal Western Europe. Nor did they want the rest of western Europe to form a federation without Britain. Such a development would be a challenge to British might. This not only irritated other European leaders, it also irritated Washington. Politicians and officials there believed in the need for a European union including Britain. They greeted with mounting derision the British claim to being special. Truman even told Churchill privately not to get ideas above his station. If there was any nation in Europe with which the Americans were particularly keen to deal, it was France not Britain.[14] Meanwhile governments elsewhere in western Europe got on with the job of building a series of pan-European institutions, with or without British involvement.

Ernie Bevin was the first to experience this. On 9 May 1950 he received news that the French Foreign Minister, Robert Schuman, had just held a press conference announcing the intention to bring the iron and steel industries of France and Germany under joint control. This was an event of potentially huge significance, yet Bevin had not been informed, let alone consulted, about the plan.[15] He was humiliated – and in consequence, all the less likely to be pro-European.

It would have taken a very strong and European-minded Chancellor of the Exchequer to have altered British attitudes. Hugh Dalton was not such a man. Since becoming an MP in 1924 his main area of policy interest had been foreign affairs, but unfortunately he was fanatically anti-German, which rather stood in the way of being pro-European. Apparently Dalton had never forgiven the Germans for the First World War, and particularly perhaps for the death of Rupert Brooke, after whom he had lusted while at Cambridge. During the more recent war he had advocated letting the Soviet Union overrun Germany so that they could use the German people as forced labour. The Russians, he remarked approvingly, are 'a most ruthless people'.[16]

Cripps had more imagination. Initially as Chancellor he was keen to see the removal of trade barriers within Europe, and the coordination of economic planning across Europe. But domestic and currency problems soon overwhelmed him, and he became sceptical of the value of physical controls at home, let alone at the European level. So European integration disappeared from his agenda. For Hugh Gaitskell, European cooperation had never been an option: Edmund Dell writes that Gaitskell 'epitomised the insularity of postwar British economic policy'.[17] Dell's charge sticks: a few years later, as Leader of the Opposition, Gaitskell would rant that British entry into the European Economic Community would mean the end of 'a thousand years of history'.

Of the Conservative Chancellors, Butler was pretty hostile to Europe. He was, in any case, hardly the man to pick a fight, and perhaps his reputation as an appeaser still hobbled him. It was unfortunate that the key moves to turn Schuman's Iron and Steel Community into a customs union or common market came about during Butler's Chancellorship, and when the strongly anti-European Anthony Eden was Prime Minister.

By then Harold Macmillan was Foreign Secretary. Macmillan had in the past been actively pro-European, and might have been expected to stand up to Butler and Eden. In 1951 Macmillan had written to Eden, then the Foreign Secretary, protesting at his anti-European attitudes and at the distorted arguments contained in a Foreign Office paper that declared, improbably, that it would make no difference to Britain whether or not the other nations of Western Europe formed a single federal economy.[18] But Eden ignored Macmillan, who was then merely the housing minister, and when Macmillan insisted on raising the issue in Cabinet, only David Maxwell Fyfe supported him. Macmillan then complained to Churchill that the Government had reversed the strong pro-European policies that it had espoused during its years in opposition. He contemplated resignation, but decided realistically that such a gesture would be futile.

But when Eden moved to 10 Downing Street and Macmillan became Foreign Secretary, he shifted his ground on European integration. He made no protest when Eden refused to allow any ministers to attend the critical conference in Messina where the plans for the Common Market were being discussed. Eden was, in Ian Gilmour's words, 'every bit as blinkered and blimpish as Bevin ...' and Macmillan seemed to want to emulate him.[19] When the six European governments invited Britain to send somebody to the meetings of the technical group charged with drawing up the future Treaty of Rome, Macmillan sent only a middle-ranking official, explicitly charged with trying to undermine the whole project.

So when Macmillan became Chancellor, and then in turn Prime Minister, the damage had mostly already been done, and some of it by himself. Whenever possible Macmillan as Prime Minister liked to appoint Chancellors and Foreign Secretaries willing to do his bidding, and so he allowed no new pro-European minister to rise to the top of the Cabinet. He alone made serious policy – or failed to make it.

In January 1958 Macmillan sulked at the news that the Common Market had at last come into being, with six members led by Germany and France. When in May of that year Charles de Gaulle became French President, Macmillan pleaded to him to abandon the Common Market, lest it cause war between Britain and Europe.[20] Instead, the President ordered an end to discussions of the Grand Design – a typically British plan for a much wider but shallower 'General Assembly for Europe'. Macmillan muttered privately about those who sought to create a European super-state: 'the Jews, the Planners and the old cosmopolitan élite'.[21]

By the time that the Prime Minister reluctantly saw sense, and decided to negotiate entry into the Community, it was already perhaps too late for Britain to achieve its full potential within Europe, even assuming that the Europeans were willing to admit Britain. In any case, Macmillan in 1960 was still keen to keep intact Britain's preferential trading arrangements with the Commonwealth, not least because of the cheap food that the Commonwealth provided. The French said 'non': the British refused to believe them. Edward Heath sought to negotiate a deal to which Macmillan was only partially committed and which de Gaulle never really wanted: it all fell apart when Macmillan enraged the French President by signing the Nassau agreement with the Americans over nuclear weapons. The French veto was a huge humiliation. Labour failed to exploit it fully because of its own anti-European stance, but it contributed to Macmillan's decline in confidence, and his resignation as Prime Minister a year later. 'All our plans are in ruins,' he lamented.[22]

European Payments Union

Perhaps we should not blame the Chancellors of the Exchequer who served in the forties, fifties and early sixties for failing to promote full British participation in Europe. Membership of the European Community was more of a Foreign Office or Board of Trade remit. Yet the European issue was of such profound economic significance that any decent Chancellor who favoured entry should have made it his business to win success in Europe, whatever the pattern of departmental demarcations. It was attitudes, not opportunities that were amiss.

Furthermore, there was a critical European dimension to the evolving challenge of managing the post-war global monetary order, which was very definitely within the remit of the Chancellor. Yet in that more specialist area too, British Chancellors showed little interest in working with their European counterparts.

As Prime Minister, Harold Macmillan coined the notion that Britain stood in relation to the United States as Greece had once stood in respect to Rome. The conceit tickled Kennedy but was not especially apposite. The reality was that if Britain was to have any prominent role it would have to be as a voice of Europe, not as the voice of past glories. Since the British would not think in such a way, they consigned themselves to a back seat. Britain and the United States alone had negotiated the Bretton Woods deal, and the rest of western Europe had merely signed the charter. By the end of the decade the Americans and Europeans were talking directly to one another. They were reassembling the Bretton Woods system according to new rules, and giving the British no more special status than anybody else. Most Chancellors of both parties contented themselves with that, and commented on the initiatives that others were taking, but seldom made the running on the evolution of the post-war economic order.

The key to progress was American recognition that, at Bretton Woods, they had got it wrong. The four great crises of the early years – the scramble for the American loan, the convertibility débâcle, the Europe-wide devaluations of 1949 and finally the need for Marshall Aid – were all manifestations of the fact that in New Hampshire, the Americans had negotiated too tough a deal. Since isolationism was not a sensible option, the United States was going to have to bankroll the world economy. The generosity that Keynes had originally advocated was triumphing over White's parsimony.

The Americans had to acknowledge the lessons of experience. They had under-funded the IMF, and as a result they were now obliged to provide loans or grants directly to foreign governments. Frequently they would make the cash available on terms less stringent than those laid down by the IMF. Similarly, the currency realignments of 1949 had been much larger than those that White had intended to permit. Furthermore, they had occurred with only cursory reference to the IMF.

Most striking of all, the provision of Marshall Aid demonstrated that White and the other American negotiators had been wrong in their attitudes at Bretton Woods. It was as much in the interests of the United States to lend generously to Europe as it was in Europe's interests to borrow from the United States. The Truman government's desperation for a prosperous Europe, plus the clear failure of the very conservative Bretton Woods arrangements, forced the Americans to accept a very different international monetary system from the one for which they had originally hoped.

The real stars of the early post-war system were proving to be exchange controls. These were helping to reduce turbulence in the international capital markets. They were also deflecting political pressures for ever-rising trade barriers that, in a world of chronic international trade imbalances, would otherwise have been irresistible. American hopes that exchange controls could go quickly were proving to be quite inappropriate.

There was a basic problem with the system then prevailing. A company in one country that had exported to a second country could not convert its resultant foreign currency earnings into the currency of a third country, with which to buy goods from that country. The only imports that it could buy were those of the country whose currency it happened to be holding. This cumbersome system, in which only bilateral currency exchanges were possible, was inimical to the rapid expansion of trade.

The obvious solution, the one agreed at Bretton Woods, was for the central banks of all countries to be willing to buy or sell *any* currency. That was what convertibility meant. Unfortunately, Hugh Dalton's 1947 convertibility crisis had cast a shadow over all of Europe. No finance minister wanted his currency to become convertible into dollars so long as the American currency was so much more in demand than any other.

The sensible option seemed to be a compromise. The European countries could go for convertibility amongst themselves, but not against the dollar. The Americans were content with this: it wasn't perfect, but it was a step in the right direction. During the late forties the American and French Treasuries devised a possible scheme. All

European governments would hold accounts with a single pan-European fund, putting in and drawing out any European currency at will, and settling up or receiving only the overall net outflow and net inflow.

The scheme looked likely to work, and in 1950 Europe's finance ministers approved the creation of the European Payments Union (EPU), which would provide for settlement arrangements throughout Europe, the sterling area and European dependencies. The Americans put cash into the fund, to make sure it was liquid, and all the participants committed themselves to tariff cuts, thereby ensuring that the EPU doubly facilitated the expansion of intra-European trade.

One European nation was a very reluctant participant in the EPU. Its identity was not a surprise. In November 1947 the new British Chancellor, Stafford Cripps, spoke to journalists. He claimed that the mooted EPU would endanger full employment in Britain. Privately he feared that the EPU would deny the British Government the right to raise import tariffs. Indeed in February the following year, he came clean and made a speech to that effect. When in September of that year, Cripps put Hugh Gaitskell (then his deputy) in charge of negotiating the EPU, Gaitskell adopted attitudes that were predominantly negative.

Meanwhile, British Treasury officials asked for secret discussions with their American counterparts. They suggested an Anglo-American payments union, in preference to the proposed European arrangement. And when Gaitskell became Chancellor in his own right, he agreed to British participation in the EPU only because he thought it would allow him to borrow larger amounts than would have been possible under a straight deal with the Americans.[23]

Rather than improve, matters got worse when the Conservatives returned to power. Despite the memories of 1947, when it seemed as if almost nobody in the world really wanted to hold sterling, Conservative ministers and their conservative officials at the Bank and the Treasury still hankered after the notion of sterling as a great reserve currency. Rab Butler and his successors thought that sterling was fundamentally different to mere continental European currencies. They failed to recognise that the best markets for British exports were no longer the old ones of the United States, the empire and the

Commonwealth, but the new ones of western Europe. It was all part of their refusal to accept that the world had changed. 'We were wrong,' confessed Reggie Maudling in his memoirs, 'and we were wrong because we had failed to recognise the historical decline in our own power and our own self-confidence.'[24]

The bias of British government policies under the Tories, as under Labour, was always to turn away from the EPU. Right from the start, Rab Butler's secret Robot plan to float sterling and introduce full convertibility would have meant Britain leaving the EPU (from which, incidentally, Britain had recently borrowed). That seemed to bother neither the new Chancellor nor those of his advisers who designed the scheme. Although the Cabinet killed Robot, in 1953 Butler, unabashed, led a delegation to Washington with another anti-EPU scheme. They hoped to persuade the Americans to agree to extra IMF funds, so that sterling could become convertible into dollars, while meanwhile emasculating the EPU. Eisenhower's Secretary of State, John Dulles, rejected the proposal out of hand.

Then, during the Chancellorship of Peter Thorneycroft, the idea of floating sterling re-emerged, and Thorneycroft also briefly contemplated withdrawal from the EPU. As it happened, Thorneycroft was more pro-European than most in his party. He might have become much more constructive towards the EPU, given time and some unbiased briefing. Unfortunately he scarcely had time to tackle the international aspects of his work before his junior ministers, Nigel Burch and Enoch Powell, persuaded him to resign over colleagues' refusal to reduce their spending levels.

Thorneycroft's successor, Derick Heathcoat Amory, was notoriously uneasy about 'abroad'. As an adolescent on holiday in Europe, he would talk to people 'in that extra-loud monosyllabic English generally reserved for the deranged'.[25] And a few years later he cut short a world tour while still only in North America, following some unspecified unpleasant incident.[26] Amory was little more than a bystander when in December 1958 the French and German Governments announced that their currencies were now sufficiently robust to be convertible into any currency, an announcement that meant the demise of the EPU and its replacement with something much like the original Bretton Woods framework. Amory hastily announced that sterling would also now become fully convertible.

What the British Government had long wanted to do, others had done first, and the Bank of England and the Treasury in London had at last got their way, but only on the coat-tails of the French and German Governments.

Worries over international liquidity

British politicians' disdain for Europe was partly just the obverse of pretensions to global political importance. During his period as Prime Minister, Harold Macmillan agitated increasingly about problems that were widely perceived to exist in the global monetary system, and which he believed acted as a brake on the growth of the British economy. Macmillan was keen for his Chancellors to address the supposed global problem.

But what was the problem? In the immediate post-war period, American governments believed that a properly functioning international monetary system was a necessary condition for the expansion of world trade, and that fixed exchange rates were a key component of a properly functioning system. They thought that such an expansion would particularly benefit American companies, since these were the most efficient in the world, and were producing the most innovative design-led products in the world.

But before long, several international monetary experts began to point out an internal contradiction to the story.[27] If American competitiveness was so decisive, then the United States would always run large trade surpluses, and its trading partners would always run large deficits. That would mean perpetual scrambles to get hold of dollars with which to buy the imports from the United States. The result would be never-ending upward pressure on the dollar. That would last until the dollar was at a height that cancelled out the American competitive advantage. Thus the devaluations of 1949 were likely to be only the first of many, and currency stability in a world of American economic superiority was a chimera.

As it turned out, the analysis had been broadly correct, but back to front. The European and later the Japanese economies produced robust recoveries. By the end of the fifties it was the United States that was the persistent deficit nation. Europe consistently ran trade surpluses. It was because of this that the countries of Europe were able to restore currency convertibility in 1958 without any of the trauma that Britain had experienced in 1947. But it also meant that, from then on, the pressure for exchange-rate adjustments would usually be for a dollar *devaluation* against the major currencies of continental Europe.

Compounding this was the tendency for the Americans to pay for their imports in dollars, rather than in the currency of the country selling them the goods or services. The world economy had too many dollars, not too few, and the value of the foreign exchange reserves that non-Americans held was always at risk of collapse. Indeed when de Gaulle became French President he explicitly threatened to sell all of France's dollar reserves and hold gold instead, on the basis that the dollar was a poor risk. Furthermore, the expansion of world trade and the increase in world liquidity meant that the $8.8 billion IMF fund now looked ludicrously small.

The major governments took several steps to help remedy the under-funding of the IMF. In 1958 the fund received a small increase in its assets, and these were boosted by 50 per cent a year later. In 1961 the ten largest industrialised countries agreed to lend the fund $6 billion, and 1966 saw a 25 per cent rise in the size of the fund. But even after all of these boosts, the IMF's resources were still too small – especially since it seemed increasingly likely that the biggest debtor of all would be the United States itself.

The problem for the world's finance ministers and central bankers was that a currency could only act as an alternative reserve asset to the dollar if it enjoyed a large and liquid market. The only currency to fit that description was sterling. Unfortunately, sterling was the one major currency to suffer from exactly the same adverse fundamentals as the dollar. Clearly, this was a particular problem for Britain, and a challenge for its Chancellors of the Exchequer. In his 1958 Budget speech Heathcoat Amory talked of how sterling played a crucial role as a liquid reserve asset that other nations might hold, from which he concluded that it was highly important to bolster international confidence in sterling.

Alas, Amory had no idea how to engender confidence. He was new to the job, well-meaning but not much interested in it, and it is doubtful if he understood the issues about which he was offering such opinions. Amory was doing little more than take his script from

Harold Macmillan. The Prime Minister believed that the British economy could not expand as rapidly as he wanted it to, because of international lack of confidence in sterling. And he believed that the way to boost confidence was to alter the international monetary system, rather than alter British economic policies.

Macmillan's somewhat tendentious view was not shared by the Americans. They denied that there was a problem with the international system, and thought that the British should put their own house in order. Nor was it accepted by the Europeans. Only a Chancellor of serious intellectual power could have articulated Macmillan's argument effectively – a Lawson, say, or a Healey, Jenkins or Gordon Brown. Macmillan had only Amory, who was out of his depth, and who could not hope to persuade anybody of the rightness of the Macmillan view. So too was Amory's successor, Selwyn Lloyd. Although in some respects a significant figure in the evolution of post-war British economic policy, Lloyd was never really the sharpest knife in the drawer. He did not begin to justify Reginald Maudling's claim that he enjoyed 'a considerable reputation in the international financial community'.[28] He had no success in arguing the Macmillan case in the international arena.

Then in 1962 Macmillan appointed Maudling himself to the Chancellorship. Reggie Maudling was not a good European but he certainly had the intellectual ability as well as the inclination to put the arguments that Macmillan wanted advanced. Thus at the World Bank meeting in Washington in 1962, Maudling proposed an arrangement designed to address the liquidity problem, and boost confidence in sterling and the dollar. His proposal was that a proportion of the dollars and sterling being held as international reserves should henceforth receive backing from the IMF, which would undertake to protect the value of those reserves.

The proposal, known as the Maudling Plan, got nowhere. The implication that American government-backed dollars had become a poor risk offended Washington. The British Government, isolated in Europe, was unwilling or unable to pressure others to adopt its ideas. Despite the eloquence of its advocate, the Maudling Plan got nowhere.

Unfortunately for Macmillan, Maudling, having failed, showed little interest in trying again. Dogged perseverance had never been his style. Maudling's successor Jim Callaghan was no great thinker, and was too worried about sterling to concern himself much with the abstruse (although related) subject of global liquidity. So British Chancellors continued as fairly minor players on the international monetary scene, while the initiative passed to the French. In 1964 the French Government proposed the creation of additional resources for the IMF. These would be denominated by an index of average currency values. That would make them virtually free of exchange rate risk. The French and the Americans spent the next few years arguing the issue. Sometimes they swapped positions, until eventually they agreed with one another that the new assets – 'Special Drawing Rights' or SDRs – should be introduced in 1970. Their introduction would boost the lending power of the IMF and hence raise global liquidity. Everything was agreed. The British were consulted, but only briefly. Not even the replacement of Callaghan by the brighter and more internationally-minded Roy Jenkins produced any increase in British involvement in international deliberations.

As it happens, the SDRs were a good idea when they were conceived and a bad idea when they eventually arrived. For by 1970 the world had experienced several years of American fiscal irresponsibility. That, together with increasingly generous monetary policies in both the United States and Europe, meant that the world now needed not *more* liquidity but *less*. The fact that the United States, because of its balance of payments problems, was set to be the major recipient of SDRs only made matters worse. (Indeed the promise of SDRs to come had been one of the factors encouraging the Americans in their pursuit of otherwise unsustainable fiscal policies.)

If anybody was taking responsibility for the international monetary system it was now the Bundesbank, which was struggling against the odds to support the dollar. Yet the German central bank felt guilty that in the process it was neglecting its domestic duties. By printing deutschmarks with which to buy dollars, it was perhaps creating inflationary risks at home. Unfortunately the American authorities refused to cooperate and moderate the expansion of their domestic economy. So, in the spring of 1971, the Bundesbank decided that enough was enough, and abandoned support for the dollar.

Initially the Americans did not believe what had happened. They were used to perfidious Albion but not perfidious Deutschland. Finally on 15 August 1971 Treasury Secretary John Connolly retaliated. He announced that the American Government was abandoning the principle of a fixed exchange rate for the dollar. He also announced a 10 per cent tax on all imports into the United States. There was no suggestion of consulting the British Chancellor. The Americans did not even take the Germans into their confidence. Such precipitate actions, and the absence of any domestic economic deflation, called into question everything for which Bretton Woods stood. The world was apparently moving towards an anarchic world economy. If the year-old Conservative Government was to make a contribution to restoring some semblance of order, then it needed a Chancellor completely on top of his brief. What it had was Tony Barber.

The self-effacing Barber seemed unlikely to provide much leadership. When Barber assumed the Chancellorship following the death of Iain Macleod it quickly became clear that Ted Heath would make most of the big decisions, and that the international monetary system was not a matter of much interest to the Prime Minister. Extraordinarily, Heath makes no reference in his memoirs to the world crisis provoked by the precipitate American action. Heath himself had already cold-shouldered the Americans, on the rather inadequate grounds that they were not Europeans. The combination of this and Tony Barber's lack of impact seemed set to bury any chance of the new British Government influencing events.

Yet Barber, to his credit, did make the effort. A month after Connolly's bombshell, the British Chancellor made a speech at the annual IMF meeting. He proposed a new settlement to replace the Bretton Woods Agreement that the Americans had just broken. The essence of the Barber Plan was that instead of all governments stabilising the value of their currencies against the dollar (all governments except the Americans themselves, who under Bretton Woods stabilised against gold), they would all (including the Americans) stabilise against the value of the SDR. In addition, central banks would no longer hold individual currencies (notably dollars) as reserves, but would hold SDRs instead. On a day-to-day basis, they would buy or sell any currency against which their own was moving out of line. They would borrow from each other or from the IMF (or some other fund) for that purpose. At the end of each month, the governments would settle all such debts in SDRs. There would also be an agreed method for creating SDRs as needed, thereby managing the rate at which global liquidity expanded.

Barber's was a bold plan – like so many British plans, it would later be called the 'grand design' – but it was not well received. The Americans were particularly dismissive of the fact that they were to be treated no differently to any other country. This affronted their dignity, but it also threatened genuine problems. They were not keen on having to settle their debts each month. Such a tough regime would force Connolly and Nixon to tackle the underlying causes of persistent American deficits, namely the undue expansion of the domestic economy and the cost of the Vietnam War. That they would not do. At the IMF conference the courteous Barber was browbeaten by Connolly, a bullying Texan who made sure that Barber's experience at the conference was not a happy one.

A year later the situation improved. The pragmatic and diplomatic George Schultz replaced John Connolly at the American Treasury, and gave permission for the IMF to investigate Barber's plan. Schultz did not declare himself in favour, but he no longer said that the Americans were definitely against Barber's scheme (especially if the plan could be modified to give them an easier ride). At the 1972 IMF conference the leading finance ministers asked Jeremy Morse, a clever Bank of England official, to chair an international committee. His brief was to devise a new Bretton Woods system, along the lines of the Barber Plan. (Morse's cleverness was later recognised by the board of Lloyds Bank, who made him their chairman, and by the writer Colin Dexter, who named his fictional detective after him.) Briefly, it seemed that meek Tony Barber was about to become one of the most significant of all Britain's post-war Chancellors.

It was not to be. In 1973, with the Morse Committee still deliberating, two great shocks hit the world economy. The first was the break-up of the temporary pact which had been signed at the Smithsonian Institute in Washington on 18 December 1971. The governments of the leading industrialised nations had agreed, as a temporary measure, to modest currency realignments and the introduction of bands within which currencies could fluctuate. Under the Smithsonian Accord the United States had been allowed to continue with its policy of not offering to convert dollars into gold. It was not obliged to alter its domestic policies, but it had agreed to end the import surcharge.

The agreement was a temporary fudge, and although politicians lauded it ('The most significant monetary agreement in the history of the world,' intoned President Nixon), nobody was willing to stake much on its survival. A period of huge currency turmoil in February 1973 nearly brought down the agreement; after much struggle, finance ministers agreed a revised set of parities. Currency market pressures continued, however, and in March 1973 at a meeting in Paris the participating countries failed to agree a further set of revisions to their exchange rates. When a second meeting failed to produce an agreement, they all abandoned the Smithsonian pact. Against such a background the Morse Committee's deliberations looked somewhat academic. Then came the second shock: the quadrupling of the oil price following the Yom Kippur War. Morse and his colleagues soldiered on, but nobody really believed there was any hope. Bretton Woods was dead, and there was no prospect of a replacement.

Europe regroups, Britain on the sidelines

The break-up of Bretton Woods and the implausibility of finding a successor system produced very different responses in different parts of the world. The American and Japanese Governments were not too bothered. They thought they could cope quite easily with floating exchange rates. In contrast the continental governments of the European Economic Community, whose economies were much more dependent on international trade, and specifically trade with one another, took the reverse view. They became even more committed to increasing the integration of their economies. The British Government, and Tony Barber in particular, were quite unable to decide into which category they fell.

Already the European governments had taken the critical steps. They had received a report from a commission chaired by the Prime Minister of Luxembourg, Pierre Werner, on the conditions that would need to prevail for Europe to have a single currency. Werner had concluded that the extreme option of a common currency for

Europe would be impossible without a common fiscal policy. Although the report set out a plan to achieve full economic and monetary union by 1980, its authors recognised that such an outcome was unlikely to materialise. Politically, it was a bridge too far. The Commission members thought, however, that fixing exchange rates into quite narrow bands was quite feasible. Thus in the Smithsonian system, the EEC governments opted for greater stability between their own currencies than between other currencies. They called the arrangement the 'snake in the tunnel', the wide Smithsonian system bands being the tunnel, and the tightly linked European currencies being the snake.

In May 1972 the British Government decided to swallow its pride, accept the strict European rules, and make sterling a member of the snake. Just a month later, following heavy market speculation, sterling left. It was an act of huge political significance. In taking Britain into the EEC, Ted Heath had repudiated Britain's traditional ambivalence towards Europe. Yet here he was behaving in just the way that his predecessors might have done. In his memoirs, Heath omits to mention the episode.

Sterling was not the only currency ever to leave the snake, but it was the only major one to do so and not return. Twice the French had to leave when the franc suffered from heavy selling. On both occasions they managed to rejoin, but the experience emphasised how vulnerable the system was. For a few years problems beset the snake, and the system might have led nowhere, were it not for a convergence in the late eighties of French and German thinking on currencies. The French had long been keen on fixed rates and the German Chancellor, Helmut Schmidt, hoped that fixed currencies could lead towards a much more federal Europe. Schmidt made a deal with the French President, Valéry Giscard d'Estaing, which the rest of the European Council endorsed in July 1978. Soon after, the resultant European Monetary System came into being. The system's Exchange Rate Mechanism (ERM) was much more robustly designed than the old snake, and was invested with much more political authority. Almost everybody joined or rejoined. Britain, once again, stayed out.

By then Tony Barber was long gone. His Labour successor, Denis Healey, distrusted the ERM and ensured that Britain did not join. Healey says that he found himself convinced by the arguments of the

German politician, Manfred Lahnstein, that the ERM meant that France and Germany '... would have to pay to keep the deutschmark lower than it would have been in a free market, thus keeping Germany more competitive and other countries less so'.[29] If this curious argument persuaded Healey, then he cannot have needed much persuasion. Healey's mentor had been Ernie Bevin, and more than any other politician of his age, Healey was eager to embrace European politicians, but reluctant to embrace European policies. He managed to persuade Callaghan that Britain should stay clear of the ERM, but was unable to convince anybody on mainland Europe. In European meetings on the proposed system Healey was generally in a minority of one; in Cabinet in London he carried the day.

To his credit Healey does not, at least in his memoirs, use the specious argument of British uniqueness to defend his opposition to the ERM. He thought the ERM was bad for other countries too. But he failed then and since to address the question of what would happen to sterling if it was outside the ERM. The answer was that it was liable to experience large fluctuations, and that nobody outside the UK would be much bothered about damping those fluctuations. With no voice in Europe and only a minor voice at the global level, the Chancellor of the Exchequer and the UK economy were going to have to trust to luck.

Nigel Lawson goes to the summit

The Chancellor in question would not be Healey, however, but Geoffrey Howe – and after him, Nigel Lawson. Howe did not really have much to do on the international front. The prime importance that the new Conservative Government attached to monetary control precluded much in the way of international economic objectives. So Howe ratified Labour's refusal to put sterling into the ERM, and declined to spend time fretting about the state of the world economy.

Such attitudes were mirrored in the United States, where the Reagan government's distaste for policy activism extended from the domestic into the international arena. Eventually, however, circumstances were bound to require that the Americans as well as the British change their attitudes. Although the United States still suffered from fundamental competitiveness problems, the early eighties saw a sharp appreciation of the dollar. This reflected the unprecedented inconsistency, mentioned already, between the budgetary policies of the Reagan administration and the monetary policies of Paul Volcker's Federal Reserve. Reagan cut taxes and expanded government spending. The consequent rise in borrowing drove up interest rates, as did Volcker's attempt to slow monetary growth. The combined effect was to drive the dollar far above the level at which American industry could successfully compete.

At first the Washington administration, notably Treasury Secretary Donald Regan and his deputy Beryl Sprinkel, ignored the problems of industry. They welcomed the dollar's strength as an indication that the financial markets approved of their policies. But gradually it became clear that Congress was unimpressed. Protectionist legislation to curb the burgeoning trade deficit seemed a real threat.

If the administration was going to thwart the Congressional pressure for protectionism, then it needed to shift its exchange-rate policy and find a way to massage the dollar downwards. After the 1984 election the replacement of Regan and Sprinkel by the less ideological James Baker and Richard Darman suggested that change was likely. Gradually the currency markets began to sell dollars. Even so, both the Treasury Secretary and the President continued to make public statements welcoming the strong dollar. They repeatedly said that they saw no reason to interfere with market forces. Under the circumstances, nobody was quite sure whether the turning-point had really come.

Watching all of this from London was Nigel Lawson, first on the sidelines, then from 11 Downing Street. Lawson was one of the more internationally minded Chancellors. He was keen to play a role on the world stage, especially since reciting mantras of Monetarism in One Nation no longer did much for any politician's credibility, not even his. In his well-plumped memoirs, Lawson recounts his version of how, in January 1985, he set in train the events that marked the end of American economic isolationism and the high dollar, and the start of a new era of global policy coordination. Apparently it was on Lawson's urging that Margaret Thatcher and Bundesbank President Otto Pohl persuaded the American authorities to abandon their laissez-faire attitudes and agree to cooperative efforts to reduce the overvaluation of the dollar.[30] According to Lawson it was this episode, rather than the Plaza Accord that followed later in the year, which marked the watershed in international economic relations.

American accounts of these events tend not to accord Nigel Lawson quite the same central role. They emphasise instead how, at home, many Americans lobbied the White House and the US Treasury to change their policies. The petitioners included congressmen and senators from manufacturing-dependent states, plus Federal Reserve Chairman Paul Volcker, and Secretary of State George Schultz.

Then in September 1985 Nigel Lawson met the other finance ministers and central bankers from the five large industrialised nations – the Group of Five or G5 – at the Plaza Hotel in New York and found that the Americans had at last shifted their views. They agreed to work together to drive down the value of the dollar. To protect American sensibilities the communiqué that they published referred not to the desirability of dollar depreciation, but euphemistically to their intention to cooperate to achieve an 'orderly appreciation' of the non-dollar currencies.

We cannot deny that Lawson played some useful role in the Plaza agreement. Yet fundamentally he was not sufficiently important to have a decisive impact on the direction of events. The same was true at the next such event, in February 1987. Within a year of Plaza the dollar had lost 40 per cent of its value. By late 1986 finance ministers were worried that the dollar's descent was going too far. They met again, this time as a G7 and at the Louvre in Paris, and agreed to seek some degree of currency stability around the rates then prevailing.

Helped by American interest rate rises, the dollar then stabilised. However, there was in truth little American commitment to managing the currency. Indeed, by 1988 the dollar was again appreciating, before falling again a year later. Fortunately such benign neglect was now occurring against a background of progressively more sensible and better run American domestic policies. Presidents Bush and Clinton adopted the moderate policies that, at the Plaza and Louvre summits, the American negotiators had insisted were not on offer. The consequence was a gradual trend towards a more stable global monetary order.

Britain in Europe? Can't decide, won't decide

Meanwhile, Nigel Lawson was at last seeking to put sterling in the ERM – just as the ERM was coming under new pressures, both economic and political. In 1987 in a memorandum to ECOFIN ministers, the French Finance Minister Edouard Balladur openly criticised the ERM. He said that the system imposed all the weight of adjustment on weak currency countries, and none on countries such as Germany with strong currencies. This, he said, had to change. The way to do it was by eliminating intra-European currency crises. That in turn could be achieved by the obvious mechanism of adopting a single European currency. The French were thus demanding a shift towards an even more integrated Europe.

In making his bid for closer *economic* integration, Balladur rightly took for granted the support of the Commission; especially now that the President was the former French Finance Minister Jacques Delors. Significantly Hans-Dietrich Genscher, the German Foreign Minister, also responded sympathetically. The German Government had decided that it would be willing to subjugate its monetary policies to a pan-European authority, if in return there could be a clear move towards increased European *political* integration.

Shortly afterwards, Delors chaired a committee to consider the practicalities of achieving a European single currency. The committee, which included all of the EU's central bankers, did not bother itself with the Werner committee's insistence that, to prevent worsening unemployment in the least competitive regions, fiscal federalism should be a precondition for monetary union. Since no European government was willing to abandon control over its own budget, acceptance of the Delors view over the Werner view was the essential precondition for the EU governments to agree to monetary union. In June 1989 the Council of Ministers took that step and accepted the Delors report. That set in train negotiations to amend the Treaty of Rome. Both monetary union and eventually political union would now become possible. In 1991 the Maastricht Conference amended the Treaty of Rome.

Although the French had set the ball rolling, the German Government had managed to shape the proposed arrangements so as to assuage domestic concerns that any new system might be insufficiently anti-inflationary. In contrast, the British Government could neither shape nor torpedo the policy. Prime Minister and Chancellor lacked all clout, and had to content themselves with a clause giving Britain, whose currency was now a member of the ERM, the right to opt out of the European monetary union – EMU. In one sense this was a major concession from the other governments, but it primarily served to convince those governments that Britain had nothing to offer Europe politically. Nor did Britain seem to have much to offer economically. The fact that sterling had been the last currency to join the ERM made it a little difficult for the British Chancellor to be taken seriously within Europe. The antics of the Conservative Party made it much harder. When sterling eventually had to leave the ERM, all British influence disappeared utterly. The most that the Europeans were now willing to do was to hope for better treatment from New Labour.

Europe was to be disappointed. Labour came to power in the spring of 1997 with less than a year in which to decide whether or not sterling should become part of the Euro system on New Year's Day 1999. Tony Blair liked the idea: it fitted in with his desire for constitutional change and his desire to end Britain's isolation in Europe. But he knew that the electorate, and even more the popular Press whose support had helped him into office, would think differently.

For his part, Gordon Brown had no deep philosophical objections to the Euro, but he was very much opposed to taking apart the new framework for the management of the economy that he was carefully putting into place. Brown's rising confidence in his alternative macroeconomic policy framework, notably the independent Bank of England, made him determined not to start again from scratch with a revised institutional structure, especially since the *Pact for Stability and Growth*, agreed in the summer of 1997 at the EU's Amsterdam Summit as the basis under which Euro member countries would manage their economies, looked more stringent and less subtle than his own system.[31] Almost from day one, commentators had been calling Gordon Brown the best Chancellor in memory: why should he throw away his achievements?

Even if the Prime Minister wanted a quick referendum, which was doubtful, the Chancellor certainly did not. Gordon Brown's alternative idea was to persuade the Europeans to delay the currency's launch until Britain was ready. He was politely persuaded not to air such hubris in public. So nothing happened, and those who had wanted an immediate post-election referendum found themselves disappointed.

Journalists clamoured to be told when and what the Government would decide – and so too did the rest of the Cabinet, and the City. The impression gained ground that Blair and Brown were divided, for and against early entry. In October Brown, keen to kick the issue into touch and apparently believing that he had the approval of the Prime Minister, allowed his press spokesman, Charlie Whelan, to brief *The Times* that Britain would not join the Euro before the general election. The article provoked a blaze of attention. Blair was startled by the news: his advisers were furious. Treasury officials and Cabinet ministers were equally wrong-footed. Before long, that itself became the story. 'Labour spins into a crisis' headlined the *Guardian*, while in Downing Street, grown men shouted obscenities at one another.

However accidental or deliberate, at least the episode cleared the air for a while. Gordon Brown demonstrated his command of his brief and of the Commons when he announced five tests that, when they were met, would trigger sterling's entry into the Euro. The tests, he noted, were unlikely to be met during the present Parliament, 'barring some fundamental and unforeseen change in economic circumstances'. Critics said that the tests were so demanding, but more importantly so vague, that they would allow the Chancellor to veto entry for as long as he wished. Brown made no reply.

There remained problems. European finance ministers refused to allow Brown to participate in their debates over how the Euro system might work – they even refused to have their photographs taken with him.[32] Britain was now as politically isolated as ever. More parochially, Brown had embarrassed the Prime Minister, who was bound to try to take back the initiative – as indeed he did, when in early 1999 he announced that if the circumstances were right, the Government would hold a referendum after the next general election, and with luck would take sterling into the Euro in time for the 2002 replacement of national notes and coins by their pan-European successors.

Meanwhile, with little prospect of winning the next general election but a decent chance of winning a referendum, the Conservative Opposition increasingly mocked the Labour Government's prevarication, and presented itself as the party that would save the pound when Labour eventually came clean and admitted it was privately committed to the Euro. Ministerial colleagues of Blair and Brown grew correspondingly frustrated that the Government did not retaliate, and that it failed to run a similarly effective campaign to bolster support for the Euro. But whenever colleagues expressed mildly encouraging words about the prospects for Euro membership, they would find themselves slapped down by the Chancellor.

Then, in his 2000 Mansion House speech, Gordon Brown made the position clear – that he alone would decide whether the Government would or would not endorse Euro membership, and other ministers would have no say. Few other politicians could have made obfuscation appear quite so decisive, and the Chancellor's statement was further striking evidence that Brown was determined to control the agenda, not just of the Treasury but of the Government at large.

And that, the Chancellor assumed, was that. Except that in February 2001 the Chancellor was as surprised as everybody else when Tony Blair announced without warning that the decision whether or not to recommend entry and hold a referendum on EMU would come in the first two years of the next Parliament. It was a reasonable inference that the Prime Minister would want to be able to recommend entry. Given the unpopularity of the Euro with the British electorate, that in turn would require a pretty enthusiastic pro-entry campaign in advance of the formal decision to advocate entry. This left the Chancellor's 'leave it to me' policy completely stranded. Soon Brown would have to make the biggest choice of his career since he had stood aside and allowed Tony Blair to become leader of the party: whether or not to give the Euro his whole-hearted backing. Once again, Nemesis was floating across the English Channel, in search of a British politician whose career to break: would it be Brown's, or Blair's, or both together?

3 What sort of person does the job demand?

Getting the job

Gordon Brown and Tony Blair both know it: the Chancellor of the Exchequer can make or break the reputation of a government. Only the Prime Minister is more likely than the Chancellor, by his or her actions, to get the Government re-elected or removed from office. The Chancellor is always in the news, and always concerning himself with what all his departmental colleagues are up to. Chancellors have large responsibilities; yet they are responsible for something, the economy, that is inherently nebulous, intangible, hard to control and in truth very poorly understood. They are surrounded by snake-oil salesmen. They don't get much sleep.

So it is tempting to think that only the very mightiest of politicians could expect to get the chance to be Chancellor. And indeed, Gordon Brown's presence as Chancellor has been so commanding that it is difficult to imagine who else from Labour's front bench could have done the job had he not been available. Tony Blair, Jack Straw and Robin Cook all seem less substantial figures than Gordon Brown, resembling movie actors performing parts, whereas he is the movie director who makes everything happen, who has a vision that he makes real, who does not need to be liked but who requires respect, and who expects to control most of those around him.

Such perceptions are of course suspect, created in part by the job, its trappings and the assumptions we project on to its incumbent as well as by any real differences between Gordon Brown and his contemporaries. During the 1997–2001 administration Tony Blair would have been more focused as Chancellor than as Prime Minister, Jack Straw as Chancellor would probably have been better advised and less accident-prone than as Home Secretary, and Robin Cook would have been more in tune with Treasury officials than with Foreign Office mandarins. The world could have been different than it was, and would not have fallen apart.

But we cannot deny that for half a century the Chancellorship has been a large, sometimes very large, job, and that it has not always been easy for Prime Ministers to fill the post. It has also been a job much coveted. Famously, Gordon Brown would have preferred to be Prime Minister, but with that opportunity denied him, at least temporarily, there was never any question of him wanting any other portfolio than the Treasury. Except in their wilder moments of fantasy, being Chancellor was the height of the ambition of Nigel Lawson and Norman Lamont, and legions of politicians have been frustrated by their failure to become Chancellor.

Nobody since the Second World War has turned down the job, but one or two did take it without much enthusiasm. 'I was not unhappy, or disappointed, for more than half an hour,' wrote Hugh Dalton of his feelings when offered the Chancellorship.[1] Dalton had been expecting to receive the Foreign Office until Attlee switched plans for him and Bevin at the last moment, and was disappointed by the change, which the taciturn Attlee never explained to him. That morning Attlee had allowed Dalton to believe that the Foreign Office would be his, which must have made the afternoon meeting rather painful. 'With whom did C.R.A. lunch?' Dalton scribbled in his diary that night, and for years afterwards he puzzled over who had changed Attlee's mind. Attlee later said that he had decided to appoint to the Foreign Office a tank (Bevin) rather than a sniper (Dalton), although there has always been a suspicion that the King, who could not bear Dalton, had requested the switch.

A decade later Harold Macmillan was even less happy to be moved by Eden from the Foreign Office, where he had been in place for only a few months, to the Treasury in succession to Rab Butler. The Foreign Office suited him and he suited the office – outwardly self-effacing but fundamentally vain, stiff-backed but willing to bend on ethical issues, Macmillan stood tall in a line of priggish Conservative Foreign Secretaries. And although Macmillan believed himself competent for the job of Chancellor, he did not relish the work involved, and was concerned that his opportunity to bid for the leadership – Eden was already sick when he took it on, and was not expected to last – might be compromised by the move. Butler, relieved of the burden of the Chancellorship, might rally his own cause while Macmillan became stuck in the fiscal mire. Nevertheless, having extracted a promise that Eden would not award Butler the title of Deputy Prime Minister, Macmillan agreed to go to the Treasury.

Both Dalton and Macmillan found being Chancellor more congenial than they had expected. Dalton soon began to enjoy the job, while Macmillan's shift put him in a better position to make political capital out of the Suez crisis, a year later. And another politician in a similar position to Macmillan, John Major, was glad to return to the Treasury after his brief sojourn at the Foreign Office. He too was soon able to exploit a great political crisis, and move from the Chancellorship to the Premiership in almost exact emulation of Macmillan's move two generations earlier.

Dalton and Macmillan were exceptions. Most politicians have been delighted with the news that they are to be Chancellor, even if they have accepted the post with understated gratitude and protestations of a due sense of the demanding task ahead, concealing their true feelings of giddy elation. Few have been more giddy than Iain Macleod, who perhaps saw less need than most to dissemble. Macleod's biographer reports that the new Chancellor was 'cock-a-hoop' when he entered the Treasury for his first day's work, and quotes William Rees-Mogg as saying 'he was full of the joys of having become Chancellor ...'. Patrick Jenkin (a junior minister to Macleod) recalled Macleod's 'joy at being back in office, and his joy at being in the Treasury'. 'Isn't it absolutely marvellous, here we all are,' Macleod told Jenkin and other colleagues at the time. And clearly he meant it.[2]

Another man not ashamed to celebrate was Hugh Gaitskell, surprised over the telephone by the news of his own appointment. Gaitskell was in New York when his moment came, and in a mood of high exhilaration he went dancing in Greenwich Village, dragging his unworldly civil servants with him.

When Margaret Thatcher appointed Nigel Lawson to succeed Geoffrey Howe, she famously told him to get his hair cut. As a further measure of their relationship she said that she had decided that he would not need quite such a large flat in 11 Downing Street as then existed, and that one of the apartment's three floors would be requisitioned for her own burgeoning staff. Lawson did not mind:

excitedly he telephoned his wife, who in turn was so agitated by the news that she burnt a hole in his shirt, which she was dutifully ironing.[3] More recently Gordon Brown gave up the flat entirely in exchange for the smaller premises above 10 Downing Street, while the Blairs moved into Number 11.

Rab Butler was told to his face that he was to be Chancellor, in an audience with Churchill at 10 Downing Street – or at least not exactly told, since Churchill, who was in bed at the time, and who was not terribly keen on Butler, merely passed him a typed list of Cabinet appointments, grunted, and then said that after much thought and discussions with Eden he had decided to give Butler the job. Geoffrey Howe was similarly summoned to 10 Downing Street, but sadly his audience with his new Prime Minister was conducted in her study, not in her bedroom. Howe had been shadow Chancellor for four years and was less surprised than Butler had been to be made Chancellor, although he had harboured a few doubts (didn't he always?) and his appointment thus came as a relief: '... it was good to hear the actual words.'[4] Howe also gained much pleasure from being almost immediately presented with the Chancellor's great seal of office, and from being allowed to take it home for the weekend, to show all his friends.

Roy Jenkins says that the moment when he realised he was about to be made Chancellor gave him 'a sense of solid satisfaction ...' but not the same exhilaration that he had felt when winning his first ministerial job (as Minister of Aviation) a few years earlier.[5] He attributes this to his awareness of the economic problems with which he would need to grapple. But perhaps the supremely ambitious Jenkins was also conscious that, with Harold Wilson now in his sights and his rivals for the top job discommoded by his promotion, he could allow himself no idle euphoria, no lapse of self-control. At their meeting, Wilson talked a lot and said he hoped that henceforth they would have 'relations of much closer contact and mutual confidence', but Jenkins mostly kept his own counsel and longed 'to get away and commune with my own thoughts'.[6]

That is not to deny that the problems that Roy Jenkins faced were real. Furthermore, his civil servants were, in Jenkins's words, 'exhausted and demoralised' by the devaluation crisis of a few months earlier; and, it might be added, humiliated by losing a Chancellor who had merely implemented the policies that they had devised. Over the next few weeks they failed to give Jenkins the support that he feels they should have offered, perhaps in part because they were jealous that Jenkins was being portrayed in the Press as the man who would sort out the mess at the Treasury. They cannot have been impressed that, on his first day in the new job and with a hostile private notice question to deal with (from Michael Foot), Jenkins insouciantly took himself off on a lunchtime engagement that he could surely have broken. Nor were they happy that Jenkins insisted on bringing his principal private secretary, David Dowler, with him from the Home Office to replace the retiring Peter Baldwin. The Treasury's mandarins tried to prevent this affront to their dignity; when they could not, they imposed instead a patently foolish arrangement whereby Jenkins had two principal private secretaries, with their own Robert Armstrong acting in tandem with Dowler.[7]

Treasury officials also ambushed the newly appointed Jenkins with stories of imminent catastrophe. The reserves were under dire strain and the exchange rate was, they claimed, in danger of collapse. It was an old tactic, designed to get the new incumbent under control right from the start. 'Their story was of blood draining away from the system' was Rab Butler's description of how he was greeted by officials.[8] Jenkins says that his staff seemed unwilling to suggest any remedies to the various economic problems that they described, and that they did not give him the plan of action that he needed 'on almost my first day in my new office'. And when Jenkins drafted his first major economic policy speech and articulated policies of delay that, in retrospect he says were 'rather dangerous nonsense', the officials let the draft through with no attempt to alter its main thrust.[9]

Edmund Dell has said that Jenkins is being a little disingenuous and that it was up to him to insist on the immediate policy action that was self-evidently necessary. It nevertheless remains apparent that for Jenkins, the behaviour of his most senior advisers when he first took office contained an unhealthy element of gamesmanship. Ironically the civil servants' tactics were exactly the opposite of those that they had played with Jenkins's hapless predecessor, Jim Callaghan, who was stampeded on his second day in office into making a decision, in conjunction with colleagues Harold Wilson and

George Brown, not to devalue the pound. Ben Pimlott speaks for most when he says that this, the Government's first decision, was probably its worst; and that it was taken with quite unnecessary haste, for which the civil servants were responsible.

Alec Cairncross, the Treasury's then economic adviser, has been open about the mandarins' motives in 1964: they wished to force the new administration towards a crisis that would oblige it to take decisions that would otherwise be ducked. 'Devaluation might yet be necessary; but it was preferable to wait until the government had learnt its lesson.'[10] That hardly seems like proper behaviour for public servants, nor was it a very kind welcome to give to the new Chancellor. But on that occasion too the politicians were a little to blame: they could have refused to be rushed. When in 1970 Iain Macleod was appointed Chancellor on a Saturday, he was immediately informed that his new private staff were at their desks at the Treasury, waiting to start work. Macleod genially told them to go home and to come to his house the following day for Sunday lunch: work could wait.[11]

When Nigel Lawson was made Chancellor in 1983 he discovered that his new staff were delighted with the appointment: for here was a man who would answer them back, in the great tradition of Denis Healey. Knowing how to handle the civil servants would seem to be a basic skill needed by new Chancellors, and one which they have often needed to apply on the very first day of taking office.

How well qualified does the Chancellor need to be?

The excitement that most new Chancellors have felt on being appointed to the position is of course a reflection both of its seniority and of its wide-ranging influence. To be given the job is to be raised above the common herd of middle-ranking Cabinet ministers, and to be accorded more power than either the Home Secretary or the Foreign Secretary wields (and as Gordon Brown and John Prescott both know, much more power than any mere Deputy Prime Minister). So it might be assumed that Prime Ministers will only appoint as Chancellor a front-bench colleague who will not be easily brow-beaten by his civil servants and who already commands the respect of fellow front- and back-benchers.

In fact, since the Second World War, only a minority of Chancellors has really fallen into that category, with a slightly larger number being either unproven when they took office, or demonstrably second-rate. The notion that a Chancellor has to be *papabile* is not one that has always appealed to the papal incumbent.

From the point of view of the Prime Minister of the day, the ideal Chancellor is one who already has the requisite seniority yet who is not a threat to the Prime Minister himself or herself. But such candidates are rare, especially since the obligations to deliver the Budget and handle finance bills mean there is no possibility at all of having a Chancellor who is in the Lords rather than the Commons.

Knowing about economics might seem to be another basic requirement for a Chancellor. But few Chancellors have been appointed primarily because of their economic expertise; and when they were, it is not clear how much help it gave them. The most recent was Nigel Lawson. At first Lawson seemed an exemplary Chancellor, on top of his subject, doing the job for which he had long prepared, providing the Cabinet at large with much of its intellectual and ideological rigour, and using the job to implement major changes in the life of the nation. Then things went wrong, and Lawson is now generally regarded as a failure – although some commentators see nothing unusual in that.

Nigel Lawson's background was not in academic economics but in financial journalism. After leaving Oxford in 1954 he did his National Service and then applied unsuccessfully for the Foreign Office. As second best he went instead to the *Financial Times* where he prospered: he was briefly editor of the Lex column, before transferring to the fledgling *Sunday Telegraph* as its first City editor. Then in 1963 he took a critical step by moving to Downing Street to be a speechwriter, first for Harold Macmillan and then for Alec Home. After the Tory defeat in 1964 Lawson returned to journalism as editor of the *Spectator*, which he rightly believed would give him a better platform for promoting himself than the proffered Directorship of the Conservative Research Office, as well as being more fun. He failed in 1970 in his first attempt to win a seat and lost the *Spectator* editorship shortly afterwards, but remained close to the centre of politics. In February 1974, though the Conservatives lost office, Lawson became the member for Blaby in Leicestershire, having written much of the manifesto on which the Conservatives fought.

The manifesto was framed in the interventionist, conciliatory Keynesian mould to which the party still officially subscribed and which as a journalist Lawson had hitherto espoused. He had, however, already begun to doubt that approach to economic management and also doubted the ability of the Conservative old guard to embrace new thinking and hard choices. After the Tories were again defeated in the October election, Lawson moved quickly to ensure that he was on the winning side in the ensuing peasants' revolt.

In the mind of Margaret Thatcher, Lawson's financial background suited him to be first an economics spokesman, and then after the victory in the 1979 election a Treasury minister in her first government. The post of Financial Secretary is a junior one with responsibility for monetary policy, but since the party had committed itself to Monetarism and since Lawson was far more assertive than the Chancellor, Geoffrey Howe, the position served Lawson well. Both in broad outline and in detail the Medium Term Financial Strategy came from Lawson's pen, and it was Lawson who insisted that Howe keep the pretence of Monetarism going after the Chancellor abandoned its practice in 1981.

Lawson was not just a leading exponent of the new policies of Thatcherism but also an occasional confidante of the Prime Minister who, in the words of her memoirs, came to regard him as 'a genuinely creative economic thinker' who was also good at decision-making, both qualities that Geoffrey Howe lacked.[12] Others were less impressed: not surprisingly Lawson's enthusiasm struck Howe among others as ridiculous and self-promoting. Willie Whitelaw, who had a near-veto over appointments and whom Lawson had unwisely snubbed more than once, also sought to slow his preferment.

Nevertheless, promotion to Energy Secretary followed within two years and to the Chancellorship two years after that, in 1983. Lawson had clearly been aching for the job since 1979. 'His first budget speech shows what good reading economics can make,' record the Thatcher memoirs, and as Chancellor, Lawson renewed the Government's overt commitment to Monetarism.[13] For many in the academic economics establishment that commitment and Margaret Thatcher's praise merely showed how shallow was Lawson's grasp of economics. He was an enthusiast rather than a sceptic, and that was not what 'professional' economists were supposed to be at all. Nevertheless it is hard to doubt that, given his intellectual and personal qualities and given the set of values and policies which the Conservative Government had been elected to advance, Nigel Lawson was absolutely the right person in 1983 to become Chancellor in Margaret Thatcher's government. He deserved the job, just as he deserved his subsequent comeuppance.

Another politician clearly fully qualified on paper to be Chancellor was the first incumbent of the post-war period. It must have seemed to Clement Attlee that nobody was better suited than Hugh Dalton to be Chancellor. 'Dr Dalton of the LSE' had been educated at Eton and Cambridge, where he studied first mathematics and then economics, and was taught by both Keynes and Alfred Pigou who, at the precocious age of thirty-one, had just succeeded the legendary Alfred Marshall as Professor of Political Economy. Pigou was a socialist who argued with great intellectual force that inequality was economically inefficient as well as morally disagreeable. It was he rather than the liberal Keynes who shaped the thinking of the young Dalton, and when in 1911 Dalton won the prestigious Hutchinson Research Studentship at the LSE, he embarked on a doctorate on the economics of inequality.

After war-service Dalton returned to a junior academic position at the School, followed rapidly by appointment to the Cassel Readership. Admittedly the LSE was still a small institution, academic appointments were less hotly and less fairly contested than today, and the war had probably eliminated possible rivals for the job. Nevertheless, merit alone justified Dalton's appointment to such a high position. His doctoral thesis was later published and is still well regarded, and a subsequent publication on public finances became a set text.

Dalton chose to be an academic because it would not interfere with his real ambition: to become a Labour MP. He achieved this in 1924, but soon found his hopes of early promotion to high office and thence to the party leadership thwarted, sometimes by Labour's electoral problems, sometimes by his own unappealing personality. At his worst Dalton resembled the villain in a cheap melodrama – six foot four inches tall with a face on whose exaggerated features false bonhomie often seemed a mask for something calculating and wicked. It was said by contemporaries that when they were not rolling, Dalton's eyes were blazing with insincerity. His personal life was a failure, and many of his contemporaries suspected that his loudly proclaimed socialism, like his marriage, was a sham.

Dalton nevertheless became a major figure in the Labour Party of the thirties and played a pivotal role in the reconstruction of Labour thinking following the débâcle of 1931, and on both economic and foreign fronts. As chairman of Labour's Finance and Trade Committee, Dalton made major contributions to the formulation of new economic policies for the party, while he also contributed substantially to foreign policy thinking and did much to steer Labour away from appeasement. For a while he was spoken of as a possible party leader, although admittedly of a much diminished party.

During the Second World War Dalton served as a minister in the coalition government, but not as a member of the War Cabinet, where the real power lay. Churchill loathed him, but recognised his competence and made him first Minister for Economic Warfare and then President of the Board of Trade. Then in 1945 came Labour's unexpected victory. Dalton had barely hoped to be re-elected and, now in his late fifties, was considering what to do in his retirement. Instead he found himself at last in government, even if at the Treasury rather than the Foreign Office.

Dalton's belief in 1945 that the Treasury offered too small a canvas for the exercise of his talents was a conceit to which another politician, also with a background in academic economics, was immune. Hugh Gaitskell came from a similar if less baroque social background to Dalton's (the Dragon School, Winchester and New College rather than Eton and King's). He taught economics for the WEA in Nottingham, and was then encouraged by no less a triumvirate than H.A.L. Fisher, G.D.H. Cole and Lionel Robbins to accept a lectureship at University College London (UCL). But as an academic Gaitskell published very little and his critics have tended to label him, not as an academic who strayed into politics but as a temporary wartime civil servant who became a politician on the back of the 1945 Labour landslide.

That claim is unfair. Gaitskell's job at UCL brought him into contact with Dalton, whose political protégé Gaitskell became. (Dalton, although a monster in many ways, was genuinely and generously concerned to advance the careers of younger men whom he admired.) Not that Gaitskell seemed to need much help: his biographer Brian Brivati has rather confirmed that the young Gaitskell was clever and imaginative as well as already politically committed. During the early thirties Gaitskell wrote pamphlets and articles that helped in the slow task of bringing some sanity into the economic policies of the Labour Party, while running the dashing, carefree life of a socialite. But finding himself in Vienna in early 1934 during the declaration of martial law and the killing of 1,500 socialists, Gaitskell also showed bravery: he risked his liberty and perhaps his life to protect and smuggle survivors out of the country. After Austria, according to his colleague Noel Hall, 'you could no longer joke about politics with him', and Gaitskell quickly became a strong anti-appeaser '... more deeply even than Dalton, not so loudly of course because Hugh Gaitskell was deep rather than loud'.[14]

It is true that during the war Gaitskell was a temporary civil servant; he worked as Dalton's secretary at the Ministry of Economic Warfare and then as his assistant at the Board of Trade. When the war ended he was offered an economics chair at UCL but instead went on to the back benches as MP for South Leeds. While biding his time waiting for a ministerial post he helped to draft the bill nationalising the Bank of England. Soon he was a junior minister at Fuel and Power, then the senior minister. Since there was a massive nationalisation programme to be forced through and the nation lived under constant threat of a fuel crisis, the position, though not in the Cabinet, was far more senior than it would be today. Gaitskell was already moving nicely up the political ladder, but mainly on the basis of a high level of general political ability, not a specifically economic expertise.

The key episode in Gaitskell's ascent was the leading role that he took among a group of ministers pressing for devaluation in 1949. The Chancellor, Stafford Cripps, was unwell. Attlee's response to that would today be unthinkable: he temporarily shared out Cripps's responsibilities between Gaitskell, the two junior Treasury ministers Douglas Jay and Glenvil Hall, and Harold Wilson at the Board of Trade. Of these, only Wilson was in the Cabinet and neither he nor Gaitskell was in the Treasury. Job demarcations were less rigid in those days, but even so it was a striking arrangement, through which Attlee recognised the need to shift responsibility away from his own generation of politicians and on to younger shoulders. Gaitskell acquitted himself so well that he was moved into the Treasury above Jay's head, and within a year he was Chancellor, and the fourth most senior politician in the Government.

On the face of it this was merely the elevation of a technocrat to perform a job for which his training had well prepared him. But if that was all there was to Gaitskell's appointment as Chancellor then there would never have been the need for the ensuing civil war in the Labour Party. Gaitskell's elevation over the heads of others who were already in the Cabinet, notably Nye Bevan and his little dog, Harold Wilson, did much to instigate the divide that would debilitate the party for the next four decades. In part the Bevanites were simply jealous of Gaitskell's rapid preferment and in part they distrusted what they saw as Gaitskell's lack of socialist credentials. But the strength of their dislike also testifies to the fact that they saw him as much more than a technocrat. The Bevanites recognised in Gaitskell a man with an opposing philosophy, whether socialist or social democratic, and with the determination to impose that philosophy on the party.

The same thought was probably in Dalton's mind when he sponsored Gaitskell's ascent and possibly in Attlee's too when he agreed to promote Gaitskell. More than that, these men also saw Gaitskell as the politician most likely to get things done: they recognised the need to reinvigorate the Government and they respected Gaitskell's practical skills. Again, therefore, it was not just or even primarily because he was an economist that Gaitskell became Chancellor but for other attributes; and there is no evidence that the Chancellorship was a post that Gaitskell had ever especially coveted.

Learning in opposition

Lawson, Dalton and Gaitskell were the three Chancellors with the most relevant intellectual backgrounds for the job, and in that sense at least they were all of them well qualified for the post. But others earned their appointment as Chancellor by having successfully shadowed the post while in opposition. They divide into two pairs: the pugilists Iain Macleod and Denis Healey and the earnest Geoffrey Howe and Gordon Brown. There is a good case for saying that between them they are a more convincing bunch than the more academically trained three.

Iain Macleod was Roy Jenkins's shadow, both in the parliamentary sense and in the sense that the two men closely resembled one another. Both were stocky and balding, urbane and clever, fiercely ambitious and yet slightly aloof, and destined to feature on the ranks of the 'best Prime Minister we never had' lists that political journalists periodically assemble. The position was very much a second best for Macleod, who had stood twice as a candidate for the party leadership, and although the Chancellorship was not a post he had especially sought, he clearly had the seniority for the job. Indeed, with Reggie Maudling failing to stay the course, Macleod was really the only leading Tory whom Edward Heath could not bully, and that implies that he was absolutely the right person for Chancellor in 1970. His death within a month of his appointment left the Prime Minister dangerously short of weighty counsel.

In 1974 with inflation, public finances and the balance of payments all out of control and the nation traumatised by a succession of industrial conflicts culminating in the miners' strike, it should not have been a complete surprise that the electorate sacked the incumbent Conservative Government and restored Labour to office. Nor was it a surprise that Denis Healey took over at Number 11. Healey's 'hinterland' (his own expression) was famously without equal: a Northern grammar-school boy, he studied Greek poetry at Oxford, served in intelligence in Italy in the war, was in Berlin during the blockade, helped to set up an institute for the study of military and political strategy, learned about painting and photography, and in the first Wilson government was Britain's most influential post-war defence minister.

In 1967 Healey had been a candidate to replace Jim Callaghan as Chancellor. When Roy Jenkins quit the Labour front-bench over the party's European policy, he was the obvious person to become shadow Chancellor, and hence in 1974, Chancellor. Obvious, not because he had any special disposition towards economics, but because of his intellect and aggressive personality: it was these qualities which meant that Jenkins as Chancellor had always been careful to consult Healey on economic policy, and these rather than economic expertise which in the troubled seventies seemed most necessary for whoever became the new Labour Chancellor.

With hindsight we can see that, if there was a sense in which Healey was not the right man for the job in 1974, it was that he was superficially aggressive but fundamentally compliant. Either he lacked the vision to see just how brutal he needed to be in modernising Labour Party thinking, or if he had that vision, he never articulated it. Like almost every other leading Labour Party figure of his time, he remained wedded to the notion that maintaining party unity was the ultimate objective of his craft.

Whether anybody else would have been any tougher is unlikely, however, so in that sense Healey was by far the least bad candidate then available. The only other possibility was Roy Jenkins who, disappointed in his bid to win the Foreign Office (Jim Callaghan clinched it instead), wanted to become Chancellor once again in 1974. If Jenkins had been Chancellor, he might well have chosen to rip apart the cracks that Wilson and Callaghan sought to paper over, and which Healey was willing to straddle. Certainly Harold Wilson distrusted Jenkins, and backed him into the Home Office instead of giving him the Treasury, for which he was in other respects supremely well qualified.

A clear example of a politician who used the shadow Chancellorship to prepare for the real thing is Geoffrey Howe, who, under Margaret Thatcher's leadership, used his post as shadow Chancellor to reshape his party's policies; something which Denis Healey had failed to do. Howe was an unlikely radical. He had entered the Tory party leadership contest in 1975 only after Margaret Thatcher had already toppled Ted Heath, and not because he had any expectation of victory. He merely hoped that a decent showing might get him elevated in the shadow Cabinet rankings. He achieved equal third place in the ballot, alongside Jim Prior and ahead of the since forgotten John Peyton, but he was well behind both Thatcher and Willie Whitelaw.

Geoffrey Howe did not even expect elevation to mean specifically the shadow Chancellorship, since that seat seemed reserved for Keith Joseph, whose public conversion to free market economics and rejection of Heathite corporatism had been the catalyst for change within the party. Joseph was too politically inept to profit fully from the change he himself had wrought, and he had not ascended to the

leadership, so the shadow Chancellorship seemed an obvious consolation for the party's new economic thinker.

But Margaret Thatcher took a sterner view, and concluded that
Joseph was too accident-prone even to be shadow Chancellor; she
was also perhaps leery of appointing somebody to the post who was
bound to stand up to her in an argument. In contrast, Howe's combination of experience, intelligence, willingness to work hard and
self-effacing nature made him ideally suited for the position. Thus he
became shadow Chancellor.

As a lawyer Howe was happy to accept Monetarism as a brief, but
he showed no great commitment to the new creed and his performances at the dispatch box were invariably lacklustre, hence
Healey's infamous dead sheep taunt. Thus his appointment to the
Chancellorship in 1979 disappointed rivals such as John Nott and
David Howell who were more in tune with the leader's thinking, and
who on the surface seemed more likely than Howe to make a success
of the job.

It is to her credit that at this time, long before she lost her grasp on
reality, Margaret Thatcher fully recognised Geoffrey Howe's
qualities – irritating though he must surely have seemed to her. Her
great strength then was to know what compromises to make and
what not to make. Compromises were, after all, necessary: in May
1979 her grasp on the party leadership was still dangerously weak.
She had got rid of Ted Heath, and for that the parliamentary party
was grateful; but in retrospect they mostly regretted that, in their
over-excitement, they had failed to vote for Willie Whitelaw. True,
they had now won the general election, but Labour was in such a
mess that the Tories would probably have won under any leader;
now Thatcher would have a year or two in which to prove her
mettle, or risk a counter-revolution.

In these circumstances the new Prime Minister felt obliged to
compromise over the membership of her Cabinet; and to give senior
posts, not to those men with whom she felt the most sympathy but to
those who would by their stature add most credibility to her government. Whitelaw himself was first among those; other senior figures
were, like Whitelaw, mostly grandees – Soames, Carrington, Hailsham and Pym, plus Jim Prior who represented Heath's rump.

And there was Geoffrey Howe, who moved in next door: where he began to wrestle, not yet with his conscience, but with turning the evangelism of opposition into practical ministry. Later on the Prime Minister might choose a more intellectually muscular and abrasive figure (as of course she did); but at that stage, sticking with Geoffrey, who was loyal to her yet respected by the party's old guard, seemed to be her best strategy.

Finally in this list of shadows who became Chancellor is Gordon Brown, of whose suitability for the job, at least within the terms established by the 'New Labour' project of which he was a prime creator, there was never any doubt. Gordon Brown taught politics briefly at Glasgow College of Technology, entered Parliament in 1983, quickly became a front-bencher and served as industry spokesman under Neil Kinnock and then as shadow Chancellor under John Smith. When Smith died in 1994 there was briefly a possibility of Brown becoming leader – but only in the improbable event that the less industrious, less intelligent but more flirtatious and winsome Tony Blair did not want to stand. The pact between them never to fight one another for the leadership, but even more so Blair's ruthless charm and speedy positioning, meant that Brown felt obliged to step aside, not even contesting the deputy leadership, but tucking away a grudge for the future.

Had Gordon Brown wanted to change portfolios that was his moment. He chose not to. From then on it was certain that, disaster aside, Blair would be Prime Minister and Gordon Brown Chancellor in any future Labour Government. Brown was not simply Blair's closest ally and conspicuously able: the modern style of politics meant that it was inconceivable that Prime Minister Blair would make last-minute decisions about major appointments in the way in which Attlee, Churchill and Wilson had all done. So when Brown entered Downing Street he knew already what he wanted to do and who his key staff would be: the Treasury found itself running to keep up with a Chancellor who joked to the *Financial Times* that it was much more fun taking decisions than talking about them. His early decision to give the Bank of England operational independence brought Brown widespread acclaim: *The Times* commented that the new Chancellor had 'hit the ground not so much running as sprinting', while the *Independent* commended 'Flash Gordon' for his boldness and the *Economist* went to print with 'The amazing Mr Brown' bannered across its front cover. Although Tony Blair had undoubt-edly been the dominant figure of the election, Brown briefly looked likely to be the central figure of the new administration.

Experienced ministers

A third group of Chancellors is made up of those promoted into the job from other departments, following the failure of a less able, mis-placed, exhausted or just unlucky colleague.

Hugh Dalton had served only two years before, tired and failing, he resigned over a budget leak. His successor, Stafford Cripps, was among the most experienced and also the most remarkable and con-troversial men in the Cabinet. Denis Healey once compared Cripps to Tony Benn and called him 'a political ninny of the most superior quality', and it might seem surprising that such a man could ever have deserved to become Chancellor. But Cripps in his time was a vastly impressive as well as popular figure, in a way in which Benn never was, and to many people his appointment as Chancellor in 1947 was the very least that his political abilities deserved.

Cripps's route to the Treasury was an extraordinary one. Over the years his politics had changed hugely, and his migration was in the opposite direction to that chosen much later by Tony Benn. In the thirties, the decade when the politics of ideology and the politics of personality were different facets of the same currency, it was Cripps, together with Churchill and Mosley, who seemed to represent the populist future of British politics. Cripps was the unambiguously left-wing member of the three, who campaigned for a Popular Front of socialist and communist parties against the National Government and who sought a far more radical transformation of society than Labour's leaders, scuttling towards respectability year by year, wanted. In a decade when Labour was seeking to redefine itself, Cripps sought to redefine society and the nation itself.

Cripps was also fiercely anti-fascist, and thus it was to him and not the imprisoned Mosley that Churchill turned for help in 1942 when the beleaguered coalition government was in need of support. As Leader of the House and a member of the War Cabinet, Cripps was soon demanding from Parliament and the nation at large the total commitment to the war effort that he himself exuded. When the fall of Tobruk threatened Churchill's authority, it was Cripps who seemed most likely to succeed. As it was, Cripps helped to hold the Government together until the end of the year, when American troops entered the war and eventual victory at last became a possibility.

Cripps received few thanks for his support for Churchill. On the contrary: with the crisis over and with his position further strengthened by victory at El Alamein, the Prime Minister moved Cripps to the low-profile post of Minister of Aircraft Production. Cripps, who had been expelled from the Labour Party in 1939, received little support from the likes of Bevin and Attlee, and so was unable to protest. Instead, he took the demotion with dignity. He did his new job well, displaying a real talent for administration, and he buried his former desire to build a radical socialist society in Britain.

From 1940 until 1942 Cripps had been Churchill's ambassador to Moscow, and contact with the realities of Soviet communism converted him to a new creed, in which labour and capital needed only to find ways of working together harmoniously for the common good. Thanks to that conversion, in 1945 the wily Attlee readmitted Cripps to the Labour Party and gave him a seat in the Cabinet, as President of the Board of Trade.

By the time that Cripps became Chancellor he fully epitomised the new realism that had overtaken macroeconomic policy making. Dalton had been a cavalier: Cripps was a puritan. Sir Stafford began each day at four in the morning with a cold bath. Despite hypochondria and insomnia he worked terribly long hours. He ate no meat and eschewed liquor, and believed that for the nation, austerity was morally virtuous as well as economically necessary. He also believed, very much, in a protestant God.

In 1947 the public lost confidence in the Attlee administration. As has already been indicated in Chapter 1, so too did both Stafford Cripps and Hugh Dalton. They blamed both Attlee himself and also Herbert Morrison. As President of the Board of Trade with responsibility for promoting exports, Cripps was foremost in advancing the case for a planning ministry to take firm control over the economy, rather than the fudged arrangement of Morrison as planning overlord but with few powers of his own.

This unrest manifested itself in a series of aborted coups. In the spring of 1947 Cripps persuaded Dalton that Bevin should be appointed to a new job of planning minister, allowing Dalton to fulfil his frustrated ambition of becoming Foreign Secretary, to be replaced in turn by Cripps as Chancellor. The two men put the scheme to Attlee, who not only would not agree, but who promptly set up a National Planning Board within the Lord President's Office under Morrison.

The result was to make Attlee himself the subject of the next plot, in which Dalton figured more prominently than Cripps, and which foundered when Bevin would not lend it his name. Then in September and following many machinations among Labour's senior figures, Cripps went to Attlee with a new plan: that Attlee should resign as Prime Minister but become Chancellor; that Bevin should become both Prime Minister and planning minister, with Cripps as his planning deputy; and that Dalton should go to the Foreign Office. This plan was an ultimatum – if Attlee would not accept it, then Cripps demanded that the Prime Minister stand down in favour of Cripps himself.

Attlee adroitly headed off the challenge. He subsequently claimed that he employed the simple expedient of telephoning Bevin and asking whether he wanted the top job. When the Foreign Secretary said not, Attlee bought off Cripps by making him Minister for Economic Affairs with control over all economic policy-making other than those things that were the Treasury's specific remit. Shortly afterwards Dalton resigned and Attlee, the subtlest of all political operators, made Cripps Chancellor and overall economic supremo.

Harold Macmillan did not have anything like Cripps's record when he was appointed Chancellor, but he was nevertheless an established and highly regarded politician whom Eden thought could restore credibility to the Treasury where Butler had, he felt, rather let things go. The repressed son of a ruthless middle-class mother, Macmillan had learnt self-discipline and a rather distant respect for the ordinary courage of his men as an enlisted Guards officer in the First World War. He subsequently married the daughter of a Duke and became an MP, but refused office under Chamberlain partly because he piously rejected the Government's unwillingness to act to reduce unemployment. Macmillan held junior office during the war – a suggestion that he be made Viceroy of India was vetoed on the grounds that insanity ran in the family – and he only really came to wide public attention in the 1951 Government, as the minister responsible for the construction of the promised 300,000 council homes a year.

Macmillan's subsequent promotion to Minister of Defence ought to have meant that he was a rising star. Even on his own admission, however, his period in that job was not a distinguished one. When Eden became Prime Minister, Macmillan nevertheless moved up to be Foreign Secretary, and then across to the Treasury when Eden felt it necessary to replace Butler. Hitherto, Macmillan had never seemed like much of a candidate for the top job, but by eclipsing Butler and getting out of Eden's shadow, he had altered perceptions substantially.

In 1961 events repeated themselves. Macmillan was himself now Prime Minister and determined to rid himself of a supposedly weak Chancellor, Selwyn Lloyd, who seemed to be sapping the Government's credibility. Lloyd was unpopular with the electorate, and in July Macmillan, egged on by the great miscalculator, Rab Butler, fired Lloyd and replaced him with Reggie Maudling, who could be relied upon to deliver the policies that Macmillan and the electorate both wanted.

Maudling was not a man to rock the party boat: on the contrary, with his large frame and cheerful disposition, there was more than a touch of Nicely Nicely about him. Nobody could call the forty-five-year-old Reggie Maudling lean and hungry, but he was ebullient and clever. Maudling had been a scholarship boy at Merchant Taylor's and had read Greats at Oxford, and was a sort of classy Ken Clarke, but without the enemies. Maudling was self-confident without being distant: senior civil servant Frank Lee dubbed him a rich man's Harold Wilson. He was clever but not pleased with his own cleverness. His middle-class origins left him with neither a Heathite chip on his shoulder nor a Macmillanesque desperation to be thought a toff. He was politically ambitious but not tediously so. He did not share the predilections of his former colleagues Enoch Powell and Iain Macleod for offending people. He liked a good lunch.

Ted Heath's biographer quotes a comment on Maudling when he was contesting the party leadership against Ted Heath, that he was '... backed by those who value brainpower above energy and judgement above drive'.[15] Maudling's judgement would later come into question, both for his famous 'Dash for Growth' and for his involvement with the crooked property developer John Poulson; but at the time of his appointment as Chancellor, Maudling was clearly the leading politician of his generation in government. He was the only one widely spoken of in the same breath as Butler or Hailsham as a possible successor to Macmillan. Indeed, Maudling was really the last of the old gentleman Conservatives to stand a chance of reaching the very top, before the new professional politicians – Heath, Thatcher, Major, Hague – took over.

The next but one Chancellor, Roy Jenkins, had more than a touch of the Reggie Maudling about him, despite being a Labour man. In fact Jenkins's fondness for good living, and his refusal to believe that politics should be pursued as a twenty-four-hour occupation when the small hours provided such amusing divertissements, harked back to Gaitskell, Jenkins's mentor. The two Labour Chancellors were alike in another way: they received accelerated promotion from outside the Cabinet straight to one of the highest posts, without having to work every step of the way. Jenkins was catapulted into the Home Office; his subsequent transfer to the Treasury to restore credibility after the 1967 devaluation fiasco made him favourite to succeed Harold Wilson in any palace coup.

Of course that never happened, any more than it did in a similar situation when a powerful Chancellor supported rather than toppled a weak Prime Minister. Ken Clarke is very different to Roy Jenkins: much more connected to his East Midlands roots, clever but determined not to be branded an intellectual, with wide experience in a series of Cabinet posts before he became Chancellor, but no Treasury background. He was appointed Chancellor in 1993 when it became clear that the beleaguered Norman Lamont was too great a liability in the post, and he was charged with restoring credibility to the Government.

The appointment was a gamble, but one which John Major had no choice but to take. Clarke's record in previous jobs had been mixed: as Health Secretary and Education Secretary he had cheerfully antagonised doctors, nurses, ambulance drivers and teachers, and as Home Secretary he was now proudly fighting against prison officers, prison governors and the police. Whereas his shadow, Tony Blair, had primly professed to be 'tough on crime and tough on the causes of crime', Clarke was happy to appear tough, full stop. But he was also the most robust and persuasive defender of the Government's economic policies. In the days that followed sterling's departure from the ERM, the minister who mainly spoke on television for the Government was not Lamont but Clarke. The Home Secretary's strength was that he was no more afraid of Jeremy Paxman than of anybody else. So when the time finally came to lay Lamont to rest, Clarke inevitably took over.

Controversial appointments

Other politicians became Chancellor with far less justification. Two of them got the job only because of the sudden death of the preferred candidate. In 1951 Churchill's first choice as Chancellor, Oliver Stanley, had died just nine months before the election, which had robbed the Conservatives of one of their leading figures and left Churchill curiously short of senior talent. One possible candidate for Chancellor, Oliver Lyttelton, was a poor Commons performer and was distrusted in the City, while Anthony Eden was a foreign affairs specialist without knowledge of, or interest in, economic policy. So the post of Chancellor of the Exchequer fell largely by default to Rab Butler.

Churchill did not trust Butler, partly because Butler had been an appeaser before the war, but perhaps also because Butler had led the modernisation of the Tory Party and made possible its 1951 victory. As Chairman of the party's research department, Butler had persuaded the Tories to commit themselves to the pursuit of full employment and to the promotion of the welfare state, burying the party's image as the uncaring party of mass unemployment and of rigid social divisions. While on the surface this would seem to have made Butler eminently suitable as a candidate for Chancellor, and ought to have appealed to the Whig in Churchill, the old warrior perversely saw Butler as an armchair politician who was in politics simply because it was pleasant to be so, and who had no real driving purpose of his own.

Such scepticism about Butler was at least partially justified. In appearance Rab Butler was a sort of prototype Willie Whitelaw: a large man, whose face when young had been oval and rather flat, without much expression, but which by 1951 was passing through wistful *en route* to mournful. As a schoolboy at Marlborough and later at Cambridge, Rab had always affected to be ambitious, but he had never seemed willing to exert himself sufficiently to achieve much under his own steam. For a while an obscure life as a public servant or perhaps an academic had seemed to be in prospect, until in 1926 he made a brilliant marriage into the Courtauld family. As well as a bride (of whom he seemed to be fond) Butler gained an annual income, the loan of some Impressionists, and a country house. In those days a man with the financial and social advantages that Butler now possessed could easily find a safe seat, and Butler promptly did so. Politics was, after all, one of the less demanding careers on offer. Whereas Churchill felt impelled to be a politician, Butler treated politics as if it were superior footwear, conveying him comfortably through life.

Tony Barber – such a nice man – was similarly Chancellor by default following Iain Macleod's death. A politician with a singular war record (he had escaped from a prisoner-of-war camp, suffered recapture, and then studied successfully for a first class law degree while still a prisoner), Barber was nevertheless much given to standing in the background. He had been chairman of the Conservative Party in opposition and had been given responsibility for negotiating Britain's application to join the EEC. After politics he went on to chair a small bank, which suited him well. (John Major briefly worked for the same bank, but at a far more junior level.) Heath greatly overshadowed Barber, and appointed him to be Chancellor partly because Barber could be easily upstaged: although to be fair, neither of the heavyweights Lord Hailsham nor Alec Douglas-Home was suitable for the Treasury. Reggie Maudling was a better option and not so tainted with the reputation as a profligate Chancellor as people today allege, but the Prime Minister was unwilling to make the appointment, which Maudling himself would almost certainly have been delighted to accept.

Both Butler and Barber were pushed into the Treasury unprepared for its particular demands. Jim Callaghan had no such excuse. Callaghan had been persuaded to stand for the party leadership in 1953 by Gaitskellites who had begun to realize too late that their preferred candidate, George Brown, was not really a match for the

Bevanite Harold Wilson. The problem with George Brown was no secret. 'Are we going to be led by a neurotic drunk?' asked Tony Crosland.[16] But the right had no other senior candidate, and the shadow Cabinet was worried. In the absence of any better idea Douglas Jay suggested Jim Callaghan, whose daughter had recently married Jay's son Peter and who, although still only a lightweight, had the rare ability to be both ambitious and widely liked at the same time. Jay, Crosland and others urged Callaghan to stand, as did the Deptford MP, Leslie Plummer. Callaghan, unaware that Plummer was an agent provocateur from the Wilson camp, agreed.

'You have ruined my chances and I shall never be leader of the Labour Party,' said Brown to Callaghan.[17] In the first ballot, Callaghan scored only 41 votes to Brown's 88, but they were enough to leave Brown trailing well behind Wilson's 115 votes. But to many people's surprise, Wilson as leader kept Callaghan in post as shadow Chancellor, while supporting Brown's continuation in the post of Deputy Leader, and duly made Callaghan Chancellor when electoral victory came in 1964.

Wilson let it be understood that by giving prominent jobs to his former rivals he was demonstrating his determination to give no oxygen to the old Bevanite–Gaitskellite feud. Nevertheless, many observers questioned whether Callaghan was really up to the job of Chancellor. His original appointment by Gaitskell as shadow Chancellor had caused a few raised eyebrows and the suspicion remains that Wilson kept him on, first in the shadow position and then in the job proper, precisely because he doubted Callaghan's grasp of economics, and wanted in effect to be his own Chancellor, fulfilling an ambition nurtured as an academic and government economist, but frustrated by Gaitskell's preferment in 1949.

Two other men became Chancellor following the traumatic resignation of the previous incumbent. Derick Heathcoat Amory replaced Peter Thorneycroft and John Major replaced Nigel Lawson. Amory has been described as 'the sort of man who makes up for not being first class by pretending to be third class, and so receives a quite disproportionate amount of credit for being top second class'.[18] (It's a cheesy remark, but hard not to make, that Norman Lamont illustrates the opposite type of politician. A top second class man pretending to be first class, he failed to bring it off and appeared in

consequence to be third class, which he was not.) Amory was educated, in the gentlemanly sense, at Eton and Oxford. He became a
Member of Parliament because that was what his particular position
within the squirearchy enabled and required him to do. Like many a
Tory at the time, he obtained his nomination in the town, Tiverton in
Devon, where his family were the major employers. He rose largely
without trace, spent his unexpected time as Chancellor doing
Macmillan's bidding, and as soon as possible gave up the job and
faded away, again largely without trace.

By rights, Major's story should have been similar. He entered Parliament in 1979 and was quickly taken on to the government payroll.
In 1987 came his big break. Margaret Thatcher wanted Major for
Chief Whip, but when John Wakeham declined to be Nigel Lawson's
deputy as Chief Secretary, Lawson persuaded Thatcher to give him
Major instead. So John Major, Lawson's second choice, found himself in the Cabinet.

Nigel Lawson says that he was attracted to Major's 'mastery of detail and likeable manner' and that he had been impressed by Major's
ability, as social security minister, 'to put the government's case
across in a firm, clear and agreeable way'.[19] But it is well known that,
at least initially, Lawson worried that he had made a mistake and
that Major was not up to the job. 'He would come and see me at
Number 11, ashen faced, to unburden himself of his worries and to
seek my advice.'[20] And although Lawson adds that his deputy soon
got on top of the job, he also says that Major never made any contribution to Treasury discussions beyond his own narrow field of
public spending control.

Two years later Margaret Thatcher decided to demote Geoffrey
Howe and elevate John Major to the job of Foreign Secretary. Again
Major, with no background in foreign policy and no experience running his own department, seemed out of his depth. Thatcher says
that she gave him the job because it would bring public recognition
to a man who deserved to be considered for the party leadership one
day, and whose modesty would otherwise leave him in the shadow of
rivals who were better self-publicists.[21] This is difficult to take seriously. Giving the Foreign Secretaryship to such a junior figure was a
snub to the departing Howe and to Nigel Lawson, both of whom she
now considered to be her enemies. Most important of all, Major

would, she knew, do as he was told and would not, she thought, be a direct threat to herself.

Nor need we take too seriously Margaret Thatcher's claim that John Major was reluctant to accept such rapid promotion to Foreign Secretary and also reluctant to accept his subsequent return to the Treasury as Chancellor, following Nigel Lawson's resignation.[22] Admittedly and like Macmillan in similar circumstances, Major had been Foreign Secretary for only a few months (Thatcher says weeks, which is a bit of an exaggeration). He was probably struck by the indecency of moving again so quickly. Nevertheless the Foreign Office had never made Major welcome, and he knew that the Treasury would. It was also a move that gave him great power: having endorsed him twice, the Prime Minister would look ridiculous if she now fought with Major in public, as she had with both Geoffrey Howe and Nigel Lawson. So John Major became Chancellor, and set the Conservative Government on its slow course to electoral defeat in 1997.

In contrast to Major's, Selwyn Lloyd's reluctance to take on the Chancellorship was very real and very well justified. As Chancellor he would be held responsible for policies that his Prime Minister, Harold Macmillan, would choose for him. He would be the fifth Tory Chancellor in less than a decade, and with economic problems mounting, his own tenure in office was quite likely to be short. So Lloyd told Macmillan that he would only take the job if he was guaranteed to keep it for the rest of the Parliament. The Prime Minister readily agreed.[23] Then two years later, Macmillan sacked Lloyd.

Two men, Peter Thorneycroft and Norman Lamont, became Chancellor when the previous incumbent moved up to be Prime Minister. Perhaps it is unfair to class Thorneycroft among those who did not deserve to be Chancellor. Peter Thorneycroft had spent five reasonably successful years at the Board of Trade, was amiable and a good Commons performer and held views similar to those of his new Prime Minister. His promotion above the heads of colleagues seemed a good move. In contrast, Norman Lamont's promotion to the Chancellorship provoked some surprise. As a junior Treasury minister, Lamont's performance had been lack-lustre, neither bad enough to get him sacked nor good enough to get him promoted. Nigel Lawson claims that in 1988 he persuaded the Prime Minister to make Lamont Chief Secretary, only out of sympathy for a colleague who had been repeatedly passed over and who clearly would not get another chance.[24] Perhaps Lamont's management of Major's campaign inevitably meant a debt for the new Prime Minister to repay, but the headship of a large government department, such as Environment or Defence, ought to have sufficed. Instead an inexperienced and uninspiring Prime Minister appointed an even less experienced and quite unconvincing colleague with whom he did not even have close relations to the second most important job in the Government.

Those who missed out

On most occasions the choice of Chancellor has been fairly straight-forward, even if not always terribly convincing. Only a few politicians have been left fulminating over how they were denied the job which really should have been theirs. Two early cases were Nye Bevan and Harold Wilson, both of whom wanted to succeed Cripps as Chancellor and who were angered by Gaitskell's promotion over their heads.

The two men's backgrounds were very different. Bevan's, famously, was solidly working class. As a young politician Bevan, like Cripps, opposed the National Government, criticised Labour's leaders and was expelled from the party for advocating a Popular Front. Unlike Cripps he continued with his stand during the war, and loudly criticised Labour for throwing away its socialist principles within the coalition government. But before the war ended Bevan had relented somewhat, and he was in the process of earning his rehabilitation even before Attlee's bold decision to make him Minister of Health in 1945.

Nye Bevan's success in that post has justly made him famous, and he played a wider role as the voice of Labour's conscience and the champion of its principles (although it was Ernie Bevin who was the real keeper of the cloth cap, rather than Bevan with his unashamed taste for high living). Bevan built up a huge popular following within the party and was highly thought of by colleagues and civil servants for both his departmental and his parliamentary work, both of which were outstanding. Many took it for granted that within a few years, Bevan would lead the party. Yet he showed great loyalty towards Attlee, and refused to join in Dalton's 1947 plot against the leader. At a deeper level, from 1945 until 1950 he trod the path towards ideological moderation, accepting for example that a success had to be made out of the recently nationalised industries before it was sensible to contemplate further nationalisations, and arguing the virtues, not just of a mixed economy, but of encouraging increased competition amongst private firms.

Despite this, Attlee consistently failed to promote Bevan. In 1948 when Hugh Dalton resigned the Chancellorship, the Prime Minister did not even consider Bevan for the role but gave it instead to Cripps. This was not too surprising, given Cripps's seniority and the fact that as Minister of Economic Affairs, he had just taken over responsibility for many aspects of economic policy-making; so Bevan accepted the decision with good grace. But he was bitterly disappointed not to succeed Ernie Bevin as Foreign Secretary when Bevin resigned through ill-health. When he was again passed over for the Chancellorship in 1950, Bevan's patience finally snapped. He wrote Attlee a bad-tempered letter of complaint, which the Prime Minister characteristically ignored, and he bent the ear of any parliamentary colleague unfortunate enough to cross his path.

The other politician who was disappointed by Gaitskell's appointment as Chancellor was Bevan's Cabinet familiar, Harold Wilson. A grammar-school boy from a comfortable middle-class background who won a scholarship to Oxford, and then a First in PPE, Wilson's early career, much like Gaitskell's own, seemed tailor-made as preparation for the Treasury.

Admittedly, Oxford's academic snobbery, itself possibly a disguised form of social (especially Wykehamist) snobbery, deemed that Wilson was extremely clever but not very imaginative. His economics tutor, Maurice Allen, said that Wilson was diligent but lacked originality, and at the Institute of Statistics where he subsequently worked, Wilson's colleague Arthur Brown thought him '... not top flight technically ... more of a practical chap'.[25] And indeed, when the war drew Wilson into government it was as a statistician not as an economist. Soon, however, he was forecasting the nation's manpower requirements, first in the new Economic Section of the Cabinet Office, then in the Ministry of Labour. After that he went to the

Board of Trade to calculate coal production statistics, where he won the praise of Hugh Gaitskell and came temporarily under the patronage of Hugh Dalton.

The end of the war saw Wilson elected both to an economics fellowship at University College and to Parliament as part of the Labour landslide, gaining almost immediate appointment to the Ministry of Works as Parliamentary Secretary. Two years later, when Attlee gave Morrison's job of coordinating economic policies to Stafford Cripps, Harold Wilson, already a minister at the Board of Trade, became its new President and the youngest Cabinet minister for a century and a half. Giddy with such rapid promotion, Wilson came to think of himself as Chancellor of the Exchequer in waiting.

Gaitskell quotes others as saying that Wilson was 'inordinately jealous' when Gaitskell himself was made Chancellor.[26] Ben Pimlott, in his biography of Wilson, says that any such jealousy reflects badly on Wilson's judgement, since he should have recognized that his flawed performance at the Board of Trade was making further preferment unlikely for at least a while.[27] That is probably true, but perhaps slightly misses the point. It was quite reasonable for Wilson to feel that Gaitskell's promotion impeded his own long-term aspirations in a way which would not have happened if Nye Bevan had become Chancellor. Wilson's career plan at that stage seems to have involved himself becoming Chancellor under Bevan as Prime Minister; he had no reason to expect what actually did happen: that within a few years Gaitskell as Opposition leader would give him the shadow Chancellorship, and that he would himself step directly from that position into the leadership, following the deaths of both Bevan and Gaitskell.

The jealousies aroused by Gaitskell's assumption of the Chancellorship were to be partially replicated a few years later, when Wilson had to choose a successor to Jim Callaghan at Number 11. The Prime Minister believed, probably wrongly, that as Chancellor he needed somebody from the Gaitskellite wing of the party, both to maintain internal harmony and to sustain the confidence of the City (and maybe the civil service). Callaghan had failed, and George Brown had been an unsurprising disaster as head of the Department of Economic Affairs. Wilson resolved to make a choice between Gaitskell's young postillions – Oxford contemporaries of one another and near contemporaries of himself, Roy Jenkins and Tony Crosland.

Like Wilson, Crosland had been an Oxford economics don before entering Parliament, and since then his book *The Future of Socialism* had turned him into Labour's philosopher prince. But Crosland's intellectual haughtiness unsettled Wilson, who instead favoured Jenkins. The latter was prone to bookishness and to flirting with high society, but Wilson found comfort in the fact that Jenkins at least came from the same social background as himself, and at heart shared his own instrumentalist rather than theological approach to politics. Most of all Jenkins was decisive, which Crosland was not, which Wilson rightly believed mattered a lot.

Crosland found the appointment of Jenkins very hard to swallow. Like Tony Blair and Gordon Brown more recently, the two men were friends and close allies as well as contemporaries and hence rivals, but of the two it was Crosland (like Brown) who started off as the more senior. But whereas Crosland had been first into Cabinet, it was Jenkins who moved ahead through his appointments first as Home Secretary and then crucially as Chancellor. Crosland was far more deeply humiliated than Wilson had been when he had been leapfrogged by Gaitskell, and although he was dignified in his defeat, there was a cooling in the friendship between Crosland and Jenkins. Nobody knew it at the time, but over the next decade and a half this hairline crack between allies would spread and weaken the cohesion of the Labour right, and help to make possible the party's capture by the left.

A final candidate can be offered for the role of most cruelly (if also somewhat justly) passed over would-be Chancellor. Over four years from 1970 until 1974 Tony Barber served as an undistinguished Chancellor, ripe for replacement, while at the Department of Education and Science Margaret Thatcher busied herself as an effective Secretary of State, yearning deservedly for promotion. From her own perspective of the time, her one failing was that she did not resist the tide towards comprehensive rather than selective secondary schools, although that hardly debarred her from promotion, given that it was party policy for local education authorities to be granted comprehensive regimes if they produced apparently workable schemes.

Thatcher promoted the Open University and pre-school education against much Tory prejudice, and while she bravely faced down her

critics and abolished free school milk, on spending issues she generally out-argued the Treasury. She also demonstrated her greed for
work. Hugo Young quotes the praise given to her by her Permanent
Secretary Sir William Pile (with whom she fought constantly) that
'She worked to all hours of the day and night. She always emptied
her box ... She was always a very good trouper ...'[28]

Her problems were twofold. Obviously, Ted Heath already
loathed her, and would have cheerfully sacked her from Education if
she had ever given him cause. Less obviously, she failed to establish
herself as a politician with opinions on matters outside her departmental remit, let alone as one whose opinions should be listened to,
either because of their inherent persuasiveness, or because they represented the views of a phalanx of actual or potential supporters. Indeed much the same could be said of the rest of the Cabinet, none of
whom attempted to secure more robust policies or demanded fresh
blood at the top. Meanwhile Heath became progressively more reliant on William Armstrong, his Cabinet Secretary, a mistake that
none of his political colleagues had the bottle to challenge.

Even after Labour's electoral victory in February 1974, Thatcher
made no bid for promotion and Heath offered her none, transferring
her instead to be environment spokesman. It was only the second
and more decisive Labour win in October 1974 that changed things.
By then Keith Joseph had broken ranks and declared that the Conservatives needed a radical rethink to counter Labour. Fortified by
his example, Margaret Thatcher showed her first glimmer of ambition. She asked Heath to make her shadow Chancellor.

With great ineptitude, Heath gave Thatcher responsibility for attacking Labour's Finance Bill in the Commons, but insisted that she
should be only a junior spokesman under his lacklustre friend Robert
Carr. Thus Edward Heath managed simultaneously to absolve Margaret Thatcher from any obligation of loyalty towards himself, while
putting her in a position from which she could show off her adversarial skills before the back-benchers. Being denied the shadow Chancellorship was the making of Margaret Thatcher's political career. When
the time came for somebody to topple Heath, as everybody but the man
himself knew would be soon, the vengeful Thatcher would be perfectly
placed to succeed. But if the Treasury thought that it had been spared
or denied her overlordship, then it would soon discover otherwise.

4 Cabinet government: relations with colleagues

Prime Minister and Chancellor

It is often said that Margaret Thatcher took very seriously her position as First Lord of the Treasury. Indeed, she said it herself. Geoffrey Howe commented, 'She warmed instinctively and possessively to the Prime Minister's formal title, First Lord of the Treasury,' adding waspishly that 'it almost made up for never having been Chancellor herself'.[1] Since the First Lord does not have financial responsibilities, and is instead mainly required to appoint Church of England bishops, Thatcher's pleasure was somewhat misplaced. Even so and even without grand titles, the modern Prime Minister has to be concerned to some degree with economic policy-making, and Geoffrey Howe's success was heavily dependent on his relationship with his Prime Minister. They annoyed one another and frequently fought one another, each despairing of the other's obduracy, but on the big issues they supported each other. Wise Howe gave credibility to strident Thatcher before she had amassed enough of her own; brave Thatcher gave cautious Howe the courage he needed in adversity. It was one of the defining relationships of the British political system, doing much to determine the way in which we think today about the appropriate structure of good government.

And indeed the Chancellor's relationship with the Prime Minister has to be crucial to the success or failure of any government. The Chancellor not only carries responsibility for issues that will have a major impact on both the economic success of the nation and the political success of the Government, but he is also bound to come into conflict with many senior colleagues, especially over spending plans, but also over the general thrust of policy on which most ministers usually have strong opinions. The way in which the political system works means that Chancellors get into lots of fights, and they cannot afford to lose many of them. So today's Chancellors need the backing, and hence the confidence, of their Prime Minister if they are to avoid warfare with other colleagues, while today's Prime Ministers need to take a close interest in the work of their Chancellors if they are to maintain their own grip on government.

It is hardly a surprise, therefore, that the troubled relationship between Tony Blair and Gordon Brown has generated more words and more attention than any other relationship in modern British politics. The two men are very different but also very close. As a student in Edinburgh the young Gordon Brown engaged in student politics with huge determination, whereas at Oxford at much the same time Tony Blair played the guitar and posed nude for an artist friend. The two men entered Parliament together and shared an office. Brown impressed Blair with his brains, his knowledge, his determination.

The partial eclipse of the sun, which began in 1994 when Blair rather than Brown became leader, will be painful to Brown for as long as it lasts, and Brown in turn will make sure that it is painful for Blair too. The two men fight frequently, but as is often said of married couples, at least they are still fighting. Margaret Thatcher and Nigel Lawson stopped speaking to one another long before he resigned, and the conduct of economic policy clearly suffered: Blair and Brown probably speak to each other more than any other Cabinet ministers.

On the surface it is Brown, the intellectual bully and loner who hates to be argued with, who is the troublemaker. Blair fights back, but cajoles Brown into accepting peace. This does not necessarily mean that Blair is the weaker of the two: there may well be value to the Prime Minister in having a bellicose Chancellor who frightens other ministers while he himself appears reasonable and pacific.

But perhaps there are other problems: deeper ones. Nobody needs to be told that the fighting is not confined to private arguments between the two principles, but involves and is often precipitated by their hot-headed followers, for whom feuding sometimes seems to overshadow any other objective of government. What the electorate wants most from its leaders is competence and orderly behaviour, not disarray in the streets and the enforced resignations of press secretaries and senior ministers. A government at war with itself is a government in danger from the voters, as the first post-war Labour

Government and the last post-war Conservative Government of the century both found to their cost.

Secondly, but more ambiguously, there is the problem of genuine policy disagreements between Chancellor and Prime Minister – disagreements that they apparently find difficult to resolve. On taking office Tony Blair's initial philosophy was to let the Chancellor have his way, recognising but not becoming bitter about Gordon Brown's determined hegemony. When Brown announced near-independence to the Bank of England it came as a great surprise to the Bank, but the Prime Minister had been no less surprised a few days earlier when his Chancellor demanded instant approval for the imminent move on the very day of their election victory. Tony Blair has allowed the Chancellor to chair the Cabinet's economic policy committee, rather than chairing it himself as his predecessors did; and he went along with the Chancellor's early tax and spending policies, even though they were not his own. The Prime Minister was also tempted to go for early entry to the Euro: the Chancellor said 'no': it did not happen.

Of course, Gordon Brown's power is very definitely not absolute. The shift in government spending priorities, two-thirds of the way through Labour's first term and already described in Chapter 1, showed the Chancellor coming into line with the Prime Minister's view. Perhaps the Chancellor had planned that all along: he says as much. It is too early to judge whether or not Brown was right to focus initially on job-creation and fiscal probity at the expense of hospitals, schools and transport; but what we can say is that it was a gamble, both politically and economically. The same is true of the Euro policy.

For the conservative observer of the conduct of government, it is bound to be a little worrying that the Chancellor largely took the gambles himself, winning no more than the grudging acceptance of the Prime Minister, and doubtless with little input from the civil service either. In some respects this merely mirrors similar concern over the much reduced role in government of both senior career civil servants and of Cabinet. But Gordon Brown presumably has little time for such observations, seeing conservatism as precisely the problem. And perhaps he is right. Many commentators equally lament the absence in modern British politics of any large men of conviction, intent on changing the system just as Margaret Thatcher did. Brown, much more than Blair, is such a person. Thatcher was isolated in her Cabinet: Gordon Brown is too, except that Tony Blair supports him. It is probably not a stable arrangement, destined to endure; but while it lasts it is still an impressive one.

Attlee, Bevan and Gaitskell

Chancellors do not always get such support, and clearly suffer as a result. Neither Attlee nor Churchill nor Eden showed much interest in the work of their various Chancellors. The major Prime-Ministerial interventions of the pre-Macmillan years were the occasions when Attlee and Eden respectively and belatedly elbowed Dalton and Butler out of office; in each case the hapless Chancellor had already lost the confidence of colleagues and of the wider policy-making community, and the Prime Minister was therefore responding to, rather than shaping, events.

Hugh Dalton was initially not too bothered by Attlee's neglect: he saw himself as the Government's troubadour, the figure who told the others what they stood for and why they were in government and why they were going to succeed. He believed that it was his mission to raise the confidence of party, Government and nation, and in public he radiated great good cheer. Cartoonists frequently depicted Dalton as a laughing cavalier, and he played the role of confidence-builder with over-powering style, grounded in great competence. Richard Crossman wrote of Dalton's 'sheer intellectual and physical power' and Michael Foot said that Dalton's parliamentary speeches made him 'virtually the dominant figure in the Government'. 'He bestrode the world,' said Jim Callaghan, from the right of the party, and Barbara Castle from the left said he brought 'socialist gusto to everything ... a big man in every sense of the word'.[2]

Dalton's ascendancy did not last long. Within three years doubts began to grow about his stewardship of the economy, and meanwhile Bevin and Bevan were gaining public respect through the apparent successes of their foreign and health policies respectively. Within government circles, Stafford Cripps too was eclipsing Dalton in repute. Partly for those reasons and partly because he was growing physically tired, Dalton's flame was fading long before he lost the Chancellorship. In any case Labour now needed to impose policies of renewed austerity, and in that sense the anchorite tendencies of Cripps were more appropriate to the job in hand. They were not, however, particularly useful when it came to infusing the Government with any sense of a new mission. Roy Jenkins, who was a young backbencher when Cripps was Chancellor, says that Cripps's speeches 'were masterful pieces of disdainful lucidity', but disdain is not an emotion around which a government can rally.[3] And when the crucial test of Cripps's Chancellorship arose – the need to devalue in 1949 – the Chancellor was away from his desk sick, leaving the management of the crisis to others.

Nor in turn was Cripps's successor an especially impressive figure during his Chancellorship. Hugh Gaitskell's authority was fiercely contested, just as Dalton's had been, and although the split that opened up between those who would soon be the Gaitskellites and those who would be the Bevanites had a lot to do with Bevan's wounded pride, it also had something to do with Gaitskell's haughty Coriolanus streak, and his desire not just to confront his opponents but to sneer at them and bully them. Gaitskell had convictions and ambitions but no roots, and refused to romanticise horny-handed sons of toil in the ways in which Bevan and Harold Wilson did; he offered the Cabinet and party intellect but not yet intellectual leadership.

In part the lack of a well-defined relationship between Chancellors and colleagues reflects the phenomenon discussed in Chapter 1 – the long time it took for the Chancellor to become second amongst equals in government. So long as the Chancellor's job was mainly to juggle a bit with taxes and take the advice of the Bank of England on monetary policy, there seemed little for the Prime Minister to worry about, and little reason why colleagues should treat the Chancellor as anybody special.

It is also true, of course, that it was not exactly in Clement Attlee's nature to lead from the front. He was good at taking decisions, but weak at identifying the issues on which the decisions needed to be taken. Hugh Dalton found him intensely annoying, rather as Norman Lamont would much later claim to find Prime Minister John Major's weak leadership unbearably irritating. Indeed the comparison is an obvious one: as a one-time local councillor, Attlee was rather looked down upon by Dalton, Cripps and Labour's other toffs, just as other Conservatives later looked down on the boy from Brixton whose father once sold gnomes. As it happened, Attlee, unlike Major, came from a comfortable background – his wealthy solicitor father had been President of the Law Society, and Clem was called to the Bar. But he never really succeeded as a barrister, and instead took work as the general manager of a Stepney boys' club, from which he moved into local politics. Attlee also had a very high opinion of himself, which made him a famously good butcher of weak colleagues; but again like Major (who also had a high opinion of himself when Prime Minister) he was no good at ridding himself of strong, troublesome ones.

Worst of all for Attlee's standing amongst colleagues, there was always a suspicion that he had become leader of the Labour Party only because, at the crucial moment, there was almost nobody else in the parliamentary party to choose from. Attlee had been one of the few Labour MPs to hold on to his seat in the disastrous 1931 election, and had thus become deputy leader, largely by default. The party leadership followed four years later when colleagues failed to choose between the more exciting alternatives of Herbert Morrison and Arthur Greenwood. Attlee then clung to that position, and from 1945 to 1951 to the premiership, with great tenacity in the face of repeated plots to unseat him. He was helped in that by the remarkable loyalty of Ernest Bevin, who apparently did not mind that Attlee was about the least inspirational politician of his day.

In retrospect we know that no government since then, not even the Thatcher administration and certainly not Tony Blair's, has pushed through anything like as much social and economic change as Attlee's did. It is also clear that Attlee's grip on the machinery of government, exercised through a web of committees, was extremely tight and that he was diligently working to a very clear plan – Labour's 1945 manifesto. On one or two issues such as housebuilding and Indian independence Attlee even gave explicit leadership, and in the party at large, he was generally popular and respected.

But on economic issues Attlee was, in Harold Wilson's words, 'tone deaf'. He seems not to have understood just how profound were the economic crises of 1947 and 1949, and it was only the efforts of men such as Cripps in 1947 and Gaitskell in 1949 that averted disaster. It was on Cripps's advice, rather than his own judgement, that Attlee made Gaitskell Chancellor in 1950; and it was thanks to Attlee's neglect that in the following year the inexperienced Gaitskell found himself free to run completely out of control.

From 1945 until 1950 Nye Bevan had been a volatile and voluble but fundamentally loyal middle-ranking Cabinet minister of enormous political potential, whom Attlee consistently failed either to promote or to sack. By 1949, like most of his Cabinet colleagues, Bevan had reluctantly come to recognise that his great pride, the National Health Service, was costing rather more than had originally been expected. Cripps half-persuaded him of the obvious truth: that the introduction of charges would be an effective method not just of raising revenue, but of moderating the pace at which the demand for healthcare was growing. It was not, however, an easy thing emotionally for Bevan to confront.

Accordingly, although Bevan piloted a bill through the Commons announcing that charges on dentures and spectacles and on prescriptions would be introduced at some point, he could not quite bring himself to take the step. He consistently failed to announce the precise date at which the charges would take effect. Instead, he simply asked for more funds for the NHS.

Bevan's consistent ability to secure from Cabinet the funding that he wanted, when other ministries had to accept repeated disappointments, irked both the Treasury and the ministerial heads of those other departments. 'Nye was getting away with murder,' was Morrison's summary of colleagues' views.[4]

In 1950 as Minister of State in the Treasury, Hugh Gaitskell begged Cripps to stand up to Bevan and establish the same Treasury control over health spending that applied to all other spending. But Cripps would not, and Attlee would not make him. But when later that year Gaitskell became Chancellor, he resolved to draw a line in the sand and announce in his 1951 budget an imminent date for the introduction of health charges.

By then Nye Bevan had moderated his once-radical views on many issues, including the mixed economy, and in Cabinet meetings in February he also accepted Gaitskell's demand on health charges – overcoming both his own instincts and the strong mutual dislike that had built up between himself and the new Chancellor. Bevan had recently been moved sideways to be Minister of Labour, and he was having to face the likelihood that his long-standing loyalty to Attlee would earn him nothing more by way of recognition and responsibility.

There was, however, one issue which burnt even more harshly than the health service on Bevan's conscience. In August 1950 Bevan expressed strong opposition in Cabinet to Gaitskell's proposal (presented via Cripps, since Gaitskell was still only the Minister of State) for an expensive rearmament programme. Gaitskell had intervened personally to raise the military's spending requests, to ensure that Britain devoted the same share of GDP to military spending as did the United States. Bevan disagreed with the policy, much to the alarm of the Cabinet Secretary, Norman Brook, who refused to minute Bevan's 'opposition' to the plans and had to be forced even to mention Bevan's 'grave misgivings' in the Cabinet record.[5]

Then in January 1951 Gaitskell, now Chancellor in his own right, asked for an even steeper rearmaments programme. The previous year, Cripps and Bevin had both advocated substantial rearmament in response to the North Korean invasion of South Korea; both were now gone, and neither Attlee nor the new Foreign Secretary, Herbert Morrison, was disposed to take the lead on the issue. Gaitskell assumed the mantle. He told the Cabinet that to fund higher military spending it would be necessary to cut expenditure on luxury items. Then he promptly announced his intention to introduce prescription charges.

This move by Gaitskell was a clear affront to the easily affronted Bevan, and although he initially accepted even this policy, his conscience was tragically torn. At the last moment Bevan changed his mind and asked Cabinet to do likewise, and deny Gaitskell his desired health charges.

The amount to be raised from the charges was trivial – £23 million – and Bevan's opposition was largely symbolic. So too was Gaitskell's determination to levy the charges. He had resolved himself to establish the principle that there was no bottomless pit of money for the NHS, and was even more determined to establish that as Chancellor, he had the right to decide all spending and revenue numbers. Gaitskell picked the fight. As Brian Brivati says, 'Politically he [Gaitskell] needed to be backed by the Cabinet to assert his ascendency over Bevan.'[6]

For the sake of a quiet life most senior ministers were initially inclined to humour Bevan, as they had often done in the past. Over the next couple of months Morrison, Bevin and others repeatedly tried to persuade Gaitskell to give way. Early in April, with a week to go before Gaitskell presented his first Budget, Bevan told a meeting in Bermondsey that he would not remain a member of a government that imposed charges on 'teeth and spectacles'. Hugh Dalton tried to persuade Gaitskell to back down: the Chancellor said that he himself would resign if he did not get his way, and carried on with his preparations.

On the morning of 9 April 1951 Hugh Gaitskell presented to the Cabinet the Budget that he intended to deliver the next day in the Commons. It included the disputed NHS charges. If the Cabinet asked him to remove the charges, he would resign and not present the Budget. When Gaitskell came to describe his proposed charges, Bevan objected. Gaitskell insisted. The Cabinet adjourned until that evening. When it reconvened, only Harold Wilson and the Education Minister George Tomlinson supported Bevan. Gaitskell had won – or nearly so.

There was one problem. Attlee, semi-incapacitated in hospital, had not been at the Cabinet meeting. The next morning, with only hours to spare before the speech, Gaitskell visited Attlee. The Prime Minister, not wanting to see Bevan, Wilson and perhaps others resign, asked Gaitskell to compromise. Gaitskell refused. Attlee argued with him. Gaitskell was adamant. Eventually Attlee gave way. 'I am afraid they will have to go,' he murmured. He was so indistinct that Gaitskell thought for a moment that the Prime Minister had said, 'Very well, you will have to go.' That afternoon Gaitskell delivered his Budget.

Attlee's support for Gaitskell had been less than total. The Prime Minister had made no attempt to avert the emerging crisis. In part that was because of his ill-health, but that was not much of an excuse. Bevin was sicker than the Prime Minister, and he did more; in any case the issue of health charges had been alive for two years, during which time Attlee had never sought to achieve anything more than a fudge. And although Cripps had agreed to compromise in 1950, the form of compromise – we will introduce charges but not just yet – was hardly one that could be sustained indefinitely.

Furthermore, Attlee's sickbed contributions were focused on

getting Gaitskell to accommodate himself to Bevan just as Cripps had done, rather than vice versa; only when all else failed did the Prime Minister back his Chancellor rather than the Minister of Labour.

Attlee's government thus came within a whisker of being unable to offer a Budget to the House. When Gaitskell got back from hospital on the morning of 10 April Edward Bridges, then the Permanent Secretary, said that it was 'the best day we have had in the Treasury for ten years' – which beggars imagination about what the bad days must have been like.[7] Certainly there is scant evidence in the story of the Treasury and Chancellor possessing either the overarching power or the Prime Ministerial backing that are today taken for granted.

Bevan did not resign immediately. But on 14 April Ernie Bevin died, to be succeeded as Foreign Secretary not by Bevan but by the manifestly incompetent Herbert Morrison. Bevan could no longer see any reason for being in the Government, and resigned two days later.

There is no doubt that on the issue of health charges, the Treasury and the Chancellor were right and Bevan was wrong – as he himself knew. Charges were needed to slow the expansion of demand for health services, and to help pay for those that were demanded. The idea that all healthcare should be provided completely free at the point of delivery had, with retrospect, always been a mistake.

But there is equally no doubt that on the far more momentous issue of rearmament – the issue that really underlay Bevan's resignation – Gaitskell and the Treasury were disastrously wrong. When the American Government had originally asked the Attlee administration to demonstrate support for American intervention in Korea by embarking on a programme of accelerated rearmament, it did at least promise to provide enough American cash to protect the British balance of payments from damage. That was the plan over which Bevan had his 'grave misgivings'. Although he was severely opposed to the Soviet Union, Bevan quite rightly scorned the notion that the rearmament programme would weaken the Soviet or any other Communist regime; he was affronted by the illegality of, and sceptical of the likely success of, the American invasion of North Korea; and he quite rightly doubted that the British economy could withstand rearmament, even with American help.

Soon it transpired that the Americans were not going to finance anything like the share of the proposed £3,600 million British military spending that they had originally promised. Instead of thinking again, Gaitskell flew to the United States, became obsessed with the Communist threat, and thus came up with his January 1951 plan to raise the military spending plans to £4,700 million over the next three years – or significantly more in proportionate terms than the Americans themselves were spending.

It was a ridiculous plan, hastily drawn up and motivated by Gaitskell's delusions of British grandeur and his adoption of crude anti-communism, and flying in the face of everything that as Chancellor, Gaitskell claimed to represent. By the summer of 1951 he was himself admitting that his own rearmament programme was excessive, and when the Conservatives returned to power in the autumn, they sharply cut the plans.

How did this error come about? The rivalry between Bevan and Gaitskell, and Attlee's failure to supervise or give the Chancellor a proper direction, must be key parts of the explanation. Indeed, more than that: one has a strong sense of Gaitskell seeking to fill Attlee's vacuum, and that of the terminally sick Ernie Bevin, lest others fill them first. Gaitskell was impatient with Attlee rather as Tony Blair and Gordon Brown were with John Smith during the latter's brief leadership, and in his Chancellorship Gaitskell opted for policies as much because they would advance his fight against the left as because they would immediately advance the state of the national economy.

That was not necessarily cynical. It might have been very good for the economy in the long term if several other short-term economic decisions had been sacrificed in the cause of thrashing out some political arguments. But in this case the politics to which Gaitskell had fallen prey were not especially edifying or good for the nation's long-term prospects, and the sight of the Chancellor of all ministers opting for gung-ho militarism was indeed curious.

The Conservatives in the fifties

Hugh Gaitskell's successor, Rab Butler, got off to a bad start where his colleagues were concerned by failing to convince them of his Robot scheme, described in Chapter 2, for 'saving' sterling. Butler unveiled the scheme on a Friday in late February to a small group of

Cabinet ministers. The Chancellor clearly expected them to approve the proposal without much discussion, so that he could feature it in his forthcoming Budget. He handed out copies of a paper, but demanded their return at the end of the meeting. Unfortunately for the Chancellor, Cherwell refused to return his copy, and took it away for his assistant, Donald MacDougall, to dissect. 'Long before I had finished it I was verging on hysteria,' claims MacDougall, whose sobriety in economic matters would later become legendary.[8]

Butler's paper proposed radical actions, the domestic and international consequences of which it admitted were not just unclear but might be hugely damaging, including the demise not just of the European Payments Union but also the International Monetary Fund – from which Butler nevertheless proposed to borrow. MacDougall and Cherwell spent the weekend preparing a rebuttal, and then spent the following week lobbying ministers and their advisers. They won the arguments, and Butler backed down, discredited in the eyes of both colleagues and advisers. In his memoirs he writes that 'among ministerial colleagues I could count Oliver Lyttelton alone as a consistent supporter.'[9] He complained of 'the Prof's [Cherwell's] private detective agency in economics' and of 'the marshalled arguments of Lord Cherwell and the cautious conservatism of the elder statesmen'.[10] But essentially he let himself down, by not being on top of his job, and not being on top of his colleagues.

As it happens the economy performed rather well for a couple of years, somewhat to everybody's surprise. So Butler survived until 1955. In April he produced an expansionary Budget, and then in July he introduced an emergency package of measures in the face of clear evidence that the economy was overheating. The second of the two Budgets included cuts to the investment plans of the nationalised industries and increases in coal and steel prices. It was a classic case of a Chancellor in disarray, grabbing any policy instruments that he could lay his hand on, and putting them to macroeconomic use (higher coal and steel prices being a means, however inappropriate, to take spending power out of the economy). That he was able to do this testifies to the power that even Butler as Chancellor could wield over a wide range of government policy: but he did so at a political price. Within months Butler would be politely sacked from the Chancellorship, although not before putting a Budget to the House in

October that largely reversed his April measures.

Butler had few friends in Cabinet – not Churchill, not Eden, not the powerful figure of Lord Woolton. Later he complained about the 'stupid men' who obstructed his ascent to the premiership, but as Edward Pearce notes in his essay on Butler, 'it is rather likely that over time many stupid men came to know that he thought them stupid'.[11] Butler was rational, detached, supercilious, casual about making enemies, and often more in tune with his civil servants than with his party colleagues. He was, therefore, easy to dislodge from office.

Butler's nemesis, Anthony Eden, lasted only a short time as Prime Minister. It is sometimes said that Eden's successor, Harold Macmillan, was the first Prime Minister to concern himself directly with economic policy. Richard Davenport-Hines writes that Macmillan told his ministers that he did not want 'great oratorical brilliance in the House of Commons, or great administrative ability in your departments ... all I ask of you is sheer physical endurance'.[12] Party, Government and nation were all in crisis, Macmillan was going to try to sort matters out, and about the last thing he wanted was colleagues getting in his way.

But although Macmillan cared about what happened to the economy, he did not devote himself to understanding why the economy behaved as it did, nor to any detailed arguments over policy responses. This was partly because he was unwilling to devote the time, and partly because he shied away from the intimacy with colleagues that a close involvement in their responsibilities would demand. And of course, he no longer had a huge department of specialist civil servants to advise him.

Harold Macmillan took it as axiomatic that his government's primary domestic policy objective was to restrain unemployment. The evils of unemployment had been impressed upon him in his pre-war persona of rebellious back-bench representative of recession-ravaged Stockton. Macmillan believed that controlling unemployment was a prerequisite for electoral success. But as Edmund Dell puts it, 'The economics of Stockton-on-Tees would bring Macmillan into conflict with his first three Chancellors.'[13]

In 1958 Macmillan refused to allow his first Chancellor, the proto-Monetarist Peter Thorneycroft, to cut government spending. That provoked Thorneycroft's resignation (plus that of the other two

Treasury ministers, Nigel Birch and Enoch Powell). Macmillan responded with great disdain and gave the Chancellorship to the agriculture minister, Derick Heathcoat Amory, who was not desperately bright and who could be relied on to do as he was told. To his credit, the new Chancellor recognised that he was out of his depth and refused to serve for very long, obliging Macmillan to replace him in 1960 with Selwyn Lloyd, a somewhat feline individual, who had been careful never to display too much backbone while Foreign Secretary. Even Lloyd was insufficiently compliant, however, hence his dismissal in the 1962 night of the long knives following his reluctance to expand the economy as rapidly as Macmillan wanted.

Three down: not many to go. The new Chancellor in 1962 was the young, clever and expansionist Reggie Maudling, who was never likely to be a pushover, but who shared Macmillan's belief in seeking a rapid expansion of the economy. For a while there was harmony, even if no particular closeness, between Chancellor and Prime Minister, and Maudling's 'dash for growth' came close to securing the Government's re-election in 1964. It probably would have been re-elected if Maudling himself had been Prime Minister, for by then Macmillan was gone, and Maudling was working under Alec Douglas-Home, a charming and amusing gentleman, whose hobbies included flower-arranging, but who was less knowledgeable where macroeconomic demand management was concerned. At least Home gave Maudling no complaints, and on the only real economic issue he had to deal with (resale price maintenance, or price-fixing in the high street, which Edward Heath at the Board of Trade was keen to do away with) Home was decisive and made the right choice (although some say that Heath held a pistol to his head). So for a couple of years at least, there was harmony among the residents of Downing Street.

Jim Callaghan, Harold Wilson and George Brown

When Harold Wilson formed his triumvirate in government, there was little doubt that he was at the top and Chancellor Jim Callaghan at the bottom, with George Brown somewhere between the two. Wilson began government insisting on taking the big decisions himself, and Callaghan lacked real status within Cabinet, where George

Brown treated him as a junior and where, more than once, Denis Healey savaged the Chancellor. One of Dick Crossman's diary entries in November 1964 says that George Brown was 'the man of action' while Callaghan 'sits beside him sort of bleating amiably'.[14] Crossman claims that Wilson confided to him about Callaghan, 'Yes, I'm having to hold his hand. His nerve isn't too good these days,' but Crossman also says that Wilson himself was failing to give a public lead, a function that George Brown was performing instead.[15]

Yet by February of the following year Crossman was writing that, despite all efforts to make the DEA the centre of economic policy, the Chancellor of the Exchequer 'with all the authority of the Treasury behind him' still held the power.[16] By April 1966 Crossman was writing, 'Callaghan and Wilson are now in full cahoots, with George Brown now in a weak position to oppose the deflation they both want.'[17]

Crossman is not best known as a reliable witness, and maybe we should not take these details at face value (although civil servants say that on these matters, Crossman was more trustworthy than on most issues). What is clear, however, is that Callaghan was a kind and courteous man who was nevertheless capable of being brutal in an argument; that Brown lacked self-control and any sense of proportion; and that although Wilson was often shrewd and often diplomatic, he was addicted to playing political games with and against his Cabinet colleagues. The consequence was that the status and power of Callaghan, Brown and to a lesser extent Wilson fluctuated greatly in those years, and so too did relations between them, and the views that they held on the main issues of the day.

The fundamental driving force was clear: economic conditions demanded both a deflation of the domestic economy and a devaluation of the currency, and if any of the three men held out too long against that force then he would suffer as a result. Brown and especially Wilson held out longer than Callaghan. Brown gave up the fight following the 1966 deflation, while the devaluation crisis tainted Wilson and Callaghan more or less equally.

The crisis cost Callaghan the Chancellorship, but it also robbed Wilson of his vitality and self-confidence. In consequence, Callaghan's successor, Roy Jenkins, had far more autonomy than Callaghan had been allowed. Jenkins writes that Wilson 'showed no panache of leadership, and indeed left the advocacy [in Cabinet, of another deflationary spending package] almost all to me'.[18] And although Jenkins commends the Prime Minister's 'quiet almost resigned loyalty' it is significant that when Wilson insisted that he and not Jenkins should announce the package in the Commons he bungled it, thereby weakening himself further, relative to his Chancellor.

By the time that George Brown quit the Government completely a few months later, Roy Jenkins was powerful enough to block the appointment of Barbara Castle as Secretary of State for Economic Affairs – a position from which she could have challenged Jenkins's grip on economic policy – although he was not quite strong enough also to insist on Denis Healey as Foreign Secretary in place of Brown. Jenkins says that Wilson then reasserted himself by temporarily reneging on a promise to promote Jenkins's deputy to a seat in Cabinet – behaviour which rather tends to emphasise the Prime Minister's weakness, rather than his strength. Wilson was apparently obsessed with not allowing the emergence of a pro-Jenkins majority in Cabinet, and admitted Jack Diamond to the Cabinet a few months later, only in the company of Judith Hart from the left of the party.[19]

Relations between the two of them then deteriorated markedly, largely because of Wilson's paranoia but also because Jenkins, though he felt himself not yet strong enough to challenge for the top job (even if he wanted to), failed to quell the gossip of those who expected him to make such a bid. To Wilson's relief, when the opportunity came Jenkins was too cautious to take it. In the summer of 1968 Ray Gunter resigned from the Cabinet. Like Geoffrey Howe in Mrs Thatcher's government, Gunter complained about the Prime Minister's manner of conducting government, although again like Howe his unhappiness also reflected a recent demotion – in his case from Minister of Labour to Minister of Power. Gunter's derogatory resignation letter might have provided a pretext for a Jenkins challenge, had the Chancellor been sufficiently ruthless. But fear of the shame of challenging and losing, perhaps combined with some genuine scruples, and hesitation over just how desirable the prize would be, prevented him. Jenkins had recently patched up a quarrel with Wilson over the provenance of leaks, and the Prime Minister was giving Jenkins to understand that if he would only wait, then Wilson would retire with dignity and pass the inheritance to him.

But by early 1969 Roy Jenkins's bloom had faded. A string of minor crises had weakened his reputation, and the Chancellor was beginning to wonder whether another devaluation might be needed – something which, Jenkins feared, could cost him his job, and might even bring down the Government.[20] Meanwhile Denis Healey was rising in stature, and Jim Callaghan was about to use opposition to Barbara Castle's trade union legislation as a mechanism for restoring his own political standing, even at the expense of ruining the Government's prospects in the coming general election.

In fact the worst of the economic news was now over, and over the next year Jenkins saw his deflationary policies vindicated, and his own position strengthened. That presented the Chancellor with the choice of whether to continue with another restrictive Budget in the spring of 1970 or whether to follow Maudling's example and go for a pre-election giveaway. This crucial decision, so vital for both the economy and the survival of the Government, Jenkins took almost alone. The Prime Minister gave him no direction. Crossman wrote, 'of course Roy is omnipotent now. Harold can only pressure him.'[21]

Crossman, who like many in the Cabinet thought that the Budget should be expansionary, had an unkind view of what might sway Jenkins. 'I believe the only sensible thing to do is for Harold to say to Roy "Look, if you give me the right budget, I will make you Foreign Secretary".'[22] But even without the right Budget, Wilson would soon be promising Jenkins the Foreign Office and, shortly after that, the premiership. Of course it was not to be – the election would soon be lost and the games that these men would have to play would be changed dramatically.

Barber and Heath, Healey and the Cabinet

Under Ted Heath, power swung dramatically back to Number 10 and the Cabinet Office, with Tony Barber playing very much a subsidiary role. Heath barely mentions Barber in his memoirs, and Barber in turn is tight-lipped about his experience as Heath's Chancellor. Geoffrey Howe says politely that Barber was the 'manager and not the originator' of the Government's central economic policies.[23] The Cabinet itself was generally friendly and united, but tended not to have much to do; Heath mostly made his own decisions with the help of William Armstrong, whose questionable advice to Reggie Maudling and Jim Callaghan had earned him promotion to Cabinet Secretary and head of the civil service.

When Labour returned to office in 1974, Harold Wilson was a reformed character, more relaxed, more confident, willing to let ministers get on with their work. But for his first year and a half in office, Denis Healey went along with what the Cabinet wanted. He was not yet the acknowledged leader of the right in government, and although he argued with the left he could not dictate to them. Only in 1976 did he change, insisting like Hugh Gaitskell and Roy Jenkins before him (but naturally with far more belligerence than Jenkins, and for higher stakes than Gaitskell) that Labour had to live in the real world. Healey's fight with the left was forced upon him, and his response was magnificent whereas Gaitskell's had seemed only mean; he did Callaghan's dirty work for him, until overpowered by far greater forces than Gaitskell or even Jenkins had ever had to face. In that period it was Healey who set the agenda on which Cabinet colleagues who wanted Labour re-elected had to fight, but to which half the Cabinet refused to subscribe.

Especially in the second half of his term of office as Chancellor, Denis Healey was not especially popular with his colleagues, and the point has been made in an earlier chapter that he seemed to prefer the company of politicians and officials abroad to that of fellow Cabinet members. The key tussle related to the spending cuts that Healey sought to implement in 1976. Several Cabinet ministers, including Tony Crosland from the right as well as others on the left, thought the cuts excessive, and clearly also resented that they were to be made to satisfy the IMF. Healey's problem was that Prime Minister Callaghan refused him any automatic backing, and forced Healey not just to debate all the issues, but to consider papers put up by other ministers offering alternative ideas about how the economy should be run. Healey was undergoing a similar trial to that of Hugh Gaitskell, a quarter of a century earlier, but on a much larger scale. He too came through the victor, thanks to bullying tenacity and great brain-power, but as a lesson in how not to run a government the episode was avidly studied by someone else: the new Leader of Her Majesty's Opposition.

Howe, Lawson and Thatcher

Healey the old ram was followed by Howe the dead sheep – but both men served to hold together the governments in which they served. In the early days of Thatcherism, Geoffrey Howe's evident reasonableness made it much harder for the wets in government to savage the extreme policies to which the Chancellor, as much as the Prime Minister, was committed; he made Monetarism respectable in a way in which more brittle figures such as Keith Joseph or Margaret Thatcher herself could not have done.

Geoffrey Howe has referred to his relationship with Margaret Thatcher in their first year in office as a 'practical, if unromantic, partnership'.[24] The relationship was eased by the Prime Minister's instinctive sympathy for Treasury hairshirtery, which meant that the two of them were generally allies. Thatcher also allowed Howe some worthwhile policy leeway – especially when Nigel Lawson said she should. Although the idea of declaring medium-term monetary targets (the pretentiously named Medium Term Financial Strategy) was something of which the Prime Minister was unsure, she went along with the approach (largely Lawson's idea anyway). And although she was sceptical of Howe's hobbyhorse – Enterprise Zones – she agreed to those too, brushing aside advice that the zones were a highly inefficient way of stimulating local regeneration in big cities – as the evidence has since shown them to have been.

Throughout her premiership Margaret Thatcher displayed a disturbing need for personal comfort disguised as policy guidance, but initially she was willing to take both formal and informal advice from a range of friends, officials and senior ministerial colleagues. As Chancellor, Geoffrey Howe met the Prime Minister formally once a week, breakfasted with her and other allies almost every Thursday before Cabinet, and snatched brief informal meetings with the Prime Minister several more times a week. This high degree of contact (although still less than that between Tony Blair and Gordon Brown) was essential if their joint political project was to flourish. Yet some shadow of the problems that would later wreck Margaret Thatcher's regime was already present. Howe in his memoirs says that the Thursday breakfast meetings were disorganised and unbusinesslike, and really only served to reduce the Prime Minister's sense of isolation and not being sufficiently in control, while creating an

impression of an exclusive cabal from which other Cabinet colleagues felt excluded.[25]

Furthermore, Margaret Thatcher was determined not to allow the
Chancellor's leash to grow too long. In the summer of 1980, after
only a year in office, she briskly called him to heel. In a repetition of
events when Tony Barber was Chancellor, the removal of controls on
bank lending – known as the corset – caused a huge surge in the
money supply, to which the Chancellor (on holiday in Greece), his
officials, and the Bank of England all responded with insouciance.
Howe told Thatcher that in a month or two the Treasury planned to
hold a seminar of academic, city and government economists, where
the state of the nation's monetary affairs would be debated; in the
meantime he planned to do nothing. Angered, the Prime Minister
launched an entire series of seminars at Number 10 (Howe's seminar
took place in the other-worldly confines of Church House, if you
please), where various extreme monetarists (Alan Walters from the
LSE, Jurg Niehans from the University of Berne, Alfred Sherman
from a place in his own imagination) advocated a new and much
tighter monetary regime. Howe and his ministers and officials attended, but whenever the Chancellor tried to speak he was subjected
to 'ceaseless and hectoring' interruptions from Thatcher.[26] He nevertheless refused to give way, and was obviously backed by his staff, so
that the Prime Minister felt unable to force a redirection of policy;
she had, however, now firmly marked the Chancellor's card, and
Press speculation soon developed about the possibility of the Chancellor being sacked.

In 1981 Geoffrey Howe decided to implement a cruelly deflationary Budget at a time of industrial collapse and mass unemployment.
On the Monday the Chancellor gave Willie Whitelaw, Peter Carrington, Francis Pym and Jim Prior advance warning of his decisions. All
were unhappy. 'I couldn't say enough bad against it,' remembers
Prior, and he summoned fellow wets Peter Walker and Ian Gilmour
to a breakfast the next day, where they discussed but lacked the
courage to implement a joint resignation.[27] Howe was given a very
rough ride in Cabinet that morning, and after the Budget in the afternoon many Conservative back-benchers and most of the serious
Press attacked what they thought was an economic and political disaster. Even in July the wounds were still bleeding – presenting a paper

to Cabinet on the outlook for the economy and the need, as he saw it for further heavy spending cuts, Howe found himself attacked from all sides. Some contributors were more emotional than rational: Michael Heseltine, a rising star who had never before shown rebellious tendencies, said that Howe's plans would undermine the fabric of civic society and that the time was ripe for a pay freeze. Lord Hailsham stirred himself to anger and made a speech in which he offered cod-learned allusions to the rise of fascism in pre-war Germany. Howe saw loyalists desert him: the Monetarists John Biffen and John Nott castigated the intellectual quality of the Chancellor's paper and said that the Government was in danger of carrying a good policy to absurd lengths. Perhaps the sharpest barb came from Ian Gilmour, who quoted Churchill: 'However beautiful the strategy, you should occasionally look at the results.'[28]

Ultimately the problem of the wets was dealt with by the Prime Minister, who in the autumn sacked several of them – including Gilmour. She emasculated Jim Prior by making him Northern Ireland Secretary, and she brought Norman Tebbit and Nigel Lawson into the Cabinet to tip the balance further to the right. But she was no longer happy with her Chancellor, and a few months later she humiliated Howe in front of his staff by deriding what he planned to say in the Autumn Statement. 'If this is the best that you can do,' she shrilled at a meeting that she had crashed, the night before the statement was due to be delivered, 'then I'd better send you to hospital and deliver the statement myself.'[29] Although the Prime Minister later commended the Chancellor's performance, she did so only privately and without apology for her previous public rudeness. Roy Jenkins would not have accepted such behaviour from Harold Wilson, and Geoffrey Howe hardly needed to accept it from Margaret Thatcher. He chose to do so. His comment, 'I have always regarded other people's personalities as largely beyond reform,' only diminishes him.[30]

By 1982 the Chancellor and the Prime Minister were no longer at all close – Howe refers in his memoirs to 'Margaret and her allies' of which he clearly was no longer one.[31] The Prime Minister continued her practice of sending Howe handwritten notes of praise – '... superb ... You deserve all the acclaim ... Have a good night's sleep!' she scribbled in response to the 1982 Budget – but fundamentally she no longer respected or even liked her Chancellor.

A month later Howe found himself excluded from the Falklands War Cabinet. Following the invasion and the possibility that the Prime Minister and perhaps the Government might fall, Harold Macmillan had demanded an audience with the Prime Minister. He supported her decision to send the Navy and the troops to retake the Falklands, and urged her to exclude Howe from the War Cabinet because he thought the Chancellor would put financial considerations before military ones. Thatcher says that it was this wise advice which rightly kept the Chancellor out of the War Cabinet, although the fact that the Prime Minister thought her Chancellor to be spineless surely ruled him out anyway. Instead she found a place for the vacuous Cecil Parkinson, whose jobs were to support the Prime Minister in the War Cabinet if her bellicosity outran that of the other members, and to relay War Cabinet deliberations to the party and media in ways which favoured the Prime Minister's cause.

Instead, the Chancellor had to make do with the meagre consolation prize later that year of overseeing the drafting of the party's manifesto for the 1983 election – although with Ferdinand Mount looking over his shoulder on the Prime Minister's behalf. Thatcher soon regretted the decision and the bland manifesto that resulted, but it hardly mattered, given the boost to the Government's popularity occasioned by victory in the South Atlantic.

Worse still, Margaret Thatcher's relations with her next Chancellor underwent the same downwards journey that had characterised those with Geoffrey Howe, except that the rate of descent was far steeper. The events have already been referred to and are discussed in more detail in a later chapter. Nigel Lawson moved from being more Thatcherite than Thatcher, to being much less so. He abandoned Monetarism and replaced it with a belief in fixed exchange rates that, to the Prime Minister's fury, also placed him firmly in the Europhile portion of the Cabinet. Thatcher unleashed Alan Walters and Bernard Ingham against the Chancellor, who, lacking Howe's masochistic streak, soon told the Prime Minister directly what she could do with the job. His resignation did not bring her down, but it unsettled her sufficiently so that Howe's own resignation shortly afterwards did so instead.

Nigel Lawson is generally painted as the clear hero of this story and Margaret Thatcher the clear villain. But there is a subtext which slightly undercuts those judgements. In late November 1987 the Prime Minister gave an interview to journalists from the *Financial Times*. They asked the Prime Minister why, if the Government was pursuing a policy of shadow membership of the European Exchange Rate Mechanism (ERM), ministers did not just go the whole hog and join the system. The Prime Minister was puzzled – it just was not true, that was not the policy. Now the journalists were puzzled. Sterling was being stabilised at 3 deutschmarks to the pound. Interest rates had been cut by the Bank of England to achieve that, and the Bank had also sold sterling heavily on the currency markets for the same reason – causing many City economists to worry about the effects on monetary growth and inflation. Nonsense, said the Prime Minister, sterling was free to float. Exasperated, the journalists dug out a graph and showed the Prime Minister how sterling had been stable at or just below 3 deutschmarks for nearly ten months. Such stability could hardly be accidental. There clearly was a policy of keeping the pound steady, just as if it was part of the ERM already. Acutely embarrassed (or, as some believe, acting a part), the Prime Minister stuck to her guns. 'We are always free,' she snapped. But privately she knew they were right. Yes, her government's policy was to stabilise the exchange rate. And no, she had known nothing about it.

'How could I ever trust him again? ... The question arises whether at some point now or later I should have sacked Nigel. I would have been fully justified in doing so.'[32] Margaret Thatcher's reflections in her memoirs are the palest shadow of the fury that she felt at the time. Sack him – she must surely have wanted to garrotte him.

Hugo Young has suggested that Margaret Thatcher's anger must have been flamed by the fact that for years Nigel Lawson had seen her, formally or informally and often alone, almost every day. Lawson had always made great play of the fact that he and the Prime Minister shared confidences with which neither Cabinet colleagues nor civil servants could be trusted. Despite all that, he had betrayed her. He had eschewed the alternative to secrecy – to insist on his policies and resign if he was refused – and had opted instead for hypocrisy. He had even avoided discussing the policy openly and officially with his Permanent Secretary Peter Middleton or with the

Governor of the Bank of England, lest they feel compromised and obliged to blab. Of course they realised what he was up to, but they in turn avoided asking the questions that might have required the Chancellor to make explicit what he was doing. By such evasions was the economy managed. And if the Prime Minister's awful personality was at the heart of the problem, none of the men around her spoke out against the mismanagement. Power is just so seductive.

A common purpose between Chancellor and colleagues?

Clearly we cannot assume that it is normal either for there to be a close working relationship between Chancellor and Prime Minister, or for the Chancellor to have effective power over other ministers. Neither of these is at all constant. The question is: how significant are such observations?

There are issues to be addressed about the conduct of policy and the conduct of politicians, and almost limitless scope for disapproval. Governments are no different to other organisations: fighting is exhausting and inefficient, and it has led to some important policy problems. But the fact that the least fractious Cabinet in recent history, Ted Heath's, was also one of the least successful, cautions against being too glib in this regard. In any case, beneath the issue of good conduct is the matter of commonality of purpose and division of responsibilities. Do Chancellors need to cooperate with colleagues (other than the Prime Minister) in order to deliver their objectives, because key policy instruments are under the control of those colleagues? Or can Chancellors afford to work largely independently of other ministers, needing to become involved with them only when narrow issues of public finance are concerned?

These are questions of considerable importance. A simple textbook account would say that different policy objectives have different policy instruments assigned to them, which should make it possible for the Chancellor to do his work largely independently of other ministers. On that basis, relations with colleagues are not so important as they might appear from all the publicity they receive. According to this account, Chancellors are responsible for all the instruments of macroeconomic policy (interest rates, taxes and overall spending limits) while other ministers look after microeconomic policy instruments such as trade union legislation, investment in training, industrial policy or competition policy.

There is certainly a simple story to be told in which before 1979, macroeconomic policies in Britain were geared towards fostering economic growth by the management of demand, while microeconomic policies focused on restricting inflation and improving the distribution of income. After 1979 the assignments switched, with macroeconomic policy aiming to reduce inflation and microeconomic policies seeking to improve incentives and the working of the market, in order to foster enterprise and boost growth.

But clearly life was much less clear-cut than that, both before and after 1979. The micro–macro split is an artificial one: changes to tax rates have both microeconomic and macroeconomic effects, and cuts in government support for industry might on occasions have desirable short-term consequences (a slowdown in demand expansion, and less inflation) but undesirable long-term effects (less investment and growth). More importantly, policy objectives are not independent of one another, and no Chancellor wants to see his policies undermined by mistakes in other areas. Since it is hard to promote economic growth safely in an environment of rapid inflation, it is not surprising that Denis Healey ended up spending much of his time trying to keep the Callaghan government's income policy in place. So, although it is true that there have been some laid-back Chancellors (mostly Conservatives), most Chancellors have been driven by an inherent pressure for the Chancellor and his staff to use their seniority and their institutional advantages to interfere in diverse areas of policy. And they have made themselves unpopular in the process.

But there is also a countervailing tendency for Chancellors to disengage themselves periodically from policy areas that have come to seem too messy and misguided, and to opt instead for a simpler regime with reduced (or more focused) ambitions. This is particularly true with regard to controls, such as post-war rationing, the incomes policies of the seventies and the monetary control of the early eighties, all of which came to seem counter-productive and better abolished. Gordon Brown's gift to the Bank of England of day to day control over interest rates is a different, but related, example.

This countervailing tendency is partly pragmatic – the desire for an easier life – but not entirely so. Gordon Brown's case is interesting for the reasons mentioned at the start of Chapter 1: that he gave away some powers, while increasing his control in other areas. Brown clearly has strong views about what his job involves, which go well beyond the apparent ambition of many Chancellors to continue with the policies of their predecessors and to try not to make a mess of things.

Gordon Brown's clarity also seems to intimidate other Cabinet ministers, most of whom are much less single-minded than he is. No minister has dared to challenge Brown publicly over an issue of domestic policy, although there have been semi-transparent disputes with Cabinet colleagues over entry into the Euro, provoking the Chancellor's Mansion House statement that Euro membership was an issue for him, and him alone, to decide. Yet if there is a new 'ism' around, then it is strange that it lacks a name, to set it alongside Keynesianism and Monetarism (or Thatcherism). Perhaps this is partly because the Government has sought to focus attention only on the New Labour brand, but that cannot be the whole reason: in Britain, political ideologies usually get named by academics or journalists, not by the politicians who espouse them.

Which raises the question of whether there is indeed a new post-Monetarist economic philosophy about, in which Gordon Brown's Chancellorship marks a shift in policy regime just as marked as that of 1979. Policy instruments have indeed been reassigned once more, there is a new policy objective of *stability* to set alongside growth and low inflation, and there is some sort of reawakening of concern over inequality and poverty, although very definitely not of the bleeding-heart variety. Thinking does indeed seem to have changed, and at quite a deep level. Or is that nonsense: the pathetic fallacy of politics, to ascribe philosophies to politicians? Do Chancellors really believe in anything? And if so, do Conservative ones believe in different things to Labour ones? The answer to both questions would seem to be 'sometimes', as the next two chapters suggest.

5 Economic philosophies: Tory chancellors

Safe choices

If a Chancellor is guided by a mistaken and unhelpful economic philosophy, then his chances of being a success are presumably rather less than if he is pursuing sensible objectives via reasonable methods. To make success more likely, Prime Ministers of both main parties have usually opted for Chancellors from the pragmatic centre-ground of politics. Hugh Gaitskell became Chancellor and Nye Bevan did not. Roy Jenkins was chosen and Barbara Castle was not. John Major beat Nicholas Ridley to the job. Tony Blair chose Gordon Brown, rather than Robin Cook (although only in the context of today's emasculated Labour front bench does Robin Cook look even remotely left-wing).

But like all generalisations, this one is unsatisfactory. There have been at least three self-proclaimed radical Chancellors in the shape of Hugh Dalton, Nigel Lawson and Gordon Brown. Meanwhile Rab Butler, Harold Macmillan, and Geoffrey Howe all articulated political creeds of one sort or another, which could plausibly be said to have informed their Chancellorships. Roy Jenkins did the same, although not until after his Chancellorship, and somewhat elliptically via his writings on other politicians. Finally, Stafford Cripps once held the most radical views of all, although when he eventually became Chancellor he pursued policies that were entirely at odds with his earlier opinions. Even those Chancellors who betrayed the least philosophical bents nevertheless subscribed to some broad view of how the world worked. Keynes's over-quoted claim that 'madmen in authority' were 'all the slaves of some defunct economist' perhaps went a bit far. Even so, to ignore the fact that most politicians subscribe at least vaguely to a political philosophy is to omit something important about what it is to be a Chancellor.

There have been twelve post-war Conservatives who have held the job of Chancellor. Thirteen if Iain Macleod is included, as he certainly should be. The least philosophically inclined was probably Derick Heathcoat Amory. Selwyn Lloyd ('middle-class lawyer from Liverpool' sneered Macmillan, even after he had been told that Lloyd was from the Wirral – 'funny place to come from') came close.[1] So too did Tony Barber and John Major. Of these, only Major clearly wanted the job. Derick Heathcoat Amory, for example, became Chancellor because the Tory Government was getting through Chancellors at an alarming rate, and he was the Buggins whose turn happened to be next.

Amory did nothing terribly wrong as Chancellor. Indeed, he did just what he was told. For that service Harold Macmillan appointed him High Commissioner to Canada. But then Macmillan always did have an odd sense of humour. Major became Chancellor for a similar reason to Amory, and made the fateful mistake of putting sterling into the ERM at too high a rate, but nevertheless managed to progress to a much bigger job than High Commissioner to Canada. His main qualification for elevation was that he was not Michael Heseltine. As Chancellor, Major's mantra was that 'if it isn't hurting, it isn't working', which at the time was probably true, but hardly amounted to much of a philosophy. As Prime Minister, his cod-nostalgia for an England of village cricket and warm beer was rightly scorned, along with his 'back to basics' principles – and these were the best ideas that Major came up with, as his party thrashed around for want of a unifying creed.

Wab or Hawold?

Was Harold Macmillan a philosopher prince? Nobody doubts that he was Machiavellian, that he pretended to be what he was not and to believe things that he did not. The puzzle is to decide which was the mask and which the flesh: whether he was a reactionary pretending to be a moderate or vice versa.

In old age Macmillan criticised the Thatcher government for neglecting civilised values and selling the family silver. It was a reassertion of his early persona as a One Nation rebel on the left of the Conservative Party. Throughout his career Macmillan always declared that his lodestar was the need to protect his dear working-class constituents in Stockton-on-Tees from a repetition of the horrors of mass unemployment from which they had suffered in the twenties and thirties. Yet when he was Chancellor and Prime Minister, even Macmillan's friends dismissed this as sentimentality. His enemies thought it cynical humbug. Macmillan's credibility was somewhat weakened by the fact that by the time he became a Cabinet minister he was no longer actually Stockton's MP. The town had dumped him and his party in 1945. Fortunately for Macmillan one of the few Conservative members to get re-elected in that year promptly died, leaving the safe suburban seat of Bromley nicely vacant. Macmillan moved fast, and got himself nominated and then elected. From then on he made absolutely no effort to reunite himself with 'dear old Stockton'.

Indeed, even before the rout of 1945 Macmillan had wanted to forsake Stockton for a safer seat elsewhere, but had failed to secure an offer, even after he temporarily lost his seat in 1929. (Macmillan had first been elected in 1924, and regained his seat in 1931 when Labour imploded.) In 1945 he nearly accepted St George's Westminster, a seat embracing Mayfair and Belgravia, but Beaverbrook persuaded him not to. 'It seems my fate to try to get away from Stockton but never to achieve it!' he said in 1945, just before the voters of Stockton decided to take matters into their own hands and say goodbye to him anyway.[2]

Yet we should not reject too lightly Macmillan's sincerity, nor underestimate his grasp of economic policy issues. When Macmillan was first elected in 1924, unemployment and poverty were already endemic in Stockton. The new MP, deeply distressed, busied himself trying to organise relief. In a scheme that would be considered enlightened today, he promoted and part-funded the conversion of a derelict shipyard into a training centre for the unemployed.[3] He also made a reputation for himself in the Commons for his repeated demands that the Conservative Government do more to reduce unemployment and relieve poverty.

Harold Macmillan greatly admired Lloyd George for his radicalism, and the Welshman gave him much-needed instructions in oratory. Mostly, however, Macmillan (still working as a publisher) wrote: articles about the need to encourage employment by removing the burden of business rates, and about housing and the need for slum clearance; and in 1927 a pamphlet, *Industry and the State*, in which he and three other young Tory MPs set out what was effectively an alternative manifesto for their party. Macmillan also bombarded Churchill, the Chancellor, with letters and memoranda. Churchill would have been surprised by Macmillan's claim in his memoirs that the pair of them were close. Nevertheless, Macmillan's arguments probably influenced Churchill, who in 1927 did indeed reduce business rates, and Macmillan was much emboldened by the encouragement that Churchill gave him: 'It was the making of my political life, in a sense.'[4]

Macmillan nevertheless remained frustrated, both by his own party and by Labour. In 1930 he wrote to *The Times* commending Oswald Mosley (then, if anything, a left-winger and not yet a declared fascist – Nye Bevan was one of many acolytes) for resigning from MacDonald's government rather than renege on his election commitment to cut unemployment. When in 1931 Mosley founded his New Party with a programme based on the principle of planning the economy rather than leaving it to the market, Macmillan came close to joining. Margot Asquith among others urged him not to. Macmillan held back, accepting that he should work within the Conservative Party to change its thinking. Almost immediately the New Party fell apart anyway. Macmillan promptly recruited its young Secretary, Allan Young, an ex-Marxist from Glasgow, to work for him.

Young brought to Macmillan ideas on how to build a new future now that 'the structure of capitalist society in its old form had broken down'.[5] A series of publications – some large, some small, some collaborative, some written under his own name but with Young's help – ensued. They started with *The State and Industry* and *The Next Step*, both published in 1932, followed by *Reconstruction: a Plan for a National Policy*, published in 1933, *Planning for Employment* and *The Next Five Years* in 1935, and then a journal called the *New Outlook*. Finally in 1938 Macmillan published *The Middle Way*, a book that brought together all of his (or Young's) thinking and that he believed articulated the only possible approach to the management of the economy.

In these publications Macmillan argued for a high degree of centralised planning of the economy. He wanted a National Nutritions

Board to oversee food distribution and an institution to direct investment into industry (initially an Investment and Development Board, later a National Investment Board that would replace the Stock Exchange). He also wanted a cheap money policy to reverse declining wages and prices; expansion in government spending, especially on housing, to create jobs; and trade union participation in economic policy formulation. Finally, Macmillan wanted the Government to focus on raising the living standards of those on the lowest incomes, partly through a minimum wage and partly through policies to reduce unemployment. And of all these things, it was the planning element that Macmillan thought most crucial.

Macmillan's policies contained many elements that were simply nonsense, but no more so than most of the views then doing the rounds. Indeed the real criticism of him is that on the whole his ideas were not as original as he made them out to be. What was extraordinary was that, except for a brief period in 1936 when he flirted with the idea of setting up his own centre party, Macmillan articulated these views from within the heart of the Conservative Party.

It was not a tenable position, and his biographer Alistair Horne is probably correct that if the Tories had fought a general election in 1939 or 1940, they might well have done so without Harold Macmillan. Thus the Second World War saved Macmillan's party career, just as it restored careers to even more maverick figures such as Churchill and Cripps.

For Macmillan, the wait for a Cabinet seat was a long one, but in 1951 he became Minister of Housing and in December 1955 Eden appointed him Chancellor. Yet now that he was at the centre of power, Macmillan showed little commitment to putting economic planning at the centrepiece of his policy-making.

His shift in position is understandable, if a little unedifying. Macmillan had thought that Conservatism was finished, unless it changed its ideas completely. In contrast Rab Butler had successfully articulated a less extreme view. Butler reassured Conservatives that, although they needed to side with Labour on the welfare state, they should fiercely oppose the socialists' love of direct controls over business. The electorate liked the deal. The Tories regained power and Butler became Chancellor before Macmillan. Under the circumstances Macmillan could hardly be faulted for putting aside his one-time views and accepting instead Butler's analysis, and the electorate's verdict. When in time Macmillan took a turn at being Chancellor, he continued with Butler's economic policies largely unchanged.

This implies that it was Butler who was the real Tory philosopher-Chancellor, not Macmillan. Yet it was always, and perhaps deliberately, unclear exactly what Butler's own creed of One-Nation Conservatism was supposed to mean.

Almost alone in his party, Butler foresaw the scale of Labour's 1945 victory. He believed that his party had to modernise its thinking. From 1945 onwards he used his position as head of the Conservative Research Department to bring that thinking into line with his own, and perhaps that of his father-in-law, financial backer and mentor, Sam Courtauld. Butler's great opportunity came with his appointment in late 1946 as chairman of the Industrial Policy Committee that Churchill set up following that year's mutinous party conference in Blackpool. The committee consisted of senior front- and back-bench Tory MPs. As well as Butler, its members included Harold Macmillan, Oliver Stanley and Oliver Lyttelton – so two future Chancellors and two who would just miss being Chancellor (and another future Chancellor, Reggie Maudling, acted as one of three secretaries to the committee). The committee acted with energy, canvassed opinions widely, and produced a report, the *Industrial Charter*, that mainly articulated Butler's thinking.

In the charter, Rab Butler and his colleagues advocated a degree of state planning, especially with respect to wage-fixing. They assumed full acceptance of the welfare state. Although they said it was better to 'humanise not nationalise' industry, they abandoned their party's claim that Labour's nationalisation of the Bank of England, the coal industry and the railways had been a disaster. Above all, the Charter said that governments of any party should pursue full employment. In the understanding of the time, the last of these meant that the Conservative Party should now embrace Keynesian economics.

'But I don't agree with a word of this,' said Churchill when it was all explained to him in 1947.[6] By then the party had adopted the Charter as its policy. The right wing were routed, at least temporarily. The party was committed to prevent a return to the mass unemployment of the pre-war era. Re-election was once again a possibility.

While credit for this was owed and given largely to Butler, Harold Macmillan was not averse to trying to steal a bit for himself. He tried to deliver a speech before the Charter's publication that pre-empted many of the things that the Charter said. Butler had the speech re-drafted, which rebuff Macmillan accepted without much complaint even though he must have been severely piqued. For it is not difficult to imagine what Macmillan must have been feeling. Long ago, But-ler had rebuked Macmillan for flirting with Mosley and had coun-selled him to find '... a new field for his recreation and a pastime more suited for his talents'.[7] Now Butler was wearing the mantle that Macmillan thought was his own, and was thereby emerging as a threat to Macmillan's vaulting ambitions.

It has to be said in Macmillan's defence that, alongside his plan-ning instincts, he had also understood Keynes long before either the Conservative or the Labour parties did, and with more acuteness than Butler could ever muster. Although in the thirties Keynes said he could see no point to the Labour Party, the Tories were mostly aller-gic to abstract thought, and so could see no point to Keynes. Macmillan was a rare Conservative who saw the power of Maynard Keynes's view that, to create jobs during a recession, a government must ensure that its policies acted to raise demand in the economy, not suppress it. Both men were also united in their distrust of pro-tectionism, and they advocated policies that would promote trade and growth at the global level.

Macmillan cottoned on to Keynes not least because he knew him well. In 1884 the Macmillan family had published Maynard's fa-ther's book *Studies and Exercises in Formal Logic*, and in 1891 they published his *The Scope and Method of Political Economy*. At Eton the young Maynard knew, and may have been romantically involved with, Macmillan's elder brother Daniel. They remained friends through Cambridge and Keynes visited the Macmillans often. Even-tually Daniel became Keynes's publisher when the economist grew frustrated with Cambridge University Press. In the thirties Keynes was full of praise for Harold's writings, chiding him mainly for being insufficiently radical. Macmillan in turn often quoted Keynes. They believed themselves to be engaged on the same quest. Macmillan's conclusion to *The Middle Way* that his policies aimed to avoid '... the decay and destruction of our democratic institutions ...' echoed a similar claim that Keynes made of his *General Theory of Employment, Interest and Money*, published a year earlier, in 1937.

But in the late thirties and early forties, Macmillan allowed his Keynesianism to take second place to his belief in economic planning. In contrast Butler put more faith in the market mechanism, while giving Keynesianism plenty of room to breathe. Macmillan's views were too like Labour's, and not enough those of a Tory, for his own party to love him easily. In 1946 he even suggested changing the party's name to the New Democratic Party – a mistake that the less excitable Butler would not, indeed did not, make. Thus it was Butler, not Macmillan, who was allowed to rewrite party policy in the late forties, and Macmillan largely fell into line with Butler.

Admittedly the cause of moderation was never completely dominant. The party's rearguard, of which the chairman Lord Woolton was one, never completely accepted Butler's 1947 victory in getting the *Industrial Charter* adopted. In 1949 Butler felt obliged to complain sharply in a letter to his senior colleagues that the new policies were not being vigorously publicised by the party. His complaint secured the publication of what looked like a new manifesto, *The Right Road for Britain*, with which the party would seek to topple the increasingly troubled Labour Government. That document was, however, heavily watered down for the 1950 election. That wasn't the end: the manifesto on which the party fought the 1951 election bore only a partial resemblance to that year's document from Butler: *Britain Strong and Free*. So Butler's ascendancy over party policy and hence his political position as Chancellor were rather weaker than is often supposed.

Yet once in office Butler, and Macmillan immediately after him, generally pursued full employment and protected the welfare state. Butler saw little reason to worry over-much about reversing Labour's nationalisations. Also, although Butler favoured increasing the degree of competition within the economy while Macmillan was keener on planning, neither man pushed his point too hard. Butler was pretty suspicious of public expenditure, but strong economic growth tended to keep welfare spending low (and tax revenues high) meaning that he needed to take little action himself. He did, however, rein in Gaitskell's military overspending.

Edward Pearce says that Butler 'largely devised' the social peace and steady economics of the fifties.[8] This cannot be quite true – similar patterns were present across most of western Europe. In any case Pearce contradicts himself. He notes that the social peace, in the form of a 'distinctly deferential approach to the trade unions', was Churchill's policy and in retrospect not perhaps a very good one. The fact that the unions often got away with wage rises that matched or exceeded productivity implies that the Government was not really in charge of events. Yet Butler correctly perceived that for most of the time the economy was capable of growing at a reasonably decent rate. Rather like Ken Clarke nearly half a century later, he was careful not to let his civil servants (or in Clarke's case, Bank of England officials) browbeat him into believing otherwise. 'We must not be frightened at a little more ease and happiness,' Butler wrote, 'or feel that what is pleasant must necessarily be evil.'[9] For most of his Chancellorship the performance of the economy, and the political and economic philosophies to which Butler subscribed, justified the policies of facilitating modest expansion.

Losing their way

Rab Butler always rejected the 'Butskellism' sobriquet placed by *The Economist* jointly on his views and those of Hugh Gaitskell, but there clearly were strong similarities in the policies of the two main parties during the fifties. The acceptance by both of Keynesian thinking was central to this. There were differences of course: Alec Cairncross says that the Conservatives were 'reluctant Keynesians' who 'practised demand management only so long as it did not conflict with what they took to be sound principles'; but in a period of sustained economic growth, that was not an especially difficult compromise to strike.[10] It is nevertheless true that the Conservative Party, then as so often, was not especially comfortable with any abstract ideas which had been tainted by twentieth-century thought, and was certainly not comfortable with the sensation that its own views were rather similar to Labour's. So adversarial politics coexisted alongside consensus policies.[11]

In any case, if not Keynesian, then what else could the Conservative Party be? Harold Macmillan had an answer. Although as

Chancellor he was a Butlerite, Macmillan had never completely abandoned his old planning ideas. By the late fifties when he was Prime Minister, the climate of informed (or self-informed) opinion was shifting back towards Macmillan's more interventionist way of thinking. The British people appreciated full employment and rising living standards. Unfortunately, they were becoming increasingly aware that in the rest of Europe, growth was often rather stronger than at home. The best-performing countries were probably Germany and Italy. Most attention fixed, however, on France (even though that country was probably growing no faster than Britain), and on the French system of state-run indicative planning.

In August 1961 Macmillan's third Chancellor, Selwyn Lloyd, wrote to the TUC and the four main employers' organisations inviting them to join a National Economic Development Council (NEDC). Officials had loosely modelled the council on France's Conseil Supérieur, which brought together politicians, industrialists and trade union leaders to discuss and agree consistent plans for the economy. Lloyd proposed that NEDC would do the same.

The idea of NEDC was Lloyd's, although he had reason to think it was the sort of thing that Macmillan would be keen on. To modern Tories the council epitomises the folly into which in those days their party fell. Yet Lloyd was far from being an appeaser. He had already announced a pay freeze for state employees, and had urged the private sector to follow suit (this was the 'pay pause' mentioned in Chapter 1). Lloyd was a firm opponent of union ambition, and was less interested in planning in the Macmillan sense than in creating a system for curbing wage rises. He hoped that NEDC would produce agreement on wage moderation. Furthermore, although Lloyd claimed that lower inflation would lead to faster growth, he offered no arguments to back up his claim. The suspicion must be that the lower inflation was itself Lloyd's real goal.

Lloyd, remember, was no economic philosopher. Nor, however, was he stupid (except perhaps for putting up with Harold Macmillan). And nor was he alone in his thinking. Frustrations with the trade unions, and anxieties over inflation, were causing many Conservatives to feel that Butler had been complacent and that Macmillan was leading them up a blind alley.

The Prime Minister remained adamant that it was politically impossible to abandon the post-war commitment to full employment and the welfare state. Yet other Tories worried more about inflation and disliked the full-employment commitment. They began to seek out the path that would eventually lead their party to the revolt of the mid seventies.[12] One who hankered after the old pre-Keynesian religion, and who in the fifties was a frequent adviser to Conservative Treasury ministers, was Lionel Robbins. A former assistant to Keynes now installed as an LSE professor, Robbins had repudiated Keynes in 1951. He urged fellow academics and policy makers to return to the principles of the pre-war quantity theory of money that Keynes thought he had overturned.

Few economists, let alone politicians, were quite sure what in practice the 'quantity theory of money' was supposed to mean. Apart from anything else, monetary data were not then collected in the way they are today. There was thus no visible 'quantity' of money about which to have a theory. But Robbins's view, that the authorities ought to prevent rising inflation by controlling monetary growth, seemed in sympathy with something that *did* look like common sense. The Treasury repeatedly argued that, as part of the need to restrict the expansion of demand, the Bank of England needed to improve its control over bank lending. To many, the difference between that and Robbins's Monetarism seemed rather minor. Even Harold Macmillan was willing to accept that monetary growth and inflation might be linked. His key principle was a different one. He remained adamant that his government would not seek a rapid reduction in inflation if that required a sharp rise in unemployment.

In 1956 Milton Friedman published in Chicago his seminal paper restating the quantity theory of money in a way which he believed dealt with Keynes's critique.[13] In that same year the Treasury and the Bank of England conducted a joint inquiry on the subject. They made the politically significant observation that government spending, unless funded from taxes or gilt sales, would increase the money supply. Thus traditional Conservative dislike of government spending elided into the new Monetarist account of the monetary causes of inflation. For the Chancellor of the day and his two Treasury colleagues that was enough. Suddenly they had a new justification for insisting on greater government spending restraint than either their officials or their colleagues thought necessary or politically appropriate. When in 1957 the rest of the Cabinet refused to humour them, the three men in question, Peter Thorneycroft, Nigel Birch and Enoch Powell, all resigned in protest.

Macmillan's argument with the three of them was mainly over politics, not economics. Fundamentally he was a pragmatist, as indeed was Thorneycroft, a good-hearted Staffordshire toff who had fallen into bad company and been led astray. Powell was the party's self-appointed intellectual fundamentalist, and Birch one of its leading pugilists. Their joint resignations had no immediately discernible effect on Conservative thinking. Macmillan found other men willing to serve in the Treasury, and Thorneycroft and Powell both later swallowed their pride and returned to the front-benches. Thorneycroft became a high-spending aviation minister and Powell a high-spending housing minister. So in a sense, Macmillan's 'little local difficulty' remark turned out to be pretty accurate.

It is also true, however, that Thorneycroft's successor, Derick Heathcoat Amory, insisted that he would only be a stop-gap and refused to stay long at the Treasury. His successor in turn, Selwyn Lloyd, refused to expand the economy at the rate which Macmillan wanted, and lost his job as a result. So, as Chapter 4 noted, Macmillan's three middle Chancellors were not obviously Macmillan's men. The appointment of Reggie Maudling to succeed Lloyd was a final attempt by Macmillan to deal with this tension, and to entrench the Butler–Macmillan tradition as the permanent doctrine of the Conservative Party. Time, however, was running out.

Lack of ideas

Reggie Maudling failed, as Chancellor, as Tory philosopher and as a candidate in the 1965 leadership election to succeed Alec Home. During the subsequent Heath years there was to be little in the way of philosophising. Enoch Powell wanted the Conservative Party to rediscover what he believed were its free-market doctrinal roots. Edward Heath, given control of policy formulation even before he became Tory leader, took no notice. He too was initially a free-marketeer, but for instrumentalist not theological reasons. Heath spoke of the need to modernise and increase efficiency, but he never strayed into the abstract world of Monetarism. He would

demonstrate in office that he was perfectly happy to use state intervention as a tool, if he thought that it would achieve what he wanted.

Heath distrusted and was uncomfortable with economic ideas, just
as he distrusted the Treasury. He was an instinctive rather than a
thinking Keynesian, which might have been sufficient in the fifties or
sixties but was no longer so in the tougher economic climate of the
seventies. His one economic passion was membership of the then European Common Market. Even that had something to do with reversing the personal humiliation that de Gaulle had inflicted on him
when, in 1963, the French President rejected the membership bid
that Heath had drawn up for Macmillan.

Meanwhile, as shadow Chancellor and Chancellor, Iain Macleod
and Tony Barber were similarly untouched by economic philosophy.
Macleod said that his main goal was to reform taxation, which is a
sure sign of a Chancellor with no strong idea about what to do with
the job. Barber said the same thing, and never quite picked up the
plot. As Chancellor he was famously under the sway of Ted Heath,
but then so too was the rest of the Cabinet. Heath we know was
much influenced by his Cabinet Secretary, William Armstrong,
whose main appeal was that he was neither a politician nor a thinker.
It is often said that Heath himself would have made an excellent Permanent Secretary. Intellectually, the Conservative Party switched off
in the sixties and seventies.

Might it have been different if Reggie Maudling had not faded
away (not faded literally, of course: he became more corporeal, not
less, as he grew older)? Maudling was so close to being a giant. He
studied Greats at Oxford. His results were undistinguished, but in his
case one is inclined to believe the usual excuse that he spent too much
time enjoying himself. His account in his memoirs of his university
days and his university studies is more humane, less preening, than
the similar accounts by Denis Healey and Nigel Lawson. Like those
two, Maudling was keen on philosophy, and acquired an analytical
way of thinking. He says that philosophy taught him several
principles that helped him in later life. These included the
understanding that progress comes 'not by finding the answers but
by progressively clarifying the questions', and 'the utter need to
apply the test of logic to any proposition'.[14] Less precisely, he says
that philosophy taught him about '... the relation between the

individual and the community, between freedom and order, and the connection of the one to the other'. These three lessons gave him the essential apparatus with which to become a decent amateur economist: one who was less dismissive of ideas than Healey, and less obsessive about them than Lawson.

As Chancellor, Maudling advocated a view that helped to get Keynesianism its bad name (a view that cannot be attributed to Keynes himself). This was the seeming paradox that the pursuit of faster economic growth could lead to lower, not higher, inflation. Behind this lurked some technical (and rather dubious) arguments over the relationship between growth, productivity and costs. There was also a more general claim: that inflation occurs when the speed at which the economy expands is less than the speed at which individuals want their own incomes to expand. A competitive struggle then ensues in which the demands for higher pay or profits are met in nominal terms, but not in real terms. Inflation is just the difference between the two.

Maudling's solution was to raise the growth rate, so that the aspirations could more easily be met. Simultaneously he favoured policies to diffuse the scramble for more pay and profits, in the guise of the arrangements that Selwyn Lloyd had introduced (particularly pay curbs and the NEDC). His problem, which he failed to identify properly, was that as Chancellor he could raise the growth in demand, but not necessarily increase the economy's capacity to supply. The consequent gap would mean either a worsening in inflation, or the emergence of balance of payments problems as firms abroad supplied the extra goods and services that the domestic economy was not producing. That was indeed precisely the difficulty that Maudling bequeathed to Callaghan.

Maudling left a political as well as an economic mess. His dash for growth undermined the Tories' (ill-deserved) reputation for economic probity. That added to their (well-deserved) reputation for lack of moral probity (the dash for growth was also known as the Keeler boom). The Conservatives needed to spend the mid to late sixties thinking in opposition both about their lack of political principles and, at a more technical level, about how they would revitalise the supply potential of the economy. They needed a new *Industrial Charter*. That was the task that Heath could have given Maudling.

Instead Heath left Maudling to languish with the foreign affairs brief.

Maybe Heath was right. It is possible that Maudling was beyond his best and just not up to the task. He had always been physically lazy, and perhaps now he was becoming mentally lazy too. His memoirs, published in 1978, reveal a simplistic tendency to reduce Britain's problems to the bad attitudes of workers. He criticises the absence of 'Pride in quality and consistency, the whole pride in efficient performance'. He blames the Labour movement for '... creating the impression that it is not clever to do your best but better to concentrate on ensuring you get as much for yourself as you can out of the other man'.[15] He probably had a point, but his charge was too narrow and reductionist. He ignored other possible contributory factors such as amateurish management, a failure to commercialise investment in research and development, weaknesses in the education system, and lack of competition in many parts of industry. Maudling preferred to blame a single set of villains for all of Britain's problems. His philosophical standards had slipped.

It seems unfair, though, to judge a man by the closing chapters of his memoirs, especially a man who by then had done a lot of living and spent a lot of time lunching in the City. Given a proper brief and some good advisers, it is possible that in opposition, Maudling might have sorted himself out and stretched his mind to the challenges of the age. He might have come up with a set of ideas to steer the Heath government through the seventies. He might even have come back as Chancellor.

Maudling was not asked to do so for several reasons. Edward Heath did not like to have strong men (or strong women) around him. Heath was not keen on ideas. In any case, hadn't Heath himself just conducted a review of the party's policies, and equipped the Tories with all the ideas they needed?

During the brief period when Alec Home led the Tories from the opposition benches, Edward Heath combined the positions of shadow Chancellor with the chairmanships of both the Advisory Committee on Policy and the Conservative Research Department. He took one job away from Maudling, and two away from Butler. With the possibility that the Wilson government would quickly lose its slender minority, Home asked Heath to put together a suite of policies with which to fight an imminent election. However, lacking much overall vision, Heath created numerous groups to examine and report on different policy issues, including farming, pensions and the legal system. The reports came first to Heath, to vet them. Heath then passed them to the shadow Cabinet. Although he believed that the process produced a thoroughly thought-out set of policies, Heath's method ended with an incoherent and unadventurous manifesto containing 100 disparate proposals. Maudling, had he been asked (and had he been bothered), would have produced something much sharper and more challenging.

After the 1966 election defeat Heath had more time for reflection. He did not use that time. He set out to create a fully prepared government in waiting, but again laboured over details while ignoring the big issues. Maudling was now a spent force and Ian Macleod almost as prone to tunnel vision as his leader (although for different reasons). Heath's biographer John Campbell does not hold back his criticism of his subject. He says that '... the party leadership shrank from any thought about the causes of inflation and how to control it'. According to Campbell, they hoped that '... talking continuously about competition, modernisation and efficiency would transform the economy'.[16] At the famous Selsden Park conference in January 1970, the control of inflation was literally at the bottom of the agenda. Thus the Tories stumbled into government, and got horribly mauled by the experience.

What of Macleod? Could he have made a difference? He did not do so in opposition, which makes one wonder whether he would have achieved much as Chancellor. Edward Pearce in his avowedly partisan essay on the man offers an optimistic view.[17] He says that Macleod would have avoided the excessive reflation of 1972 and would have handled the unions better than Heath did on his own. Roy Jenkins, avowedly not partisan, says much the same, as does Macleod's biographer Robert Shepherd. Certainly it is easy to agree that if Macleod had been around, many individual decisions would have come out better. But would the overall approach have been much more sensible? Perhaps the real differences are that, assuming Macleod had stayed for the whole Parliament, the Tories might not have lost the February 1974 election, and there would have been no lurching towards Thatcherism. Yet it is hard to feel inspired by this story. What would they have done for good? Even with Macleod, the Tories would surely have been an intellectually tired and direction-less party.

Monetarism in opposition and government

Many of the mistakes of the Heath government contributed to an overall sense of incompetence. In particular, the clear statement that there would be no help for 'lame duck' companies, followed by hasty bail-outs of large firms with doubtful commercial prospects, looked inept. But though notoriously embarrassing, such episodes were not hugely serious, and at worst reflected an unwillingness to face up to problems and accept unpopularity.

Some of the Heath government's other mistakes were rather more damaging. In 1970 the new administration started with a commit-ment to control inflation, a commitment not to have a statutory in-comes policy, and a commitment to maintain full employment. Later it tried to honour the first and third of these by reneging on the sec-ond. It was a strategy that did not work, partly because of an inabil-ity to handle the unions. The Government hugely accentuated its difficulties by introducing legislation to reform the unions. The aim was to reduce workplace strife, but the inept legislation made the situation much worse. That damaged growth and raised unemploy-ment, but it also made the incomes policy unworkable, which meant that the Government could not control inflation. The Heath govern-ment failed.

These problems, and Heath's isolation from his party, were perfect conditions in which Monetarism could ferment. The high priest of populist Tory Monetarism was still Enoch Powell, who promulgated the theory as part of an extreme free-market agenda. Powell's long-standing feud with Edward Heath gave a personal edge to his agenda, and was something to which many other Tories, repeatedly snubbed by their leader, could relate. After 1968 Powell's views on race, and his suggestion that people should vote Labour, meant that no respectable Tory politician could be directly associated with the firebrand. Even so, Powell's agents such as Nicholas Ridley did what they could to spread unrest amongst the peasants.[18]

Other key figures included the journalist Alfred Sherman and Alan

Walters of the LSE – Lionel Robbins's old school. In conversations with Heath's Social Services Secretary, Keith Joseph, both men poured scorn on the interventionist policies of the Heath government. Following the Tories' electoral defeat in February 1974, Joseph hoped to receive the shadow Chancellorship. Heath disappointed Joseph, but allowed him instead a roving brief to study 'the reasons for Britain's long-term decline'.[19] Joseph set up a research institute (of sorts), the Centre for Policy Studies, and installed Sherman at its head. Much to Heath's anger, he funded the exercise by luring corporate donors away from the Conservative Party. Shortly afterwards, Joseph brought Walters and another Monetarist, Jim Ball of the London Business School, with him to a shadow Cabinet meeting. Heath and most of his colleagues were unimpressed by the two academics.

Joseph, however, was making speeches, writing articles and making friends. Two shadow Cabinet colleagues, Margaret Thatcher and Geoffrey Howe, gave him discreet support. After the party's second defeat that year it was Thatcher's turn to feel aggrieved at not being given the shadow Chancellorship. Shortly afterwards she challenged Heath for the leadership, won, and made Howe her shadow Chancellor.

Back in 1965 Geoffrey Howe had nearly voted for Powell as party leader. In those days Howe was gently liberal in both his social and his economic thinking. Since then, as a Cabinet minister, he had played a critical role as the enforcer of Heath's interventionist policies on union reform and on prices and wages control. Yet somehow he had managed to let it be known that secretly he was still a bit of an economic liberal. Thatcher saw in him qualities of tenacity and reliability that she would need and that Joseph lacked. Howe could acquire the full ideology with time. As Hugo Young puts it, 'Joseph articulated ideas, Howe formulated policies, and Mrs Thatcher was the essential conduit from one to the other.'[20]

Over the next couple of years these three and other colleagues shifted the party's policies. In 1977 Geoffrey Howe contributed to a pamphlet, *The Right Approach to the Economy*, of which he was to remain hugely proud. He and his co-authors promised the control of the money supply to curb inflation, and lower taxes to boost growth. They rejected the commonplace belief that better-paid workers were entitled to see their pay differentials preserved, and they proposed to remove unnecessary regulations on businesses.

The Right Approach was a sober document, intended to set out the new policy direction without scaring the old order in the party. Indeed Jim Prior, a close supporter of Edward Heath but one who was willing to admit that the Heath government had made some mistakes, was one of those who put his name to the publication. When the Tories got into power there was a similar reluctance to create too much anxiety, and to articulate a single creed or economic philosophy. But beneath the surface, the new Government had three radical aims: to break the power of the unions, to defeat inflation and to roll back the frontiers of the state.

The first aim would require tougher legislation than that introduced by Howe himself, when he was a minister in Ted Heath's Cabinet. It also needed something more: a new attitude of mind from ministers. Margaret Thatcher ordered an end to fraternisation with the enemy: they would no longer offer union delegations beer and sandwiches at Downing Street, there would be no more negotiations over pay, no more of Labour's despised 'Social Contract'.

This meant that Howe would need to control inflation by other means. That was where Monetarism came in, and why the new Government was so ready to embrace the creed. According to Monetarist theory, inflation control was not a problem. All the Government needed to do was reduce the rate of growth of money in the economy. Inflation would come down in consequence, by one means or another. Accordingly, Howe's first full Budget introduced targets for the growth of the nation's money supply that became progressively more stringent the further out they went. These formed the centre of the grandiloquently titled, but in truth rather slight, Medium Term Financial Strategy. The strategy, the Chancellor said, would be the centrepiece of government policy.

This Monetarism was no longer the provenance of a few isolated politicians and economists. It owed much to the advice of Howe's official and unofficial advisers and his ministerial colleagues. When in late 1979 Terry Burns, an economic forecaster at the London Business School, became Howe's Chief Economic Adviser, he began to preach Monetarism within the Treasury, which was fair enough since that was what the Chancellor had recruited him to do; more worrying was the Monetarist zeal of Peter Middleton, a career civil servant who should have known better. Ministers wanted officials committed to the Monetarist cause, and a new generation of civil servants gave advice that was far less dispassionate than that of previous mandarins. At first this delighted ministers, and Thatcher and Howe rewarded Middleton by promoting him to the very head of the Treasury, but it meant that Howe embarked upon policies whose naïvety must now be an embarrassment to him.

It is true, as it so often is, that the essential traitor was already within the gate. Geoffrey Howe was not particularly devoted to the kind of abstract economic reasoning that attracted others to Monetarism. Nevertheless, he did have a predilection for any grand intellectual construct that promised to anticipate and thwart all problems in advance. His 1971 trade union legislation, written for Employment Secretary Robert Carr, was a giant machine intended to solve all industrial relations problems in one go. Unfortunately it proved quite unworkable; in contrast under Margaret Thatcher first Jim Prior and then Norman Tebbit introduced a whole series of smaller changes whose cumulative impact was far more powerful.

Partly because Howe was not really a true believer, at least not by the standards of Margaret Thatcher or Keith Joseph, the Medium Term Financial Strategy was short-lived. Although the Chancellor continued to pretend that Monetarism was the guiding light of policy, in truth the strategy crumbled in the 1981 Budget, just one year after its launch. It seemed that monetary growth was uncontrollable, just as the Government's critics had warned.

Many believers insisted that the Treasury needed to tighten monetary policy. But Howe the pragmatist was not convinced. Inflation was falling sharply, despite the overshooting of the monetary targets. The reason was that, although very high interest rates failed to control the money stock, they did succeed in dampening spending and output, thereby creating unemployment of nearly 2 million. Not surprisingly in the circumstances, wage claims came down sharply and inflation fell. The growth of money turned out to be irrelevant.

So although in 1981 Howe announced new and even more stringent monetary targets, he made little attempt over the remainder of his Chancellorship to attain them. On the contrary he allowed interest rates (and as a result, the exchange rate) to fall, thereby allowing a restoration of economic growth from a starting point of low inflation.

Although he did not really believe in Monetarism, Geoffrey Howe did believe in something: that the Government should curtail its borrowing, whatever the circumstances. 'I'm just an old Welsh fundamentalist,' he used to say, by way of explanation. That was why he offset his relaxed attitude to monetary growth with £3 billion of very visible tax increases. If it had not been for the cuts in interest rates and the fall in the exchange rate, these tax rises would have pushed the economy yet deeper into recession. Instead, recovery followed.

As pure economics the Monetarist experiment was half-baked: an over-simplified theory which never produced the policy conclusions that its advocates claimed. In practical terms, Monetarism was just one of several attempts to find a way of controlling inflation and to establish a clear policy anchor in a world without Bretton Woods. The attempts moved through trade union legislation and incomes policies to monetary control and then fiscal tightening, before returning to a more effective attack on trade union power, coupled with more general market deregulation, widespread privatisation, and the extension of private enterprise into activities traditionally performed by the state. It was in these areas that the real policy shift took place.

Free markets

Geoffrey Howe and the rest of the Conservative Government believed in pushing back the frontiers of the state. Where taxes and government spending were concerned, they largely failed. Economic policy under Howe evolved into a regime in which taxes were probably about the same overall as they would have been under Labour, but skewed more towards lower earners and less towards higher earners. Although the Chancellor cut many areas of government spending, other spending programmes increased to fill their places. Government spending was probably no lower than it would have been under Labour, but more of it went on welfare payments, since unemployment was higher. There was a sharp increase in the proportion of the population who depended on the state for their income. In that sense the Government failed completely, frustrating those on both the left and the right of politics simultaneously.

The real policy improvements of the period were the refusal to featherbed industry (for which Keith Joseph deserves credit), the quiet but systematic erosion of trade union powers (largely the work of Jim Prior, although the high unemployment for which Howe was partly responsible was also hugely important), a refusal to countenance the reintroduction of incomes policies (Margaret Thatcher's strong point; one suspects that Howe could easily have gone soft on this), and above all a willingness to brazen out high unemployment (Thatcher again, but also Howe). These policies, soon to be followed by widespread privatisation, the encouragement of inward investment and cuts in corporation taxes, were implemented in ways and for reasons that were morally distasteful, but they led to changes in institutions and in attitudes that had long-lasting and substantially beneficial consequences for the UK economy.

Privatisation had been hinted at in the Conservatives' 1979 manifesto and in Geoffrey Howe's first Budget, and several small sales quickly followed, but it only really took off in 1984, with the sale of shares in British Telecom. To the Government's relief the sale went very well, and further sales followed. The Treasury, especially Nigel Lawson as Financial Secretary and later as Chancellor, was keen from the outset – not least because it received the proceeds of the sales – although the Prime Minister was initially more cautious, as was Geoffrey Howe. Ministers justified the sales on the grounds that they promoted wider share ownership and encouraged competition, although neither was necessarily true. In particular, the privatisations frequently replaced a public sector monopoly with a private sector one – an outcome that John Major's government felt obliged to address, some years later.

The real significance of the privatisations was that they were associated with a marked erosion of employee power, job cuts and hence improved productivity, and with a more general freeing of top managers, and a fundamental change in business attitudes. Any doubts on the part of pre-privatisation managers, and indeed employees, were often tackled by starving the industries of funds before privatisation was announced, and then providing financial help to ensure that the flotation would go well. Yet these were not features of privatisation that the Government had any desire to trumpet: and the whole process had an unfortunate tendency to resemble a money-raising activity, pure and simple.

The widespread impression that the Government lacked principles was something that Nigel Lawson was keen to correct when he became Chancellor. Lawson had been the most important member of Howe's early ministry. In 1979 Margaret Thatcher had shrewdly adopted Harold Wilson's old policy of placing a junior minister whom she trusted in the department of a senior minister whom she distrusted. At the Treasury she had two: John Biffen, who didn't work out, and Nigel Lawson who did. As Thatcher's nark, Lawson was supposed to report back to the Prime Minister on the Chancellor's conduct, and thus help to keep Howe on the path of correctness. Lawson's Monetarist passion struck Geoffrey Howe among others as ridiculous and self-promoting, although naturally it earned Lawson favour with Margaret Thatcher, whom he sometimes saw more frequently than did the Chancellor.

Indeed, since Nigel Lawson was a close confidant of the Prime Minister, he could go further and frame policies that were more rightly the responsibility of the Chancellor. The Medium Term Financial Strategy was the prime example: both in broad outline and in detail it came from Lawson's pen, and not from either the Chancellor or his officials. And, as already noted, it was also Lawson who insisted that Howe keep the pretence of Monetarism going after the Chancellor abandoned its practice in 1981. When Lawson became Chancellor in 1983, he attempted to restore adherence to the creed.

Nigel Lawson had not always thought that way. The sobriquet that attached to him of the best-prepared Chancellor of the century reflected his years as a financial journalist. Until 1974 Lawson was a fervent opponent of the sort of policies that he would later advocate as Financial Secretary and attempt briefly as Chancellor. This background is something that seems to trouble Lawson. His memoirs are over 1,000 pages long, yet he glides quickly over the views that he expounded in his columns for the *Financial Times*, the *Sunday Telegraph* and then the *Spectator*.

Nigel Lawson drafted the Conservative Party's manifesto for the 1974 election. Though he was elected in February of that year the party was not. Lawson suddenly rejected the Keynesian and interventionist policies that he had hitherto advocated, and became a proselytiser for free market economic policies.

Over the next few years the simple doctrine that control of the money stock would produce low inflation exerted considerable influence over Lawson – precisely because it was a simple doctrine. Alan Walters, the Prime Minister's economic adviser and Lawson's nemesis-to-be, was one of those who reassured Lawson when he was Chancellor that, under Geoffrey Howe, Monetarism had failed because of technical mistakes in the policy's implementation, and not because the theory was wrong. By redefining 'money' and by changing the control instruments, Nigel Lawson hoped to bring the facts more closely into line with the theory.

Any hope of success was, however, soon utterly undermined by Chancellor Lawson's parallel policy of financial deregulation. By removing credit controls and by taking away the barriers that prevented the building societies from competing with the banks, he stimulated a boom in financial sector activity. The money supply increased sharply, but so too did the prices of financial assets and of other forms of wealth, including house prices. The economy entered a boom, but one that failed to have any impact on unemployment, which remained embarrassingly high at more than 3 million.

By 1985 the evident overheating of the financial system ought to have caused Lawson to raise interest rates sharply. Unwilling to risk higher unemployment in the run-up to the next election, he failed to take action. Over the next year this inconsistency increasingly worried the foreign exchange markets, and Nigel Lawson's credibility declined, taking the pound with it. In September 1986 a currency retreat became a rout, and Lawson found himself in a currency crisis no less serious than those that Cripps, Callaghan and Healey had suffered in 1949, 1967 and 1976. Forced to borrow from the Bundesbank, the traumatised Chancellor decided to replace the management of the money supply with the management of the exchange rate as the centrepiece of his policy.

Again, Lawson over-inflated the economy. The interest rates needed to keep sterling stable against the deutschmark were too low to stem an excessive expansion in demand. At first the Chancellor comforted himself with the belief that the expansion was not in fact excessive. He believed that the Government's many supply-side reforms, notably privatisation, had raised the supply potential of the economy, making it possible to get more growth without more inflation. Yet it soon became apparent that there was little evidence in support of such optimism. The much-trumpeted productivity gains of the Thatcher government consisted primarily of poorly managed firms taking to cost-cutting with alacrity, thereby making temporary gains in productivity, but not making the investments in new processes and products that would allow them to respond to new markets and increased demand. Many outsiders had been telling the Treasury this, but had not been listened to: Lawson made great sport out of knocking the economists of the City, denouncing them as 'teenage scribblers'. But pretty soon it became apparent, even to the Treasury, that the economy was overheating. Either inflation, or the balance of payments, or both, was bound to create problems.

Lawson had already slammed on the brakes when his impatience with Walters's carping caused him to storm out of the Government. By then it was already hard to take Lawson seriously as a coherent economic thinker. He remained a formidable intellect, but not a convincing theorist. His political feud with Margaret Thatcher, much more her fault than his, had taken away his time for basic thinking and his parliamentary colleagues' inclination to listen. As the eighties gave way to the nineties, Lawson should have been the person to define a new Conservative philosophy, to refresh their values and their popularity and keep them in power. Instead his career fell apart, and with it his capacity for new thinking. He wrote a cookbook. And although many things were written about Lawson's memoirs, first published in 1992, nobody found in them any inspiration for where the Tories should go next.

The absence of new thinking about the economy is still a problem for the Conservative Party, a decade after Nigel Lawson's departure from government. After him came John Major and Norman Lamont, with neither of whom do we need to bother much in a discussion of Conservative philosophers (although Lamont's macroeconomic policy reforms were useful steps towards Gordon Brown's rather larger policy reformulation). Then came Ken Clarke. Like the others he was – is – not an obviously philosophical man. Indeed he insists on being obviously *not* philosophical. But we should not take the bluff blokeish exterior at face value. Ken Clarke was a Chancellor with intellectual bottom. He has not, however, defined a new Conservatism, despite a modest attempt to do so.

As Chancellor, Clarke repudiated the idea of a minimalist safety-net welfare state, and declared a halt to aspirations for a radical reduction in the size of the public sector. He strongly favoured full participation in the European Union, apparently on the grounds that the pressure of surviving in Europe was good for the British economy. And he remained committed to attacking vested interests, wherever he saw them.

None of this made Ken Clarke popular in the Conservative Party of the day. Since the party was no longer remotely popular with the electorate, that was not necessarily a reason for criticism. It did, however, leave hanging the question of how a string of Chancellors with powerful intellects, albeit interspersed with some rather dull ones, had left the Tories so bereft of any economic philosophy that they could call their own.

6 Economic philosophies: Labour chancellors

Roots

In what does Gordon Brown believe? He talks a lot about the fundamental importance of macroeconomic stability, and about the need to keep inflation consistently low. But he always maintains that these are just means to an end. He says that his real objectives are sustained growth, the elimination of poverty and the achievement of high, perhaps even 'full' employment. And although one can never be sure, it seems likely that these claims are sincerely meant. Behind Gordon Brown's slogan 'prudence with a purpose' is a commitment to politics with a purpose, and a moral purpose at that.

Gordon Brown's objectives put him squarely in the centre of the Labour tradition. But that certainly does not mean that they separate him completely from the Conservatives, many of whom have claimed to have the same goals in mind. Several Tory Chancellors were clearly irritated by how callow their colleagues were: Rab Butler, for example, said that perhaps those who talked of the need for a large pool of unemployed people should simply be thrown into the pool. Yet the fact remains that these men were willing to make the compromises that allowed them to be members of the Conservative Party, whereas Brown has not made those compromises (although perhaps he has made others instead).

At the same time, Brown's commitments to growth, jobs for all and the elimination of poverty do not imply any corresponding commitment to any particular policy simply because it is the kind of policy that Labour has traditionally pursued. Indeed he has been as willing to drop Labour totems as Tory ones. He carries no baggage. In his separation of means and ends, Brown resembles Tony Crosland, but Brown is far more ruthless than Crosland was. As a result, and in stark opposition to Crosland, most of Brown's senior colleagues dislike him. And although attempts are often made by both friends and enemies to portray Brown as the guardian of Labour's moral and political heritage, in contrast to closet-Tory Tony Blair, it is by no means clear that Brown does have much attachment to Labour's past, or indeed that Labour's intellectual past is one that any reasonable politician would wish to attach himself to.

If there is a modern Labour intellectual tradition then it must start with the policies that the party adopted in response to the 1931 débâcle. In 1931 the Labour Government under Ramsay MacDonald and Chancellor of the Exchequer Philip Snowden was as convinced as its Tory predecessor that it should pursue policies of extreme fiscal and monetary rectitude. Ministers blamed the economic problems facing the country on the legacy of the First World War, and particularly on the failure to restore the policies and institutions that had prevailed before the war. Pre-eminent among these was the Gold Standard. Leaving left-wing radicalism to the Liberals, the Labour Government sought to balance the budget, keep sterling tortuously high at its pre-war level, and yet maintain low interest rates.

In August 1931 the tactics failed spectacularly. MacDonald and Snowden found themselves in the midst of a currency crisis. Apparently New York's bankers were refusing to cover the UK's current account deficit so long as Labour was in office. It seemed that even when a Labour Government pursued Tory policies, it failed to secure the trust of the financial markets. That left two options. One was to adopt the principle that, if the markets would not tolerate a Labour Government, then a Labour Government should take control of the markets. The second option was to give way, and hand government back to the Conservative Party. MacDonald and Snowden chose the second route.

First, Stanley Baldwin persuaded MacDonald that if he would only bring some Conservatives into government under MacDonald's leadership, then the crisis would go away. MacDonald took the bait and formed a coalition, but largely without the support of his own party and hence highly dependent on the Tories (just as the wily Baldwin had expected would happen). Then Snowden, who had remained Chancellor, became a blistering critic of his own party. When MacDonald called a general election that October, Snowden delivered a radio broadcast in which he said of Labour Party policies

'This is not Socialism. It is Bolshevism run mad.' Snowden's words helped to wipe out the Labour Party in Parliament and to return the Conservatives, thinly disguised as a National Government, to power. At which point Baldwin thanked MacDonald and Snowden for their services, and sent them both into retirement.

The 1945 and 1997 humiliations suffered by the Conservative Party were trivial compared with the agony of Labour in 1931. Labour, which in the twenties had manoeuvred the Liberals out of office, had now been out-manoeuvred in turn – but more suddenly, far less scrupulously and with its own leaders complicit in the act. The policy of allowing the markets to run the economy had apparently been destroyed by the hostility of the financial markets to Labour. Doing a deal with the Tories had made matters vastly worse. That seemed to push the party back to the other extreme option of having to deal with market hostility by taking control over the markets. 'Bolshevism run mad' was to be the way forward.

The well-known punchline to this story is that the financial markets' opposition to Labour had never been as extreme as MacDonald and Snowden had been led to believe. Reports of the hostility had been greatly exaggerated, not least by the Conservatives, who found their paranoid Labour opponents easy to dupe. But in 1932 the myth of the bankers' ramp dominated Labour thinking. That year's party conference boldly proclaimed that as soon as Labour returned to government it would nationalise the banking system and thereby secure real as well as nominal power over the nation's economy.

The policy was largely bravado, based more on emotion than on analysis. For one strand of Labour thinkers, emotion was all that was needed. Much of the party moved to the left and stayed there, masturbating against the leg of Joseph Stalin. Beatrice Webb announced grotesquely that, just as old ladies often fall in love with their chauffeurs, so she had fallen in love with the Soviet Union. Others realised that all this was nonsense: that nationalising the banks, let alone more extreme dirigiste policies of widespread control over all prices, output and resource allocation throughout the economy, would achieve nothing. They were sure that Labour should not stand for Bolshevism. Their problem was that they did not know what it should stand for instead.

Several individuals, including two future Chancellors, engaged themselves on the project of devising new policies for Labour. Often they met together as clubs. The New Fabian Research Bureau, which included Hugh Gaitskell as well as the fiendishly bright Evan Durbin, was one. Another was the XYZ group which included Douglas Jay and the wealthy Nicholas Davenport, and which was mainly interested in banking and monetary questions. Their work came together in a 1937 manifesto, *Labour's Immediate Programme*, which dropped the commitment to nationalise the high-street banks but nevertheless announced that 'the community must command the main levers which will control the economic machine. These are Finance, Land, Transport, Coal and Power.'

The manifesto planned the nationalisation of the Bank of England, the creation of a National Investment Board, schemes for public investment and methods for encouraging industry to move to depressed regions. It sold 300,000 copies, and a subsequent pictorial version sold 400,000 more. The programme provided a new central vision for Labour, based on a limited degree of planning linked to nationalisation, and without the extremism and the naïvety of the far left. It restored the party's confidence that it could succeed in government. Its editor and prime author was Hugh Dalton, who had survived the October 1931 rout, had himself published in 1935 an important book, *Practical Socialism for Britain*, and was now an important figure in the party, even if not quite so important as he himself hoped.

The intellectual justification for Dalton's policy of pursuing some planning and some nationalisation, but not too much, was never very clear. The question of where the line was to be drawn received no robust answer. Still less was there much explanation of how nationalisation was to achieve full employment, other than the rather tautological thought that if planning was 'socialist' then it was bound to have such an outcome. Certainly there was still no intention to stimulate the economy through demand-side expansion: interest rate cuts, or tax cuts, or increases in government spending, any of which might in turn stimulate increased private sector confidence and hence further private sector spending. On this issue, Snowden's views still held sway. Taxes were to be kept high and spending held down so as to curb borrowing and, via that route, achieve low interest rates – and hence, Dalton and colleagues hoped, economic expansion.

Dalton's compromise, which combined ultra-orthodox macroeconomic demand-side policies with moderately radical microeconomic supply-side policies, was not especially persuasive. Oswald Mosley in 1931 and Harold Macmillan through much of the decade had a lot more to offer by way of policies than did Labour's future Chancellor. Macmillan's Investment and Development Board was a lot like Labour's National Investment Board, and indeed Macmillan adopted the latter terminology. But, especially in his later writings, Macmillan also offered explicit monetary, fiscal and labour market policies aimed at raising living standards and reducing unemployment, to put alongside his Labour-like belief in planning.

Macmillan also had the advice of Keynes. The Labour Party in the thirties was generally not too keen on Keynes. This was partly because Keynes was not too keen on Labour and also probably because Dalton in particular was discomforted by Keynes, whose languid self-confidence contrasted with Dalton's social and physical clumsiness. At Cambridge, where Keynes had taught Dalton, the latter had been excluded from the Apostles, just as at Eton he had been excluded from Pop; Keynes, of course, had been welcomed by both. Dalton's humiliations were several: whereas Keynes's love affairs with handsome young men were many and unashamed, Dalton at Cambridge stumbled between being repressed and rebuffed. According to Ben Pimlott, 'Keynes regarded Dalton, not exactly with contempt, but with a kind of amused scorn.'[1] No wonder Dalton as an economist was no Keynesian. On the contrary: he used his position as chairman of Labour's Finance and Trade Committee to uphold the same conservative macroeconomic view that Keynes had argued against at Cambridge, that he had himself taught at the LSE and that had informed Snowden's policies as Chancellor.

But Labour's commitment to an uncomfortable combination of planning and nationalisation on the one hand and conservative macroeconomic policies on the other had deeper roots than Hugh Dalton's personal unease with Keynes. Even without Dalton, Labour would probably have been unwilling to embrace the new ideas that Keynes and others were promoting. At the heart of the new economics, and this was the point that Keynes himself saw most acutely, was the notion that there was too much thrift in the economy and too little willingness to spend, and that government should stimulate others into spending by spending rather more itself. To the cautious men of the Labour Party (Bevan and Bevin were yet to make their marks, Cripps was out in the cold) this was just as heretical as it was to the stuffy men of the Conservative Party.

Had the Labour Party not been so conservative, Keynes might have publicly thrown in his lot with Labour: after all, the Liberals had been even more decimated in 1931 than Labour, so he had little to lose in that respect. Instead Keynes gave up on the politicians and returned to Cambridge to write his general theory, leaving the Labour Party to pursue its half-baked notions. The likelihood of sensible policies under a Labour government thus looked even lower than the likelihood of a Labour government.

The wrong direction

Clearly the war changed matters. Conservative macroeconomic policies suddenly became irrelevant, while planning temporarily assumed a much greater importance than Dalton and colleagues had ever anticipated. Events thus shifted Labour away from its unpersuasive compromise, towards a more full-blooded commitment to planning. And although for a while the continuation of wartime controls on production and prices into peacetime could be justified on pragmatic grounds alone, Labour sought an additional intellectual justification for those policies by harping back to its pre-war planning ideas.

The unfortunate result was that planning ideas became entrenched in many people's understanding of what it was to be a British democratic socialist. The same was even more true of Labour's commitment to widespread nationalisation. The party adopted a constitution that embraced a far more widespread commitment to nationalisation than that incorporated in the 1937 document, *Labour's Immediate Programme*.

At first Hugh Dalton was very much in the vanguard of this way of thinking. 'Yesterday it was coal. Today it is cables. The socialist advance, therefore, continues,' he said of the nationalisation of Cable and Wireless. But gradually Dalton became frustrated by the failures of planning, while Cripps and Gaitskell went further and embraced the Keynesian view that the way to expand the economy was via boosts to demand. The left, in contrast, saw such Keynesian ideas as an unhelpful diversion from the true goal of taking control over the supply-side levers of power.

A key figure in maintaining an interest in the old planning ideas was the man whom Gaitskell made shadow Chancellor when he himself succeeded Attlee as leader: Harold Wilson. It was an appointment that Gaitskell quickly regretted. Wilson, always keen to ingratiate himself with the left of the party, was often disloyal to his leader, even though he had campaigned for Gaitskell against Bevan in 1955. In 1960 Wilson even challenged Gaitskell for the party leadership. Unfortunately for him he lost by a large margin, and before long Gaitskell shuffled Wilson into the post of shadow Foreign Secretary, in order to minimise his influence.

The two men were deeply opposed. Gaitskell had come to reject class antagonisms and now favoured welfare paternalism, as set out in Rab Butler's *Industrial Charter*, as well as in Crosland's *The Future of Socialism*. Wilson, in contrast, partly influenced by Balogh (as noted in Chapter 1), still believed that the old order had decayed, and that modernisation through planning was both necessary and likely to be electorally popular.

As a way of thinking, planning's veneer of certainty, and its rejection of ambiguity, accorded with the way in which, as an undergraduate, a researcher, a don and a civil servant, Harold Wilson's mind worked. Wilson's first job after graduating was as a research assistant to Beveridge, recently installed as Master of Oxford's University College. The project was a study of the causes of the trade cycle and hence of the causes of cyclical unemployment, and Beveridge's approach was obsessively statistical rather than theoretical (he was a sworn opponent of Keynes, whom he regarded as a charlatan). Wilson railed against Beveridge's overbearing personality, but significantly he was happy with the older man's plodding methodology.

'... [S]ocialism, properly applied, is the only means to full efficiency,' wrote Harold Wilson in 1945 in a pamphlet, *New Deal for Coal*, calling for coal nationalisation. Shortly afterwards he entered Parliament as part of the Labour landslide, gaining almost immediate appointment to the Ministry of Works as Parliamentary Secretary. That post gave Wilson part-responsibility for the nation's post-war physical reconstruction, a task impeded by shortages of bricks and other essentials, but also by the refusal of other Whitehall departments to cooperate. For Wilson, the coordination of the economy and the coordination of government had long been inseparable; now they were a personal challenge.

In 1948 at the Board of Trade Wilson was in public a fervent advocate of decontrol, hence his bonfire of controls on 5 November 1948. But in private and helped by discussions with Balogh, he sought to develop an intellectual case to justify the Government's intervention in industry. In a never-published 1950 paper that was nevertheless much discussed by senior ministers, Wilson set out an argument for continued control over key aspects of the economy, including prices, industrial location and capital flows. He also proposed that government representatives should sit on the boards of major corporations and that the state should take control of badly run companies. This paper, *The State and Private Industry*, was about the first attempt to see planning as a way to modernise the economy, rather than either a mechanism for getting through crisis or a redistributive device. It was the foundation stone of the policy changes that Labour would seek to introduce in 1964, under Harold Wilson's leadership, and the precursor of much that was written and suggested by others.

In 1963 Hugh Gaitskell died and Wilson took his place as leader. By now, Wilson was excited by the opportunities offered by science and technology. His clear rejection of the past accorded Wilson an electoral appeal denied to Gaitskell, and helped Labour towards a narrow victory in 1964. As a revolutionary, albeit a minor one, Wilson was able to ridicule effectively first Macmillan and then Home, in a way that Gaitskell had never managed.

As shadow Chancellor and then as Chancellor, Wilson inherited Jim Callaghan. In contrast to Gaitskell, Wilson and also Tony Crosland, Callaghan lacked any formal background in economics. But Callaghan was respected by Crosland – supposedly Labour's best economics brain – and he quickly accepted an invitation to spend time at Nuffield College, being tutored in economics by a gaggle of Oxford dons and other sympathisers who had volunteered for the task.

At the time, Tommy Balogh complained that the group were too mainstream and insufficiently socialist. Callaghan wisely ignored him. In any case a belief in the efficacy of planning was more of a mainstream idea than Balogh was willing to admit, and at Nuffield Callaghan absorbed the approach. As Callaghan's biographer Kenneth Morgan emphasises, planning was a core theme at the Nuffield seminars, and Callaghan put his name to a publication stating that 'planning means introducing a sense of purpose into our national life'. He also endorsed the idea that the Government should have a National Plan for production targets for key industries.[2] In any case Selwyn Lloyd had already established the National Economic Development Council (NEDC) and its supporting office of staff (NEDO), and these innovations would provide some of the foundations on which Labour would eventually build their own planning department.

It was also true that if planning was to continue living under the Labour roof, then it had to share a bed with policies of a broadly Keynesian nature. Keynesian economics was deservedly in the ascendance both academically and, within the Conservative government at home and other governments abroad, politically. Keynesian ideas ruled over free market ones, and kept planning ideas in their place. So Callaghan at Nuffield was instructed in the Keynesian arguments, as well as the planning ideas.

What Callaghan did not realise until it was too late was that the Plan that the Labour Government would eventually introduce would be pursued by a powerful department set up explicitly as a rival to the Treasury; that the department would be led by a volatile politician who regarded Callaghan as his deepest enemy; and that the contents of the Plan would be entirely inconsistent with the policies that he, at the Treasury, would be pursuing. Gradually in the run-up to the 1964 general election, these things became clear. Callaghan repeatedly fought with George Brown, seeking to curb his colleague's ambitions. The feud continued for the first year of government. Only once it became clear that the failings of the DEA were even worse than those of the Treasury itself did Callaghan relent, and leave Brown to swing in the breeze. From early 1965 onwards, although Callaghan continued to criticise the National Plan, he essentially regarded it as a naïve irrelevance, rather than a matter of substantive importance.[3]

In 1970, when Labour went into Opposition with Harold Wilson inappropriately still its leader, the myth developed that the National Plan had failed, largely because it was never given a proper chance to work. The planners had never been in control, so it was no surprise that their aspiration to increase GDP by 40 per cent had not been achieved. According to the myth-makers, the obvious solution was to take even greater control over the economy.

Neither Callaghan's successor as Chancellor, Roy Jenkins, nor Jenkins's successor as Shadow Chancellor, Denis Healey, was readily disposed to believe such nonsense. Unfortunately with Labour in opposition, power shifted away from them and the rest of the front bench, and towards the party's National Executive Committee and its Annual Conference. In neither of those bodies had there ever been a shortage of credulity, and now they lurched sharply leftwards, partly in response to the failures of the Wilson administration, and partly as an element of a wider social phenomenon. Urging the party in that direction were such figures as Tony Benn, a fellow traveller in the old administration, with a Keith Joseph-like desire to distance himself from its failures, and Stuart Holland, a minor academic turned Labour back-bencher, who managed to become quite well known in certain circles for rather a short time.

The centrepiece of the new strategy that Labour espoused in the early 1970s was to be a National Enterprise Board that would take minority stakes in up to twenty-five of Britain's largest manufacturing firms and lend them cash. (There was a brief moment when they nearly opted for 250, but apparently nobody could count that high, so the National Executive dropped the idea.) The banks and the large insurance companies were to be nationalised. Like a confetti of National Plans, there were to be planning agreements between employers and unions in each industry. Measures of industrial democracy would be introduced to improve the performance of individual companies. There would be a tax on the wealthy, with the proceeds (such as they would be) going to the poor (who under these policies would be many). There would be a system of import controls. That would oblige Britain to leave the European Economic community, which itself was regarded as rather a bonus.

The policies were extraordinary, and as the 1974 election approached the Labour leadership did its best to ignore them. Harold Wilson had lost most of his illusions, and was in any case not keen on policies dictated to him by the party's unwashed. He rather crassly told an anxious Shirley Williams that the National Executive was merely going through a 'menstrual period'.[4] (Wilson had frequently failed to turn up to the National Executive's meetings, which had perhaps not been the smartest of tactics.) Tony Crosland said the policies were 'idiotic'. Edmund Dell later said that no other government in the century entered office armed with policies of such 'intellectual and political incoherence'. Roy Jenkins subsequently admitted that he neither wanted Labour to win, nor thought that the party deserved to win.[5] Yet to everybody's amazement and many people's horror, win it did.

The 1974–9 Labour Government made no attempt to implement the majority of the planning and nationalisation policies on which it had been elected. If Harold Wilson had lost his illusions, Denis Healey had never had any, and made it no part of his job to facilitate the party's programme. The National Enterprise Board was created, but starved of funds, and took almost no stakes in major companies, other than British Leyland which it bought when the car manufacturer went broke. The banks and the insurance companies stayed in private hands. Planning agreements were signed only with Chrysler, who agreed to sign only because they were being given government cash, and the National Coal Board, who were part of the public sector; and even these were watered down. To Labour's embarrassment the trade unions did not like the industrial democracy that the Government offered them, and the subject was quietly dropped. There was a tax on the wealthy, but the poor stayed poor. The electorate were given a referendum on the European Economic Community, and said they wanted to remain members. The massively restrictive import controls were thus a non-starter.

'Betrayal!' shrieked the left. In a way, they had a point. The Labour right were proficient at ignoring the party's policies, but failed to articulate, let alone win support for, a real philosophy of their own. In these circumstances it should not have been a surprise that after the 1979 defeat, the party demanded another bout of dirigiste thinking, with widespread nationalisation, withdrawal from the European Community and centralised control once more on the agenda, backed up by party rules that forced the leadership to pursue the policies of the party, rather than its own inclinations.

178 Second Amongst Equals

The policy was known as 'the Alternative Economic Strategy', although self-evidently it was none of those things. Even more than before, Tony Benn roused the rabble, especially with respect to the need for greater democracy within the party. The new Shadow Chancellor was Peter Shore, who had briefly headed the Department of Economic Affairs under Harold Wilson. Shore, an ally of the new leader, Michael Foot, was a worthy but uninspiring believer in both planning and a siege economy. Shore lasted until 1983 and the party's well-earned defeat. His successor, the essayist and man of principle Roy Hattersley, made little impact, and never seemed comfortable with economic complexities. Then came John Smith who discreetly, resolutely but slowly devoted himself to dismantling the party's economic policies. That left Gordon Brown with a clean sheet of paper, but little by way of guidance from the party's past to help him decide what to write.

Hugh Gaitskell, Denis Healey, and the alternative tradition that never was

One Labour Chancellor who might have carved out an alternative Labour economic philosophy, to put alongside Tony Crosland's political philosophy, was Hugh Gaitskell. It was Labour's great tragedy that Gaitskell never actually did so. This was not entirely for lack of opportunity. Gaitskell became a minister in 1946 and Chancellor in 1950, yet it was not until the late 1950s that, as party leader, Gaitskell set himself the task of modernising Labour thinking – prompted in part by the challenge posed by Macmillan's assumption of the Conservative leadership. By then, time was running out. As Chancellor, Gaitskell had battled against Bevan's romanticism and self-promotion, but had never offered an alternative philosophy. Gaitskell famously fought and defeated Bevan for the introduction of prescription charges. As has already been suggested, he did so to reject the principle of a government commitment to foot an unlimited health bill in its entirety; and also to assert the principle that on all spending matters, the Chancellor has final say. Both were good principles to uphold, but neither reached to the heart of the nation's economic dilemma or to the need for Labour to rethink how the economy should be run. Gaitskell at that time lacked an independent view of what Labour stood for, had few oratorical skills, and as a minister tended to behave rather as he had done as a war-time civil servant: implementing rather than devising a brief.

If planning was the general preoccupation of Labour policy-makers at the time, then nationalisation was its major manifestation. In his first job as Manny Shinwell's Parliamentary Under-Secretary, Hugh Gaitskell participated without apparent qualms in the nationalisation of the mining, gas and electricity sectors. His quiet competence contrasted favourably with the histrionics of his vain and incompetent boss. After the 1947 fuel crisis Attlee demoted Shinwell and put Gaitskell in charge of the Ministry of Fuel and Power, although without a seat in Cabinet. The new minister worked hard but as his biographer, Brian Brivati, notes, 'Gaitskell, like the rest of the Labour government, put far too much faith in the nationalisation programme.'[6]

When Gaitskell became Cripps's deputy he quickly emerged as a major player in the Government, admired by Attlee for his grasp of technicalities and his ability to lead arguments towards proper conclusions, destined already to succeed Cripps as Chancellor, and take on the responsibility of making whatever further corrections to the Government's course that would prove necessary. His career had received much encouragement from Hugh Dalton, who persuaded Attlee to give Gaitskell the post of Minister of State at the Treasury, and later (in company with Cripps) the Chancellorship itself. Dalton commended Gaitskell for his 'quick intelligence, or bright ideas, or diligence or methodical administration ...' and for his '... power to resist high-powered advice.'[7] Dalton did not commend Gaitskell, however, for any special vision, or willingness to challenge Labour party (as opposed to civil service) thinking. Gaitskell offered nothing that matched the romantic ideals of Bevan and the left.

As Chancellor, Gaitskell's economic thinking was curiously unimpressive. Taking on Bevin's mantle, he became preoccupied by his desire to expand military spending in response to the Korean War. Rightly or wrongly, Gaitskell allowed his economic duties to take second place to his commitment to fight against totalitarianism. In such circumstances his Chancellorship never stood a chance. The dispute with Bevan overwhelmed Gaitskell's Chancellorship, and hastened the Government's demise.

After Gaitskell came the misguided Harold Wilson, and after him came the worthy but intellectually limited Jim Callaghan. And then in 1968 came the learned Roy Jenkins, appointed by Wilson in preference to the more analytically-minded Tony Crosland. Jenkins took the job without any profound plan regarding what he wanted to do. Nor did Jenkins develop any plans while in office: his task was just to get the economy under control, and then move on to greater things. He did the former with great mastery, but the latter with less success. Indeed when it came to the crunch he was not sure if he wanted to move. Jenkins's visions were not economic ones, but the job's position at the centre of power attracted him to the Chancellorship, and he half-wanted to stay in 1970, and half-wanted to go back in 1974. It was not to be.

Instead, responsibility for economic policy passed to another man who was similarly uninterested in economic thinking. But at least when Denis Healey became Chancellor in 1974 he had been given three years in Opposition in which to decide how to tackle the economic problems left to him by Ted Heath and Tony Barber, and in which to sort out a fundamental analysis of what the economy really needed.

Alas, there was not much evidence of preparation. One would like to say that when he became Chancellor, Healey saw the nation's economic situation for what it was, knew what to do, but lacked the power to take the necessary steps. In truth his views were less clear than that. After his first two distinctly shaky years he eventually became a powerful fighter for economic realism, but even then he made some compromises which left him well short of greatness, and which reflected his own thinking as well as the circumstances that faced him. Denis Healey was better than most of those around him, and poorly served by his Prime Ministers and Cabinet colleagues, but as Chancellor he was neither a hero nor an original thinker. Healey saw things half clearly, which in easier circumstances would have been good enough, but which at that time was not.

This is all the more painful because Denis Healey was amongst the sharpest, best educated, most intellectually sophisticated Chancellors of our age. Healey sought to occupy a position between that which would later be filled by Nigel Lawson, who always wanted to be thought of as an economic thinker, and that assumed by Ken Clarke, who pretended not to be an intellectual at all. Healey's boast was that he understood but rejected the economic ideas of his age, and so turned to an older intellectual tradition. 'I abandoned Keynesianism in 1975,' says Healey in his autobiography *The Time of My Life*, and attributes this decision to three weaknesses that he believed existed in the Keynesian way of thinking: a lack of sufficient understanding of how social institutions, especially trade unions, work; an absence of an account of a nation's economic relations with the outside world; and finally the impracticality of doing what Keynesianism was all about: manipulating demand to achieve a particular objective for employment.[8]

Unlike many of his time who had similar crises of faith, Denis Healey refused to espouse the doctrines of the growing Monetarist church. Instead, he claims that as Chancellor he turned back to Joseph Schumpeter, a German émigré to the United States who took a more historicist and institutional view of the economy. Healey quotes Schumpeter's 1946 analysis that '... a socialising government cannot possibly tolerate present trade union practice ...' and he notes Schumpeter's assessment that although England (*sic*) was the place in which democracy stood the best chance of taming the unions, '... the road to solution may be tortuous and long'. Amen, says Healey: 'I spent my five years as Chancellor discovering how right he was.'[9]

We should not take too literally the notion of Healey using Schumpeter for guidance on how to run the economy. Like an old-style Tory, Denis Healey always trumpets his learning a little too loudly: that is part of his appeal. He quotes, not only from the obvious poets – Homer and Blake, Shakespeare, Yeats and Auden – but from less obvious ones such as John Cleveland, a Cavalier poet whose collected verse Healey presented to Adlai Stevenson shortly before the American's death. Conspicuous display of learning is partly a defence – what point arguing with a man so much better read than oneself – but in the case of economic theory, the result is not entirely convincing.

Healey's criticisms of Keynesianism may work as criticisms of the reductionist policies of the Treasury and of many journalists, but they do not do justice to the full richness of Keynes's school of thinking. Meanwhile, Healey's unwillingness to commit to Monetarism seems to have had more to do with a refusal to adopt the anthem of his Tory enemies than with any critique that he was able to offer of the underlying logic of the Monetarist ideas themselves.

Denis Healey devotes quite a lot of space in *The Time of My Life* to explaining why demand management is a fiendishly difficult policy to implement.[10] The historical data on which, as Chancellor, you must base your judgement is unreliable; and forecasts are even more so. You do not know whether any tax cut will be spent or saved, and if it is spent you do not know whether it will go on domestic goods or on imports. If it is imports, you do not know whether that will alter the exchange rate. You do not know whether more demand will mean more output or just higher prices, and what the effect of higher prices will be anyway. And so on.

But is there an alternative? Healey seems to have taken the view that, despite the problems, he should continue to try to manage demand, which makes his claim that he abandoned Keynesianism seem a bit odd. Admittedly after 1975 he also tried to influence the growth of the money supply (or in the great tradition of British monetary policy, pretended to do so); but that didn't mean he had abandoned his earlier policy. Indeed, in opposition Healey would chide Geoffrey Howe for only being interested in monetary control: a policy that Healey compared to a golfer using only one club. And his description of himself as an eclectic pragmatist ducks the issue of whether Keynesian economics was correct in theory but too difficult in practice, or just not correct in theory.

The correct answer to this, which Healey gives only obliquely, is that when he came into office he uncritically continued the Heath–Barber policy of trying to achieve far more from Keynesian policies than those policies could possibly deliver. In previous periods governments had generally been pretty moderate in their Keynesian interventions, even though not moderate enough for many later commentators. The economy had grown at historically high rates, thanks initially to post-war reconstruction and then to the expansion of world trade. The beneficial impact of Keynesian policies on growth came from the use of emergency deflation in times of crises (although it never needed Keynes to point out the need for such actions) and perhaps from their beneficial effects on business confidence, rather than from their direct expenditure-raising effects. But the downswing of the mid seventies was so problematic, and the degree of success to which the Heath and Wilson governments aspired was so considerable, that failure was inevitable. What Denis Healey abandoned in 1975 was not Keynesianism but a fantasy approach to policy-making that had moved far away from its original Keynesian groundings.

Similarly, although Healey was right to identify the position of the trade unions as the central issue of the day, it is fanciful to suggest that reading Schumpeter helped him with that judgement. Reading the newspapers, let alone working as a Cabinet minister, would swiftly have led anybody with any common sense to the same conclusion.

Healey expresses sorrow that the unions did not respond to his two 1974 give-away Budgets by restraining their pay demands, and says that in the circumstances, curbs on pay rises rapidly became unavoidable. He personally wanted statutory controls: silly Michael Foot and disingenuous Jim Callaghan insisted on voluntary limits with statutory powers held only in reserve, and to this compromise Healey agreed. Whether or not some more profound restrictions on, or remodelling of, the unions was in truth necessary is something that Healey was for a long time reluctant to discuss. Despite the appalling events of 1978 and 1979, when delinquent trade unions destroyed both themselves and the Labour Government and handed power to the Tories, Healey stayed quiet.

This is not because Denis Healey was personally in thrall to the unions. That charge could be levelled with only a little unfairness against Jim Callaghan but emphatically not against Healey. But the party was in hock to the unions, and Healey was loyal to Labour, however disloyal the party was to him and to the electorate. When he was Chancellor and for a while in opposition Healey, despite everything, wanted to safeguard his chance of leading the party. Perhaps too he believed that, if he ever became leader, he would need the unions to fight with him against Tony Benn and the extreme left. Only much later would Denis Healey admit that '... the pressure by Thatcher to make union decisions more democratic was absolutely right ...' and that the unions '... were the obstacles to the election of a Labour government ...'[11] By then the assessment was commonplace, and Healey's views no longer mattered. All that was left was to wait for Tony Blair and Gordon Brown, and their New Labour ideas; alas the wait was to prove a long one for the party.

Politicians espouse philosophies partly because they need follow-ers. There never were and never would be Healeyites, and so there was little need for Healeyism. That was a great loss to the Labour Party, and was part of the reason why for eighteen years it could not get itself re-elected. Some consolation is to be had from the fact that, despite Peter Jay's best efforts with father-in-law Jim, Labour never fully succumbed to Monetarism, and Denis Healey deserves his party's thanks for that. But the absence of a sensible alternative Labour philosophy was a fatal flaw.

New Labour, new thinking?

If not from the past, then from where does New Labour get its ideas? And where does it think it is taking them? The one incontrovertible thing to say about New Labour is that, at least in the short run, it is about having a party that is electable. Neither its adherents nor its detractors would deny that. (In the long run, Tony Blair's real project may be the transcendence of the party itself, but that is another mat-ter.) The harder question is what, if anything, New Labour embodies by way of political and economic philosophy. The rejection of old Labour ideas is explicit. So what does it offer instead?

The rapid turnover in credos – 'communitarianism', the 'stake-holder society', the 'third way', they last a year if they are lucky – at-tests to the possibility that New Labour insiders are as confused about where they are coming from as the rest of us. Take the 'third way'. The Macmillanesque phrase is not necessarily a worry: it is not a bad rule of thumb in politics to identify the two great strands of thinking of your time, and then opt for a compromise between them. Rab Butler before he was Chancellor and Denis Healey after his pe-riod in office, both seeking to save their parties, did just that.

Such an approach is, however, low reward as well as low risk (just ask Butler and Healey). Compromise is a good idea if your party has its back to the electoral wall, as was the case before Labour won its 1997 landslide, and your aim is to survive the next couple of years. It is a bad idea once you have attained a firm grip on power, and when you are seeking to change society and the economy – and by doing so, seeking to remain in office for a generation. Voters want to see the purpose behind the prudence.

Fortunately, it is reasonably clear that Gordon Brown genuinely does have a purpose. He sincerely abhors the existence of poverty in an otherwise prosperous society. This is more than just an intellectual pose. It aligns him with a diverse bunch that includes supposed Labour right-wingers such as Clem Attlee and John Smith, but which contrasts him with Hugh Dalton and Tony Benn, to take two of many examples of Labour politicians from privileged backgrounds, for whom being a good socialist always seemed like the pose of a clever schoolboy whose face got stuck when the wind changed. The abhorrence surely motivates much of what Brown wants to do as Chancellor. In that sense he is fundamentally, and not just contingently, a *Labour* not a Tory Chancellor. Gordon Brown does not see his ultimate purpose as the promotion of wealth or enterprise, and nor is he ideologically rootless in the way in which Tony Blair clearly is.

And yet in Brown's philosophy, the main way to relieve poverty is to get people into work, through a combination of carrots and sticks, rather than through macroeconomic job-creation: an approach that has little basis in Labour traditions, and which helps to engender such equivocal attitudes towards him. The New Deal, introduced in 1998 for young people but subsequently extended, was one of the clearest examples of Brown's new philosophy of 'welfare to work'. The scheme, which partly built on the Workfare programme of the Government's Tory predecessors, abolishes unemployment benefits for many of the unemployed, and obliges them instead to work, train, or do without. The scheme's severity has been ameliorated by the provision of job subsidies and decent advice for those taking paid work, and its major effect has probably been to encourage people to take work which they could have taken anyway. But its undoubted success has occurred against a background of sustained strong growth in the British economy. One wonders whether in less favourable macroeconomic circumstances, it would have been so successful.

Another example is the Working Families Tax Credit. The Government now pays tax credits to low-wage parents with children, to bring their incomes up to a minimum level. The idea is to end the old

poverty trap, whereby unemployed people on benefits had little incentive to take low-paid work, since the benefits foregone typically
exceeded the pay on offer. Critics, such as the former social security
minister, Frank Field, say that (at least for adults with children) the
new system shifts the problem higher up the income scale, so that
those on low wages now have little incentive to work harder and
earn more, since by doing so they will lose their tax credit.[12] But if
the single most important step that the Chancellor wishes people to
take is to leave the benefit system and enter work – any work – then
that is presumably a price worth paying.

The fact that the tax credits go only to parents with children points
to a second strand in Brown's thinking. That strand is also revealed
in the fairly generous way in which he has raised Child Benefits in
successive Budgets. The conclusion that is often drawn is that Brown
is 'pro-family'. The real point is that the Chancellor is not just anti-
poverty, but is especially opposed to child poverty – not just for sentimental reasons, but also because he knows that childhood
deprivation damages a person's prospects throughout their whole
lives. Here again we see Brown the socialist who refuses to play to
the galleries in the way in which many in his party have done. Harold
Wilson famously exaggerated in a speech by saying that when he was
at school, many of his fellow pupils were so poor that they attended
barefoot. (Macmillan no less famously retorted that if the infant Wilson himself wore no boots, it was probably because he was too big
for them.) Gordon Brown would make no such mistake, but privately he is said to carry with him the memory of the village poor,
who came to his father's manse when he was a child, in search of
charity.

It is critically important here that the raising of Child Benefits and
the introduction of the Working Families Tax Credit, even more than
the New Deal, were very much the Chancellor's personal policies.
They and the Chancellor's other ideas have been hugely expensive,
and for the first three years of the Labour Government they have
crowded out spending on health, education and transport – all of
them, as noted already, dearer to the hearts of the Prime Minister, his
Deputy and most of the rest of the Cabinet than to the Chancellor's
heart. Gordon Brown really does not like poverty, welfare dependency, and the culture of the perpetual claimant. A hand up, not a

hand out, is what all ministers are instructed to say they now offer – although at least it is a genuine offer, not the cynical one that an equivalent Chancellor from the modern Conservative Party might decide to make.

Although Gordon Brown once wrote a PhD thesis on Scottish politics (specifically the relationship between the trade unions and the Labour Party in Scotland), and although he has been known to claim some intellectual affinity with Tony Crosland, his debts to the domestic tradition of Labour thinking are in truth modest – at least as far as the intellectual, as opposed to emotional, origins of his views are concerned. Brown's modern beliefs are transatlantic in origin. A visit that he and Tony Blair made to Washington in 1993 is emblematic of this. Brown and Blair met the two leading intellectuals of the Clinton era – Labor Secretary Robert Reich and Treasury Secretary to-be Larry Summers. And while Blair readily absorbed the new-Democrat message that to be elected you must first be electable, it was Brown who concerned himself with more technical questions, and who took on board what the Americans were saying about the best ways to run a modern mixed economy. So proficient did he become in American political economy that had Brown not entered the British Cabinet in 1997, he could probably have wangled himself a seat in the American one.

The Americans taught Brown that above all else, the welfare system should promote, not discourage, employment. Which was handy because they also taught him that macroeconomic policies could not promote full employment, or at least not in the way that the Keynesians had once thought. The authority figure here was Larry Summers, recent Harvard mentor to a Kennedy scholar, Ed Balls, who had since been writing for the *Financial Times*, and who would soon work for Brown ('it's not Brown's, it's Balls!' as Michael Heseltine memorably said of Labour economic policy). So precocious was the young Balls that it was he who introduced Brown to Summers, rather than Summers who introduced Balls to Brown. Pretty soon, Summers's new macroeconomics – Balls has called them Post-Monetarism – were a key part of Gordon Brown's portfolio of policies.

The new macroeconomics of Gordon Brown are neither Keynesianism as it used to be taught, nor Monetarism as it used to be practised; neither interventionist nor free-market. The approach is self-consciously non-political. The core belief, as articulated in the Treasury's 'mission statement', is that the role of government is to deliver macroeconomic stability, understood in terms of low and stable inflation and a sustainable path for public finances, and that the institutions of government should be shaped to that purpose. If this is done, if the policies to encourage people into work are in place, and if there are other supposed growth-promoting policies in place such as support for innovation or an expansion of higher education, then Mr Brown claims that the outcome will be strong and stable growth and full employment.[13]

But all governments say they favour stability. What is new? The answer is that Gordon Brown favours a rather clever middle path between those who advocate fixed rules (the ERM is a classic example of such a rule, and so too was the Monetarism of the early Howe years) and those who favour no rules and making it up as you go along (step forward, Ken Clarke).

The argument is that targets for the exchange rate or for monetary growth or any other such indicator are intended to promote stability but that, slavishly applied, they often perversely do the reverse – as happened when sterling was ejected from the ERM, or when Geoffrey Howe's efforts to get monetary growth under control helped to send the exchange rate soaring to a level that was bound to be followed by a collapse. These targets may look sensible when they are adopted, but in a changing world they quickly become inappropriate; pedantic adherence to them then destabilises the economy and pushes it in the wrong direction.

Equally, unbounded discretion allows ministers to pursue self-serving short-term policies – and even when the ministers do not do so, nobody believes them, which is almost as bad. That is what happened when the markets interpreted Ken Clarke's refusal to raise base rates as cynical electioneering, so that long-term interest rates rose on fears of future inflation fuelled by a Chancellor deemed to be irresponsible.

Instead, Gordon Brown subscribes to a regime in which those who implement policy are given very clear targets for their ultimate goal (a rolling target of 2.5 per cent inflation in two years' time, in the Bank of England's case) but have wide discretion about how they meet the target along the way (hence the Bank's freedom to let actual inflation move away from the target, and to raise or lower interest rates as it sees fit). Similarly, fiscal policy is set to achieve a stable ratio of debt to GDP, and borrowing is permitted only to fund investment, but these rules apply over the course of an economic cycle rather than within a single year.

The obvious analogy with devolved management in large private businesses is an apposite one: indeed, there is a good case to be made for the notion that business-school theory is the new political ideology that Labour has picked up, and that the Tories have yet to embrace. But we also need to remember the transatlantic academic roots of the policy, so that when the Governor of the Bank of England commends a consensus among finance ministers and central bankers on 'macroeconomic stability as a necessary condition for sustainable growth', what he is really drawing attention to is the current dominance of American thinking on policy makers around the world, and not just in Britain.[14]

Linked to that approach is a strong sense in the Brown worldview that macroeconomic policies must be sustainable. This is not a cynical nod in the direction of the environmentalists, whom New Labour keeps at arm's length lest they dribble, but instead simply says that operating policies that anybody can see are going to collapse is probably not sensible. It is a lesson that Stafford Cripps, Jim Callaghan, Nigel Lawson and Norman Lamont, among others, could have usefully applied. Since sustainability is the quintessential test that financial markets apply, the use of such a principle reduces governmental vulnerability to the whims of markets – indeed makes the markets the enthusiastic fans of those governments with the wit to follow sustainable policies. Far from fearing unfettered global capital markets, Gordon Brown consciously sets out to impress them.

The third strand in Gordon Brown's commitment to stability is to gain the confidence of markets, electors, employers and individuals; partly by the Chancellor being as transparent as possible about what he and his officials are doing and why, and partly by him making it as hard as possible on himself to do one thing, while claiming to be doing another. This means, for example, disclosing the basis for how the fiscal sums are done, as set out in the Code for Fiscal Stability, getting the National Audit Office to check the Treasury's own figures and assumptions, and giving the Bank of England operational independence, with a Monetary Policy Committee (MPC) whose deliberations are made public. Again, it is an approach that other countries have also adopted, and which reflects the thinking of mainly American academic researchers.

Unfortunately these principles have proved less clear in practice than in theory. The MPC's pursuit of stable, low inflation has caused a damaging exchange rate appreciation, in much the same way that Geoffrey Howe's pursuit of stable, low monetary growth did from mid 1979 until early 1981. Sustainable trends in public finances have not protected the economy from anxieties over unsustainable trends elsewhere, such as in the equity market, or in personal savings (consistently too low to fund future pension needs) or in Far Eastern economies. And the new policy transparency has been clouded by surreptitious tax rises and spending sleights-of-hand.

If the radical new approach to policy seems less radical by the day, then we should not be completely surprised. Gordon Brown is not the first politician to disguise continuity as change. Many of his reforms continue a trend set in motion by Norman Lamont, who introduced both inflation targets and a panel of independent economic forecasters whose views were made public. Ken Clarke took a step further when he published the minutes of his monthly meeting with the governor of the Bank of England. So although Gordon Brown and his advisers like to argue that they have rethought economic policy-making from first principles, the truth is that the Treasury and the Bank of England had evolved towards similar ways of thinking under the old Conservative regime. Indeed, Norman Lamont claims that when he was Chancellor he argued for Bank of England independence, but was turned down by John Major; the claim would not be surprising, given that by then, the intellectual case for central bank operational independence had been established beyond almost any doubt, and was set out in large numbers of learned articles published around the world.[15]

Is Labour now working?

The remarkable feature of the Brown Chancellorship is that it remained largely trouble-free throughout Labour's first term of office. This was not just because of new and better theories, but also because of lucky timing. The unexpected growth and stability of the world economy, emanating particularly from the United States, and from the new information and communications technologies, meant that lots of finance ministers around the world looked pretty clever too. The new technologies raised growth internationally, while lowering inflation, and inflation itself gained from the liberalisation that had occurred in economies around the world. That in turn helped the British economy to withstand an exchange rate that, thanks to the Bank of England's need to meet a tough inflation target, rose to a level that would otherwise have been ruinous for the economy.

To the question 'What do you do in a crisis?' the Brown philosophy replies, with some justification, that it seeks to make a crisis less likely. But to the repeated question, 'Yes, but what do you do in a crisis?' the economics of Gordon Brown become somewhat tight-lipped. The framework, because it allows inflation and public finances to deviate in the short term from their long-run targets, and because it avoids the classic high-risk element of an exchange-rate target, ought to be able to withstand minor squalls; but how it would cope with a major storm of the sort that wrecked (for example) Tony Barber's Chancellorship is less clear. For how long and by how much does one allow inflation and public finances to deviate from their long-term paths? The answer requires judgements about the future, and in particular about the length and severity of the economic cycle, and hence it is not just a matter of mechanically applying formulae. And where good judgement is concerned, there are certainly no guarantees.

7 What happened to the economy

Received wisdom

The thrust of Edmund Dell's accusation in *The Chancellors* is that the British economy grew far too slowly in the half century following the end of the Second World War, in large part because of the failings of those who held the office of Chancellor. Dell clearly believes that Chancellors habitually ducked their responsibilities and chose popularity over duty; and that even when they were guided by principles, they mostly adhered to the mistaken ideas of the left and the centre-ground, rather than the true precepts of sound finance, a strong currency and monetary restraint. 'More culpable than *papabile*' might summarise Dell's thesis.

The view that the British economy has under-performed since the Second World War is widely accepted. But we need to be careful not to paint too bleak a picture of British under-performance. The increase in British living standards since the Second World War has almost certainly been greater than in any comparable period in recorded British history. Nor can this be dismissed as a materialist conceit: improvements such as greatly reduced child mortality, better housing for the majority of people and better care for the elderly are real gains which cannot be gainsaid by the common observation that conventional measures of well-being such as GDP conceal nearly as much as they reveal.

Even in terms of international comparisons, Britain does not do quite as badly as is commonly supposed. Comparisons in the immediate post-war reconstruction period are pretty meaningless, so it is only from about 1950 that it is sensible to measure British performance against that of other countries. And certainly in the period up until the mid seventies, output per head in the UK tended to rise by only about 2.5 per cent a year, compared with about 3.5 per cent a year in the world's twelve large industrialised economies.[1] But since then, trend growth has declined in most of the larger economies, so that in the eighties, average growth rates of the twelve large industrialised economies fell to about 2 per cent, or about the same as that in the UK in the same period. In the last decade, the UK has at least kept pace with the pack, and today there are as many commentators saying that the once mighty economies of Japan and Germany should be remodelled along Anglo-American lines as used to say the opposite.

How do we square this assessment with perceptions of severe and sustained problems in the British economy? Part of the explanation is that the 1 per cent a year gap between growth in Britain and elsewhere may not sound much, but over a period of nearly a quarter of a century it had a large cumulative impact. It allowed other countries, and especially their manufacturing industries, to catch up with British productivity and living standards and in many cases overtake and leave them far behind. The performance gap also created problems with the management of the British economy, and dissatisfaction amongst the British people, notably downwards pressure on the exchange rate, chronic balance of payments problems and persistent inflation. These in turn generated the sense of perpetual dissatisfaction and crisis that Dell and others have chronicled, and that many people remember all too well. In the seventies the accumulation of problems, on top of new difficulties in the global economy, created economic conflicts and emergencies that overwhelmed the Heath government and, even more so, its Labour successor. And although the situation has stabilised since then, and countries abroad have moved into a less unusual 'post-boom' growth path, British policymakers have still not found ways to recover the ground lost in the fifties and sixties. Nor is it clear that they ever will.

Post-war reconstruction

The obvious question is why the British economy participated only partially in the golden age of the fifties and sixties boom. Many commentators have blamed the legacy of the preceding Labour Government. On the face of it that is a harsh judgement: after all, the greatest project of the Labour Government from 1945 until 1951 was the reconstruction of the nation's economy after the disruption of war: a remarkable achievement, well delivered. During the Chancellorships of Dalton, Cripps and Gaitskell, Britain's industry gradually shifted from a preoccupation with the production of war materials to a focus on the manufacture of peacetime products. Output generally increased, and 9 million jobs were found for demobilised servicemen, and for those no longer needed in the munitions industries. With jobs available for almost all of those (men at least) who wanted them, unemployment in the reconstruction period remained low, at about 1.5 per cent of the labour force.

In a sense this was an indirect achievement, for there was little that the three Chancellors needed to do themselves to boost production: companies were mostly eager to produce, and consumers were eager to buy. The politicians' job instead was to prevent other problems from getting in recovery's way. Dalton, Cripps and Gaitskell did that with a broad degree of success – not single-handedly, and not totally, but with far more on the positive side of the balance sheet than on the negative side. (One negative was the nationalisation of various industries, which though in the short term not hugely harmful economically was not especially beneficial either, and was a political distraction for ministers with more than enough else to do.)

An ingredient of their success was that inflation stayed in check. An inflationary surge would have forced whoever was the Chancellor of the day to suppress heavily the rate of growth of demand in the economy, probably to the extent of pushing the economy into recession. So Labour Chancellors used high tax rates to moderate the pace of recovery, without choking it off completely. They and their Cabinet colleagues also persevered with the legal constraints on price rises that had been so important during the war, and they persuaded trade unionists to moderate their wage demands, by the commitment to full employment, and by keeping out of industrial relations matters. By and large these measures worked: inflation averaged a tolerable 5 per cent or so, and there was never any need to slam on the brakes.

The other, even more remarkable, achievement of Dalton and his successors was the one described in Chapter 2: getting the balance of payments at least partially sorted out. The nature of the problem is worth reiterating. The war had left the nation heavily in debt, and the Government of the major creditor, the United States, was keen to obtain rapid repayment. But American businesses had secured for themselves many of the trading links on which pre-war Britain had depended, while the war had in any case disrupted Britain's ability to produce the goods which it needed for trade, for investment and for home consumption. So long as isolationism prevailed in the United States, the global economy was likely to be stymied by shortages of finance for lubricating trade and investment flows; that too meant that in 1945 and 1946 Britain's balance of payments problems looked both dangerous and almost insoluble.

So Britain ended the war, not just in debt, but getting ever deeper into debt – a situation that could persist only for so long as foreigners were willing to lend funds to cover the shortfalls. If not, then just as with excessive inflation, the Chancellor of the day would have needed to invoke a recession in the domestic economy, to curb the nation's appetite for imports. But with the American Government's 1945 cancellation of Lend-Lease, overseas financing was bound to be problematic, since Britain lost both the American funds themselves, and the confidence that such funds might have engendered in other potential lenders.

Yet through a combination of negotiating alternative arrangements, and the implementation of fierce import controls, capital controls and domestic rationing, and helped by growth in the American economy, disaster was averted, and by 1950 the balance of payments was back in current account surplus. In the meantime, finance of one sort or another flowed into Britain. A big help came from the United States, where policy-makers increasingly realised that a hard line did nobody, including themselves, any good: American factories could hardly be expected to produce goods for export if the export markets were not there; American banks and institutions gained no benefit from holding British assets if Britain could not afford to honour its debts. But much was also achieved by the continuation in Britain of rationing and of direct controls on the economy.

Reconstruction thus occurred, and Labour honoured its election commitment to maintain full employment. It also maintained for most of the time stable fixed exchange rates, reflecting a view that such stability was necessary for the health of the larger international economy, and for keeping Britain's vaunted place within the international system.

Alongside reconstruction and the strong pound came the establishment of the welfare state: the National Health Service, a proper state-funded education system, welfare benefits for the unemployed, pensioners and others in need, and local authority housing for those on low incomes. There were also food and farming subsidies, and many other, smaller initiatives outside the welfare sphere such as the creation of the National Parks and the Arts Council.

The welfare state was not the child of Chancellor Hugh Dalton, but there is no doubt that he was its midwife. 'No Chancellor of the Exchequer, before or since, has been such a soft touch for social-spending ministers,' says Peter Hennessy.[2] Michael Foot, in his biography of Nye Bevan is more positive: 'After Bevan,' he wrote, 'Dalton was the chief architect of the NHS.'[3] And funding the emergence of the welfare state was something about which Dalton boasted: he did it, he said, 'with a song in my heart' (although he said the same of several other policies too).[4]

The welfare state, which for a while was easily funded by the high tax regime that Labour inherited from the wartime government, was not as vital economically as the reconstruction programme, but politically it was equally so.[5] Against the backdrop of the hardships of reconstruction, and the remembered hardships of both the war and the pre-war depression, the introduction of the welfare state, together with the commitment to full employment, amounted almost to a new constitutional settlement – a commitment by the state to pay better regard to the needs of the people.

To modern eyes it seems strange that, given the problems with the balance of payments and the official reserves in the early post-war period, the Government did not ease the situation by slowing down on the introduction of the welfare state. The argument for doing so was that, even though the new arrangements were being reasonably well funded from taxes (Dell's jibe that it was 'socialism on credit' is just plain wrong, at least in those early days), they nevertheless contributed to the expansion of demand in the domestic economy, and hence to the balance of payments problem.

Dalton, however, seemed not to make the connection (he was an economist, but not one with much imagination), or if he did, he refused to acknowledge it. And indeed the Chancellor could not reasonably have done otherwise than fund the welfare state, even if he had wanted to. It was impossible for any sensible person to doubt in 1945 that Britain needed a publicly funded welfare state, and that it was Dalton's job as Chancellor to make such a system possible. The British experience in the Second World War had been unique: the nation had been under almost constant and direct attack, mobilisation had been near-universal, and the war had ended in victory. Key elements of the welfare state had emerged during the war: housing for those who were bombed-out and had nowhere to go, free medical treatment for civilian wounded as well as military wounded, healthcare for the sick to enable them to go back to work, nutritional advice to people forced to live on rations, free schooling for evacuated children. Going back on all of that was not an option.

So in Britain the warfare state became the welfare state, which rescued the nation state; in France, Germany, Japan, Italy and elsewhere, political unrest would in time require far more explicit constitutional deals to achieve the same result.

Or perhaps the point should be put the other way round: the 1945–51 Labour Government was so fearful of political change, so politically conservative, that it made sure that its reconstruction and welfare state programmes were powerful enough to forestall significant political upheaval. And ministers were quite reasonably proud of their efforts, at least in the early days. Hugh Dalton rightly said that the period from July 1945 to January 1947 was the high point of his career, when he felt 'gay, confident, tireless, influential and on the whole successful'.[6]

But the Attlee government's emphasis on planning the economy was a severe mistake, and one which stifled the emergence of the economic dynamism that the British economy would need in subsequent years, and that other economies would acquire, alongside their greater political turbulence. Britain in the reconstruction period eschewed any sharp shock of market liberalisation, of the kind that in 1948 Ludwig Erhard (then the economics minister and later the German Chancellor) imposed on Germany. In Britain, all was sensible and careful: too much so. Import controls helped to get the balance of payments back into current account surplus, but they also protected British companies from any pressure to improve their products, processes or marketing efforts. A softly-softly approach to anti-trust policy was an effective way to buy the cooperation of industrialists with respect to controls on what they could buy or sell, but it took away some of their need to compete with each other, and so made them lazy. The commitment to full employment and to non-interference by government in industrial relations meant that the unions moderated their wage demands, but it also encouraged those unions to expect such policies as a matter of right, whatever the circumstances. And at least until the devaluation of 1949, the maintenance of a high exchange rate was good for Labour's reputation at home and abroad, but hampered the competitiveness of British industry.

Clearly, Dalton, Cripps and Gaitskell did not see the limitations of their governments' policies with the clarity that hindsight offers us – how could they? But they did have their doubts: more than their critics give them credit for. They knew that raising productivity was crucial to future prosperity. The metal and engineering industries had expanded rapidly and haphazardly in the war, but lacked the scale, organisation, products and marketing expertise they would now need. Traditional staple industries had been run down, and their markets taken by competitors abroad – in the case of textiles, from India, for example. Important industrial towns and cities had been severely bombed. Ministers, not surprisingly, thought that planning was needed, but nobody had any strategic idea what such plans should contain. Still less could any adviser offer an articulate justification for letting market forces sort out the problems. The result was the worst of both worlds – industry was heavily controlled, but not planned in a forward-thinking sense.

In contrast, the Treasury had copious, though not always coherent, advice to offer on the country's short-term problems: the financial crises that always seemed about to overwhelm the British economy, and that demanded the three Chancellors' never-ending attention. Low inflation, stable growth, full employment, a recovery in the overseas balance of trade in goods and services, and the successful creation of the welfare state, were achievements, hard-won in an atmosphere of perpetual crisis. Dalton and Cripps were broken in the process, and even Gaitskell, who was much younger and who came later, did not have an especially easy time. The commitment to a stable currency was a constant problem for Dalton and, until 1949, Cripps. The funding of the welfare state (especially food and farming subsidies) gradually became a problem for Dalton, remained so for

Cripps, and, when accompanied by the cost of rearmament, came to overshadow Gaitskell's Chancellorship via the fight with Bevan.

For the population at large, the exhaustion of politicians was of little importance compared to the exhaustion that they themselves felt. This is partly because some of the crises affected ordinary people very directly: over 2 million people were unemployed during the 1947 fuel crisis, plus another half a million, stood off work on full pay. But even in less exceptional circumstances, life could be tough. While the economic historian looks back comfortably and sees a period of reconstruction, the population of the day experienced austerity and self-perpetuating bureaucracy. Food, clothing and fuel were all rationed, often more stringently than during the war, and shortages of other goods were common. The planning regime seemed to create as many problems as it solved. The Government persuaded car manufacturers to limit their sales on the home market, because steel for car production was scarce, but the steel was scarce because of lack of fuel, which was scarce because of shortages of labour and transport. So where was the planning? Coal-mining, along with textiles and agriculture, was officially described as an 'undermanned' industry – somewhat galling for the 2 million demobilised women, many of whom had left the labour market against their wishes.

The abolition of controls began in 1948, but it was too little and too late, both for the economy and for the reputation of the Labour Government. The popularity of the welfare state was increasingly outweighed by public irritation with continuing austerity, bureaucracy and obscurantist economic controls. The public became progressively more disillusioned with Labour, and began to contemplate alternatives. By 1950, Labour's landslide majority was down to just six seats. A year later, it was gone completely.

The complacent fifties

One of the last great mistakes of the 1945–51 Labour administration had been Gaitskell's decision to reverse Cripps's cautious husbandry of the economy, and to commit Britain to a programme of rearmament which proved to be even more expensive (relative to the size of the economy) than the American programme. Government borrowing rose, and business investment fell, crowded out by the switch to military spending. Exports fell too. The balance of payments plunged back into deficit. The exchange rate came under severe strain, and the foreign reserves began to haemorrhage. The economy was once more in crisis.

But now it was Rab Butler's problem. The Treasury proposed various initiatives that Butler mostly declined or was unable to implement, not least the Robot scheme discussed earlier. He did cut back the rearmament programme, and in 1952 he introduced an austere budget. Recession followed, but not for long. The economy recovered remarkably easily, and the financial problems of the late forties and early fifties seemed to melt away. The economy embarked on its golden age of historically (though not internationally) high and stable growth, during which it would seldom be necessary to implement Keynesian demand management policies with anything more than a light touch.

With the economy growing steadily, Butler and his various Tory successors as Chancellor oversaw unemployment rates that mostly varied between 1 and 2 per cent. At the time they were understandably proud of their achievement. Later commentators and Conservative politicians have been less kind, however, and a common criticism of policy in the fifties is that unemployment was too *low*, providing an insufficient margin for flexibility, and for reallocating labour away from old jobs and industries and towards newer opportunities. And it can be argued that softness on unemployment was part of a larger failure on the part of the Conservatives (more so than Labour, and with less excuse) to overhaul and modernise the British economy; a failure that may be attributed to lack of thought, lack of nerve or lack of commitment, or some combination of the three, and which partly explains why Britain missed out on the full benefits of the golden age of the fifties and sixties.

The kinder interpretation is that in this period, successive Chancellors were as worried as in any other about inflation, but believed that the maintenance of full employment was, as a minimum, a necessary measure to appease the unions, and thereby keep inflation under control. At most, it was an essential element of a much larger political compact, and one which was also a social good in itself, and for which they liked to believe that the Second World War had been fought.

In any case, from the perspective of the time, unemployment always remained a background threat and sometimes a source of immediate anxiety. Between 1951 and 1952 the number of people on the unemployment register increased by two-thirds, reaching almost half a million, and much the same thing happened again in 1958, when the half million barrier was breached. While the numbers involved were not large by the standards of the eighties and nineties, the rises were sufficiently rapid to generate a sense of crisis on each occasion, and they provoked criticisms that the Government was failing in its obligations.

Fundamentally the Tories, much more explicitly than Labour, set out to deliver economic growth – and for the most part with much success. From 1950 until 1964, while annual growth in the UK averaged an historically impressive 2.5 per cent, inflation averaged just 4 per cent, or even less than in the reconstruction period. Neither Butler nor any of his Conservative successors ever claimed that it was they alone who had *caused* the period of rapid growth, although not surprisingly they asked for credit for eschewing policies that would either have prevented the growth from happening, or would have allowed it to get out of hand. To them, it seemed that they had got the balance of policy roughly right.

In his pursuit of economic growth, Rab Butler was advised by Roy Harrod, an Oxford academic who had reworked Keynes's analysis of how to stabilise economic activity at a given *level* into a much more dynamic account of how to (and indeed why to) stabilise economic activity at a given *rate of growth*. Harrod argued that there was a sustainable growth rate for the economy, and that so long as the private sector believed that the Government was ready to nudge the economy back on course when necessary, businesses and consumers would expect stable sustained growth, and those expectations would generally be self-fulfilling. If, however, the Government allowed the economy to deviate far from its stable growth path, then it would tend of its own accord to wander even further off, and it would become increasingly difficult for policy-makers to bring the economy back on course.

Harrod's story was incredibly appealing, and long after Butler had left the Treasury, his views and those of economists who thought like him continued to carry considerable weight. Macmillan stuck with

Harrod's analysis, and so for the most part did Thorneycroft and Amory. By Selwyn Lloyd's time, however, Harrod's vision of a government deftly maintaining the economy in a state of equilibrium was beginning to look rather precious: partly because the real-world stabilisation problem seemed much harder than the textbook problem, and partly because of Harrod's silence (and that of academic economists more generally) on what were the underlying determinants of the growth rate.

The dash for growth

In the late fifties and early sixties economic growth became a major cause for concern to the Conservative Government. The British could no longer ignore the evidence that their growth rate, although high by historic standards, was low in comparison with what was being achieved in other countries, particularly Germany (and people believed, France). This was a problem partly because of pride, but more importantly because relatively low growth was linked closely to relatively low productivity rises, and these in turn meant that progressively more people were needed in Britain than in Germany to produce the same amount of output. Together with another worrying development, a tendency for British wage and price increases to be higher than that of other countries, that meant declining competitiveness and problems with the trade balance. So it seemed that Dalton's balance of payments worries were coming back to threaten his Conservative successors.

Much of the discussion about relatively slow growth focused on two possible explanations: a relatively low rate of investment, and poor industrial relations. The two were possibly connected: poor industrial relations made it hard for firms to invest in the latest technology, hard for them to get the best out of what investment did take place, and so hard for them to raise employment and wages as fast as the workforce would like, damaging industrial relations and creating a vicious spiral.

Modern empirical research tends to substantiate that story, but also points to the importance of other factors that received less direct attention at the time.[7] These included a lack of expenditure on research and development, other than in the defence and aviation sectors which offered few commercial spin-offs; lack of investment in vocational training; and the ability of poor managers and directors to remain in charge of their companies, almost irrespective of how badly they performed.

The last of these seems at first sight rather odd, for the fifties were a decade of sharply increased takeover activity, thanks to the 1948 Companies Act. Alongside the 1956 Restrictive Practices Act, which outlawed cartels, this ought to have sharpened management practices. But mergers and takeovers were largely about creating firms whose market size was too large for their predation to be a possibility, and the managers of the enlarged firms showing little willingness to put one another to the sword. And while the restrictive practices legislation made it harder for managements to agree not to compete with one another in the home market, managers still showed little understanding of the need to compete with firms abroad, especially firms from elsewhere in Europe.

In the late fifties and early sixties, worries over industrial relations produced a number of attempts by the Macmillan government to broker deals between the unions and management. As a result, and also because of concerns over investment rates, Selwyn Lloyd in 1962 introduced the National Economic Development Council (NEDC), to advise and provide leadership in those areas. When Reggie Maudling became Chancellor two years later he created a National Incomes Commission (NIC) to encourage pay moderation. Two years later, the NIC having failed ignominiously, Labour's new Department of Economic Affairs also took on a remit to encourage pay moderation across the economy.

These initiatives were not especially successful and did little to curb wage demands. Despite that, Harold Macmillan remained strongly committed to a rapid expansion of economic demand. So too did the Prime Ministers who followed him. In July 1961 Selwyn Lloyd informed the Cabinet that he proposed to run the economy at a more rapid growth rate than it had so far achieved: 4 per cent a year. Reggie Maudling stuck with the 4 per cent target, as did Labour in 1964: the target appeared little changed as the centrepiece of Labour's National Plan.

Worse still, Macmillan tended to panic about any signs that rapid growth was not being achieved, and also about his scandal-ridden government's growing unpopularity. In particular, he was very un-happy that Lloyd's 1962 Budget was too tight. That was a view that Lloyd came to share, and the Chancellor quickly cut interest rates. But Macmillan was impatient. In July 1962 Lloyd was considering tax cuts and a further cut in interest rates when Macmillan removed him from office.

Ironically, by sacking his Chancellor and other ministers Macmillan made himself look ridiculous, not decisive, an impression that his aristocratic successor, Alec Douglas-Home, also tended to convey. So Jim Callaghan inherited an economy growing far too fast, and suffered in consequence from severe balance of payments problems from which he as Chancellor never recovered. 'Sorry to leave things in such a mess,' chirped Maudling to Callaghan, sticking his head round the door of the Chancellor's office.[8] Then he popped on his trilby and sauntered off.

Maudling's spell in office had been more interesting than it is usually painted. Initially he was less inclined than Lloyd to reflate the economy, not more, and in his early days he came under a lot of pressure from advisers, politicians and financial journalists alike to boost demand. Among the journalists was Nigel Lawson, then a great reflationist, editing the *Daily Telegraph*'s City page, while among the advisers was Alec Cairncross, a man of great experience, and one who was initially discomforted by Maudling's tendency not to follow, or even seek out, the advice of expansion-minded officials.

To the Treasury, the evidence in the summer of 1962 seemed clear that the economy was in distress. A cold winter at the start of the year had damaged construction and industrial activity, and GDP had fallen. Unemployment was rising and now manufacturing investment was falling.

But Maudling cautiously refused official requests to reflate the economy, insisting that any package should be delayed until the autumn. Many observers assumed that Maudling was merely delaying so as not to embarrass his predecessor by an immediate overthrow of Lloyd's policies. That was not the whole reason. The Chancellor, like his critics, was concerned by the signs of slow growth in the economy, but he attributed this partly to sluggishness at the global level. Exports were suffering from the weakness in the world economy, and as far as could be judged, neither world industrial output nor world trade was growing. The American economy was in recession, Wall Street was wobbly, and people were talking about a repetition of 1929.

Maudling hoped that if he could persuade other governments to act, then the scale of domestic expansion on which he would need to embark would be lowered. The advantage of an internationally co-ordinated expansion was that it would not damage the trade balance and hence would not put downwards pressure on sterling; whereas a go-it-alone domestic expansion would.

These thoughts were part of the reason why, at the World Bank meeting in Washington in 1962, Maudling argued for his scheme, discussed in Chapter 2, to expand global liquidity and hence avert a serious global recession. Only when the Americans and the Germans rejected the scheme did the Chancellor decide that he would have to act domestically.

So, in the autumn of 1962, Maudling announced tax cuts, spending increases and relaxations in credit controls, designed to speed up the economy. Then in April 1963 the Chancellor placed a give-away Budget before the House, with reductions in income tax and measures to help under-performing regions of the economy.

No sooner had the Chancellor done so than the economic indicators turned round, picked up their skirts and ran. Fixed investment and stockbuilding soared, unemployment tumbled. The balance of payments was causing problems and the official reserves were draining away. So in 1964 Maudling changed his mind and introduced a deflationary Budget. It did little to slow the economy, but contributed to the sense of a government still in disarray. That autumn, Labour regained office.

In part what went wrong was not so much an excessive tendency to want economic growth and falling unemployment at any cost, but naïvety in the interpretation of official statistics. When the economy failed to respond instantly to Maudling's autumn 1962 reflation, the Chancellor and his advisers assumed that more was needed, hence the give-away Budget of 1963. What they should have done was give the initial measures sufficient time to take effect (rather as the Bank of England is now told to target inflation two years out, and not to be panicked because inflation today is above or below target). Instead they generated an excessive expansion in the economy and a need for a sharp correction: indeed a sharper correction than either the outgoing Conservative Government, struggling to avoid defeat, or the incoming Labour Government, elected on a wafer-thin majority, was politically able to offer.

Furthermore, the Treasury failed to recognise that normal seasonal fluctuations were exaggerating the extent of the slowdowns in 1962. A sharp rise in unemployment at the end of the year persuaded Alec Cairncross that reflation was needed; only in retrospect did he notice that the rise was merely the result of winter weather (little work in the tourism sector, the building trade or farming, and in those days only a modest Christmas boom to compensate) and would not last. 'I take no pride in my record as an adviser in 1962,' Cairncross confesses.[9] The result was a period marked by the kind of stop-go policy swings that are often, but erroneously, associated with the entire post-war but pre-Thatcher period.

In part there was a deeper error on Maudling's part, and one that makes the stop-go mistakes seem somewhat ironic. Like many Chancellors since, Reggie Maudling entered office wanting to end the practice of forever altering policy: stimulating activity to reduce unemployment or stimulate investment, dampening it down a few months later because of worries over inflation or the trade balance, and then stimulating again in the next year because of renewed worries over unemployment or investment.

But unlike Geoffrey Howe and Gordon Brown, whose policies in this regard have already been discussed, Maudling sought, as we noted in Chapter 5, to achieve medium-term stability, not by the modern method of opting for stability around *low* or moderate growth, but by going for *strong* growth. For the reasons already mentioned, Maudling believed that faster growth would not, as had been traditionally assumed, necessarily mean higher inflation and a weaker trade balance: on the contrary, higher growth could lead to *lower* inflation and a *stronger* trade balance. The trick was to break through from a low rate of productivity growth to a high rate, and going for faster output growth might just bring that output.

At the time there was a respectable academic pedigree to this view, even if it was far from being Treasury orthodoxy. Something like it had been articulated many years before by a Dutch economist, P.J. Verdoorn, in an article published rather obscurely in Italy in 1949. A few years after Maudling's Chancellorship, in 1966, the Cambridge economist and Labour Government adviser Nicholas Kaldor would publish a book, *Causes of the Slow Rate of Economic Growth of the United Kingdom*, which would develop and improve upon Verdoorn's argument and empirical analysis. (Kaldor, like Balogh, was Hungarian and the two men were known at the Treasury as Buddha and Pest.) And although the idea would subsequently fall into disrepute, it does have some resemblance to modern 'endogenous growth theory', which underlies in part Gordon Brown's thinking on growth and stability, and which generated Michael Heseltine's 'not Brown's but Balls" jibe.

Of course, we should not be naïve: it is doubtful whether Maudling spent much time studying academic articles. It is true that Douglas Jay said that Maudling was the only politician of their generation whose grasp of economics matched that of Hugh Gaitskell, who used to teach the subject.[10] And Alec Cairncross says that Maudling was 'always well informed ... at home in economic arguments and [he] took an intellectual interest in them ...'[11] Despite that, Cairncross despaired of Maudling, and of Lloyd, and said of them that 'Neither had any insight into the mainsprings of economic growth, especially if that is taken to mean growth in productivity.'[12]

Cairncross's criticism has considerable justice, for although Lloyd and Maudling (and behind them, Macmillan) tapped into an idea that had some intellectual merit, neither fully understood the argument. Verdoorn and Kaldor only applied their theories to manufacturing industry, and did not suggest that the results could be generalised to the economy as a whole; today's endogenous growth theories are even more restrictive and apply the arguments only to education, research and innovation activities in the economy.

Also, at the heart of the Verdoorn and Kaldor arguments was the notion that larger factories and larger companies were more efficient; so economic growth was beneficial through an 'economies of scale' route. But when Lloyd and Maudling pumped demand into the economy through tax cuts, spending rises, lower interest rates and the relaxation of restrictions on bank lending, there was no justification for assuming that exploitable economies of scale would quickly result. The policy was just not fully thought through. The dash for growth, on its own, was clearly a mistake.

The abyss, and after

The challenge to Labour was to do better. Maudling had been too confident about the beneficial impact of faster economic growth on productivity and hence inflation, and he had been insufficiently disturbed by the threat that any productivity gains would be wiped out by increased wage claims, consequent on lower unemployment. In 1964 the incoming Labour Government promised to address these issues. Labour offered a National Plan that would set out a rational long-term path for the economy to follow; and to buttress it, Labour promised to negotiate with the trade unions a voluntary code of wage moderation.

In a disturbing parallel to the 1997 promises of Tony Blair's administration, the new government also said that it would provide help to high technology industries and to exporters, promote increases in research and development and in vocational training, improve the educational system, and thereby restructure the economy. Harold Wilson even created two special ministries, one dealing with the National Plan and incomes policy, and one dealing with technology, to make it all happen. And he appointed George Brown and Tony Benn to run the new ministries.

Whether, given a favourable background, any of these Labour ideas would have worked is debatable but also academic, since the new administration clearly did not have a favourable background to work from. It had inherited from Reggie Maudling a balance of payments problem that demanded immediate action, yet the new government resolutely refused to pursue either of the two policies – devaluation or deflation – that might have had a chance of easing or even resolving the problem. Had the Tories been re-elected then Maudling would quite possibly have floated or devalued the currency: Labour in general and Harold Wilson in particular was determined to do no such thing – and equally determined not to deflate. A crisis was thus inevitable, literally from day one: something which, as has already been noted, the civil servants understood but about which they kept quiet.

The first exchange-rate crisis came in November 1964, and the following July there was another one, and then another one in July 1966. The Government responded with a tax on imports and other tax rises, modest but nevertheless unpopular spending cuts, interest rate rises, and, at the insistence of the American Government, a six-month statutory freeze on pay rises.

The particularly severe deflationary package introduced in 1966 represented the end of the expansionary policy phase which had existed since at least 1962 and Selwyn Lloyd's removal, and perhaps since 1956 and Peter Thorneycroft's resignation. The package made a mockery of the National Plan, which was all but abandoned, and George Brown tendered his resignation from government, but instead moved to the Foreign Office. (The other principal planning minister, Tony Benn, established a pattern for the future, and did not resign.)

It all helped, but not enough; and in November 1967, following yet another currency crisis, the Government devalued sterling. By then, unemployment had burst the half million barrier. The world had changed, and not for the better. The Chancellor, Jim Callaghan, knew it, but did not understand why or what to do. In close anticipation of events under Norman Lamont, Callaghan had watched the official reserves drain away, thanks to an overvalued exchange rate fixed for him by his Prime Minister; and he had watched and watched, and (partly because, as in Lamont's time, the Government's majority was so slender) he had done very little.

Callaghan soon swapped jobs with Home Secretary Roy Jenkins, who proved to be much tougher on public finances (too tough perhaps), but who failed to grasp control of the most important item on the political agenda: policy towards the trade unions. Jenkins was not even consulted when Harold Wilson and Barbara Castle decided to use legislation to improve the framework for industrial relations, an initiative that lost the Government the support of the trade unions for its incomes policies. And Jenkins stood on the sidelines when Jim Callaghan shamelessly attacked Wilson and Castle in public, thereby costing the Government its little remaining public support. With Callaghan's help the trade unions were now undeniably out of control, and by 1970, Labour was out of office.

The next decade would be dominated by problems with inflation. The unions were not wholly or even mainly to blame for that, but nor were they the innocent victims that they outrageously claimed to be. A better government would have helped. Ted Heath entered office intending to reverse the Wilson/Castle defeat and curb trade union power through legislation, but he also wanted to maintain low inflation through voluntary wage restraint, even though it was abundantly clear from Labour's experience that statutory controls over union power precluded voluntary cooperation over wages restraint. As if that contradiction was not enough, the new Prime Minister also wanted to reduce unemployment while simultaneously reducing inflation. This was the politics of Houdini; but nimble is probably not an expression that anybody has ever used of Ted Heath – 'a good man without fingertips', as Edward Pearce says.[13] His government never stood a chance.

Nor as we noted in Chapter 5 did the Conservative Government have much in the way of ideas. The Tories fought the 1970 election on a manifesto that promised to disengage government from the workings of the economy and promote free enterprise. It was not a policy that they had thought through in any detail, nor was it one to which they had any very deep commitment. Its main purposes were to distinguish the Conservatives from Labour and to give the party faithful something to incant. The policy of disengagement did not tell them what to do when faced with a 'new and ... baffling combination of evils' as Tony Barber put it in his first Budget – high unemployment combined with high inflation (and he could have added, problems with the trade balance and with public finances too).[14]

If Reggie Maudling had been Chancellor he might have had some idea what to do. But when Iain Macleod had died the job had gone to Tony Barber – a clever man but lacking, as we have already noted, the intellectual self-confidence of either Macleod or Maudling. So Heath received no policy proposals to conflict with those of his Cabinet Secretary, William Armstrong, who clearly thought that the country should be run in the same way as the Government was run. All permanent secretaries are accustomed to issuing instructions, and then taking it for granted that the instructions will be implemented after a due process of decent bureaucratic delay. That was how Heath, advised by Armstrong, ran his administration. The Government became as interventionist as its predecessors, yet even more insensitive, and more out of touch.

Ted Heath's administration was also an unlucky government. In 1972, with a favourable balance of payments position and mounting unemployment at home, it initiated another inflexion in the British economic policy regime, corresponding to those of 1951, 1962 (or 1958 if Thorneycroft's departure is rated more important than Lloyd's) and 1966. It embarked on reflationary policies at exactly the wrong time: just before world commodity prices and then oil prices soared, and it opted for an extreme rate of reflation that would have been questionable even without the external problems. The resultant period of balance of payments problems and hyper-inflation was almost without precedent, and would have been hard to deal with at the best of times, but the poor industrial relations bequeathed by the previous Labour administration clearly made matters a lot worse.

Furthermore, the Heath government had a knack of making its own bad luck worse. In the autumn of 1971 Tony Barber authorised a shift in the methods of controlling the rate of growth of bank lending, towards one that fostered increased competition between the hitherto highly regulated high street banks. As Chapter 1 recounted, the result was a big surge in bank lending, just when the other inflationary factors were kicking in. It was not a clever move, and should have been spotted at the time.

From about the middle of 1972 onwards, the Heath government aimed to use incomes control – statutory if necessary – to reduce inflation, despite having introduced a very provocative Industrial Relations Act in 1971, and despite also pursuing a remarkable white-knuckle growth target of no less than 5 per cent a year, in an effort to get unemployment down to about half a million. In October 1973 Opec hiked oil prices, and the National Union of Miners (NUM) rejected a 13 per cent pay offer and introduced an overtime ban. The next month, Heath and Armstrong introduced a state of emergency. Tony Barber raised interest rates and reversed the 1971 relaxation of bank lending. In January 1974, the NUM voted to strike and a few days later the Prime Minister called a general election. Shortly after, and much to his own amazement, Harold Wilson returned to Downing Street.

For a while the new Chancellor, Denis Healey, set about making matters worse. Although the industrial relations climate was initially a little easier than it had been, nothing fundamental had improved, and in any case there were major problems with both the balance of payments and inflation. Yet Healey authorised large increases in state spending and an unsustainable rise in government borrowing, and blamed the economy's problems on others: the mess bequeathed to him by the Tories (although from 1970 to 1974 they had pursued much the same policies that Labour would surely have adopted); international events; poor Treasury advice; and the emergent irresponsibility of the trade unions.

The Healey spending boom produced a lot of criticism at the time. There was a general sense of alarm in the country, well articulated by two Oxford economists, Robert Bacon and Walter Eltis, who wrote a series of articles for the *Sunday Times* (later turned into a book) in which they argued that the British economy had long suffered from a tendency for excessive public spending ('non-market' in their typology) to crowd out private sector entrepreneurial activity, thereby depressing the sustainable growth rate of the economy.[15] Meanwhile two American economists, Karl Brunner and Alan Meltzer, wrote an article in *The Banker* which received a lot of City attention, and which argued that public sector borrowing (as opposed to spending, the Bacon and Eltis subject) also tended to crowd out private sector activity.[16] Both arguments were well received: indeed Bacon and Eltis's work provoked a response in the *Sunday Times* from Denis Healey himself, in which the Chancellor at least partially accepted their view.

Neither analysis has exactly stood the test of time unscathed, with the Bacon and Eltis argument the target of considerable academic scorn.[17] Even so, there is no doubt that Healey's public sector spending boom, like the Barber private sector boom that preceded it, helped to generate an immediate and severe crisis in the economy, as imports poured in and pay claims rocketed. In 1976 the crisis obliged Denis Healey to draw up plans for severe offsetting deflationary policies, geared around reversing the earlier spending increases. But the Cabinet, lacking leadership from the new Prime Minister, Jim Callaghan, rebelled. Healey stood his ground, and Callaghan eventually stood by him. By then international confidence in sterling was, not surprisingly, almost non-existent. So Healey obtained emergency funding from the IMF, in return for a promise to get the situation under control. International confidence rallied, helped by the arrival of the first drops of North Sea oil. Inflation fell. For a short while it looked as if the situation had stabilised.

But the unions were livid about Healey's spending cuts, and about the fact that the Government was more willing to jump to the IMF's tune than to their own. They were willing to agree to some degree of wage restraint, but not lightly so: they made Healey, charged with the negotiations, sweat for every percentage point of moderation. Even then, the moderation was more on paper than in fact, and the Chancellor could not prevent inflation from rising once again. When in late 1978 the Prime Minister unilaterally announced his unrealistic 5 per cent norm for pay rises, Healey was appalled: he knew that the unions would use it to justify abandoning all cooperation. There followed the Winter of Discontent, with its rising pay demands, lengthening and unpleasant industrial disputes, attitudes of class warfare, and its patently exhausted Prime Minister and Chancellor. 'Labour Isn't Working,' said Saatchi and Saatchi, on the Tories' behalf. They had a point, and the electorate agreed.

The Thatcher revolution and its legacy

Unemployment was coming down when Geoffrey Howe took over in May 1979, although it was still a staggering 1.25 million people. But by the time Howe left the Treasury, in June 1983, there were over 3 million people unemployed, a figure that no previous Chancellor would have thought remotely tolerable. If a Chancellor's job is to run the economy in such a way that most people who want work can find it, then Howe was surely the greatest disaster of the post-war era. Maybe Labour hadn't been working, but the Tories were quite literally twice as bad.

Indeed, some Conservative ministers thought so and said so, and duly became ex-ministers. For they had missed the point. As we noted in Chapter 5, the Chancellor and the Prime Minister had consciously decided to risk anything where unemployment was concerned, in the name of changing the underlying psychology of the economy. They did not expect that unemployment would pass 3 million, but if it did, then so be it. Some ministers did not care, may even have relished the pain – after all, not all politicians are nice people. Others, not least the Chancellor, did care but believed that the situation was not their fault; or that if it was, then it was merely a temporary evil that would in time contribute to a permanently lower unemployment level. In his own eyes, Howe was a good guy, not a bad one.

Inflation fell during Geoffrey Howe's Chancellorship, although after an initial period when it went up, not down. Then during the Chancellorship of Nigel Lawson unemployment fell sharply without any new severe problems with inflation, which seemed to exonerate the much-maligned policy of Monetarism – at least to those people not much affected by the sense of civil collapse that had been as pervasive under the new Tory Government as under the old Labour one. The experience had been a nasty one, but it kind of looked as if psychology had changed as a result. And indeed wage demands did moderate, and the unions did find themselves emasculated (through, for example, the demise of the closed shop, but also through the sheer decline in their membership). But the Thatcher government was in part saved by increasing employment in service sector activities, for which it can claim little credit, and which helped to offset manufacturing job losses. The new jobs were often less secure and less well-paid than the old one, taken by women, and lacking trade union representation, and that made it possible for employment to grow without engendering a revival of inflation.

For a time, Lawson was widely regarded as the most successful Chancellor in living memory. Then inflation, public finances and the balance of payments all began to deteriorate, and the fall in unemployment was eventually recognised for what it always had been: the consequence of a profligate boom of precisely the kind that Chancellor after Chancellor had repudiated in name, if not in practice. Just before the end of his Chancellorship Lawson tightened policy in a belated attempt to correct his error, and John Major and Norman Lamont followed through; none got many thanks, and unemployment climbed back towards 3 million.

The increased unemployment sorted out the problem of inflation, some highly unpopular tax rises got public finances under some semblance of control, and the improvement in competitiveness after sterling left the ERM helped with the balance of payments, boosted output and turned rising unemployment into falling unemployment. This, it seemed, was the real legacy of Thatcherism: a rapid return to old stop-go policies, and hence no real legacy at all from the point of view of improving macroeconomic management. The new Chancellor, Ken Clarke, did not protest: he was the happy beneficiary of the start of the new upswing; but the electorate, its confidence severely dented, recognised a government that did not really know what it was doing, and asked it to leave.

Jim Callaghan and Denis Healey had both inherited an economy that was growing too fast and that needed to be dampened down. Both delayed acting, indeed made matters worse by fiscal irresponsibility, and thereby helped to create crises that would cause lasting damage to the reputation of their party and contribute to their governments' subsequent election defeats. Gordon Brown had read his history and was keen not to repeat the experience. He resisted pressure for increased government spending and increased borrowing: indeed he stood still while public finances soared into huge surpluses. He gave the Bank of England responsibility for the management of inflation, thereby cheering up the business community and the financial markets no end, and he introduced a whole range of carrot and stick schemes to attract or compel the unemployed into work. Unemployment, which was already below 2 million and falling fast, was now set to decline even faster.

Apart perhaps from Nigel Lawson, no Chancellor since the Second World War has entered office with so clear an idea of what he wanted to do as Gordon Brown. His policies have been thoughtful, un-doctrinaire (and hence 'post-Thatcherist' in more senses than one) and undeniably successful. But Brown has also been superbly lucky with his timing, and that probably accounts for the larger part of his success. Ken Clarke spent much of his time as Chancellor rebuffing the Bank of England's unsubstantiated belief that inflation in Britain was about to soar and that interest rates needed to rise. His arguments, everybody said, were politically tainted, but Clarke was right and the Bank was wrong. As Chapter 6 noted, the world had entered a new era of low inflation in which Britain was a participant. Markets for raw materials, manufactured goods, services, money and financial assets, and for labour, were all now more open and liberalised than they had been at any time in living memory. In such a world, inflationary pressures were low: it was a good time to be Chancellor. Clarke gained from it briefly: Brown for much longer.

Who did Brown have to thank for this? Geoffrey Howe, Nigel Lawson and indeed just about every minister from the previous Conservative administrations of Margaret Thatcher and John Major can claim some credit, not for their flirtation with Monetarism, but for their pro-market reforms – privatisation, trade union legislation, financial and other deregulation, cuts in tax rates and benefits, and the contracting out of former public sector activities.

These initiatives were not without cost and many were crazy: privatisations which simply turned public sector monopolies into private sector ones achieved little, for example, and had to be rethought later, and it was only in the late eighties that the Government lifted its eyes above narrow market economics and showed any regard for the importance to growth of education and vocational training, with the introduction of the Technical and Vocational Education Initiative and the Education Reform Act. But from the point of view of keeping inflation low, the market reforms were more useful than anything done at the macroeconomic level. And although it could be said that pre-Brown Conservative ministers were merely participants in a larger American-led global policy change, they were nevertheless active participants, and often proselytisers too. They bequeathed a valuable gift to their New Labour successors.

Adding to these benefits, as we also noted in Chapter 6, have been the gains that have arisen from the new information and communications technologies, which improve economic performance in much the same way that new transport technologies (steam trains, steam ships, jet aircraft, and so on) did in the past – but with the added twist that they are so effective at lowering costs that they too are helping to keep inflation in check. It is also possible that the new technology is helping to repair the economic damage caused by the negative side of market liberalisation: for increased competitive pressure can often be a severe deterrent to investment in innovation, as firms sacrifice their capital spending in order to save costs. (Significantly, business investment was low in the early years of the Thatcher government and only recovered when the pressure from the Treasury was taken off.) Even if the new technology is not actually *raising* growth, about which it is too early to say, it is certainly helping to keep growth going.

The ERM episode

Gordon Brown, like Ken Clarke before him, has also clearly enjoyed the fruits of sterling's September 1992 departure from the Exchange Rate Mechanism (ERM) of the European Monetary System. Membership of the system had involved an uncompetitive exchange rate, and high (although not sufficiently high) interest rates to support the currency against downwards pressure in the markets. Between them, these factors severely deflated the economy, especially since they came on top of the fiscal squeeze that was still being used to unwind the profligacy of Chancellor Lawson. Departure meant a corresponding boost to the economy, and an easy time for whoever was lucky enough to be Chancellor.

The ERM had first been put together when Denis Healey was Chancellor. As Chapter 2 reports, Healey rejected entry. In his memoirs he offers technical reasons for his decision, but one suspects that there were political considerations too. Healey had enough on his plate, trying to keep unions, employers, Cabinet colleagues, backbenchers and the Opposition under control; he cannot have welcomed the idea of another constraint on his actions. As somebody whose attitudes towards Europe had always been lukewarm, Healey was also distrustful of the purely political arguments for entry; and maybe he was influenced by the fact that his old rival Roy Jenkins had been one of the system's original sponsors.

Healey's opposition to ERM was continued by Geoffrey Howe, on the perfectly correct argument that membership of the system was incompatible with any serious attempt to run a Monetarist economic policy, and that view was also held by Nigel Lawson, until his abandonment of Monetarism in the mid eighties. Lawson could not, however, persuade Margaret Thatcher. His successor, John Major, favoured ERM because Treasury officials did, and proved better at weakening the Prime Minister's resolve than his confrontational predecessor. Major got his way, and sterling joined the ERM in October 1990, at an exchange rate high enough to cause a serious threat to British industry, and much higher than the markets would soon believe could be sustained.

Within a year and a half, the only rational way forward was a realignment of sterling within the ERM. Apparently nobody in government, whether minister or official, had the clarity of mind to see that imperative, let alone persuade colleagues to act upon it. Nothing was done, and eventually confidence became so weakened that withdrawal became a more attractive option than realignment. The damage to the reputations of John Major and Norman Lamont was mockingly balanced by the boost that the subsequent recovery gave to the reputations of Ken Clarke and Gordon Brown. Norman Lamont remarked that it hardly seemed fair. Critics said that he still hadn't quite got the hang of politics.

Enemies of Clarke and Brown comforted themselves with the thought that, in time-honoured fashion, an exchange-rate decline followed by sustained economic expansion would lead to inevitable problems with inflation. The Bank of England was sure of it. Having recently been given the freedom to make its views public, it kept on warning of inflationary problems ahead. Yet the inflationary surge always remained in an imminent future that was never quite reached. Sustained growth with low inflation: it was almost as if the remedial action of the Howe years had at last led us to a new period, in which sustained low unemployment was once again a realistic possibility in the UK. The world had shifted: things at last were better.

Underlying forces?

The way in which economists usually portray this sequence of events is in terms of a shifting trade-off between unemployment and inflation.[18] Some Chancellors have held office in periods when a low rate of unemployment was associated with low and stable inflation, and hence could be easily sustained. Other Chancellors have run the Treasury in periods when even quite high unemployment seemed unable to prevent high and accelerating inflation, thereby making low unemployment very hard to sustain, and making the Chancellor's lot an unhappy one.

So perhaps these differences in historical period determine whether or not any particular Chancellor is successful in the pursuit of low unemployment, rather than the day-to-day policies of the Chancellor himself. The way to be a good Chancellor, it would seem, is to hold office at the right time. So some humility please, Gordon Brown.

On that basis it was better to be Chancellor before the mid sixties than for several decades after, because it was in the sixties that the level of unemployment needed to restrain inflation (the 'non-accelerating rate of unemployment' or NAIRU) began to rise.

Behind the jargon lies a more obvious phenomenon: a rise in trade union militancy, and consequent upward pressure on wages. In the early sixties the old Conservative administration lost its way and then its legitimacy; and a generation of workers who had lived through the hardships of the thirties passed into retirement, to be replaced by young people who were more assertive, who took full employment for granted, and who believed that, regardless of their own behaviour, their jobs could and should be guaranteed by their employers and by government. The development of a decentralised wage bargaining system weakened the power of the TUC, and hence its ability to deliver wage moderation, while Britain's unsophisticated employers showed little ability to manage themselves out of the problem. The Wilson government bungled first the economy, then incomes policy and then trade union reform, and hence threw away its own authority. All of that occurred against a background of social unrest elsewhere in Europe and in the United States. Wage claims and the strikes that accompanied them became steadily more outrageous, and the Wilson and Heath governments in turn proved increasingly inept at managing the situation.

Something else went wrong. The international economic boom of the fifties drew towards a close, reducing the rate at which the British economy could expand without some radical improvement in its underlying efficiency. As has already been noted, economic expansion in the UK had hitherto been highly dependent, not so much on Keynesian demand management, as on growth in world trade (and before that, post-war reconstruction).[19] Now world trade was slowing, and Britain was losing its share of that trade. So, just when domestic aspirations accelerated and discipline broke down, the British economy's ability to deliver rising real incomes diminished. Nominal wages accelerated, and different Chancellors at different times allowed unemployment to rise to choke off the inflation, only to find that the level of unemployment *needed* to rein back the wage rises was rising just as fast as the *actual* rises in unemployment. In desperation, successive governments tried to impose wage restraint via incomes policies, but found that at best they merely postponed problems by a year or two. At worst they added to the adversarial atmosphere of the age: ironically so, given the attendant exhortations for everybody to pull together. The whole process reached its apogee in the Winter of Discontent, and the consequent defeat the next spring of the Callaghan government.

Geoffrey Howe laments that when he was Chancellor, relations between the Government and the unions (as between the Government and others) were so adversarial. But the need to change the psychology of the nation was real enough, and it is hard to see how this could have been done without making enemies of the trade unions. For their part, the unions were in no hurry to concede defeat.

This conflict occurred against a worsening macroeconomic background. Although, as we noted above, Howe inherited declining unemployment, this was at the cost of a worsening inflation outlook. In other words, the rate of unemployment needed to secure lower inflation was still rising, and it continued to rise for the next year and a half, as unions demanded increasingly large wage premiums for their members compared with non-unionised workers and those out of work. (The unions also demanded higher benefits for the unemployed and higher state pensions, but nobody seriously believed that these were at the top of their shopping lists.) So Margaret Thatcher and Geoffrey Howe took what was literally a 'double or quit' gamble, and imposed increasingly tough monetary or fiscal policies. The Employment Secretary, Jim Prior, backed them up with a series of restrictions on trade union powers, even though he, like others, expressed alarm at the thrust of macroeconomic policy.

Chancellors: villains or bit-players?

One story behind all of this would seem to go along the following lines. In the Treasury in the early 1980s, an over-naïve application of rather crude free-market ideas replaced the over-naïve application of over-simplified Keynesian ideas that had prevailed ever since the reconstruction period. Both periods saw a great deal of nonsense written, spoken and implemented by academics, advisers and politicians, some of whom should have known better, but many of whom could not have. Even so, the evidence on the reasons for the poor growth of the British economy in the post-war period, and specifically in the golden age of the fifties and sixties when other countries did so spectacularly well, tends to suggest that, in general, poor growth did not primarily result *directly* from poor macroeconomic management; and also that there was no significant improvement in macroeconomic policy design during the Thatcher years, whereas there probably were improvements in other areas, from which Tony Blair's administration has benefited.

As far as the golden age is concerned, it appears that some of the gap in economic performance can be attributed to low rates of private sector investment in plant and machinery, and that rather more of it can be blamed on poor rates of government investment in infrastructure and in people, poor rates of innovation by British industry, and a general failure to get as high returns from investment as many other countries obtained.

So exoneration for the Chancellors? Not quite. There has to be a strong suspicion that Britain's low rates of investment in infrastructure and in people can be blamed, at least partly, on repeated spending curbs imposed by successive Chancellors of the Exchequer, and by the Treasury's general suspicion of all claims that government investment in infrastructure, education and training generates worthwhile long-term benefits to the economy.

The reasons for Treasury caution are fairly obvious, and perfectly understandable: the need to hold down taxes and borrowing, combined with pressure from alternative spending priorities (and perhaps a less commendable belief on the part of Treasury officials that other government departments are always and everywhere up to no good). But that really just restates the point rather than removes it, and raises a question of whether past Chancellors just did not understand the need for more substantial investment in these areas, or whether they understood, but were too weak to deliver, or whether their policy priorities were simply different to those that we think they should have had.

Where poor rates of investment in plant and machinery, inadequate innovation by British industry, and the general failure of companies to get high returns from investment are concerned, it is less obvious that the Chancellors are even partly to blame. Even here, however, high corporate tax rates, high interest rates, and vetoes on adequate government support for industry may all have contributed to such problems.

A third observation may be more important than these two. For much of the post-war period, a large proportion of British managers seemed to be peculiarly reluctant to force through productivity rises, to fully exploit the benefits of new technology, and indeed to innovate generally, when compared with managements abroad. And as noted already in this chapter, the explanations for this are likely to have included a reluctance to upset employees (and especially unions), a low risk that under-performing managers would lose their jobs, and business strategies that focused on selling non-innovative products to secure but low-growth markets, using low-skill labour and low-skill management (i.e. themselves).

For this third set of failings even more than the first two, no Chancellor would be keen to accept primary responsibility. And nor indeed should we primarily blame Chancellors for such problems. But we can still blame governments for not seeing or addressing the problems, and we may well wonder whether such myopia or complacency was in part due to the repeated insistence of Chancellors of the Exchequer that resolving their own macroeconomic problems should always take precedence over resolving the problems of other ministers and departments. The hegemony of the Chancellors may not have been such a good thing, if what it meant was myopic government.

Indeed, the obvious conclusion of such an argument must be that, as a group, Britain's post-war Chancellors have done themselves no favours by stifling investment in infrastructure, skills and innovation, since (at least until the most recent decade) the consequence has been a lower rate of sustainable growth than would otherwise have been possible, and hence frequent problems with inflation and the balance of payments. As a result many Chancellors ended their careers with unnecessarily tarnished, even ruined, reputations.

More generally the point being made here is that it is possible that Chancellors prevented the supply potential of the economy from growing fast enough, both directly through their actions, and indirectly through insisting that other departments' policies were of secondary importance compared with the Chancellors' own concerns.

However, an alternative charge is that, from Dalton to Healey, the real mistake that Chancellors made was to pursue full employment. If this simply means that it would always have been better if demand had risen more slowly, then it is a dispiriting conclusion, and one which skirts the real issues rather than addressing them. A more powerful criticism is that the Treasury failed to debunk the trade-unions' mistaken belief that full employment could only be achieved if firms could be persuaded not to lay off surplus workers. What that belief led to was slow productivity growth, which generated slow economic growth, which made full employment *harder*, not easier, to achieve, and which also made low inflation, low taxes and low government borrowing hard to achieve.

The villains here were not only the trade unions, who were merely doing their best within their parochial understanding of the world, but equally the company directors, whose attitudes were often little different to those of the unions. Many believed that they themselves should be protected by trade barriers, cartels, price-fixing and other market curbs, from the risk of losing their jobs. So long as such protection existed, British managements were quite happy to buy peace on the shopfloor by sharing with unions two critical decisions: how many people should be employed, and how much they should be paid. The unions implicitly offered moderation on pay in return for indulgency on jobs.

Poor productivity performance and poor economic growth also meant that investment in industry, infrastructure and people tended to produce poor returns, thereby seeming to justify Treasury (and also incidentally City of London) parsimony and scepticism, and it got in the way of industrial change and restructuring, and of institutional arrangements such as incomes policies which worked in other economies but not in slow-growing Britain.

Academic research since then has confirmed that in the fifties and sixties, British firms frequently failed to take advantage of new technology to improve their competitiveness, because of union vetoes over job cuts.[20] Managers put up with the problem because there were no sanctions against poor performance. In industries such as tobacco, brewing and car manufacturing, the result was a shift in production to competitors, or to subsidiaries abroad.

The situation was particularly difficult because of the prevalence of large numbers of small craft-based unions, which put their own fragmented interests ahead of the companies or industries for which their members worked, and which were able to exercise leverage over company decision-making that belied their own small size. (In countries abroad, where unionisation had come later, the unions were more rationally structured.) When combined with firms that often struggled to get their products sold in the marketplace, this made it very hard for managers to raise productivity as fast as in countries abroad, even when they could be bothered to make the attempt.[21] Worst of all, the ability of unions to secure for their members large shares of the returns resulting from new investment (more jobs than there should have been, although not at especially high wages) tended to dampen the investment rate, and hence dampen growth through that mechanism too. [22]

This was a vicious or self-reinforcing circle: just the kind of problem that cries out for government intervention to break the cycle. The absence of effective intervention raises doubts about the politicians of the period and their advisers, who should have been able to take a more strategic view, but who failed to see with sufficient clarity what was needed, and who failed to provide the appropriate leadership, and to steer unions and management towards more positive ways of thinking. In this context, the Chancellors can hardly be singled out for special blame, although nor can they escape the general censure.

Then in the seventies, when Tony Barber and Denis Healey were at the Treasury, the unions became actively mischievous. They had already brought down Wilson's first government. Now they ceased to be concerned primarily with their forlorn fight to maintain full employment by the cock-eyed mechanism of restricting productivity growth; they developed larger agendas, and an irrational belief that they could raise their members' living standards by demanding inflationary wage claims.

At first the politicians failed to see the full significance of what was going on, and when they did realise, they found themselves unable to deliver a suitable response. One individual was at the eye of the storm: Chancellor Denis Healey. The fact that he took a stand against the unions, with some backing from Jim Callaghan, and the fact that he lost his fight, provided the Conservative Opposition with its vital lesson. Two governments had now fallen to union pressure: Callaghan's was about to be the third. Compromise was clearly no longer on offer. But Margaret Thatcher did not like compromise anyway, and was equally determined not to be bullied – she believed strongly that only by fighting anybody and everybody on any issue that arose could she personally have a hope of surviving at the top. She probably did not realise just how far such attitudes would carry her, nor how much of a bully she herself would soon become.

Up until then, there had always been two ways to break out of the trap into which the economy had fallen. One – by no means guaranteed to succeed – was to put further pressure on the economic system, to force it to change. Early entry into the Common Market might have had such an effect, by exposing British companies to tougher competition. Tough anti-cartel legislation in the UK might have been similarly helpful. With luck, the results would have been pressure on firms to compete via quality rather than price, thereby requiring them to invest in new products and processes, and requiring them to increase investment in skills so that the products and processes could be used effectively. But it would only have worked if government support for industry, for the unemployed and for the regions, was focused on supporting change and restructuring, rather than on reducing the pain caused by failure to adapt.

The second tactic was to refute directly the underlying premise, that the trade unions needed to be humoured in their belief that productivity gains were bad for their members. That meant undermining both the rights of unions to be consulted on manning levels, and the ability of unions, whether consulted or not, to use industrial action to impose their own views on management.

Taken together, these two notions suggest that in 1964 the incoming Labour Government was right to think that demand management alone was not enough, but was wrong on just about everything else. Instead, the policies that this account favours look more like those introduced in 1970 by the Heath government, abandoned shortly afterwards, and then revived in rather different forms by the 1979 Thatcher government (strong on standing up to the unions) and the 1990 Major government (strong on making the economy more flexible and competitive).

The Heath government's U-turn was unsurprising, largely because it did not believe in the new policies that it introduced, and nor did almost anybody else at the time, but also because it faced external shocks that provoked an understandable loss of nerve, and a return to older tried and tested policies. The Thatcher administration was able to get away without a U-turn only because the traumas of the preceding two governments gave it the necessary legitimacy, while simultaneously leaving it without many alternatives. Even then, the Thatcher government depended on the collapse of the Labour Opposition and post-Falklands electoral euphoria to secure re-election in 1983.

Furthermore, the policies of the Thatcher and Major governments tend to look much more rational with hindsight than they seemed at the time, and more useful against the turn-of-the-century backdrop of a global economy that was growing rapidly thanks to an American-led technological revolution, than in the less positive economic climate faced by Chancellors Lawson, Major and Lamont. Had it not been for a strong but stable global economy helping to generate sustained low inflation and low growth in the domestic economy, the benefits of the Thatcher and Major reforms would probably have been more theoretical than real. This makes the Thatcher legacy look more like a necessary condition for the success of Gordon Brown's policies than a sufficient condition.

New Labour – continuity or change?

Finally there is the question of whether the New Labour Government has achieved its own policy revolution. The suggestion in Chapter 6 was that although the origins of the Labour Government's policies are to be found largely in the United States, where Gordon Brown (and Tony Blair) went shopping for ideas once they realised that Labour's domestic policy tradition was devoid of anything useful, there are also domestic origins to the policies. After all, policy ideas require soil as well as seed. These domestic origins are to be found, not in the Labour tradition but from the policies being implemented at the Treasury when Norman Lamont and Ken Clarke were in charge. The abandonment, first of monetary targets and then in 1992 of exchange-rate targets, had left a need for a new policy framework, and first Norman Lamont and then Ken Clarke, guided by officials at the Treasury and at the Bank of England, moved macroeconomic policy in the direction that Gordon Brown himself wanted.

The Labour Government has also embraced most of its predecessor's pro-market economic liberalism. It has, for example, tolerated job losses in the motor industry, in textiles and in farming, that pre-Thatcher governments would not have accepted. But Gordon Brown also claims that he is blending free-market liberalism with a very un-Tory commitment to public sector investment in the long-term supply side of the economy – in education and skills, in the innovation process and in the nation's infrastructure – thereby addressing for the first time the real deficiencies that academic commentators have identified in British economic policy-making.

If this claim is true, then it is not just a rare convergence between what the academics say is needed and what the policy-makers say they intend to deliver: it represents a no less rare determination by a Chancellor to relegate short-term macroeconomic policy-making to its rightful place, and to tackle the bigger issues on which long-term economic prospects really depend.

It would be a pleasure to leave the matter there, without feeling the need to add a sceptical note. Unfortunately, ideals seem to have moved ahead of practice. Gordon Brown's first Comprehensive Spending Review left education, training, business support and transport spending clearly under-funded, while none of the relevant government departments has been able to put together quickly a clear and simple plan of what it needs to do, and then get on with it. The Department for Education and Employment and the Department of Environment, Transport and the Regions have both seemed overwhelmed by their tasks, while the Department of Trade and Industry is now just a small department without much budget, whose ministerial offices seem to provide little more than motel facilities for politicians travelling up or down their respective career paths.

In 1997 Tony Blair promised 'joined-up government' and said that for Labour, the time had come to stop talking and start acting. Numerous White Papers, discussion documents and task force reports later, neither of these statements has been delivered upon. This may be partly because the Chancellor has never built the kind of relationships with colleagues that such a policy regime requires, or it may simply be because 'post-neoclassical endogenous growth theory' is even harder to turn into practical policy actions than it is to say. Whatever the reason, it remains too early to conclude that a corner has definitely been turned in the post-war history of the management of the British economy, whatever Gordon Brown might say to the contrary.

8 How they dealt with crises

Stafford Cripps and the 1949 devaluation

No Chancellor, indeed no senior minister, has the right to regard himself or herself purely as a victim of circumstances or of colleagues' myopia. The general criticism to be made of Britain's post-war Chancellors is that they failed to take control of the course of events and alter the rules. 'Except for me' might be Gordon Brown's response. It might also be Brown's response to his colleagues who find him over-mighty, and to his critics who say that he sets himself even above his rival and sometime friend, the Prime Minister.

To this criticism, many Chancellors might say in their defence that dealing with the great fundamental issues – Europe, the trade unions, industrial innovation, and so on – was never really their main job, much as they would have liked it to have been. Their real task was a more demanding and more vital one: to deal with crises, and it is with regard to that area of work that Chancellors can be most fairly judged.

It is indeed probably true that on the whole we remember Chancellors for the crises that befell their periods of office, rather than for what happened between the crises, and that we tend to judge them on the extent to which they were responsible for the crises, and the ways in which they dealt with them. We also, inevitably, tend to remember most clearly the recent emergencies, perhaps failing to put them into their historical perspective, in which they might look less disastrous, and the Chancellors of the day less peculiarly inept.

The first two post-war Chancellors, Hugh Dalton and Stafford Cripps, both faced traumas during their Chancellorships as acute as any faced by recent incumbents. For Dalton it was the 1947 convertibility crisis, already discussed, which helped to weaken his authority and hasten his departure from government. For Cripps it was the 30 per cent devaluation of sterling that he was forced to concede in

1949. Perhaps what was most extraordinary about that event was that the Chancellor, residing in a Swiss clinic and nursing his health, took little part in the decision. Or then again not so extraordinary: big events sometimes require that the principal actor be safely out of the country. The 1931 devaluation was decided when the imperious Governor of the Bank of England, Montague Norman, was in mid-Atlantic, having been sent abroad for a rest-cure. In 1966 when Harold Wilson was in Washington his ministers plotted about a devaluation, and in 1976 Denis Healey, a good reader of history, turned back at Heathrow airport rather than fly to Hong Kong during a major sterling crisis. And although the exchange rate was not the immediate issue in dispute, it was striking that Margaret Thatcher was in Paris on the day when her parliamentary colleagues decided not to renew her contract.

Stafford Cripps's crisis started in the usual way. During the early summer of 1949 sterling came under extreme pressure in the currency markets. The possibility of a devaluation was widely discussed, forcing Cripps to declare clearly that no devaluation would occur. Having said it, the Chancellor believed that he had to stick to it. Then on 19 July he departed for Switzerland, leaving Hugh Gaitskell, Douglas Jay, Harold Wilson and the more junior Glenvil Hall in charge of economic policy, reporting to Attlee. Less than a week later, on 25 July, Gaitskell, Jay and Wilson met the Prime Minister. Gaitskell and Jay said there should be an immediate devaluation – Wilson to their surprise agreed.

Over the next few days Harold Wilson would change his mind several times, damaging his chances of becoming Chancellor in his own right, and damaging too his relationship with Jay and (crucially) Gaitskell. Attlee, however, quickly sided with Jay and Gaitskell, especially when the Treasury's senior officials told him directly that they too thought devaluation inevitable, and when Dalton (back in the Cabinet as an elder statesman in a minor job) supported the two ministers. On 29 July the decision was taken.

Wilson volunteered to travel to Zurich to secure Cripps's agreement. Attlee accepted the offer – but judiciously arranged for a senior civil servant to travel separately, carrying a letter to Cripps, which the President of the Board of Trade would merely hand to the Chancellor on Attlee's behalf. Cripps read the letter, made no real protest although he still disagreed with the new policy, and merely asked that the devaluation be delayed until the autumn, so that he could accept responsibility for it himself in London.

When Cripps returned in August, he did what he could to persuade his colleagues to postpone the devaluation for as long as possible – ideally until there could be an election on the issue. Majority opinion and the currency markets were both against him. At the end of the month Cripps and Ernie Bevin sailed to America, charged with deciding between them the scale of the proposed devaluation, although in fact the two men scarcely spoke while on board ship. In Washington, Cripps informed the American Government, and on 18 September he gave a radio broadcast in which he announced the devaluation to the nation.

Cripps felt that he had failed, and was wounded by the hostility that he received – Churchill, for example, commended him in private for making the right decision but castigated him in public. Cripps's reputation for scrupulous honesty was now damaged, and so too was the recovery in the Labour Government's credibility that had begun with his appointment as Chancellor two years earlier. He desperately wanted to resign: colleagues said he could not. Cripps soldiered on for another year, his health and his spirit both failing.

The testing of Norman Lamont

These events provide a perspective on similar but more recent episodes. When the currency gets into difficulties, the Chancellor will be blamed whatever he does or does not do, and whether or not he played much role in creating the original problems. Fairness is unlikely to be much in evidence. Most obviously, people today say that Norman Lamont messed up his Chancellorship, without considering how much of his problems were not of his own making, and how they compared in magnitude with those of Nigel Lawson or Geoffrey Howe, let alone Tony Barber or Jim Callaghan, Hugh Dalton or Stafford Cripps. We also perhaps underrate how much greater are the pressures under which a modern Chancellor such as Lamont works, compared with the days of deferential journalists and slow-moving financial markets. And perhaps people today are more likely to take pleasure in the discomfiture of politicians than people of a generation ago.

In 1992 the problems that Norman Lamont faced as Chancellor were especially acute. The economy was in recession. If the Conservatives were to stand a chance of winning the next election, then relief was needed urgently, especially since with only a narrow Commons majority the calling of the election could easily be forced upon them. But Lamont had no room for a fiscal relaxation, because he had proclaimed his determination to reduce the high borrowing bequeathed to him by past policy errors (including, it has to be said, some of his own when he was an over-generous Chief Secretary). But nor could he reduce interest rates, because sterling was at the bottom of its Exchange Rate Mechanism (ERM) limits. The markets clearly anticipated a devaluation within the ERM, but Lamont would not countenance such a step, partly for political reasons and partly because his officials had warned him that to devalue would be taken as a sign of weakness and would probably lead to further troubles and higher, not lower, interest rates. Ideally Lamont, a Eurosceptic of the grumpy rather than messianic variety, would have liked to take sterling out of the ERM altogether. But that was clearly not an option available to him. Instead, all he could do was make speeches, encourage the Bank of England to intervene with what limited funds it possessed, and look for help from abroad.

Lamont's only real hope was to persuade the Bundesbank to relax its policies. The German central bank was deeply resentful that during reunification its Government had opted to allow former East Germans to convert their marks to deutschmarks at parity: an indulgence that the Bundesbank thought was dangerously inflationary. So the central bank was pursuing an offsetting policy of high German interest rates, thereby placing on the ERM the strains from which sterling was suffering. The Bundesbank also thought that the German Government's approach was a disturbing precedent with regard to the way in which European monetary union might be handled. Fiercely jealous of its independence, unhappy with the prospect of being replaced by a more liberal pan-European central bank, and focused by law purely on German self-interest, the Bundesbank was not minded to do much to help the governments of countries with weaker currencies. Britain was one such country; Italy and Spain were others. Britain plus the Mediterranean fringe: the usual poor performers. The Bundesbank would not easily be moved.

In Cabinet and in private discussions with the Prime Minister, Norman Lamont had never been an especially effective advocate of his views. Although his arguments were frequently strong and well made, Lamont lacked the personal authority necessary to make his views stick. He was too quick to get annoyed, and too close to the issues, to adopt the hauteur of Michael Heseltine or Douglas Hurd, or the expansive self-confidence of Ken Clarke. But Lamont's position as Chancellor (and the skills of his civil servants) gave him both status and power within government. So long as he had those, he stood at least some chance of getting his own way.

Alas, being Chancellor of the Exchequer cuts little ice with the President of the Bundesbank. On 5 September 1992, while chairing a meeting of European finance ministers and central bankers, Lamont abandoned his consensus-building role as chairman and, in the opinion of many people there, got carried away. He asked Helmut Schlesinger, Bundesbank president, to cut German interest rates – the sort of explicit demand that finance ministers and central bankers do not normally make of one another in such venues. Worse still, Lamont castigated Schlesinger for mismanaging German monetary policy. Schlesinger, not happy about being told in public by a British politician that he did not know how to do his job, stonewalled. Lamont asked again. Some finance ministers who shared Lamont's views also spoke up, but others who knew that Schlesinger would never succumb to an open assault watched in disbelief as, four times, Lamont demanded a rate cut. Schlesinger hinted at a willingness to cut rates as part of a realignment of currencies, but Lamont either did not notice, or was simply unwilling to accept anything less than an explicit announcement of a change in German policy. It is said that as the meeting spiralled into disarray Schlesinger, furious at his treatment, prepared to walk out. His finance minister, Theo Waigel, whom Lamont also attacked, restrained him.[1] Schlesinger later said that he had never been treated so badly. 'Well, perhaps he had not lived very fully,' remarked Lamont later, unrepentant that he had made an enemy of the only man who could have saved his policy.[2]

But then perhaps Norman Lamont did not want to save the policy. ERM membership had never been his idea, and was a policy with which he had never been happy. It was placing severe strains on the

British economy, his policy-making and indeed on himself. Lamont claims that on two separate occasions he tried to persuade John Major to consider leaving the ERM, and that on both occasions the Prime Minister refused to discuss the issue. 'The only remarks he made about withdrawal to me were to the effect that he wasn't prepared to discuss it.'[3] Others disagree. Certainly Lamont did not appear to push for a realignment within the ERM. Such a step would have been difficult but not impossible – indeed, the Italians did it. Any more general realignment would have had to exclude the French, who were understandably unwilling to devalue their currency in advance of their referendum on joining the single currency, or would have had to wait until after the referendum. Perhaps that was the hope – but there is no evidence that it was ever a plan.

Helmut Schlesinger was about to get his revenge. On 16 September two newspapers, one German and one American, carried an interview in which the Bundesbank president said that the recent ERM realignment, involving only the lire, had not been enough: more currencies would soon have to be devalued. Nobody doubted that he included sterling in his judgement. When Lamont talked sterling up, nobody listened. When Schlesinger talked sterling down, even obliquely, the markets not only listened, they acted. It seems likely that Schlesinger thought that his remarks would be off the record, and would have little impact. Since they were not, and since he declined to withdraw them, that was no comfort. When the currency traders read the interview, they sold sterling. And once they had started, they did not stop.

By eleven o'clock in the morning it was clear to Norman Lamont and his officials that the game was up. They had spent huge sums of reserves and had just raised interest rates by two percentage points, with no impact at all on the currency. This was a landslide, and the only sensible policy was to step aside, suspend ERM membership, and allow sterling to keep on falling.

Lamont could not make such a decision alone. Even the interest rate rise had needed Prime Ministerial approval, as such rises always did before the Bank of England gained independence. But the Prime Minister was anxious to keep up appearances, and decided not to cancel all his other business. He was also determined to involve Michael Heseltine, Douglas Hurd and Ken Clarke in the deliberations on what to do about sterling, dipping their hands in the blood, as Clarke put it, so that none could subsequently distance themselves from any decisions taken by Major, and thereby threaten the Prime Minister's own position. Lamont, aghast at the consequent delay and the huge cost in terms of foreign exchange reserves in defence of sterling, could do nothing but wait, and try to make his ministerial colleagues see sense. Heseltine, Hurd and Clarke were scrabbling around, trying to understand the problems so unexpectedly thrust upon them, and none acquitted themselves with much distinction, insisting on a second interest rate rise, as if determined to maximise the appearance of governmental incompetence. Eventually they relented, and the Chancellor got his way. The next day Lamont remarked to his Cabinet colleague Peter Lilley, 'Now I have got the economic policy I want, I don't see why I should resign.'[4]

One has to say that at no point in the ERM débâcle was Norman Lamont able to set the agenda, either of events, or of European economic policies, or of his own government's policies towards the ERM. Intellectually he may have been up to scratch, but politically not at all so. Later, after he left government, Lamont said that the Major administration gave the impression of being in office but not in power. In Lamont's case and with regard to the ERM, that was more than an impression. It was the reality. Norman Lamont was an isolated Chancellor, close to his officials but not to others, inside or outside his own government. The ERM problems that he faced were systemic, and demanded that solutions be driven forward by a politician able to marshal cooperation within and between governments. Lamont was not such a person.

Nor, as he concedes in his memoirs, did Lamont recognise at the time what a disaster Black Wednesday was for him personally. He failed to appreciate how ridiculous he looked. A swift move to another department, followed if he wished by some discreet briefing of the Press to apportion blame for the crisis on the Prime Minister, and then some policy triumphs of his own, would have been to Lamont's advantage. Instead, he soldiered on, doing some good work to improve the technical conduct of economic policy, but generally regarded as a bit of an embarrassment, and becoming increasingly resentful of his indenture to John Major. Had Lamont been in office in a period of favourable economic circumstances, such as Ken Clarke and Gordon Brown enjoyed, his reputation might have been pretty high. But no Chancellor can really expect such luck, and indeed, few get it. Lamont was unlucky, but he did have a rare gift for turning bad luck to his further disadvantage.

Jim Callaghan – victim or villain?

The acknowledged model of how to behave in such circumstances is provided by Jim Callaghan. When first told in late 1967 by Alec Cairncross, the Treasury's senior economist, that imminent devaluation was inevitable, the Chancellor received the news calmly and with dignity, even though devaluation was a reversal to his long-established policy, and even though he had no doubt that it would cost him his job. 'His demeanour was that of a man who has thought it through, come to a firm conclusion, and is incapable of being ruffled,' wrote Cairncross in his diary. In subsequent meetings the Chancellor remained calm and good-humoured, and although when he made his post-devaluation statement to the Commons Callaghan initially appeared demoralised, he made a strong speech winding up the debate, free of bluster and excuses, sombre but businesslike, and predicated on the common assumption of speaker and listeners that Callaghan would do the decent thing and relinquish the Chancellorship just as soon as was practicable. Dick Crossman called it one of the best parliamentary performances he had ever heard, and before long Callaghan was embarking upon the most successful political comeback of the modern period.[5]

Indeed, such was Callaghan's gravitas that many politicians and commentators speculated that he would be the ideal person to replace Harold Wilson, if the Prime Minister's position became untenable, as seemed possible after he made an unpersuasive television broadcast, telling people that the pound in their pockets had not been devalued. There was no other candidate: in the last few years George Brown had repeatedly made an ass of himself while Roy Jenkins, although a rising star, was not yet fully risen. Callaghan had already offered his resignation from government, but had been persuaded by Harold Wilson to wait and move to another department. Initially the two men had been supportive of one another, behaving well in the face of adversity; but before long Press reports would appear, claiming that for years Wilson had been preventing the Chancellor from running a rational exchange rate policy, so that it was the Chancellor who was the victim of events, and the Prime Minister the culprit. The fact that the author of the most prominent story was the Chancellor's son-in-law, Peter Jay of *The Times*, caused much unease in the Wilson camp, and fuelled anxieties of a coup.

Callaghan himself never explicitly tried to shift the blame for the devaluation crisis on to the Prime Minister – unlike Norman Lamont, who has often said that the ERM was not his policy and so not his mistake. But then Callaghan was in office for the entire period before the crisis came, whereas Lamont had simply taken over John Major's policy, so that Callaghan's scope for disassociating himself from events was clearly much smaller than Lamont's. Which leads back to the questions of whether or not Callaghan was indeed to blame for the crisis, by letting problems fester in the previous three years, and whether he could have acted sooner and hence made the devaluation less wounding to the Government.

From 1964 onwards, the only really effective way to avoid a de-valuation crisis would have been to sharply tighten fiscal policy, with significant tax rises and spending cuts. In this regard, Jim Callaghan was just not tough enough: he deflated, but not by enough, and the imbalances in the economy remained unresolved until the foreign ex-change markets forced the issue. But it would have been surprising if the Chancellor had been tougher, and it is surely unreasonable to blame a Labour Chancellor in the 1960s for thinking like a Labour politician of the 1960s. Callaghan's Labour heritage, the views of his political colleagues, and also the academic orthodoxy of the age, all got in the way of tougher policies.

The puzzle is why the case for deflation was not put more clearly and more constantly by advisers and officials. Perhaps it would have been ignored, but the case should have been put. The essence of the answer has already been given, in Chapter 3: the advisers believed that it would take a crisis before ministers could be expected to make the right decision. So on the evening of their first day in office, when Callaghan, Wilson and George Brown were urgently briefed by Treasury and Bank of England officials about the plight of the bal-ance of payments, the need to deflate the economy was not raised.

The currency markets were already nervously trying to sell sterling on the assumption of an annual deficit of a few hundred million pounds; now the civil servants confided that they themselves feared a huge deficit of £800 million for the full year, with similar numbers likely in later years. This dwarfed the nation's available foreign exchange reserves – an imbalance which, once it became known as eventually it must, would create justifiable financial panic in the absence of any policy response.

The civil servants told the three senior ministers that they needed to take an immediate decision, and offered them three alternatives. The menu did not include the option of deflating the economy by raising taxes or cutting government spending, even though that would have helped the balance of payments and was widely favoured in the City. Instead, the ministers were asked to choose, and to choose immediately, between devaluation, import quotas, or a tax on imports, euphemistically called a 'surcharge', though with strong advice not to take the first of the three options, and with quite a leaning towards the third.

Later that night, meeting privately without their officials present and accepting without apparent question the civil servants' claim that an immediate decision was essential, the three men indeed opted for a surcharge.

So there is no question that at least some of the blame for the crisis that was to emerge was due to Treasury officials rather than to Callaghan and other ministers. The Government's advisers had not omitted to argue for deflation in 1964 because they thought it unnecessary: on the contrary, they believed that it was essential. But the Treasury's permanent secretary, William Armstrong, and his colleagues took it for granted that the Labour Government would not consider such a move until forced by circumstances to do so. The civil servants believed that only in crisis would Labour ministers make the right decision, and so they recommended policies that they knew were likely to make such a crisis inevitable. The policy advanced by the Treasury in 1964, that the Government should immediately introduce a tax on imports, was outlawed by GATT, and was liable to be interpreted by the markets as a panic measure from a government which knew it had to devalue, but which was afraid to do so. The Treasury thus tacitly recommended a policy that, more likely than not, would put the economy on a path towards a major currency crisis. The politicians, knowing no better, accepted the advice.

Accordingly, the Chancellor contented himself with introducing various measures that he had been persuaded would contain the balance of payments problem. As well as the tax on imports of manufactured and semi-manufactured goods, the measures included subsidies for exporters to cover the costs of oil, petrol and vehicle licences, the opening of discussions with the IMF about the use of UK drawing rights to finance the balance of payments deficits, and the cancellation of the Anglo-French Concorde project, which was going horribly over budget.

Already, thanks in some measure to the advice of its officials, the Government felt itself under siege. It had to raise interest rates, and borrow $2 billion from the Federal Reserve. The November 1964 Budget was poorly received by the markets, who sold sterling and declined to buy government debt, for fear of what lay ahead. A few days later in his Guildhall speech the Prime Minister sought to reassure the markets by asserting his complete refusal to contemplate devaluation.

But while Wilson meant what he was saying (he was sceptical of the benefits of devaluation on both economic and political grounds – the latter reflecting his government's slender three-seat majority in the Commons, and his belief that devaluation would lose Labour votes in the repeat general election that he would soon need to call), the Chancellor was secretly having second thoughts. Callaghan was unwilling to be merely Wilson's poodle (having once been Dalton's), and accordingly had already begun to think the unthinkable. It was he who was closest on a day-to-day basis to the drain on the nation's currency reserves, and he who was thus under most personal pressure. Now Callaghan was privately questioning the Government's opposition to devaluation.

So, late one night, Callaghan confided his thoughts to George Brown – that devaluation might be the lesser of two evils. Brown was appalled at Callaghan's heresy, and decided to make the first of his many resignation threats. In the kind of farcical act that was to become so typical of the Wilson administration, he summoned Donald MacDougall – now Brown's adviser as he had once been Cherwell's – from his bath and ordered him to draft a letter to Wilson. The letter was to say that if the pound was devalued then he, George Brown, deputy leader of the Labour Party, would resign from the Government.

MacDougall, still moist from the bath, complied and wrote the resignation letter. But Callaghan took no immediate action, and Brown sheepishly decided not to send the letter. The episode established that although Callaghan was less experienced and less expert than either Wilson or Brown, he was more open-minded. But it also established that the Chancellor lacked his own view, and lacked the ability to dictate the terms of the policy debate. Unsure whether or not to devalue, the Chancellor was not strong enough, either within the Treasury or within Cabinet, to get the question of devaluation addressed by government in a rational way. Just as the civil servants were unwilling to put hard choices to the Chancellor, so he himself was unable to put strong views to his colleagues. He was not yet in command of his brief.

Nor was the Prime Minister about to let Callaghan take control. Wilson's Guildhall speech had failed to reassure the markets, who decided that, in the absence of the cuts in government spending for which they lusted, only an increase in interest rates would provide convincing evidence that the Government was serious. For Wilson, of course, the purpose of his assertive speech had been precisely to obviate the need for such action. But following a modest run on the pound, the markets interpreted a decision not to raise base rates on 19 November (a Thursday, the day when rates were normally altered) as a sign that the Government lacked any determination to defend the currency. Then, when Callaghan ordered an increase of two percentage points the following Monday, the move was seen as a sign of panic. It was certainly an annoyance to the Federal Reserve, which retaliated with a half-point rise in its discount rate. Each of these events weakened sterling and forced the Bank of England to sell foreign reserves to defend the fixed rate. Still the pressure continued, and a devaluation would have been inevitable had not the Bank for International Settlements and central banks in Europe, the United States, Japan and Canada stepped in two days later with loans of $3 billion to save the pound.

This amount was sufficiently large to convince the Prime Minister that there really ought to be no more problems with the currency, so long as damaging speculation could be avoided. To that end, Harold Wilson now made it clear that there was to be no further discussion under any circumstances, by ministers or officials, however senior and however secretly, of the subject of devaluation. Nobody, not even Callaghan, was to be allowed to question this central policy, even though it was one which fell squarely within the Chancellor's remit, and although it was a policy that many colleagues and advisers believed was already undermining the Government's every purpose, and which might yet lead to its loss of office.

In one limited respect, Wilson's judgement was right. Partly thanks to the import surcharge, the current account of the balance of payments was about to move into a brief period of surplus, taking the pressure off sterling and removing the need, at least temporarily, for devaluation to be considered. This was the situation which prevailed through much of 1965, and which persuaded Wilson to seek a general election in March 1966, before the temporary benefits of the surcharge wore off and sterling once again came under threat.

Labour's decisive victory in the election was Harold Wilson's greatest moment, but was quickly followed by renewed speculation over the currency. On the home front, the trade unions had been holding back wage demands in the pre-election period, and had agreed to a system of voluntary prices and incomes policy; with the election now over, they were less inclined to do the Government any favours. In May 1966 the National Union of Seamen, who had seen doctors, judges and senior civil servants all receive pay increases which breached the incomes policy, demanded a deal on pay and hours of work that would similarly break the Government's rules. Wilson, Callaghan and Brown met and decided that if they now stood up against the union, the pound would strengthen; accordingly they backed the employers and criticised the union, most of whose members were low paid and working in difficult conditions. So on 16 May the seamen went on strike. With the nation's trade now blocked, the pound immediately fell, proving ministers seriously mistaken in at least one respect. Harold Wilson promptly called a state of emergency and denounced the strikers on television and in Parliament, but that did nothing to help the trade figures, which began to deteriorate alarmingly, taking the pound down with them.

The seamen eventually gave way, and the strike finished on 1 July.

For the government it was a pyrrhic victory. Frank Cousins, Minister of Technology with a seat in the Cabinet, resigned soon afterwards; as an ex-union leader he felt unhappy with incomes policies in general and Wilson's handling of the dispute in particular. Cousins was not a great loss – he was no Ernie Bevin – but his resignation weakened the Government's relations with unions and provoked a further loss of confidence in sterling. Once again the decline in the reserves was beginning to look dangerous, and the possibility returned of an imminent and enforced devaluation.

In theory, Wilson's prohibition against mentioning devaluation was still in place. In practice, the line was becoming hard to hold. George Brown was generally known to have changed his opinion – something which put the onus on Callaghan to have opinions of his own, and not just take orders from Wilson. Back in 1964 Callaghan had largely deferred to the judgements of Wilson and Brown against whose united belief in the wrongness of devaluation he could scarcely argue, even if he wished to do so. Now, that could change. And since Brown had become an apostate while Wilson had stuck to the faith, Callaghan's opinion was clearly crucial.

Callaghan says that in early July 1966 he was 'strongly against devaluation, and believed it could be avoided, but I reluctantly concluded that our lack of action was rendering it inevitable.'[6] The very conditional nature of this opinion (intellectually more respectable, incidentally, than the more extreme views of either Wilson or Brown) opened up the possibility of the Chancellor being persuaded either way. That in turn led to a period of political machinations which showed the Wilson administration at its most deplorable.

For the Prime Minister, scared of a Brown–Callaghan coalition against him, the essential response to Callaghan's ambivalence was to flush him out and offer the Chancellor permission to take the action he thought necessary to stave off devaluation – action which would inevitably annoy George Brown. Accordingly, on 12 July Callaghan put a paper to Cabinet calling for tough cuts in public spending. Not surprisingly other ministers protested, causing Callaghan to contemplate and threaten resignation. Rather than give the Chancellor the immediate backing that he deserved, Wilson deferred a decision until the end of the month when he returned from a visit to Washington, where he would be negotiating for more help in supporting sterling.

The next day, Callaghan lobbied Brown and won his agreement to a new policy encompassing both devaluation and spending cuts, which Brown presented to Wilson on his return. But Callaghan was not yet a match for the Prime Minister, who promptly persuaded Brown that deflation was a great evil that should be postponed for as long as possible. Wilson said that they two should unite against the Chancellor, and that if Callaghan insisted on resigning then he would be no great loss. Brown could take over the Treasury, just as Cripps had done when Dalton resigned. Brown, giddy with excitement, switched sides.

When presented with this, Callaghan backed down, remaining as Chancellor to fight another day. Wilson told the Commons that deflation looked inevitable, but not just yet. But Callaghan's day came quickly, as he knew it would: within a week the Cabinet insisted that if there had to be deflation, then it should come before the Prime Minister next flew to Washington, since that might help Wilson in his negotiation on support for sterling. This in turn left George Brown feeling bitterly betrayed, and he launched a frenetic campaign to persuade Cabinet colleagues to agree to a devaluation even if it meant Wilson's resignation. He might have succeeded had it not been for the corollary, which was Brown's elevation to the premiership. Those who rejected Brown because he was too right-wing were joined by those who rejected him because he was a drunkard. For the time being, Wilson was safe.

The Prime Minister knew, however, that he had lost the argument and his personal authority. Almost nobody else of any stature except Douglas Jay at the Board of Trade still opposed devaluation. Wilson now started to tell friendly colleagues such as Dick Crossman and Barbara Castle that he too was quite in favour of devaluation, but from a position of strength, not weakness, probably in the spring in 1967. It was a disingenuous claim, but that was what he put to the Cabinet in a five-hour-long meeting on 19 July, at which he sought to regain control of his government. Those who spoke against the Prime Minister on this, the first occasion when a discussion about sterling had been permitted, included influential ministers such as Dick Crossman and Tony Crosland from the left and right respectively, as well as George Brown. Crucially, however, Callaghan went with his instincts rather than his head, and agreed to accept Wilson's proposed delay. So too did Roy Jenkins, the rising star at the Home Office, whose opposition to the Prime Minister might have been nearly as fatal as Callaghan's would have been. Others such as Denis Healey, that supposed paragon of cleverness and toughness, mainly kept their heads down. Brown was thus isolated and outmanoeuvred. He muttered about resignation, but nobody took much notice. The Cabinet followed Callaghan's lead and backed the Prime Minister. There would be no devaluation in 1966.

No devaluation simply meant, however, that the Government was obliged to introduce an emergency package of measures in lieu of the devaluation and to make its decision on the currency workable. The very next day, the Cabinet met again to approve the Chancellor's plan for propping up the pound.

Jim Callaghan's mini-Budget of November 1964 had been broadly neutral in its impact on the economy, even though demand in the economy had clearly been rising very rapidly, thereby contributing to the balance of payments problems, and even though he presented it as a tough Budget made necessary by Tory profligacy. His first full Budget, in April 1965, was a little more clearly deflationary, thanks to increases in indirect taxes buttressed by the introduction of capital gains tax and corporation tax and by cuts to defence spending (including the cancellation of the TSR-2 bomber). In May 1966 the Chancellor then took a further step when he introduced a tax on manufacturing jobs – Nicky Kaldor's ill-conceived selective employment tax. Taken together, these Budgets all reduced the economy's growth rate a little; they did not, however, do much to reduce the country's balance of payments problems, and hence they did little to benefit sterling.

In contrast the July measures, like those that Denis Healey would introduce in similar circumstances a decade later, were more severe than most ministers had been expecting, and perhaps more severe than any since the Second World War. Callaghan cut his spending plans by £500 million, and announced a statutory wages freeze. George Brown said little in Cabinet, implying thereby that he wished to wash his hands of government economic policies. Ministers from the Left such as Tony Benn tried to argue for devaluation without deflation, but there was no suggestion that they expected to win their argument, or that they would make trouble afterwards. More by attrition than anything else, Jim Callaghan had got his way.

Rather than press home his advantage, Callaghan continued with his resolve to try to avoid devaluation, in the hope that the deflationary measures would be sufficient to stabilise the balance of payments and make the currency's value appear more sustainable. He remained convinced that a devaluation would be a disgrace, and tried to avoid it as best he could. For a while the current account did improve before deteriorating again in 1967. A variety of temporary factors were adduced for the deterioration, and right up until the last few days the Chancellor continued to hope that he could avoid humiliation. But it was not to be.

Callaghan's repeated unwillingness to grasp the nettle and devalue (while at the same time being unable to act sufficiently decisively to avoid a crisis) was fed by the apparent inability of his staff to assemble any crushing arguments, in which they all believed, with which he himself could be persuaded, and with which he could at least try to persuade the Prime Minister. A more intellectually aggressive Chancellor might have forced his advisers to recognise that he needed to know how to go beyond muddling through, and towards a genuine resolution of both arguments and basic economic tensions.

Callaghan's opposition to devaluation also had other roots. He was heavily influenced by political considerations: a confused belief that a sterling devaluation would be a betrayal of the trust that the electorate had placed in the Government, and a desire to please the American Government of Lyndon Johnson, which was very averse to a British devaluation. The Americans feared that if sterling was devalued then the markets would expect the same to happen to the over-valued dollar, forcing a currency crisis on Washington; and Callaghan was excessively keen to keep the Americans happy.

Callaghan had been given three years in which to take decisive action to avoid a devaluation or, if not, then to achieve it in an orderly fashion. By always seeking to do the minimum that he thought he could get away with, he failed. The Chancellor's ability to avoid becoming rattled by events, which would heighten his stature after devaluation, contributed to the chain of events that brought the devaluation about. His resignation was, in truth, better deserved than his rehabilitation.

Denis Healey and the IMF crisis

With the benefit of hindsight we can see the 1967 devaluation as the first of a wave of problems to hit the international monetary system. The American fear that if the pound fell then the dollar would follow proved quite correct. Within a few years the whole of the so-called Bretton Woods system had collapsed. When in 1992 sterling burst out of the exchange rate mechanism of the EMS, it was similarly clear from subsequent events that the British currency was a participant in a larger international drama, and that ministers at home were not exclusively to blame for the mess.

Denis Healey had no such excuse. His own crisis began on 28 September 1976. As Healey sat at Heathrow airport waiting to fly to the Commonwealth Finance Ministers' conference in Hong Kong, and then to the annual IMF meeting in Manila, the man who had recently beaten him in the competition to lead the Labour Party was speaking in Blackpool at the party's annual conference. Jim Callaghan, perhaps remembering his own Chancellorship, spoke of years in which Britain had lived in a fool's paradise, and had believed in a 'cosy world ... where full employment would be guaranteed by a stroke of the pen'. He proclaimed that 'We used to think that you could just spend your way out of recession,' and that 'I tell you in all candour that that option no longer exists.' He said that a refusal to face facts and to make fundamental choices had left the economy exposed to inflationary pressures, and that inflation itself caused rather than avoided the high unemployment that his party hated. 'That is the history of the last twenty years,' he thundered.[7]

Callaghan's speech rejecting the post-war belief that, thanks to Keynesian policies, full employment was always possible was aimed as much at the currency markets as at the fraternal delegates. For months, sterling had been under severe selling pressure. The last few weeks had been particularly bad. To stem the flow, Healey and Callaghan had raised interest rates and had authorised large sales of foreign reserves by the Bank of England. Neither had worked. Now the Chancellor was sitting at Heathrow airport, receiving reports of turmoil in the currency markets, and wondering what to do. Decisive action was certainly needed, and perhaps immediately. The flight to Hong Kong would take seventeen hours, during which Healey would have few opportunities to speak to London. So, since no politician on a junket abroad is entirely safe when there is a crisis at home, Healey did the thing for which he will be best remembered: he abandoned his flight and returned to the Treasury. From there he telephoned Blackpool, and secured Callaghan's agreement that Healey should announce that the Government would ask for a massive loan from the IMF.

In his memoirs Denis Healey says that 'For the first and last time in my life, for about twelve hours I was close to demoralisation.'[8] Such a sentiment is understandable: the economy was in a dangerous situation, he was about to supplicate himself in front of the IMF and ask for the largest loan in that organisation's history, and far from supporting him, much of the Labour movement – parliamentarians, trade unions, even fellow ministers – seemed intent both on vilifying him and on making the underlying situation worse. The currency crisis had been occasioned in part by industrial unrest at British Leyland and among the seamen; now the Ford workers announced that they too were going on strike. If anything was likely to undermine any vestigial confidence in sterling and in the Government, this was it.

Healey hid his despair. He offered to speak personally to the Labour conference. Callaghan at first refused, saying that such a step would imply panic, but then changed his mind, perhaps fearing that if Healey was not there, then he himself would receive the full weight of the party's anger. So the Chancellor took on the conference. Since Labour's drift to the left meant that he was no longer a member of the party's executive, Healey had to speak from the floor of the hall, and to limit himself to just five minutes. From that diminished position he told delegates that they must accept '... Things we do not like as well as things we do like'. He spoke of cuts in public spending and of holding down pay settlements. 'I come from the battlefront,' he cried.[9] Some delegates cheered, but many booed.

Inevitably the Chancellor looked slightly ridiculous, but he managed to give the markets some reassurance. Now he had to negotiate a policy that would satisfy both the IMF and his own party. He did so with little support. Indeed he was particularly poorly served by Jim Callaghan, who despite his brave talk at the conference continued in his old habit of not facing up to things. Healey had, the previous year, already switched from expansionary to deflationary policies and these, he proclaimed in Blackpool, would form the basis for a deal with the IMF. But the Chancellor came to the conclusion that, in the negotiations that would soon follow, he would be obliged to offer more. Callaghan was unhappy: he feared the resultant unpopularity and at first he wanted Healey to stick to existing policies, while he himself scurried about uselessly, trying to get the American, French and German governments to provide aid on easier terms than the IMF might demand.

Then on 6 October Healey told the Prime Minister that he would also need to increase interest rates. The Prime Minister refused. Healey said he would raise the matter in Cabinet. Callaghan said he would oppose him in Cabinet. Healey did not need to say that in that case he would resign. The two men parted. Later the Prime Minister sent a message: he had merely been testing Healey, who of course could have his rate rise. It was a strange way to run policy in a period of great instability.

Nor was Callaghan finished. When the IMF team arrived in London on 1 November, the Prime Minister ordered Treasury officials not to meet them. For two weeks the two sides were forbidden to talk. Meanwhile Callaghan's old friend and Healey's rival, Tony Crosland, was whispering to the Prime Minister that the underlying situation was not nearly so bad as everybody supposed. Crosland argued that the modest further tightening that the Chancellor proposed, itself much less than the IMF's demand, was unnecessary. The Prime Minister wavered. Healey insisted that, whatever the underlying reality, the markets had to be placated and that required an IMF deal. Meanwhile the Press (notably Samuel Brittan in the *Financial Times*) said that Healey lacked all credibility and that what the markets really wanted was not so much an IMF deal as the Chancellor's head.

It is clear that Healey won his argument with Crosland through the strength and stamina of his intellect. Edmund Dell calls it Healey's 'supreme achievement', made all the more so by the intolerable strain that the Chancellor was under.[10] The Cabinet tried to wear Healey down, with Crosland joined in his opposition to the IMF deal by other less intellectually able but nonetheless vocal ministers such as Tony Benn. But the Chancellor won, and Callaghan finally gave Healey his total support. On 15 December the Chancellor announced to the Commons the details of the spending cuts and other policy changes that would be made in return for the IMF loan. Although many called it a day of shame, there was no doubt that Healey had turned crisis into triumph.

But as Chancellor, Denis Healey had been partly responsible for the emergence of the crisis. In 1974 and 1975 he had been too indulgent towards spending ministers, too interested in the redistributive role of taxation rather than its revenue-raising role, and insufficiently attentive towards the state of industry and the trade balance. He blames this on poor economic advice, citing technical problems with forecasting and the breakdown of the Keynesian theoretical consensus. But the larger, more important, reason was that the Labour Party had been drifting and that he had drifted with it.

As Chancellor, Healey's inheritance had been especially difficult. Almost alone amongst major governments, Ted Heath's administration had responded to the global recession and global inflation of the early seventies by expanding rather than contracting domestic demand, and so had burdened both itself and its successor with large problems of indebtedness. But Labour had increased the debt burden to appease the unions, with Healey overseeing the policy to appease his colleagues.

Labour had entered office not just ill-prepared for government, but in many areas unwilling to govern. Harold Wilson sidelined strong colleagues such as Roy Jenkins and Barbara Castle to Cabinet posts unworthy of them, while giving the key job of dealing with the unions to the inexperienced Michael Foot, a one-time polemicist now turned sentimentalist. For his first crucial year in office, Foot allowed the unions almost anything they wanted in terms of wages and legal immunities. Meanwhile Wilson allowed Tony Benn to flout collective Cabinet responsibility and campaign for both withdrawal from the European Community and the siege economy of the so-called alternative economic strategy. Benn gained influence outside Cabinet by offering party activists the right to dictate Cabinet policy, and by doing so gave the electorate strong reasons to get Labour out of office as soon as possible and keep it there. Healey made no protests, accepting the curious wisdom of first Wilson and then Callaghan that the honourable course was always to compromise.

In 1975 two significant policy changes offered the hope that the Labour Government would get itself in order. Jack Jones, leader of the transport workers, persuaded the TUC to offer a policy of wage restraint; and Tony Benn lost the referendum on withdrawal from Europe. If Denis Healey could now get public finances under control, then there was at least the possibility that Labour would be able to restore confidence and steer the economy towards some kind of stable growth with relatively low inflation. But Healey lacked the authority to do that, and perhaps also the inclination, until the autumn of 1976, when the IMF provided him with suitable cover.

Geoffrey Howe – double or quit

A common theme of these examples is the personal trauma that they occasioned for the Chancellor concerned. Of the three most recent cases, Norman Lamont, although initially the least worried by the experience, was the one whose career and reputation were most damaged. He was a less substantial politician than Callaghan or Healey, less able to rise above his circumstances or fight back against his enemies. Callaghan made the fewest attempts to justify himself, but instead relied on his strong party roots (and ruthless ambition) to support his political rehabilitation. Healey never had the opportunity to rebuild a band of loyal followers, but then he had never really had such a band in the first place. Like Lamont, he told his story in his memoirs – useful where history's verdict is concerned, but too late for one's career.

In general, Chancellors in difficulty cannot expect much support from ministerial colleagues, and mostly rely on Treasury officials for solace. For those such as Hugh Dalton with a tendency to make enemies of their officials, this can be a bit of a problem. But one Chancellor *was* supported in a series of crises by his officials and his Prime Minister, although not much by other colleagues.

Geoffrey Howe's story is even more remarkable because the various crises of his Chancellorship verged on the intentional. Howe had inherited from Denis Healey an economy in a mess, but, egged on by Margaret Thatcher, he engineered further problems in order to achieve a radical change in the nature of the macroeconomy. Geoffrey Howe implemented policies that most observers thought would make matters much worse. As Chapter 7 recounted, their anxieties were well-founded: unemployment rocketed to 3 million, inflation refused to fall, public finances and monetary growth proved hard to control, and the Government quickly became dependent on disarray within Labour and warfare in the South Atlantic for its re-election. But Howe stared down his opponents, and eventually the economy improved, partly just in a cyclical sense, but perhaps in more fundamental ways as well.

The crisis broke in early 1981 and has been described already. The economy was in deep recession, crippled by a high pound and high exchange rates, and the Government was hugely unpopular. Many in the Cabinet wanted a change of policy, or of Chancellor or Prime Minister – whatever it took. Old-fashioned Keynesian common sense said that the forthcoming Budget should be expansionary; and some Tories muttered that if that meant an incomes policy to avert inflation, then so be it.

But the Treasury was worried that public sector borrowing was already too high, and Monetarist advisers and officials (by now, close to running the Treasury) wanted a cut in borrowing, not an increase. Geoffrey Howe was never in doubt that Monetarist principles should prevail, and that in the forthcoming Budget, steps should be taken to cut public borrowing and hence, with luck, monetary growth. A slower rate of monetary expansion would give him the confidence to cut interest rates, which would weaken the pound and thereby stimulate economic recovery from a position of stable finances. In the meantime there should be only modest help for industry and little to encourage job creation. And in practice any cut in borrowing had to come at least partly from higher taxes. So Howe proposed that his £4 billion squeeze on the economy should be partly funded by a rise in income tax.

The main opposition to the tax rise came from the Prime Minister. Margaret Thatcher was unhappy to adopt a policy that seemed likely to lose the Government the next election, and that might lose her the leadership before then. It is said that she told Alan Walters, her economic adviser, 'They may get rid of me for this.'[11] But she presumably had the sense to realise that if she allowed herself to be captured by her critics, then she would probably be disposed of anyway. Although Margaret Thatcher was paranoid about threats to her position from her colleagues, her response, in complete contrast to that of Harold Wilson or Jim Callaghan, was to face her enemies, and fight back. So she took a chance and approved Howe's Budget plans.

The Cabinet's response has been described in Chapter 4. Several members were unhappy, but none had the strength of character to resign. Outside commentators were predictably divided between those who could not comprehend the stupidity of a government implementing a large fiscal squeeze in the depth of a severe recession, and those who could scarcely believe that Howe had the courage to put fundamental principles above short-term expediency. The *Financial Times* said that the Budget was an admission of defeat, *The Times* that it was the most unpopular Budget in memory, and there was a fair amount of unrest on the back-benches. But on balance the Budget went well for the Chancellor, now regarded for the first time as a tough operator in his own right and not merely as a journeyman politician.

When in July the Chancellor revealed to the Cabinet a new plan to cut £5 billion off their spending plans for the following years he found his colleagues determined to defend their departmental spending targets as if they were protecting the honour of their maiden aunts. Their attitudes were greatly strengthened by the worsening crisis in the economy. A wave of inner-city rioting seemed to reflect, at least in part, government indifference to the plight of the unemployed and disadvantaged. Critics claimed that the Conservative Government had lost touch with basic human values. In such circumstances, the usual Cabinet wets were joined in their criticisms of the Chancellor by more serious figures, alarmed at rising unemployment, falling votes and the prospect of stern looks from their permanent secretaries for giving way to the Treasury over spending.

This rebellion in Cabinet, provoked by economic disarray and by the Chancellor's assault on the fundamental desire of the civil service and departmental ministers to spend money, was more than the Chancellor could deal with alone. Willie Whitelaw gave Geoffrey Howe support, but failed to impress anybody. The Chancellor needed a stronger ally. Fortunately for him, he had one. Whereas earlier Prime Ministers such as Clement Attlee and Jim Callaghan had stood aside at key moments when their Chancellor was attacked, Margaret Thatcher once again stood side by side with her Chancellor. She made it clearer than ever before to all her ministers that she would risk everything, rather than abandon her mission. She casti-gated the rebels, closed down the argument and ended the meeting, delaying decisions until the autumn. By then, she had sacked or de-moted most of the troublemakers.

Shortly afterwards the foreign exchange markets began to sell ster-ling heavily, generating real prospects of an economic recovery. Pub-lic finances improved. Nigel Lawson commended the Chancellor's 'sturdy resilience in the face of the most appalling pressures' and Margaret Thatcher his 'quiet confidence'.[12] By the time of the 1982 Budget, the Chancellor felt that he had enough 'room for manoeuvre' to produce a mildly reflationary package, with a focus on relief for industry. After so much pain, for both the economy and the Conser-vative Government, the Budget was received with huge relief, and the Prime Minister reported that 'the troops were delighted'.[13] Geoffrey Howe was now once again in the Prime Minister's favour, and there seemed at least the glimmer of a possibility that the Conservative Party might escape the annihilation that the next general election had seemed likely to bring.

Conclusions

So faced with a crisis, Geoffrey Howe stood firm and weathered the storm. But his predicament was fundamentally different to those of Lamont, Callaghan and Healey (and Cripps, and Lawson, and oth-ers). They were faced with a collapsing exchange rate that threatened to obliterate the nation's currency reserves: if the situation got suffi-ciently extreme then there was nothing that they could realistically do but give way. The pressures that Howe faced were political and perhaps moral: standing up to them was a viable option even if an uncomfortable one. And had he not been given the clear support of his Prime Minister, Howe might not have done so.

It is in comparison with the early give-away periods of the 1964–70 and 1974–9 Labour Governments, and with the Conserva-tive Governments of 1951–64 and 1970–74, that Howe looks strongest. And maybe even that judgement implies a questionable distinction between strength and obduracy. To repeat an earlier and obvious remark: had it not been for the Argentinian invasion of the Falklands and the disintegration of the Labour Party, the Tories would certainly have lost the 1983 general election, and Thatcher and Howe would have been to blame. Geoffrey Howe's reputation would have been that of a politician who fiddled while the economy, especially the inner cities, burned. His reputation would have mirrored that of Tony Barber, as a Chancellor too weak to stand up to an overbearing and misguided Prime Minister.

But the Conservatives did win, exhaustion and fratricide overcame the Government's critics, the economy improved, and evidence began to emerge that the first few years of 'Thatcherism', while in many respects damaging to the economy and to society, had also produced, as Chapter 6 noted, important long-term benefits.

The central change was one of psychology. Fear of unemployment, and the gradual realization that the Government had little sympathy and absolutely no shame, were new sentiments that had both positive and negative consequences. Some members of the population became dispirited, or used the new social climate as excuses for anti-social behaviour; but others became less demanding, more self-reliant and hence in time more capable and more productive. The manner in which the Government brought about the change was all the more effective for frequently being distasteful, even immoral. The response to the 1984 miners' strike epitomized the new mode of governance, with the police using new powers to prevent miners from picketing peacefully, some coal villages finding themselves placed under near-siege, and violence erupting from both sides of the dispute. The Government defended itself on the basis that its opponents, the miners, were behaving far worse than its agents, the police; which may have been true, but was nevertheless not an argument that any British Government since the thirties had felt inclined to advance. The post-war consensus was definitely cancelled.

Geoffrey Howe played his part in the new way of doing business. His refusal to tackle the crisis of unemployment reduced inflationary expectations and helped to weaken the institutions (particularly the trade unions) who fed off and encouraged such expectations. The result was that future Chancellors, if they were careful, could achieve a better balance of unemployment and inflation than had been available to Howe and his predecessors. (The fact that the next Chancellor, Nigel Lawson, was not at all careful was hardly Geoffrey Howe's fault.)

The two Chancellors who most resembled Howe, in that they kept their heads in periods of great historical crisis, were his immediate predecessor, Denis Healey, and the first of the post-war series, Hugh Dalton. Healey had his IMF crisis and his dramatic turnaround at Heathrow airport: but these episodes marked the emergence of Healey as the man who came closest to saving his government from the annihilation that its enemies were attempting to achieve. Dalton had his chronic currency problems and in particular his convertibility crisis, but before that he had successfully stewarded the economy out of war and into peace. He was not by any means a great figure, and certainly not a likeable one, and he did not act alone; but he did act, and lay foundations on which others might build.

What these equivocal comments suggest, therefore, is that dividing Chancellors into those who were good in a crisis and those who were not is a rather fruitless task. Some like Healey started badly and ended well, others like Dalton followed the reverse trajectory. Some like Cripps prevaricated, and others like Butler allowed themselves to be panicked. Norman Lamont was dealt a bad set of cards which he then played badly; Ken Clarke exuded huge confidence, but was never really tested by events, and so clearly cannot be judged.

Such a conclusion contrasts with the clearer judgements which one can make of Prime Ministers. In particular, we cannot identify a clearly lamentable Chancellor with anything like the certainty with which we can identify a clearly lamentable Prime Minister: Anthony Eden, who marched the nation into a ludicrous war against Egypt, and then took himself off to Bermuda to calm his frayed nerves while his troops were still in danger. Some of the Chancellors may have been just as incompetent as Eden, but none can be so clearly identified as such, because none stands out in relief as obviously as do many recent Prime Ministers. The exact role of a Prime Minister in events is easier to spot than the role of a Chancellor: for Prime Ministers are more likely to take decisions alone, have more capacity to choose which issues are important and which are not, and their strengths and weaknesses are more visible than those of the men who stand slightly in their shadows.

Finally, a Prime Minister usually has power over a Chancellor's career and reputation; the opposite is less true. It was Norman Lamont, not John Major, who on 16 September 1992 stood blinking in front of the cameras in the central courtyard of the Treasury and thereby took the blame for sterling's departure that day from the ERM. And it was Major who would later sack Lamont, for bringing the Government bad luck. Prime Ministers do tend to outlast their Chancellors, and most gain stature (though not popularity) simply from longevity. Macmillan went through four Chancellors, Attlee and Thatcher three each. Even Anthony Eden and John Major managed two each. When things go wrong, the Prime Minister usually outlasts the Chancellor, so that the memory of the crisis sticks to the Chancellor, not the Prime Minister. History is always written by the victors.

9 Resignations and reputations

Sacked Chancellors

Which post-war Chancellors are remembered at all? The three early Labour Chancellors, Dalton, Cripps and Gaitskell, have all been the subjects of important biographies, and as a result are well known to the readers of such books. Macmillan is remembered because he became Prime Minister, and Butler is remembered by aficionados because, despite several opportunities, he did not. Thorneycroft resigned from the Chancellorship, and so was rather hip in the Tory Party in the dying days of the Major administration, when it was *de rigueur* to hold views that excluded oneself from government. Jim Callaghan, Roy Jenkins and Denis Healey can still occasionally be glimpsed, feeding off the young. Geoffrey Howe and Nigel Lawson made and then unmade the Thatcher premiership. John Major and Norman Lamont made themselves look ridiculous. Kenneth Clarke looms large, but only because he is so close to us – he will not be famous two decades from now. It is too soon to say whether or not the same is true of Gordon Brown.

The old adage about Chancellors is that the way to get out with your reputation intact is to get out early. It is a poor rubric, but it reminds us that, despite the job's seniority and power, it helped only Harold Macmillan and John Major ascend to the premiership. In Macmillan's case the advantage was essentially that by becoming Chancellor he ceased to be Foreign Secretary and so was not directly implicated in Suez; while as Chancellor, Major acquired the aura of being, in the expression of the time, a 'safe pair of hands' but did not really display any greater talent for high office than several of his Cabinet colleagues. Jim Callaghan had to wait nearly a decade to live down the memory of his performance as Chancellor before he could inherit, while Ken Clarke is the latest of many Chancellors who must suspect that the job impeded rather than helped their ascent to the very highest rung on the ladder.

Few Chancellors are loved by their parties, even in memory, let alone at the time when they hold office. Chancellors of the Exchequer carry with them an odour of mortality, and of thwarted dreams. Yet the observation made in the last two chapters, that macroeconomic management has probably done little harm as well as little good, despite all the attention devoted to it, and that no Chancellor has been solely responsible for either creating or mishandling a crisis, also leads to the conclusion that Britain's Chancellors of the Exchequer have not been quite as culpable for Britain's poor economic performance as is conventionally supposed.

Most Chancellors' careers have ended painfully. Even so, and given the general discontent with the performance of the British economy, and the nastiness of politics, it is surprising how few Chancellors have been openly sacked. The only recent example was Norman Lamont, felled by an economy unable to cope with the implications of ERM membership, and personally by his inability to inspire any confidence. Even Lamont was not strictly speaking sacked from the Government, since John Major offered him another Cabinet post which he declined. At the time of Black Wednesday, Major made it clear to the Chancellor that he did not want him to resign, probably because so long as Lamont was in place, the Chancellor would be the focus for criticisms of the Government, and not Major himself.

Unfortunately for the Prime Minister, by keeping Norman Lamont, John Major added to his own appearance of weakness. The Chancellor engendered little respect, within or outside the Government, and was unable to establish a decent working relationship with his boss, or indeed with Cabinet colleagues. The occasion in October 1992, mentioned in Chapter 1, when Lamont stormed out of a meeting on government spending with Michael Heseltine and Ken Clarke, was not unique: he did the same to the Prime Minister the next year, and to lesser figures too. When eventually the axe fell, Lamont behaved with considerable ill-grace, which only made him look more foolish, and thereby rather tended to justify the decision. Lamont has confessed that he refused to read the letter sent to him by the Prime Minister, and peevishly threw it away unopened.[1] He made a resignation speech in the Commons which failed to make as much impact as he had hoped it would. He told his friends that he was not bitter 'but both my children told me bluntly that I was'.[2] He got a job with Rothschilds, but lost it because of his tetchy opposition to the Government, and he became a cast member in the dramas of lesser politicians, notably John Redwood.

Norman Lamont was the first Chancellor to be sacked since Selwyn Lloyd in the night of the long knives. Lloyd did not want to go, and unlike Lamont he was not even offered an alternative post. Like Lamont he had not been a huge success as Chancellor, but unlike him he had never really wanted the job, and did not regard himself as especially well suited to hold the position, a view which others also held. Lloyd always gave the impression of trying too late to tackle events which he did not fully understand, and his 'pay-pause' was ineptly introduced in a way which implied that the lower-paid should restrain their pay, but not the better-off (a precursor here of Lamont's VAT on fuel and light). Like Norman Lamont, Selwyn Lloyd was a technical innovator who failed to inspire, and was identified in the public mind as emblematic of how the Government at large had lost its grip and its way. The back-benchers wanted reflation, Macmillan agreed, Lloyd was not keen, and so was told to go.

Macmillan was a cad, who famously treated Cabinet colleagues like servants, hiring and firing them without conscience: when the Earl of Kilmuir lost the Lord Chancellorship in the night of the long knives, he reportedly complained that his cook would have had more notice of dismissal, to which Macmillan retorted that it was harder to get a new cook than a new Lord Chancellor. Even so, it is hard to credit the manner of Lloyd's dismissal. Rab Butler, who had himself been turfed out of the Chancellorship a few years earlier and who should have known better, encouraged Macmillan to remove Lloyd and then leaked the story of the impending dismissal to the *Daily Mail*. Macmillan panicked and sacked Lloyd the following day, along with a third of the Cabinet. A fortnight later, Lloyd agreed to dine with Macmillan, who told him that it had all been a dreadful mistake and that Butler was to blame. Lloyd was struck by Macmillan's 'utter ruthlessness, and his determination to retain power by the sacrifice of even his closest friends'. Macmillan, he concluded, now saw Lloyd as a threat, and was trying to regain his loyalty.

Lloyd was allowed some revenge. His dismissal contributed to Macmillan losing the confidence of the parliamentary party, and when in an act of bathos Alec Douglas-Home replaced Macmillan, the new Prime Minister invited Selwyn Lloyd back into the Cabinet, as Leader of the House. The trouble with knives is that they can be used against you.

Rab Butler was the only other Chancellor to be clearly sacked, although he accepted another job, albeit only that of Leader of the House. The move came after an exchange-rate crisis, when Butler had already lost the confidence of his colleagues and the public, and Lamont-like had come to be seen as a liability (although in those gentler times Butler did not have to face the ridicule heaped on Lamont). Eden would have cheerfully sacked Butler earlier, when he himself replaced Churchill as Prime Minister, but held fire because Butler's wife had recently died. By 1955, however, Eden was both dissatisfied with Butler and annoyed with Harold Macmillan, who was proving to be a thoroughly uncompliant Foreign Secretary. So Eden asked Butler to stand aside for Macmillan, whom Eden insisted had to be moved. Ever willing to be out-manoeuvred, Butler agreed. Macmillan went on to become Prime Minister, and Butler hung around for another decade, until Harold Wilson cut him down and made him Master of Trinity.

The sacking of Rab Butler was a symbolically important event. Butler's should have been the pivotal Chancellorship of the post-war period, setting the economy on a new more optimistic course and rendering him unassailable. Reconstruction was giving way to a new post-Festival of Britain era, and Britain now had a party in government that purported to be pro-enterprise but which, especially with Butler at the Treasury, accepted the necessity to maintain and finance the welfare state. This should have been a powerful combination, and in the sense that economic growth did indeed pick up, it was superficially successful. But even Ian Gilmour, who claims that Butler was 'an excellent Chancellor of the Exchequer', recognises that in the Butler period British economic performance was below that of most other industrialised economies, and that with hindsight, Butler's was a rather wasted Chancellorship. 'Unquestionably,' Gilmour writes, 'their policy bequeathed problems to their successors.'[3]

In his memoirs, Butler says that his policy could be summarised by one word, 'expansion', but that he was himself quite aware that the expansion was only possible if 'the fresh winds of freedom and opportunity were allowed to blow vigorously through the economy'.[4] Yet Butler did little to cause such winds to blow, and little to persuade other ministers. There was no push towards Europe, no anti-cartel legislation, no introduction of full sterling convertibility and no attempt to forge a new political settlement with the unions. Butler confined himself to modest economic ambitions, and even in that regard – Keynesian demand management, plus some cuts in taxes and subsidies – he found the job rather harder than perhaps he expected, and came to seem rather accident prone. He was far more dispensable than he had ever expected to become.

Edmund Dell's view is characteristically uncompromising: he regards Rab Butler as a failure, because Butler was willing to run the economy at too rapid a pace of expansion, paid little attention to sound financial discipline, and allowed himself to be deflected from the Bank of England's objective of moving rapidly to full convertibility for sterling.[5] But Butler was a more conscientious Chancellor than this implies, and was persuaded by the overwhelming consensus of the day that a combination of Keynesian demand management and cooperation with the unions would deliver the best combination of low unemployment and low inflation. The pace of economic demand was no more than was needed to hold down unemployment, public finances appeared to be satisfactory, and convertibility would have placed a great squeeze on living standards, undermining the implicit contract between government and unions.

This implicit contract was something that Winston Churchill was famously keen to maintain. It reminded him of his wartime administration, and also helped him to forget his reputation as the man who in 1911 sent in the troops against the strikers of Tonypandy, and whose bellicosity during the General Strike of 1926 had caused much ill-feeling. In the fifties the leaders of the major unions were men of moderation, and politicians of the time were hardly being unreasonable if they favoured voluntary agreement over tough legislation. There was particular concern over the economic damage that strikes might provoke, which was why in 1951 Churchill gave Walter Monkton responsibility for trade union matters. Monkton was an emollient figure, who until recently had not been particularly identified with the Conservative Party: he had once been an adviser to the Nizam of Hyderabad, and before that to Edward VIII. Monkton made it his business to establish friendly relations with the trade unions and to avert threatened strikes. Everybody agreed: consensus was a good thing, and the Tory Government was right to favour it.

The problem with this approach, when it was over-extended over the next decade and a half, has been discussed already in Chapter 7. The mistaken premise – that the way to achieve full employment was to safeguard existing jobs – appealed to those in the Conservative Party who were, or pretended to be, landed gentry: Butler himself, but also Macmillan, Churchill, and just about everybody else who mattered. Their paternalism, affected or real, manifested itself as a belief that employees should be looked after and protected from disturbing pressure for change (never mind that change might bring opportunities). There were to be no 'fresh winds of freedom and opportunity' blowing vigorously through the economy, as Butler had once promised, only a government in which the ministers liked to dress like Edwardian gentlemen, and liked to make a great fuss about spending the season shooting, rather than in London.

Butler was a gentleman who thought that the time had come for his party to be run by players, but who could not bring himself to be the man to make it happen. His career was overtaken by that of Macmillan, a player who pretended to be a gentleman. Butler said he wanted change, but once in government he never pressed the point: he failed to follow through and develop the radical thinking of his Industrial Charters, and failed to grab control of the party. A lesser man, Anthony Eden, pushed him aside; a less scrupulous man, Harold Macmillan, kept him there.

Resignations

The tragedy of Butler was that he never resigned, and just took whatever job was going. There is a lot to be gained from a good resignation. The Chancellor who most clearly took the blame for a policy failure and voluntarily resigned was Jim Callaghan, and he ended up as Prime Minister.

Hugh Dalton was another who took the blame for policy mistakes: he certainly resigned, and he certainly felt some despair over what had happened to his policy, but whether his resignation was voluntary or whether he was pushed, and if so, why, are fine judgements to make.

The immediate events have already been alluded to. Seconds before entering the House of Lords to deliver his fourth Budget speech (the war damage to the Commons having still not been repaired) Dalton confided some of the contents of the Budget to the lobby correspondent of the *Star*, a London evening paper, now defunct. The Chancellor's speech was remarkably short, less than an hour in duration, but in those days the printed Press were much quicker than they are today to get news on to the streets. Even before the Chancellor was telling MPs about his tax proposals, a few Londoners in the vicinity of Fleet Street were reading the details in the *Star's* Stop Press. For the most part the details were described merely as the expectations of John Carvel, the journalist concerned. But they were clearly too accurate to be just a guess, as rival journalists on the *Evening Standard* and the *Evening News* subsequently realized. They quickly appraised various Conservative MPs of the facts.

The next day a right-wing Tory back-bencher, Victor Raikes, asked a written Private Notice Question about the leak. Dalton readily confessed, and apologised to the House, on whose behalf Churchill then extended to the Chancellor 'our sympathy with him at the misuse of his confidence'.[6] The Leader of the Opposition clearly thought that it was Carvel, not Dalton, who should be ashamed of himself. However, many Tory back-benchers were unwilling to be as magnanimous as their leader towards the hated Dalton. They had him, in Raikes's words, 'wriggling on a hook'. Under pressure from his own party, Churchill now wrote to Attlee saying that the Opposition intended to ask for an inquiry by a Select Committee.

This was an affront to the Government, though hardly a serious one, and sufficient Labour members were more than willing to defend their Chancellor, who had himself been so ready to apologise for a mistake which had been entirely without mischief, both in its intent and in its consequence. Clement Attlee, however, was in a different mind, as were other senior ministers with whom the Prime

Minister discreetly consulted. Dalton had made too many enemies in Cabinet. He had plotted to have Attlee removed, and had made little effort to conceal the contempt that he felt for most other colleagues. A year earlier Ernie Bevin had vowed that one day Dalton would be 'properly dealt with'. Now it was about to happen.

So, when on the afternoon of the 13th, Dalton met Attlee and firmly repeated an earlier offer to resign, Attlee accepted the offer. According to Dalton, Attlee 'was much more deeply moved that [*sic*] I was at this meeting. He said he hated – hated – he repeated this word several times – hated to lose me.'[7] But although Attlee may have said that, he surely did not mean it. Like Margaret Thatcher four decades later, Attlee was unwilling to sack his Chancellor but quite happy to face life without him. 'Dammed fool, always talked too much,' was Attlee's verdict on the episode.

The puzzle is why Dalton offered Attlee such an opportunity. Ben Pimlott's view is hard to disagree with. It is very unlikely that Dalton consciously engineered the crisis so as to provide himself with an excuse to go. Only with penny-dreadful cunning could Dalton have planned to give away his Budget secrets: and if he had done, he might have opted for a more secure mechanism than sending his minder, Douglas Jay, off to get a glass of water, thereby giving Carvel his brief couple of seconds in which to approach him alone in the lobby.

But at a less calculating level Dalton had perhaps given up the will to survive. Just as the months of negotiating the American loan had precipitated Keynes's early death, so the crisis of 1947 had damaged Dalton's health. The Chancellor was taking drugs to make him sleep and others to keep him awake, and he was suffering from a variety of stress-induced skin ailments. The exhaustion that made him bad-tempered and dismissive of colleagues also made him paranoid. Dalton believed himself to be surrounded by enemies, including Attlee and Herbert Morrison, who refused to take the actions needed to avert an economic catastrophe. He believed that, in contrast, his own November Budget was the kind of difficult step from which the others had flinched. So, having had the courage to take the step, Dalton was able to leave Attlee and the rest to get on with things, his own honour perversely intact.

In contrast to Dalton in 1947, Nigel Lawson in 1989 seemed determined to hang on at the Treasury and sort out the problems created by his Chancellorship. But for approaching a year, Alan Walters had been publicly criticising Lawson, even intimating that the Chancellor ought to quit. Since Walters was Margaret Thatcher's personal economic adviser, his views were taken to be representative of her own. Even if Walters was not acting on Margaret Thatcher's instructions, it certainly seemed likely that he was articulating the policies that would prevail as soon as Lawson could be eased out and a more congenial alternative (ideally in the Prime Minister's mind Nicholas Ridley, or failing him John Major) inserted into the Chancellorship. Since Walters was demanding a currency depreciation, there was predictable downwards pressure in the currency markets. Indeed it was that, rather than the humiliation, which Lawson claimed was the factor that made his job undo-able so long as Walters remained.

So on the morning of 26 October 1989 Nigel Lawson told the Prime Minister that he believed it necessary for Alan Walters to leave her employ, and that if not then he, Lawson, would have to resign. 'At first I could hardly take him seriously. I told him not to be ridiculous.'[8] Margaret Thatcher told Lawson that she would not sack Walters and asked him to go away and think again. Lawson claims that the Prime Minister said that 'If Alan were to go, that would destroy *my* authority' – somewhat implying that Walters ('A devoted and loyal member of my staff ... always acted within the proprieties') had indeed been speaking with her authority.[9] Thatcher and Lawson met twice again that day and the announcement that he had resigned was made on the six o'clock news. The currency promptly tumbled and the Bank of England felt obliged to provide support.

The shock was no less marked for being such an obvious resolution of preceding events: although not at all obvious, the Prime Minister claimed, to herself. Then and later she maintained the fiction that the resignation was both unexpected and patently unnecessary, and that neither her own behaviour nor that of Walters could conceivably explain that of Nigel Lawson. She claims that the Chancellor's determination – 'indecent haste' – that the resignation be announced immediately was because he feared that she would speak to Walters, who might resign first and thus deprive him of the excuse he wanted.[10] Why anybody would imagine that she would do that, or allow Walters to do it, is not clear. The point which really seemed to rankle most with the Prime Minister was surely that Lawson had seized control of events, and he was not about to let go. And rightly so: if Bernard Ingham had been given time to brief the Press, he would doubtless have found a way to twist events to Lawson's disadvantage.

As we noted in Chapter 4, in few accounts of these events does Margaret Thatcher come off well, and nor does she deserve to. Yet nor, as Chapter 4 also indicated, should Nigel Lawson be allowed to escape without blame for what happened. He had been a disastrous Chancellor. Back in 1986 his expansionist policies had generated increasing concern in the foreign exchange markets, and his credibility had declined sharply, taking the pound with it. In the September 1986 currency rout, Lawson had found himself in a currency crisis no less serious than those which Callaghan and Healey suffered in 1967 and 1976. Forced to borrow money from the Bundesbank, he had switched from targeting monetary growth to targeting the exchange rate, without telling the Prime Minister what he was doing. To cover his tracks, he bribed the electorate with massive increases in government spending and the largest tax cuts in history.

The result of the 1987 pre-election Budget was predictable: a stunning electoral victory, but a post-election surge in inflation and a deepening balance of payments crisis, both of which forced Lawson to reverse the give-away Budget in 1988, raising taxes and cutting spending. That provoked uproar, and those Conservatives (all of them) who had lionised Lawson for winning them the 1987 election mostly now turned against him, suspecting with justification that he could not be trusted. As the economy slipped towards recession the Prime Minister not surprisingly also became disenchanted. Some commentators believe that she was already beginning to suspect Lawson's secret exchange-rate policy. Already slipping into paranoia, the Prime Minister added Lawson's name to her list of traitors.

For Nigel Lawson, final meltdown began in early October 1989 on the eve of the Conservative Party conference. He and Geoffrey Howe had already forced the Prime Minister to agree privately that sterling would join the ERM, but nothing was happening. On the contrary: Howe had been removed from the Foreign Office, and Alan Walters had been installed in 10 Downing Street as an alternative Chancellor. With its usual lack of tact, and despite the strength of the deutschmark, the Bundesbank had just raised German interest rates. Lawson was obliged to raise sterling rates in response, and the *Sunday Times* published a story saying that Walters had opposed the rate rise and that Margaret Thatcher sided with Lawson only reluctantly. Neither Walters nor the Prime Minister denied the story. When Lawson slipped away from Blackpool mid-conference, the Press reported that he was scared to face party members. The *Daily Mail* called Lawson 'this Bankrupt Chancellor'. His country house in Stoney Stanton was besieged by journalists.

The conference itself went surprisingly well for Lawson, and perhaps in response Alan Walters promptly tipped off the *Financial Times* about an article that he was about to publish in which he called the ERM 'half-baked' and said that it lacked 'even a minimum level of plausibility'. Walters told the *Financial Times* that the Prime Minister concurred with such views.

In the Commons first Neil Kinnock and then shadow Chancellor John Smith mocked Lawson, Smith with particular effect. In his memoirs Lawson downplays the event, describing Smith's 24 October speech as 'witty' and saying that the shadow Chancellor merely addressed the 'confusion and disarray' in government policy.[11] Certainly Smith asked to know who was in charge, Walters or Lawson. But the speech, which was not just witty but coruscating, was as much concerned with the mounting evidence that the economy was in a mess as with the activities of Walters. And Smith's nastiest barbs were thrown at Lawson's own vainglorious claims in the Budget that Britain had achieved an economic miracle comparable with Japan's or Germany's. Lawson was humiliated. That morning he had confided to Geoffrey Howe that he saw little point in carrying on, and the following evening he told the Prime Minister on her return from a visit to Malaysia that Alan Walters was a problem about which they had to talk. The next day he resigned.

Under the circumstances, Lawson's departure was long overdue and Margaret Thatcher's desire to sack him quite understandable.[12] She did not do so for fear that it would undermine her attempts to claim that the economy and the Government were both in excellent shape. But the fact that she allowed Alan Walters to do her dirty work for her does her no credit at all. For his part, Nigel Lawson admits in his memoirs that he wanted to resign much earlier but that he felt obliged to remain and 'undo the inflationary surge over which, regrettably, I had presided'.[13] There is too strong a note of vanity in such a sentiment to allow Lawson quite as much sympathy as one might otherwise give him. Caring too much for your reputation is the politician's quintessential vice.

The other Chancellor who resigned was Peter Thorneycroft, who also believed that he was not being given the support he needed to do his job. Thorneycroft, unable to secure Cabinet agreement to spending cuts, had first threatened resignation late in December 1957. Harold Macmillan responded by urging colleagues to support the Chancellor, but over the next few weeks declined to do so himself. When Thorneycroft hectored the Cabinet in early January, annoying the other members and worsening his own position, Macmillan sided against him. Thorneycroft repeated his threat to resign. Macmillan suggested a compromise, but Thorneycroft reserved his position. Macmillan said that if no compromise could be reached then he would tender the whole Government's resignation to the Queen. Still Thorneycroft would not compromise. But he knew that Macmillan had given him an ultimatum, and so he went back to his ministerial colleagues Nigel Birch and Enoch Powell and asked them if he should back down. Powell, lacking as ever a sense of proportion, claims, 'I put my hand on my left breast and said "It won't do."'[14] The others agreed, Thorneycroft said he would resign, and his two lieutenants said that so too would they.

Quite possibly, and despite the amateur dramatics, the three ministers did not really mean it. Macmillan was about to leave on a six-week tour of the Commonwealth, and perhaps the Treasury team thought that their resignation threat would force him to delay or cancel the trip and parlay with them. Even if they then had to give way, at least they would have drawn a little blood.

If that was their reasoning they were wrong. Thorneycroft was friendless in Cabinet and Macmillan had no intention of making himself the same, let alone friendless with the public. He accepted the resignations entirely without argument, whipped the doughty Derick Heathcoat Amory into the Treasury, made his apparently casual but carefully prepared remark about 'a little local difficulty' and, asking Edward Heath to 'look after the shop', insouciantly set off on his trip, leaving the suddenly unemployed Thorneycroft somewhat stunned.

Rejected by the electorate

A rather larger group of Chancellors, Gaitskell, Maudling, Jenkins, Barber, Healey and Clarke, lost their jobs because their parties lost general elections. Significantly, in none of those cases would one say that the election result was a clear and direct rebuttal of the Chancellor's efforts alone, so much as a much more general rejection of the Government.

In Maudling's case the reverse view is more commonly advanced: that Maudling behaved irresponsibly by seeking to win votes with his pre-election dash for growth, and that it serves him right that it didn't work. But as we have already seen, Maudling was a more thoughtful politician than either he or his critics wanted people to think. Alec Cairncross acknowledges that Maudling was careful about considering policy risks, and it is probably fair to say that Maudling was a careful and thoughtful Chancellor, much guided by economic arguments, and not the irresponsible chaser of electoral popularity that he is commonly supposed to have been. Alas, being careful did not prevent him from being wrong, and did not save the Conservatives from their narrow electoral defeat in 1964, and their more resounding defeat two years later.

Maudling went from office cheerfully enough, and in general losing an election is probably a less painful experience for any minister than being singled out for dismissal. Even so, Roy Jenkins in his memoirs talks affectingly of the embarrassment he felt when, suddenly no longer a minister, he carried his own heavy suitcase ('... off which I had hurriedly torn a 'Chancellor of the Exchequer' label ...') on to a railway platform full of commuters, waiting for the train that would carry them to their jobs, and him to 11 Downing Street to clear his desk.[15] The stationmaster saved the situation by shepherding Jenkins swiftly onto the train, and at Euston his principal private secretary Bill Ryrie was there to meet him 'looking sympathetic and depressed'. Then for Jenkins and his wife it was down to the chores of ordering the removal van, packing and saying goodbye.

Jenkins's stoicism was sustained partly by the assumption, hugely mistaken, as it turned out, that this was a temporary reversal, and that a long ministerial career lay ahead. It must have seemed then that his chances of becoming Prime Minister were still largely intact. In the meantime he welcomed a period when the pace of work might slow. He was conscious of his own role in the defeat – 'It was broadly my policies on which Wilson had chosen to fight and on which we lost' – but consoled by the belief that Labour had deserved to win.[16]

Jenkins describes calling in to see Harold Wilson and finding him 'appallingly battered, but … wholly calm and unrecriminating … He was altogether rather impressive, and the occasion moving.'[17] Denis Healey in contrast says almost nothing in his memoirs about his own experience of losing the Chancellorship and nothing about how Jim Callaghan must have felt at losing the election. One gets the impression that Healey's frustration with Callaghan, to whom he has been loyal ever since, was riding high. Callaghan's post-defeat failure to move aside and give Healey the leadership must surely have seemed like a betrayal. Perversely, Callaghan told Healey that he was hanging on to make things easier for him: 'taking the shine off the ball'.[18] He recalled that in the fifties Attlee had hung on to the leadership to prevent it falling into Morrison's hands, and that as a result Gaitskell had inherited. Yet Attlee's delay enabled the rift between the Bevanites and the Gaitskellites to deepen, and thus kept the Tories in power for thirteen years; Callaghan's delay had a closely equivalent effect, with a Labour schism, Conservative rule for the next seventeen years, and Healey denied the premiership, rather as Gaitskell was.

The reputations of both Roy Jenkins and Denis Healey have risen since they lost office. Both men became deputy leader of their party and produced bold responses to a period of extreme political crisis: Jenkins became the champion of full British involvement in Europe and then of domestic political realignment, while Healey almost single-handedly kept Labour from complete disintegration. Before 1980, Healey had never been much of a campaigner, but as the attacks on the party grew more dangerous, and as the opposition crystallised into a single figure in the shape of his former colleague Tony Benn, so Healey began to tour the country, urging the party not to lurch so far to the left as to render itself unelectable. In the autumn of 1981 Benn even challenged Healey for the deputy leadership of the party. Healey won a large majority of the votes cast, but because most of these were cast by rank and file trade unionists whose leaders felt no obligation to consider their members' views, Healey held on to his post by only a tiny margin.

Denis Healey says, doubtless rightly, that the tough things he had to do as Chancellor had severely damaged his popularity in the party and perhaps cost him the leadership. (In the late thirties, he and his fellow communist undergraduates used to debate the question 'Who will do the dirty work under socialism?' Healey says that when he became Chancellor, he discovered that the answer was 'Denis Healey'.) But it is also possible that the experience of being Chancellor gave him some of the extra toughness he needed in the years to come. And although we should not overstate this (Margaret Thatcher and Tony Blair did not need to be Chancellor to learn how to be tough, while Rab Butler and Tony Barber are Chancellors for whom a roasting at the Treasury did their careers no great favours), it is noticeable that on the two occasions when an incumbent Prime Minister resigned amidst farce and crisis, it was the Chancellor of the day who took over.

Illness

Harold Macmillan and John Major aside, only two Chancellors since the Second World War have really left the Treasury of their own free will. Geoffrey Howe left the linoleum of the Treasury for the marble floors of the Foreign Office, while Derick Heathcoat Amory left government entirely. By a sorry symmetry, ill-health cut short two Chancellorships: most horribly so in the case of Iain Macleod in 1970. The Conservatives had won the 18 June general election and as expected Edward Heath appointed Macleod Chancellor two days later. That afternoon Douglas Allen, Treasury Permanent Secretary, attended the Mayfair home of the new Chancellor's daughter and son-in-law. Macleod, although clearly delighted with events, felt unwell. He had suffered from severe and painful neck problems for twenty years, and also from kidney problems, but this new discomfort was different. It was, he told Allen, probably just food poisoning, although he may have been keeping more serious doubts to himself. Certainly the next day he told Bill Ryrie (he who had met Roy Jenkins off the Euston train for the last time a few weeks earlier) that he intended to work only from ten o'clock until five with no long lunches or official cocktail parties, and that he would take no work home in the evenings: an unlikely regime for either an ambitious Chancellor or a socialite, but a sensible one for a man worried about his own health.

Over the next few weeks Macleod proved himself decisive, quick-witted and resolved to take action on issues such as inflation, spending control and tax reform, thereby allaying civil service anxieties over his short working hours. Macleod's officials were largely unaware that the pain the new Chancellor had experienced on the day that he took office was still with him. On the morning of 7 July Macleod consulted a doctor who diagnosed possible appendicitis and advised immediate hospitalisation. Instead the Chancellor took Treasury questions and, now in great pain, delivered a much below-par speech. That night he was admitted to St George's Hospital, then still at Hyde Park Corner. An operation followed: not, it transpired, for appendicitis but for a hernia. Although Macleod's delays meant that the hernia had ruptured, there was little reason to doubt that he would make a full recovery. Yet several days later visitors found him weak and tired.

Iain Macleod left hospital on 19 July but was still confined to bed for most of the time. His post-election euphoria had left him and he seemed depressed. Perhaps he was grieving: his mother had died less than two months earlier, yet first the election campaign and then the demands of his new job had prevented him from properly absorbing the event. But the following day, on the evening of 20 July, he got up for dinner. At 10.30 p.m. on his way back to bed he felt severely ill. Unhappily his dinner guest – Mathew Forster, his own doctor – had just left. Another doctor was sent for, but within little more than an hour, Iain Macleod was dead.

It was not the spinal problems that did for Macleod, nor renal failure, nor the hernia, and certainly not appendicitis, but a heart attack, probably the result of a blood clot consequent upon his operation. So bad luck, as well as bad health, was apparently to blame. Edward Heath moved quickly, as he was obliged to do, and made Tony Barber Chancellor. A gap had nevertheless opened up in the heart of government, even more than it would do if Tony Blair had no Gordon Brown, and it remained unfilled. Admittedly Macleod had previously said to friends that because of his poor health he would do only three years as Chancellor and then leave government, so maybe the gap would have emerged anyway. But by then there might have been somebody in Cabinet with the stature fully to replace him.

Stafford Cripps's demise was less sudden than Macleod's. He spent longer in office at the Treasury, although still not very long, and he did not actually die in harness. Nor did his death occur at the birth of the Government of which he was a member, but when the Government was already well into decline. The political blow was still severe, however, for it was Cripps who had seemed to offer the best chance of reversing that decline, and of restoring public confidence in the Government.

The 1945–51 Labour administration was racked with health problems, partly reflecting the exhaustion of leaders who had carried heavy burdens through the Second World War, and who had then assumed equal peacetime responsibilities. Ellen Wilkinson was an early casualty, weakened by pneumonia in the terrible winter of 1947 and then killed by pills. Bevin died in 1951. Attlee had periods of hospitalisation, while Dalton and Morrison were dogged by minor but disabling ailments – even to the extent that on one occasion Dalton got a septic finger from tapping the dispatch box too hard and too often.

Stafford Cripps had never been healthy. Chris Bryant in his biography says that, having spent much of the First World War as an invalid, Cripps felt guilty for ever after. That drove him to take on more work than was reasonable, which precipitated exhaustion and illness and then more guilt. Others saw him as a hypochondriac, and the two interpretations are not necessarily inconsistent. Colitis, a ruddy nose (the surprising result of taking the waters at Baden Baden), fainting, spondylitis, exhaustion, cancer, TB, leukaemia – these were no doubt all genuine enough, but the pattern of conspicuous overwork followed by virtual collapse creates suspicion. Alternative therapies, naked swimming and running, and a diet eschewing meat, cooked food and stimulants (other than tobacco, which he continued to use) seemed to do Cripps no good, and even before he became Chancellor his time was already running out. He was irritable and suffering from insomnia, and it was because of the Chancellor's poor health that Attlee created a new Treasury post of Minister of State, and appointed to it Hugh Gaitskell, to help Cripps.

The Chancellor was enthusiastic about the appointment and even suggested that Gaitskell should share his office so that the two men could work in tandem. Yet Cripps oscillated between bouts of exaggerated effort one moment, and the next declaring that he needed to go off for a long convalescence. In 1950 Cripps contemplated resignation, having only been Chancellor for a few months, but Gaitskell persuaded him to stay, perhaps partly to avoid the arrival of a new Chancellor who might impede his own career progression. Meanwhile the amount of work that Cripps could actually complete was diminishing. Gaitskell was soon acting as a full deputy for Cripps, even to the extent of delivering the Mansion House speech.

As Chapter 8 noted, ill-health meant that Cripps was out of the country during the 1949 devaluation, an episode of huge significance but in which he played only a small part. The following summer he spent a long period away from the Treasury, resting at his home in Gloucestershire and saying that he might not return. Then in early October he wrote to Attlee saying that he would shortly be resigning. He travelled to Switzerland, for another rest-cure at the Bercher-Benner clinic, returned for the public announcement of his resignation, and then made his way back to Switzerland. Subsequent diagnoses included a tubercular infection of the spine (for which the treatment was for him to be encased immobile in plaster), stomach tumours, and a bone marrow cancer for which there was no treatment. Cripps survived through 1951, emaciated and often in pain, and died in Switzerland on 21 April 1952.

In his biography of Cripps, Simon Burgess says that he was the only post-war Chancellor 'to depart at the time of his choosing and with his reputation still in one piece'.[19] The time was not really Cripps's choice, but his reputation was certainly very high, despite the 1949 devaluation. The Tories respected Cripps with the same vigour that they disliked Dalton, and the public found it easier to accept austerity imposed by the saintly Cripps, who had never promised them much anyway, than by the raffish Dalton who had once seemed to promise everything and had then asked for it back, even before it was all actually given.

On devaluation, Cripps looks less impressive, putting off an act that he should have seen was inevitable. Dell also chides Cripps for not being more austere, but then Dell would: no Labour Chancellor could expect to escape from Dell unscathed. More to the point, although Kenneth Morgan calls Cripps the architect of post-war economic recovery, David Marquand has written that since Cripps assumed office at a very difficult time, and implemented policies that any Chancellor would have had to pursue, he was less an architect than a prisoner of events.[20] But many other politicians have failed to do what was needed of them, and Cripps was characterised by his refusal to flinch from his responsibilities. His civil servants greatly admired his intellect and courage. Cripps turned a terrible balance of payments deficit into a surplus, and more generally he left the economy in a clearly better shape than he found it. When Cripps retired, the Press were generous in their praise – although when Cripps handed in his seal of office, the King offended him gratuitously by failing to thank the retiring Chancellor and war-time minister for his service to the nation.[21] The terrible thing was that everybody knew that the Labour Government had lost its backbone. That was the role that Gaitskell would now seek to fill; but with Cripps gone, so too was party unity.

Judgements, criticisms and defences

The praise bestowed on Cripps when he resigned was very unusual. When Norman Lamont lost his job, one newspaper carried the headline 'Hooray, Hooray' while another printed a photograph of him leaving the Treasury, captioned, 'The picture all Britain wanted to see.' Even more succinctly, Nigel Lawson's resignation was marked in one of the papers by the banner headline, 'Good riddance'. To lose an overpowering job like the Chancellorship is bound to be a wrench, but to have one's performance harshly judged must feel gratuitously painful. Norman Lamont was hurt personally, but also concerned for the impact on his children – to his credit he went straight to see them on the day of his loss of office. Nigel Lawson says that his own response to the many letters of support that he received following his resignation was to feel, 'So what?' Lawson writes: 'The depression that inevitably follows a trauma of that kind was already beginning to set in.'[22]

There are several different issues here. Perhaps journalists, authors and pundits are too keen to condemn glibly those who have at least made the attempt to do a job (and live a life) far more difficult than those that most of us have ever taken on. Perhaps too we collude with Prime Ministers and others (civil servants maybe) who use Chancellors as fall-guys for their own errors. And perhaps at a deeper level we are wrong to personalise problems that reflect much broader sociological and institutional drivers: we are too keen on the Great Men approach to history, an approach that provides us with villains who mostly meet their just deserts – for don't all political careers end in failure, much to the satisfaction of the rest of us?

An important matter is what, with the benefit of hindsight, Chancellors have to say in their own defence. Politicians' memoirs are notoriously self-serving, but what is striking is how few ex-Chancellors have claimed that they entered office with a strong diagnosis of what the economy's real problems were, and what should be done, and then got on and did it. One who does make such a claim is Hugh Dalton. When in 1954 he republished his pre-war text book *The Principles of Public Finance*, Dalton asserted that on his unexpected appointment he quickly identified the big issues that he needed to tackle, and then decided what to do about them. This claim is probably true, given that Dalton had a powerful mind, an economic background, and was taking over the Treasury at a clearly climacteric moment. Another well-prepared Chancellor with a radical agenda was Geoffrey Howe, who justifiably describes himself as such in *Conflict of Loyalty*. If Gordon Brown writes his memoirs (hard to doubt, circumstances permitting) then he too will be able to say that he spent his time in opposition on both fundamental thinking and precise planning, and that on assuming the Chancellorship he set to work, implementing his agenda.

But these are the exceptions, and there are more examples to put in the opposite group. 'I felt it prudent once again to restate Conservative party policy; but quite unnecessary to "rethink" it,' says Rab Butler in *The Art of the Possible* of the policies on which the Tories fought the 1951 election – policies that deliberately did not stray far from the Labour inheritance.[23] The biggest policy step that Butler considered, the Robot scheme for currency convertibility, was suggested to him by officials and was neither something that he entered office already proposing to implement, nor something that he fought for with very much conviction. Roy Jenkins in *A Life at the Centre* is candid that, while he knew that he was taking over an economy in difficulty, he did not initially know what to do, and waited for his staff to make suggestions. 'Having accepted the new job insouciantly, I soon developed an oppressive sense of awe towards my responsibilities.'[24] Denis Healey writes in *The Time of my Life* that 'I entered on my new life as Chancellor of the Exchequer with less confidence than I had brought to my first cabinet post.'[25] Norman Lamont, with remarkable candour, says in *In Office* that shortly after becoming Chancellor he was startled by, and did not much care for, a suggestion from the new Prime Minister that they should have a seminar on 'what we believe in', and also that 'I was personally agnostic about the ERM.'[26] No suggestion here from Lamont that he could see much need to rethink the policies that would soon lead him into such difficulties.

Most Chancellors, it seems, enter office under-prepared and with little idea what they want to do with the job, and most find they do not enjoy it much once they have got it. At the end of a stint at the Treasury, a note often struck by ex-Chancellors, in their memoirs or elsewhere, is what painful work it all was. Denis Healey is typical: he says of being Defence Secretary that 'I loved every minute of it' whereas being Chancellor was 'exceptionally hard and frustrating work, with few of the diversions which made my six years at Defence so exciting and enjoyable'.[27] Chancellors do seem to spend a lot of time feeling beleaguered, and John Major offers a remark that perhaps says more than he intended: 'the Treasury enjoys a crisis.'[28]

Most ex-Chancellors remain loyal to their ex-staff, but some break the code. The mighty Roy Jenkins writes: 'the one time in my ministerial career when I consider that I was badly advised on major questions was in my first two or three months as Chancellor.'[29] And apart from Jenkins, Rab Butler and Jim Callaghan were both undoubtedly badly advised in their early days, while there was a moment during Stafford Cripps's Chancellorship when he was dismayed to find that his staff were attempting to backtrack on the Cabinet's decision to devalue the pound. Jim Callaghan once faced open revolt from Lord Croham, the Governor of the Bank of England: a revolt that seems to have been motivated by the Governor's belief that nobody from the Labour Party should have the cheek to be Chancellor (though he didn't much like Reggie Maudling either). And both Geoffrey Howe and Gordon Brown allegedly found the Permanent Secretaries whom they inherited less than helpful, and so were keen to see them retired.

Another common complaint from ex-Chancellors is of poor support or poor leadership from the Prime Minister and his or her staff: as one would expect, Geoffrey Howe, Nigel Lawson, John Major and Norman Lamont all make this charge (although several earlier Chancellors had at least as much cause for complaint). The criticism is generally applied in the context of prevarications over immediate crises or tough spending decisions, whereas it could just as well be applied to most Prime Ministers' lack of an over-arching philosophy for tackling the nation's deeper problems. Attlee led from behind, Churchill was way past his best, Eden was inadequate, Macmillan sold out to the aristocracy, Home was just an illustration of the consequences of that sell-out, Wilson was too foxy whereas Heath was just a hedgehog, Callaghan was out of his depth (although he was remarkably good at giving the reverse impression), and Major was over-promoted.

Which leaves just two Prime Ministers: Margaret Thatcher and Tony Blair. Thatcher certainly gave her ministers leadership, although fatally she did not give them enough of her loyalty. Her huge strength was to be visionary while caring obsessively over details. Tony Blair has tried to be visionary, but he does not have much grasp for details, and so he tends sometimes to sound foolish.

In the economic arena, uniquely, this weakness of Tony Blair's has not been a problem: the Prime Minister has left well alone, and Gordon Brown has his own economic analysis which, whether it is right or wrong, is certainly clear and comprehensive. Neither intellectually nor personally does he need leadership from Blair, except in the sense that he needs Blair's loyalty, which mostly he gets. Tony Blair thinks his Chancellor is a pain, but so long as Brown delivers the goods, Blair puts up with him. And many, Tony Blair probably included, see Brown as the most successful Chancellor of the post-war period.

The general rule is simple: Chancellors do not love their Prime Ministers, and Prime Ministers do not love their Chancellors. When the end came, Clement Attlee was glad to see the back of Hugh Dalton and Anthony Eden was happy to move Butler out of the Treasury. Macmillan was at best indifferent to the fates of Thorneycroft, Amory and Lloyd. Wilson was probably pleased to shunt Callaghan to the backwater of the Home Office. Thatcher was happy to push Geoffrey Howe out of the Treasury and no doubt wished that she could have found the opportunity to push Nigel Lawson out of an aeroplane. John Major must have said goodbye to Norman Lamont with a huge sense of relief tinged with embarrassment. Turning the tables, Anthony Eden and Margaret Thatcher had to watch with gritted teeth as their Chancellors took their jobs.

Against that, Attlee was sorry to lose Cripps. It's not a very even balance.

When we look at Prime Ministers and Chancellors who went down together, the picture is only slightly different: it is mostly one of marriages that were not actually violent, but that were not exactly happy either. Attlee and Gaitskell were distant colleagues, with little to say to one another, as were Home and Maudling, and Wilson and Jenkins. Heath showed little sign that he ever noticed that Tony Barber was there at all. Jim Callaghan and John Major certainly knew that Denis Healey and Ken Clarke were there: they seem to have slightly resented their indebtedness to their junior partners. Indeed Major thought that Clarke was too keen to indulge in fights with the Eurosceptics, and that he contributed to the sense of a government always under siege. By the end of his government, Major's relations with Clarke had deteriorated substantially.

So what does it all amount to? Perhaps the real measure of a Chancellor is what he did next. Macmillan, Callaghan and Major became Prime Minister, and whatever one thinks of their performance, one has to commend their achievement. Hugh Gaitskell was elected leader of the Labour Party, but did not find much happiness in the job, and died before he could become Prime Minister. Various other ex-Chancellors took various other Cabinet posts, from which they got modest satisfaction at best.

After his stint as Chancellor, Denis Healey found himself rejected by his party, but nevertheless fought to save it from the wreckers, and then retired to write gentle and thoughtful memoirs and essays. Roy Jenkins preferred to reject his party before it rejected him, founded another one, became President of the European Commission, and also retired to write gentle and thoughtful memoirs and essays.

Judged as fully rounded individuals, who achieved great things in politics but who also did contemplative things very well, Jenkins and Healey would seem to be the most successful Chancellors of the age. Both were as capable as anybody else of talking nonsense when they so chose; but they have also (Jenkins particularly) proved themselves capable of writing wisely and at great length – something which cannot easily be said of any other members of their pack.

Of the two, Denis Healey is the one who perhaps strives a little too hard in his writing, who name-drops and shows off a bit too much. He writes of music, of military strategy and of painting. 'I am,' he remarks, 'often reminded of Donne's words,' and he recalls an occasion when 'we had to comfort ourselves by saying with Yeats ...' He quotes from the Polish poet Zbigniew Herbert. He recalls that when visiting Budapest as a young man he admired works by 'Rippi Ronai, Csontvary and Derkovits'. But none of this is wholly forced or false – his memoirs are to Margaret Thatcher's as flesh is to silicone – even if none of it is entirely ingenuous either. Denis Healey has become the ageing lush of the political classes. It's not such a bad thing to end up as.

10 Perspective

Those who defined the Chancellorship

It is unlikely to be controversial to say that, of the nineteen men who since 1945 have served as Chancellor for more than a few weeks, a handful have fashioned the job of Chancellor into the one that we recognise today. They have created standards against which others have been judged. More debatable is just who these handful are. Stafford Cripps, Hugh Gaitskell, Roy Jenkins, and Geoffrey Howe would be on most people's list, and one strongly suspects that Gordon Brown will be included by future generations. Denis Healey would be a controversial inclusion, and so too would be Hugh Dalton – but if those do slip in, then why not Nigel Lawson too, if only to redress the political balance?

So why did some men manage to define the job and others not? Let us start at the beginning. The big point about Hugh Dalton and the Chancellorship has already been made in earlier chapters: that in Cabinet, he lacked clout. This was partly because, at the time, there was generally insufficient understanding of how much power a Chancellor needs if he is to do his job. Dalton reluctantly took on what seemed to him to be a small and rather pedestrian job, only to find that the issues with which he had to grapple were by far the most important facing any Cabinet minister: important in their own right, but also important in the sense that upon their resolution depended the success or failure of all the Government's other policies. Yet not only was economic responsibility divided between Dalton and Herbert Morrison, but even in his own sphere of responsibility, Dalton could only expect to get his way with the agreement of Cabinet colleagues, including some quite junior ones.

Dalton just did not have the day-to-day authority that modern Chancellors feel they should be able to take for granted (and that Gordon Brown has perhaps taken too far). The refusal of men such

as Manny Shinwell to submit to the Chancellor's will over government spending, and the belief of Cabinet ministers that they could
and should argue with Dalton on equal terms over other aspects of
policy, meant that at several critical junctures Dalton was unable to
impose the stringency that economic circumstances demanded.

Although some of the blame for this must go to Dalton's tendency
to alienate his Cabinet colleagues, Clement Attlee's failure to give
Dalton the power that he needed was the larger source of the problem, and the direct reason why Dalton and Stafford Cripps sought in
turn to squeeze out the Prime Minister. Partly as a result, and partly
through accident, Stafford Cripps found himself in 1948 combining
Morrison's economic powers with those of the Chancellorship which
he had just inherited from Dalton. But since Cripps's authority in
Cabinet was still circumscribed by Attlee's failure to discipline other
ministers, Plowden's sobriquet ('the first modern Chancellor') seems
over-generous. In truth it was Hugh Gaitskell who, by picking a fight
with Nye Bevan and securing Attlee's reluctant but unequivocal
backing, successfully asserted the principle that on economic policies
the Chancellor conceded ground to no one, and thus first established
the authority, power and position of the Chancellor over all Cabinet
colleagues bar one.

To some extent Gaitskell was lucky. Attlee had already lost two
Chancellors: he was not inclined to lose a third. (Later on, Harold
Macmillan would be far less fastidious.) Like John Major after Nigel
Lawson's walkout and initially Kenneth Clarke after Norman La-
mont's dismissal, Gaitskell exercised power partly because a some-
what beleaguered Prime Minister could not afford to let the
Chancellor resign. More than that, however, Gaitskell was absolutely
clear why, for him and his office, it was necessary to be bloody-minded.
His clarity flowed both from the ex-civil servant 'desiccated calculating machine' side of his nature and from the passionate political side.

What Gaitskell fought for, others gave away. The Conservative
Chancellors of 1951 to 1964 were mostly poor guardians of their
own authority, and hence did little to define the job we know today.
Admittedly they suffered from being unlucky with their Prime Ministers, as did Jim Callaghan, who also suffered from a certain lack of
ability. By November 1967 the currency of the Chancellorship was
tragically debased. Then Roy Jenkins restored it, but only briefly;

Tony Barber would have pleased Harold Macmillan as Chancellor – and it is no accident that Ted Heath was a Macmillan familiar – and Denis Healey spent half his Chancellorship taking liberties and the second half chastising others for doing the same.

Denis Healey is without question the most interesting, although perhaps not the nicest, man to be Chancellor since the Second World War. A colder and less ambiguous figure was Roy Jenkins who, on his appointment as Chancellor in 1967, became without question the second most powerful man in British politics. Harold Wilson feared him. It was partly for that reason, but also because they liked his urbane intellectualism, that Jenkins's senior civil servants revered him. (In received memory they still do.) With respect to fiscal policy, Roy Jenkins took nonsense from no one, and his self-evident confidence and ability, his command of the House of Commons, the overpowering probability that he would soon be leader of the Labour Party and maybe Prime Minister, all conferred on him an authority that struggling Jim Callaghan could not possibly muster.

Or so it seemed at the time. But when Callaghan attacked Barbara Castle's *In Place of Strife* legislation, Jenkins stood disastrously on the sidelines, thereby weakening his broader political position and allowing Callaghan of all people to re-emerge as the Labour politician most likely to succeed Wilson. Had Labour secured re-election in 1970 and had Jenkins remained as Chancellor, he might have regained the initiative; had Labour won and Jenkins gone as planned to the Foreign Office, then he would probably have remained just as sidelined as he actually was.

Tony Barber surrendered without a fight the territory that Jenkins had regained. His successor, Denis Healey, was no patsy; but for all his intellectual pretensions, Healey did not think through what the job was really about until the 1976 IMF crisis forced him to do so. But then for two and a half terrible years he carried the Government on his back, and all that was right with government policy (not much) emanated from the Treasury. It was the Chancellor not the Prime Minister who was the strong man of the Government. This meant that it was the Chancellor against whom the Labour Party turned when inevitable defeat followed.

The relationship between Healey and Callaghan was reversed when the Tories took over. Margaret Thatcher provided the toughness, Geoffrey Howe the self-doubts. It proved to be a better division of labour: one that was designed to work whereas tough Healey and weak Callaghan were bound to fail. Of course it would not have worked if Geoffrey Howe did not have his own strong sense of his worth – he had, after all, stood for the party leadership, and it was he more than anybody else who eventually toppled Thatcher – but Howe nevertheless got most of his strength from the fact that for the most part he was working to the same agenda as, and with the full backing of, the Prime Minister. Ministers who criticised the Chancellor criticised the Prime Minister too – and found themselves no longer ministers. We have already seen that in 1981 several Cabinet ministers dared to criticise Geoffrey Howe's Budget and his management of the economy, and how Margaret Thatcher responded by sacking them shortly afterwards. The principle that Thatcher upheld was that although the Prime Minister was allowed to criticise her Chancellor, no other minister was allowed to doubt him, for to do so was to doubt her. How clearly that contrasted with the débâcle of 1976 when, during the IMF crisis, Jim Callaghan explicitly invited Cabinet ministers to develop economic policies that differed from those of his Chancellor.

Nigel Lawson did not need the Prime Minister to help him fight his battles. With Howe the Chancellorship had been a job of great power because the Prime Minister wanted it so; with Lawson, he himself kept it so. Lawson's colleagues feared him, even as his policies excited them. The Prime Minister initially trusted him and, until it was too late, felt no need to run him – not that she could have done. His civil servants admired his technical mastery, and journalists liked the fact that he had once been one of them. Quite a few back-benchers detested him – the scholarship son of a Jewish London tea merchant, haughty Lawson was for them a bit too Oscar Wilde in appearance and too Elsie Tanner in behaviour – but they cheered him on as he flew higher and higher towards the sun.

Then Lawson fell. He pursued policies with which he knew his chief disagreed, and when the inevitable happened, he seemed willing to pull Margaret Thatcher down with him. He instigated a new period of distrust between Chancellor and Prime Minister within which period we still live. Margaret Thatcher chose John Major to succeed Lawson as Chancellor partly because she believed he would be no threat; then Major in turn (oops!) chose Norman Lamont partly on the same basis. But Lamont lacked credibility and Major found himself obliged to appoint a heavyweight politician, Ken Clarke, just as Wilson had been obliged to give Roy Jenkins the Chancellorship after Jim Callaghan.

Even more so than with Healey and Callaghan, the new Chancellor was better in a brawl than the Prime Minister, but was still vulnerable to attacks from other colleagues because the Prime Minister would not stand by him. Even more than before, a strong Chancellor was no remedy against a weak Prime Minister. On the contrary, Clarke only made Major look all the weaker, not least through his pronouncement that any enemy of John Major was an enemy of Ken Clarke.

Is Tony Blair making the same mistake? Not yet. Blair's problem is to cope with the fact that no Chancellor has ever been as greedy for power as Gordon Brown. The present Chancellor would try the patience of a saint – which thing Blair, though pious, is not. Curiously, it is easy to feel equal sympathy for both men. From Brown's perspective, Tony Blair's lack of grasp of policy detail, weakness for platitudes and ideological rootlessness must seem dangerous to the long-term future of their mutual New Labour, New Britain project. Brown has taken upon himself and his office the governance tasks that Blair fails to accomplish: and perhaps has a right to do so, given the two men's history, their respective strengths, and the facilities that he as Chancellor has at his disposal.

From Blair's perspective, there is great danger in an often bad-tempered senior minister who acts towards everybody in government as if he himself is Prime Minister – by, for example, issuing directives to Cabinet colleagues and extending patronage to junior ministers – and who does everything with such feverish intensity that a huge policy error seems bound to happen sooner or later.

So, because of the differences in the way in which the men practise their politics, it needs neither personal jealousies nor deeper ideological differences, both of which exist, for there to be difficulties between Chancellor and Prime Minister.

So far the Prime Minister has dealt with the situation by occasional massive swipes, such as the 1998 ministerial reshuffle in which he sacked or sidelined several key Brown supporters, such as Nick

Brown the Chief Whip, whom Blair cruelly sent to the ministry of agriculture, and advanced his own such as Stephen Byers, whom he imposed on Brown as Chief Secretary. Blair was determined to make it clear: that his own office and not the Treasury was the nerve centre of government, and that the Chancellor's patronage provided no protection against his own strikes.

Up until now such manoeuvres have sufficed, leaving Gordon Brown less omnipotent than he would like to be, but still more powerful than any previous Chancellor. The fact that Blair, unlike Thatcher, is not a frustrated would-be Chancellor, and does not see economic change as the centrepiece of his radical programme, augurs well for Brown. Yet if the economy encounters serious problems, and the Chancellor gets publicly criticised for not addressing them, then Tony Blair will have to interest himself in the Chancellor's work, or risk suffering a much broader loss of confidence in the Government's grip. A re-run of the Thatcher–Lawson fight is far from impossible.

How much does the individual matter?

Is all of this stress on individual performance mistaken? Many of the obviously important decisions that Chancellors take are those that arise out of crisis. But in such cases the Chancellor does not generally have much real choice: his job is simply one of facing up to the inevitable, and making the best of the circumstances. Devaluations and most tax hikes or spending cuts come under this heading.

But there have been other decisions which were not taken in haste, which were not inevitable and which did make a difference. The clearest recent example was John Major's responsibility for taking Britain into the Exchange Rate Mechanism (ERM) of the European Monetary System. Major could have decided not to bother: to go along with the Prime Minister and eschew ERM membership. That would have displeased the new Foreign Secretary, but Douglas Hurd was in no position to insist; equally the alliance of Major and Hurd for ERM entry meant that Thatcher was in no position to resist. It was Major specifically who played the Hurd card against Thatcher rather than the Thatcher card against Hurd. He settled the course of events.

The long-term consequences were immense. The recession that

soon followed would have happened even without ERM, for the simple reason that a recession was necessary to correct Nigel Lawson's excessive boom; but the pattern of the recession was different, the appearance of government helplessness was more intense than it would otherwise have been, and the opportunity that ERM membership provided to blame Europe for the problems of the British economy was a terrible propaganda advantage to the Conservative Eurosceptics. Civil war within the Conservative Party was now inevitable, and that, together with Major's broader mismanagement of events, in turn made the return of a Labour Government vastly more likely than it had been at any time for twenty years.

Yet it still seems a little simplistic to say that all of this was John Major's exclusive doing. It was he who pressed the button, but who put the button under his finger in the first place? It is hard to believe that John Major would have favoured ERM entry had the great weight of informed opinion been against; in that sense, Major was the agent of that weight of opinion, and his direct contribution to the actual decision was correspondingly reduced.

This line of reasoning does not have to lead to the vacuous conclusion that no Chancellor is responsible for anything he does. In general, the view that people – top people – do not matter cannot be right. But the view that almost all the blame for Britain's lamentable economic performance can be placed on Britain's lamentable Chancellors cannot be right either. For one thing, the economic performance has been disappointing but not lamentable; and for another, most of the Chancellors were neither complete fools nor complete knaves.

We have to give some credence to the alternative explanation that Britain's Chancellors (although far from blameless themselves) have often been ill-served by colleagues, advisers and sometimes by officials, not just at the day-to-day level, but in terms of identifying the very large issues that need to be faced and the steps required to address them. The disappointment is that few if any of the Chancellors responded by taking the initiative themselves, and instead holders of the office have generally remained trapped in the business of managing rather than redesigning the economic system.

Or to put the point more politely: there are policy communities and policy continuities which promulgate policy approaches, which in turn encompass the decisions that individual Chancellors make. What is important is the extent to which any individual Chancellor plays a large role in creating and maintaining such a community or continuity, or just a small one.

On many policy issues, for example, Hugh Dalton had a major and personal influence. Largely because they came later and were in office for shorter periods, Stafford Cripps and Hugh Gaitskell were much less influential. On the international side Dalton's personal influence was matched only by Keynes's; on domestic aims he did far more than Attlee to establish what could and could not be done with the resources available – and it was he alone who had any understanding of how to make those resources available. In the early years he was more insistent than Cripps would have been that redistribution had to be a major feature of policy. He pursued cheap money as a personal crusade; one that other politicians did not understand and of which the experts in and out of government mostly did not approve. His acceptance that controls over the real economy were necessary was no greater or lesser than that of the rest of the Cabinet; his realisation that such controls were not sufficient to achieve the Government's objectives was for too long shared by no other politician in office.

Cripps understood that direct controls had to give way to financial controls aimed at managing the expansion of spending power in the economy. But the amount that he or Gaitskell could do was limited by the rest of the Government's unwillingness to move quickly. When the Conservatives gained power there seemed a serious risk that, while the direct controls would be abolished, the financial controls would be misapplied: that policy would focus only on low taxes and a strong pound, with cuts in government spending to achieve that. Largely because they wanted to be popular and wanted to avoid unsettling the trade unions, the Tories chose not to be so blinkered. Instead they decided to rely on the Keynesian demand management to which the Labour Government had stumbled only awkwardly.

Some people see that decision as the best one in recent British economic policy-making, and some see it as the worst decision. The truth is that the policy supported but did not generate the economic growth that carried the economy forward almost uninterrupted until the mid seventies. But there was frequent political pressure to use

Keynesian policies for something that they were not designed for: namely covering up the fundamental failings in the supply-side properties of the economy. Selwyn Lloyd was uneasy with this, but could not muster a convincing argument; Reggie Maudling and Jim Callaghan were prepared to take a risk; Roy Jenkins put his foot down, but was too quickly voted out of office for his impact to be significant. Tony Barber did not care, and nor at first did Denis Healey.

Then came the third great phase of policy, after the reconstruction period and the slightly-golden age: the backlash, which Healey ushered in but which Geoffrey Howe and then for a while Nigel Lawson pursued with genuine determination. Howe was the pivotal figure here, and hence perhaps the pivotal Chancellor of the last half-century. If he had been grumpy and equivocal in the Healey style, bemoaning the need to pursue tough policies, blaming the IMF, toadying to the unions and saying that it would shortly be possible to relax policies, then the impact of his measures would have been much less. Howe refused to offer hope to those who thought that Keynesian expansionism would return, not least amongst Treasury officials. He made Thatcherism seem inevitable, whereas Thatcher herself merely made it seem fanatical.

The Monetarist rhetoric of those years has proved insubstantial, discredited by Nigel Lawson and his spending boom, akin to a television evangelist being caught *in flagrante*. At first, Chancellors still wanted the thing that Monetarism gave them: a sense of control, of certainty; a fixed point, a comfort blanket. Fixing the exchange rate in the ERM was the response to that need, but a short-lived disaster: and now Chancellor Gordon Brown resists an even more extreme option: European Monetary Union. He has opted instead to follow the post-Monetarist thinking of modern macroeconomic theorists, and he combines tough welfare-to-work principles, conservative fiscal policies, targets for inflation, and a liberal's love of policy transparency.

Most finance ministers abroad have, to varying degrees, adopted the same philosophy; some of them within the EMU framework and some outside. But although Gordon Brown's thinking is not entirely his own, as Chancellor he has been distinctive in the intensity with which he has pursued such ideas, and the ferocity with which he has dominated his colleagues, to ensure the implementation of his policies. This self-confidence makes him, for the moment at least, stand out as a definitive Chancellor.

Perhaps we should pay less attention to what Chancellors say and do, and more attention to what they do not say and especially what they do not do. Edmund Dell concludes his study of Britain's postwar Chancellors by quoting Adam Smith's aphorism that 'there is a great deal of ruin in a nation'. Dell laments that British governments 'have learned few lessons from the history of economic management', and that political parties 'continue to promise us what they cannot deliver'. He finds one crumb of confidence, but only one: 'Since the IMF crisis of 1976 ... the begging bowl has been put away.' In other respects, he tells us, economic management has gone on much as before, and that where there have been changes 'they have not been for the better'. And he observes that 'there have been no improvements in economic performance greater than would be extrapolated from previous history'.[1] It is all rather depressing.

Dell's essential criticism is that too often Britain's Chancellors, faced with a hard but responsible option, took an easy option instead. They allowed public sector spending to rise too quickly, they were too indulgent over inflation, they were unwilling to take the measures needed to produce a strong pound. And looking back, that does often seem to have been true – indeed his book records the evidence.

But it was argued in earlier chapters that the evasions were seldom so large as to explain even the modest under-performance that occurred in the British economy, let alone the large under-performance that Dell suggests occurred. It is perhaps significant that the worst evasions of the half-century were those that took place while Dell himself was in government. Perhaps he generalised too readily from the experience of his period in office, to the problems of the age. Dell was, after all, not just a member of Britain's most ill-fated government: from 1974 to 1976 he was a Treasury minister with a Cabinet seat.

Indeed, Edmund Dell nearly became Chancellor. In 1976, when Denis Healey was discredited and friendless, Dell was an obvious alternative. But Healey's metal hardened in the crisis of that year, and in any case Jim Callaghan was too canny to sack Healey and place himself in the firing-line. So Dell had to be satisfied with the job of Trade Secretary, from which position he could observe but not really fight the fire that engulfed the Government.

Europe: a great neglected issue

In 1979 Edmund Dell put aside politics to return to history, a subject that he briefly taught at Oxford, and to spend time in business. He published *The Schuman Plan and the British Abdication of Leadership in Europe*. There is something to be said for the view that the theme of that book, or at any rate the theme of Britain's lost European opportunity, is not only larger and more important than the theme of relative decline that *The Chancellors* addresses: it also encompasses the issues addressed in *The Chancellors* within its larger framework. Where the period 1945–2000 is concerned, isolation from Europe may well be the main story, and relative economic decline a sub-plot.

There is, to be fair, no definitive quantitative evidence for that claim: no proof to the pudding. The distinguished historian Alan Milward says that 'the failure to sign the Treaties of Rome was a serious mistake' and the equally distinguished historian Peter Clarke calls it 'the most obvious missed opportunity'.[2] But neither is rash enough to claim that isolation from Europe was definitely the single biggest policy mistake of the age, let alone the single most important explanation for poor economic performance.

Nevertheless, the failure to join Europe early had widespread adverse consequences, which impinged on the performance of the economy. It meant that Britain failed to gain full access to the great European economic boom, that Britain forfeited the opportunity to help shape the great European institutions, that British companies and political institutions missed out on the modernisation and restructuring that European involvement would have precipitated, and that the British political élite was able instead to perpetuate its solipsistic self-deception that Britain was special, and that by inference the British elite was even more special. And all of that meant that the economic problems faced by the Chancellors of the Exchequer were rather worse than they would otherwise have been.

Britain's post-war Chancellors were trapped by the sentimental post-imperial thinking that engulfed almost everybody in British politics. The first Labour Government was not without guilt in this regard, especially patriotic little Mr Attlee, with his belief in Empire, and his conviction that the English were especially good at understanding and governing the Africans. But the worst culprits were Conservative ministers in the fifties, and their advisers at the Foreign Office, the Bank of England and the Treasury. When the Conservatives gained power in 1951 their attitude was very much that Labour had reconstructed the domestic economy, and that it was now up to them to reconstruct Britain's position in the world economy. Yet they actually did the reverse.

To some extent the problem here is the lack in Britain of a strong European-minded post-war leader: a Monnet, Schuman or Spaak, an Adenauer, de Gasperi or De Gaulle. But what one most notices is the absence of any broadly pro-European *movement* in British politics in the twenty years that followed the end of the war: a movement that might have generated enough of a wave for a senior politician (maybe a Chancellor) to climb aboard.

This absence reflected the broad perception that the Second World War should not be seen to have cost Britain its global role: which was somewhat unfortunate, since that was exactly what had happened. Britain was unusual amongst the nations of the world in that it had gone through the experience of the Second World War with both its political elite and its national identity intact, but with its domestic economy severely damaged and its overseas empire almost completely cut off.

On the continent, the situation was very different. Many nations had been violated, many had collaborated, some had been perpetrators of terrible sins. The Common Market and the organisations that preceded and superseded it were designed to avert future economic, political and by extension military hostilities, and thereby guarantee the future of the nation-states of Europe. This ambition had no resonance in Britain. On the contrary, the British from Bevin onwards kept on insisting to the Americans that Britain was not just another European nation, and that European integration undermined the joint Anglo-American project for free trade and free financial flows at the global, rather than the continental level. The British authorities were sure that once the Schuman Plan, and later the Treaty of

Rome, had collapsed, the Europeans would see the errors of their ways and acknowledge British leadership over them: the Americans thought that the British were daft, but by and large harmless.

The nearest candidate for the role of European champion within Britain was Harold Macmillan, who, as Foreign Secretary, Chancellor and Prime Minister, was instead the great disappointment of post-Second World War British politics. Macmillan had abandoned agitation, and had learned how to finesse: in all three top posts he balanced Europeanism with Atlanticism, thereby achieving little. Macmillan's preference was always for there to be no Common Market, but if that was not possible then for Britain to be one of its members. It was an embarrassing surprise to Macmillan to find that the Americans favoured the Common Market, a great annoyance when the continental Europeans went ahead without Britain, and a caustic shame when in 1963 De Gaulle refused to allow Britain to join late. It was the worst possible outcome.

The tortuous negotiations over European entry, and then the failure of those negotiations, contributed to public dissatisfaction with the Macmillan government, his resignation, and Labour's 1964 electoral victory. Had Macmillan been more forthright in his pro-Europeanism, then maybe he could have secured British entry into Europe during the golden age of strong growth, making life easier for those who succeeded him at the Treasury. Instead, Britain eventually joined just before the great stagflation of the seventies, and when the institutions of Europe had crystallised in ways which were uncomfortable to Britain. Membership would prove to be needlessly controversial, even after entry, giving ministers and officials plenty of opportunity to be as poor Europeans from within the community as they had been outside it, and laying the groundwork for the intense Europhobia that afflicts British politics today.

Perhaps it is unfair to complain that Macmillan, despite the SuperMac tag, was never a super-hero, never able to redirect single-handedly the direction of events. None of his Chancellors complained that progress towards European participation was not quicker, and nor of course did their Labour successors, Jim Callaghan and (tellingly) Roy Jenkins. The only Chancellors that Britain has had who were staunchly pro-European when in office were Nigel Lawson and Ken Clarke – and Lawson was only so after the collapse of Monetarism left him desperate for a new creed, and a new anti-inflationary anchor in the shape of the ERM.

Other neglected issues

And if one is unwilling to buy the view that late participation in the European community was a major failure of economic policy, then one might still want to subscribe to the view, articulated earlier, that Britain's poor industrial relations were, until the eighties, the real villains of the piece – or indeed some other explanation such as City short-termism, or under-investment in infrastructure, training and education, or ill-considered industrial policies, or maybe some broader cultural explanation.

In most of these cases it is hard to blame Chancellors directly and exclusively for such failings, and in the case of under-investment it is hard to pick out any Chancellor who was much better or worse than the rest. But one may still wonder why Chancellors have been so unwilling to point the finger of blame themselves, or to suggest what others should do to address these more basic issues. Even Denis Healey, who used his memoirs to explain at great length why others were to blame for the travails of the 1974–9 Labour Government, has refrained from offering much practical advice on how the British economy really ought to be run.

This reflects in part the point already made that, although other ministries often complain of Treasury interference, Chancellors are not generally chosen for their vision, and tend not to have grand plans for what they would like to do with the job, let alone how they would like to take over the jobs of other ministers. When they start, Chancellors often say that they will eschew short-termism, restore confidence and end the self-serving policies of their predecessors, but essentially they mostly aim to continue to do the same, only better, rather than rewrite the rules of the game. Perhaps Geoffrey Howe was an exception, and for obvious reasons so too was Hugh Dalton. Maybe Gordon Brown. But that's about it.

In his defence, Denis Healey did try to get a grip on a broader policy agenda, part-way through his Chancellorship, when it became clear that narrow macroeconomic policy instruments alone were not enough to deliver the Government's objectives. But Healey's

involvement in industrial relations was part of a general abandonment of boundaries and responsibilities, as the Wilson/Callaghan
government lost confidence in its own authority to govern; it was not
strategic and indeed it was scarcely tactical.

Indeed, one has a glimmer of sympathy for those such as George
Brown, Barbara Castle, Michael Heseltine and John Prescott who
have believed in the need, either for an alternative economic department to take on the key longer-term challenges facing the economy,
or for existing departments to be more ambitious and less subject to
Treasury strictures in addressing those challenges, whether they be
Europe, industrial relations, education, research and innovation, or
whatever.

Yet the record suggests that changing the names and remits of government departments, merging them and demerging them, makes little significant difference to the success of policies, although such
changes may make a lot of difference to the careers of politicians and
senior civil servants. It is ideas and individuals, working through institutions, which possess what little power there is to affect the outcome of economic events.

The impact of ideas on events

In the half-century since the Second World War, the problem is not so
much that British ideas about *macroeconomic* policy have been bad
ones, as that they have been used inappropriately to compensate for
muddled and generally unhelpful thinking and actions, with regard
to longer-term, supply-side, *microeconomic* issues. It is this imbalance in the quality of thinking and of action which, combined with a
profoundly warped view of Britain's position in the world economy,
does most to explain disappointment with the performance of the
British economy.

To start with, during Clem Attlee's administration, the situation
was slightly different, with problems in both the demand-side macroeconomic and supply-side microeconomic policy areas. The verdict
on the reconstruction period must be that while the founding of the
welfare state was an impressive and largely unproblematic achievement, with powerful economic as well as political benefits, the
Labour Government was rather too slow to shift from direct controls

on the economy to a mixture of Keynesian demand management and free markets for goods and services. The Attlee administration, and Hugh Dalton in particular, also mistakenly believed in cheap money, thereby depriving itself of a useful mechanism for controlling demand. And although it was assiduous in obtaining funds from the United States to fund imports and investment, the Attlee administration had an overblown view of the need for Britain to play a major role in the management of the world economy – an altogether unfortunate idea to pass on to the new Conservative Government, which needed no encouragement to indulge in national economic aggrandisement.

When the Conservatives took charge, they continued with the removal of direct controls on the economy, cemented in Keynesian demand management, and sensibly abandoned Labour's simplistic cheap money policy. Partly as a result, there followed a period of consolidation and respectable economic growth. But the Conservatives were muddled, indeed lazy, in the rest of their thinking. They were excessively worried that trade union unrest would disrupt production, and so they encouraged industrialists to surrender control over employment levels to the unions. This impeded the industrial restructuring that the economy needed, and deterred innovation, just as effectively as had Labour's dirigiste policies, especially when combined with the Government's failure to attack cartels and other anticompetitive arrangements, and above all its refusal to commit to the emerging European Common Market.

Although growth in the period was high by historic standards, it did not seem to match the aspirations of the electorate. So, under Harold Macmillan's premiership, policy started to change in the late fifties, but in the wrong way. Keynesian demand management switched from being a tool for stabilising the economy to being a tool for raising the growth rate. In this phase of policy, there was a constant struggle to find new ways to reconcile moderate or rapid expansion in demand, with the economy's blatant inability to raise production at the same rate. Problems manifested themselves in various ways, including balance of payments deficits and downward pressure on the exchange rate, while supply-side solutions were mostly botched – not least the rejected bid for Common Market membership, the return in the early sixties of the planning ideas that the

Tories had supposedly kicked out in 1964, and Reggie Maudling's self-deluding 'dash for growth'.

Little changed when Labour took office in 1964, except that the underlying economic situation was worse and the planning ideas were more far-fetched (although to be honest, largely irrelevant). Then in 1966 the Chancellor, Jim Callaghan, slammed on the brakes. It was a genuine policy reversal, marking the start of a new policy phase, but it was not enough: devaluation and more deflation followed. Unsurprisingly, this new austere and orthodox period also featured the return of a severely chastened Conservative Government, now led by the severely chaste Edward Heath. The orthodoxy, it should be noted, was in large part a Keynesian one: with demand management reverting to its original role of stabilising demand rather than boosting growth.

Where supply-side measures to support long-term growth were concerned, both Labour and Conservative governments attempted unsuccessfully to use the law to restrict the power of the trade unions. For the time being Labour turned its back on planning, and so too did the Conservatives. And despite the opposition of a large minority in his party, Heath marched Britain into the European Economic Community.

In 1972 policy shifted once more. Faced with mounting unemployment, Heath ordered a return to pre-1966 practice, a massive reflation of demand, and measures to support ailing industries (about the worst sort of planning one can have). It was an ill-considered exercise, which turned to disaster when, shortly afterwards, the worldwide system of fixed exchange rates collapsed and commodity prices (especially oil) started to soar. Heath attempted to curb inflation via wage controls, which did precious little for his credibility.

Indeed there was very little political credibility to be had. An inconclusive general election in February 1974 was followed by a similarly inconclusive election in October. Labour now formed a government of sorts, leaving the Tories to regroup once more. Legal curbs on the unions were dismantled, to be replaced by a voluntary social contract that the unions ignored. Planning guidances were also introduced, and these too were ignored. Denis Healey allowed public spending to rise without control.

In 1976 there came a hint of a real change to come: a near-bankrupt Healey accepted IMF instructions to cut spending. He claims that at about that time he abandoned Keynesianism, as if he had ever really known what it was. The Government spiralled further out of control, with Healey at least doing what he could to delay the inevitable crash, by bullying and cajoling the unions not to do too much damage, and by carefully husbanding public finances.

Then in 1979 came a Conservative Government, with some sharp theories and little conscience. A new policy era was under way. For a lot of the population it felt a little like William of Orange marching through Ireland, but for the Treasury in Whitehall it was a great relief. Order was being restored. Rational ideas would prevail.

The high theory aspect did not survive for long. The attempt to secure low inflation via monetary discipline was a fiasco: so instead, Keynesian demand management was once again used (anonymously) to curb demand, but with the unprecedented twist that unemployment would be allowed to rise as far as was needed to secure price stability. Meanwhile, the Government started on a supply-side agenda that shocked the British economic establishment. It set out to clear away the detritus of economic controls of one sort or another, while simultaneously imposing serious restrictions on the activities of the unions. And it started to sell off the nationalised industries.

This combination of tough, pragmatic and unspoken Keynesianism and market liberalisation proved surprisingly effective as a way to run the economy. Before long the toughness could be relaxed somewhat.

Then in 1987 the Chancellor of the day, Nigel Lawson, did something rather stupid: he embarked on a new policy phase, by relaxing macroeconomic policy entirely and setting off on yet another dash for growth. The result was inevitable: rising inflation, a worsening balance of payments, a currency collapse, and an emergency tightening of policy.

Lawson's problem was that the benefits of the Tories' supply-side revolution, though real, were not yet nearly as substantial as he arrogantly assumed. But having made that error of judgement, he then failed to recognise its true nature. He should have concluded that the economy needed slow growth in demand, combined with efforts to boost further the supply side. Instead, he concluded that what was needed was an alteration to the operational procedures of macroeconomic policy, involving a replacement for the discipline that monetary targets had failed to provide. The consequence was sterling's ill-fated entry into the European Exchange Rate Mechanism.

Economic policy-making at the start of the new century

After sterling's expulsion from the ERM there has followed yet another phase, characterised by a long-overdue rejection of macroeconomic gimmicks. Under Gordon Brown the new policy regime has included a strong belief in fiscal orthodoxy and a commitment to macroeconomic policies that are self-evidently sustainable, buttressed by extensive measures to get people off welfare and into work. It is, as Chapter 6 concluded, a policy that evidently works well in good weather. And to make people believe that it will not be abandoned when the circumstances get tougher, the Bank of England has been given its independence, and hard-to-break rules over fiscal policy have been proclaimed at every street corner.

But that is not the only point that needs to be addressed. In the early twenty-first century, the nation's large policy needs are threefold: to rebuild the infrastructure, to boost investment in training, research and innovation, and to reposition Britain within Europe away from a low wage economy able to specialise in basic assembly or call-centre work, and towards being the favoured location site for the highest value-added, knowledge-intensive parts of the production and service-delivery process.

On all of these three matters, Gordon Brown has all the right things to say. He seems to understand the supply-side issues in a way which previous Chancellors mostly have not. The Treasury has been slightly reorganised, to make it less focused on macroeconomics and more focused on the promotion of enterprise, employment and growth. And macroeconomic policy announcements are now typically presented as the handmaidens of supply-side policies – witness, to take a small example, the ponderous title of the 1998 budget report, *Equipping Britain for our long-term future*. More to the point, there have been numerous supply-side policy initiatives from the Government, supported and often instigated by the Chancellor. In the field of science and innovation, for example, the outdated scientific infrastructure of Britain's universities is being addressed through a Joint Infrastructure Fund (jointly organised and funded by a private sector agency, the Wellcome Trust), there is a new University Challenge Fund providing seed venture capital for the commercial exploitation of university research, and a similar Science Enterprise Challenge Scheme, as well as a Venture Capital Challenge to finance early-stage high-technology businesses, and a research and development tax credit to encourage smaller companies to invest in research and development.

But whether these and a huge host of other schemes amount to very much is a different matter. The Venture Capital Challenge Scheme was, for example, set up with just £20 million to spend: small change to an American Ivy League university. In other areas too, and even after the 2000 Comprehensive Spending Review, the scale of the policy changes being made seems inadequate, relative to what needs to be done. There is to be more investment in the London Underground, but only if the private sector will provide a lot of the cash. A supposedly massive increase in expenditure on education is actually worth only a small amount per pupil. The University for Industry (UfI) has been set up, but with a derisory launch budget of £15 million (plus anything it can scrounge from Europe). Nursery education and the élite end of higher education alike are to remain dangerously under-funded compared with provision in similar nations abroad. Meanwhile, major pharmaceuticals companies have considered removing their research efforts to mainland Europe, the Swedes and the Germans have argued over who should take over control of the London Stock Exchange, and British involvement in biotechnology and genetic engineering is declining relatively and perhaps absolutely.

In the short term none of that notices, thanks to the impetus to the economy being provided by the new information and communications technology, and the attendant surge in world trade and world growth. And the fact that this boost is driven by American private sector finance provides a warning against grandiose plans for government intervention and leadership. But the history of Britain since the Second World War provides a counter-warning: that the economy's underlying supply potential is no more transformed by government neglect and parsimony than it is by government diktat and profligacy.

Then there is the matter of Europe, and the next last great issue: European Monetary Union. Some of those who oppose British participation do so because the macroeconomic policy rules of EMU are inferior to those that Britain can adopt, and indeed has adopted, alone. This is true, but only marginally so. Others oppose EMU because they find Europe too un-democratic, too bureaucratic, too old-style socialist and perhaps too corrupt. Such people have a strong argument to advance, but it is not really an argument against British membership of EMU. Others argue on grounds of nostalgic sentimentality, or from their suspicion that the Euro is a step towards European federalism.

But what we do know is that EMU is part of the creation of a single European economy, with integrated financial and product markets, and transnational legislation covering labour markets. There is a good case for finding this distasteful, even immoral: but its economic potential is vast, and the economic cost to Britain of being pushed outside will be correspondingly large. The most successful European economies of the next decade or two will be the ones which do most to exploit the single European economy: Britain outside of EMU will surely lose ground relative to those nations, whoever they are.

It is correspondingly disturbing that throughout the Blair government's first term of office the Chancellor was so keen to preserve the British tradition of aloof disdain in the face of what is really quite a clear and simple choice. The history of the fifties has been and is being repeated, five decades later. There is something very un-Gordon Brown about this, and something very Whitehall. But then if Britain does join EMU and sterling disappears, so too will a lot of the Treasury's importance. In this respect, the Treasury and the office of Chancellor may lose something either way: the choice is between sustaining power within a diminished economy, or accepting diminished power within a stronger economy. Any company director who has contemplated merging his or her firm with a larger rival knows the nature of this dilemma. But the difference is that Gordon Brown, as a politician, can and should separate his future from that of the office he holds, and the officials who serve him.

Gordon Brown: how does he compare?

So where does Gordon Brown stand amongst Chancellors? There is no sensible way of saying which was the 'best' post-war Chancellor. It depends on whose values and objectives you use as a benchmark, and on how you assess the contribution of the Chancellor to the performance of the economy. Has Gordon Brown been a better or worse Chancellor than Rab Butler, who oversaw economic conditions reasonably similar to those of the Brown Chancellorship? Does he win plaudits or criticism for raising the power of his department? Questions like these have no absolutely right or wrong answers.

It is more useful to think of the characteristics of different Chancellors and hence of the categories into which they might fall. This can be done in an infinite number of ways, but two particular dimensions tend to capture a lot of what people have in mind when they think of what a Chancellor was really like.

First, there is the basic question of whether the Chancellor in question tended to encourage or discourage faster growth in demand in the economy. On that basis, with his large Budget surpluses, it is clear that Gordon Brown has mostly tended to restrain demand. That allies Brown with fellow Labour Chancellors Francis Cripps and Roy Jenkins, but also with Peter Thorneycroft, Geoffrey Howe, John Major and Norman Lamont from the Tory side. All the other Chancellors (twelve versus seven) can best be described as expansionary, although in some cases it may seem slightly strange to say so. In particular, much of Denis Healey's fame (notoriety) stems from the large cuts in spending and borrowing that he commanded in 1976. But since these cuts were precipitated by his own earlier profligacy, it seems fairer to put him in the expansionist camp. Similarly, most of the deflationary measures in Stafford Cripps's first austere Budget had been carried over from Hugh Dalton's regime, and Dalton had himself imposed a clearly deflationary Budget in 1949. But the 1949 Budget was generally seen as an admission of failure, and a recognition that past mistakes needed to be rectified: so that the pop-judgement that Dalton was primarily an expansionary Chancellor is probably worth sticking with.

Meanwhile, Peter Thorneycroft deserves to be put in the parsimonious basket, even if it's a slightly honorary presence occasioned by his resignation in protest at Macmillan's refusal to allow him to cut

spending. And although a close examination of the borrowing numbers casts doubt on whether Stafford Cripps was quite as frugal as
people thought he was, his reputation was just as important as his
actions, and had a large impact on the mood and behaviour of the
nation.

The second dimension that heavily influences our judgements of
Chancellors is the extent to which they seemed to want to alter the
long-term course of the economy, rather than just accepting existing
trends largely unchanged. On this basis the radical Chancellors are a
mixed bunch. Hugh Dalton, as the first peacetime Chancellor, inevitably broke with the immediate past, whereas his Labour successors seemed mainly concerned with not endangering what had been
achieved to date, and the next few Conservative Chancellors were
similarly mostly intent on not rocking the boat. It would have been
different (not necessarily better, but different) if Rab Butler had not
given up on Robot so quickly; once he did, the Treasury settled itself
into a quiet life.

Some might want to offer Selwyn Lloyd as an example of a Chancellor who tried to redirect the economy, via such initiatives as his incomes policy or the foundation of the NEDC. Lloyd may indeed
have hoped that his measures would transform the climate of industrial relations and thereby boost productivity and hence economic
growth. But he took these steps without a huge amount of conviction, and he was really more of a dabbler than a thinker, and probably just misses the title of a serious long-term radical thinker – as
does Norman Lamont, the man who abolished the NEDC that Lloyd
set up.

In contrast, Reggie Maudling fancied himself as an intellectual,
and resolved to use a rapid expansion in demand to catapult the
economy on to a new path of rapid growth with high productivity
gains. His theories have long been rejected, at least in their original
form, but theories they were, based on Maudling's recognition that
he had taken over at the Treasury at the end of a decade of lost opportunities. Maudling was a strategist not a tinkerer, albeit a strategist who failed.

In contrast to Maudling, Geoffrey Howe used deflation as a tactic
to encourage a long-term improvement in the economy's productivity performance and supply potential. His successor, Nigel Lawson,

believed that Howe's legacy and the liberalisation of the economy then under way had been sufficiently successful that they had made the economy safe for a Maudling-type boom. So Lawson went for rapid expansion, believing that thanks to market liberalisation, a new golden age had dawned. In truth the economy had not by then been transformed (it would change more during John Major's Chancellorship and premiership), and Lawson's policy was naïve and self-deceiving; but it was undeniably a bold policy, and there was no sense of business as usual while Lawson was around, any more than there was during Howe's incumbency.

For several years after Nigel Lawson, the policy framework was once again geared towards restoring a degree of balance, and avoiding anything that might endanger confidence in the economy. Then came Gordon Brown, who has carried on with that approach but who also obsesses about the long term. Brown wants to corral people into work so that they can reap the benefits of being integrated back into employed society, and so that they can contribute to growth; he also wants to use policy interventions to encourage firms to be more innovative, entrepreneurial and yet long-sighted. As with the others, he may be wrong in his policies, but he is certainly not lacking in ambition.

Of these long-sighted Chancellors – Dalton, Maudling, Howe, Lawson and Brown – only two also fall into the fiscally conservative category. They are Geoffrey Howe and Gordon Brown. The other cautious Chancellors – Cripps, Thorneycroft, Jenkins, Major and Lamont – showed little interest in trying to achieve a transformation of the economy. They would deny that, of course: Norman Lamont has particularly done so. And indeed Lamont did make some institutional changes, such as the unified Budget, which were intended to have a lasting impact. He was not, however, a visionary Chancellor, and he offered no new analysis of the nation's economic fundamentals: Norman Lamont was a technician in an age of policy-collapse, and it wasn't enough.

Looked at in this way, Geoffrey Howe and Gordon Brown stand out from the mass of Chancellors, for having been very tough in the execution of the job and its fiscal obligations, but also very keen to attempt a transformation of the economy. Significantly, Howe was backed by a domineering Prime Minister, while Brown is himself a domineering figure. Indeed it is clear that Gordon Brown is not so much the new Geoffrey Howe as the new Margaret Thatcher: industrious, intelligent, isolated, intimidating, tragically flawed, impressive. It may well be a good thing for democratic liberal values that he has so far been confined to the position of second amongst equals, and that he has to endure the irregular chastisements that his Prime Minister hands out.

Or is that precisely the sort of judgement from which British political economy has suffered for so long: the belief that if a politician has the qualities and inclination to make a difference, then it is desirable to circumscribe him or her, just in case we do not like the difference once it is made? Tony Blair is a gentler version of Gordon Brown: no less keen to centralise power, no less desirous of changing history, but perhaps less likely to succeed precisely because he is more emollient in his manner, less focused, and far more worried about what the electorate thinks.

Perhaps that is too crude. Perhaps it is best to have strong roots but supple branches. Tony Blair claims that he remains committed to his two great purposes: to reunite the Labour movement with the Liberals, thereby ejecting the Conservatives from their dominant position in British politics; and to place Britain at the heart of Europe. Just at the moment it does not look hugely likely that he will succeed with either. But if he does (and it is not impossible), then it will be less of a victory for Blair over Brown than for the legacy of Roy Jenkins over the legacy of Margaret Thatcher. That, taken together with the shift that there has been towards non-doctrinaire attitudes towards economic management and social tolerance, would mean eventual triumph for the principles of the Chancellor, Jenkins, who never became Prime Minister, and defeat for the ideas of the Prime Minister, Thatcher, who was refused the Chancellorship.

It would not be a result that would please everybody. But it would still be a result – and one that would suggest something new and important about who can really influence the long-term direction of an economy and society such as our own.

A bibliographical essay: sources and further reading

Chancellors' memoirs and autobiographies

Everybody says that politicians' accounts of their careers are untrustworthy, and to some degree at least, that must be so. But it is not obvious why politicians should be any worse in this regard than novelists or athletes or businessmen, and some politicians, once they have left office, can be remarkably candid in their recollections.

For example, Hugh Dalton's account of his career, *High Tide and After: Memoirs, 1945–1960,* Frederick Muller, London, 1962, has not been much disputed, although not surprisingly it tells us far more about his political than his private life. The memoirs are based in part on Dalton's diaries, edited by Ben Pimlott: *The Political Diary of Hugh Dalton,* Jonathan Cape, London, 1986. Pimlott's own book on Dalton is mentioned below.

Neither Stafford Cripps nor Hugh Gaitskell lived to publish an autobiography, but Philip Williams has edited Hugh Gaitskell's diary: *The Diary of Hugh Gaitskell, 1945–1956,* Jonathan Cape, London, 1983. Gaitskell was, it has to be admitted, circumspect in what he revealed. Rab Butler was more playful: *The Art of the Possible, The Memoirs of Lord Butler,* Hamish Hamilton, London, 1971, is replete in the elliptical aphorisms for which many people loved Butler, but which leave others unmoved. The Butler memoirs are, however, certainly to be preferred to Harold Macmillan's ponderous autobiography, of which *Riding the Storm, 1956–59,* Macmillan, London, 1971, and *Pointing the Way, 1959–61,* Macmillan, London, 1972, should be read only by those whose time is not too precious.

After Macmillan the scribbling stops for a while, until taken up again by Reginald Maudling, whose *Memoirs,* Sidgwick & Jackson, London, 1978, give a decent return on one's investment, even though

Maudling would have done us more of a service by being more candid. A much larger book is James Callaghan's autobiography, *Time and Chance,* Collins, London, 1987: gentle and decently written, it tends to confirm one's impression of a man who was supremely good at politicking, but who misread the great political history of which he was part. Roy Jenkins's *A Life at the Centre,* Macmillan, London, 1991, gives a very different impression. The self-questioning Jenkins hesitated as a politician, and so lost the greatest prize in that field, but as a Whitbread prize-winning biographer, his grasp of history's nuances is hard to rival.

Tony Barber's *Taking the Tide*, Michael Russell, Norwich, 1996, is a modest volume which stands in complete contrast to the autobiography of a man whose history was in some ways a little similar: Denis Healey – *The Time of My Life,* Michael Joseph, London, 1989. Healey tells us vast amounts about himself, although not always in the way in which he perhaps intended. It is another large book, as is Geoffrey Howe's nicely written *Conflict of Loyalty,* Macmillan, London, 1994, which tells of life under Margaret Thatcher, and which includes his reflections on whether he should have acted earlier or more forcefully against her (yes he should). But both books bound together would scarcely exceed in size that of Nigel Lawson, *The View from No. 11: Memoirs of a Tory Radical,* Corgi Books, London, 1993, who provides fascinating insights into Mrs Thatcher's management methods, and rather less fascinating essays on how to control the money supply. (Those who like to see big beasts preying on one another should, incidentally, read Roy Jenkins's damning review, published in *Portraits and Miniatures*, Macmillan, London, 1993.)

John Major's autobiography, not inaccurately entitled *John Major: the Autobiography,* HarperCollins, London 1999, has similar qualities to that of Jim Callaghan, a politician whom Major in many ways resembles. Norman Lamont's *In Office*, Little, Brown, London, 1999, helps us to understand why he had a difficult time in office. Ken Clarke and Gordon Brown have yet to produce.

Biographies of, and essays about, Chancellors

Where the act of biography is concerned, politicians are as much sinned against as sinning. Hugh Dalton appears as a more interesting person on the pages of Ben Pimlott's hugely impressive *Hugh Dalton*, Jonathan Cape, London, 1985, than on his own pages. 'Interesting' can be taken both literally and euphemistically, and Dalton today remains a highly controversial character, who receives an unfavourable assessment by Robert Skidelsky in his review of Pimlott's book, reprinted in Skidelsky's *Interests and Obsessions*, Macmillan, London, 1993. In contrast, a kinder view of Dalton is taken by Roy Jenkins in *The Chancellors*, Macmillan, London, 1998 – a book which starts with Randolph Churchill, and ends with Dalton.

In seeking to understand Stafford Cripps we are well served by *Stafford Cripps: a Political Life*, Victor Gollancz, London 1999, and *Stafford Cripps the First Modern Chancellor*, Hodder & Stoughton, London, 1997, by Simon Burgess and Chris Bryant respectively; Burgess places more stress on Cripps's spiritual views, while Bryant's perspective is illustrated by his title. There is also a well-known, much older but rather good essay on Cripps by David Marquand in Michael Sissons and Philip French (eds.), *Age of Austerity*, Hodder & Stoughton, London 1963, and another sensible assessment by Kenneth Morgan in his book of essays, *Labour People: Leaders and Lieutenants, Hardie to Kinnock*, Oxford University Press, Oxford, 1987.

Where Hugh Gaitskell is concerned, Philip Williams long ago published his much respected *Hugh Gaitskell, a Political Biography*, Jonathan Cape, London, 1979, but for modern tastes Brian Brivati's *Hugh Gaitskell*, Richard Cohen, London, 1996, is well-researched, judicious and probably to be preferred.

Anthony Howard was, by his own admission, an unlikely biographer of Rab Butler, but the result, *RAB, The Life of R.A. Butler*, Jonathan Cape, London, 1987, is just as good as one would expect from Howard. Butler also appears as the subject of one of three extended essays in Edward Pearce's *The Lost Leaders*, Little, Brown, London, 1997. Pearce admires each of his trinity, and is perhaps too generous about Butler's record as Chancellor.

It is nevertheless a sobering thought that Butler, who once seemed such a giant figure, is today little known to the wider public. Soon the same will be true of the great actor-manager. For the time being, Harold Macmillan takes an uncomfortable centre stage position in

Richard Davenport-Hines's incisive account of the foibles of Macmillan's whole family, *The Macmillans*, Heinemann, London, 1992. An older but still respected biography is Anthony Sampson's *Macmillan, a Study in Ambiguity*, Pelican, 1968, which sits alongside J. Turner's *Macmillan*, Longman, London, 1994. Robert Skidelsky's *Interests and Obsessions* also contains an essay on Macmillan. Meanwhile Macmillan's official biographer, Alistair Horne, although from the old school, is willing to criticise his subject a little, in *Macmillan, Vol. 1, 1894–1956*, Macmillan, London, 1988. The same cannot really be said of Gore Allen's *The Reluctant Politician: Derick Heathcoat Amory*, Christopher Johnson, London, 1958, which is delightful but rather too admiring of its subject.

D.R. Thorpe does much better with his *Selwyn Lloyd*, Jonathan Cape, London, 1989, which elicited a rightly favourable review by Roy Jenkins, reprinted in his *Portraits and Miniatures*, mentioned above. Peter Thorneycroft and Reginald Maudling both suffer unfair neglect, although there is a compelling portrait of Maudling in John Cole's *As It Seemed to Me*, Weidenfeld & Nicolson, London, 1995.

An ex-Chancellor who has certainly not been neglected is Jim Callaghan – admittedly a more important politician than most. Unfortunately, Kenneth Morgan, in *Callaghan: a Life*, Oxford University Press, Oxford, 1997, is too willing to make excuses for his subject. The same was not true of Peter Kellner and Christopher Hitchens, who gave Callaghan a famous drubbing in *Callaghan: the Road to Number 10*, Cassell, London, 1976 – written when Callaghan was new to the premiership but when, for these two commentators at least, the writing was already clearly on the wall.

There then follows a huge and almost unbroken gap in the chronology, reflecting the quite understandable reluctance of biographers and living subjects to tango with one another. Denis Healey also appears in Edward Pearce's *The Lost Leaders*, as does Ian Macleod, who also benefits from a very fine biography: Robert Shepherd's *Iain Macleod*, Hutchinson, London, 1994, which gives a characteristically measured assessment of a difficult, quixotic but admirable man. After that we have to wait for John Major, who became Prime Minister and who is thus too large a subject to be ignored. And yet, of course, Anthony Seldon's *Major, a Political Life*, Weidenfeld & Nicolson, London, 1997, does not tell us a huge amount: which fact is much more a reflection on its subject than on its author.

More recently still, Hugh Pym and Nick Kochan's *Gordon Brown – the First Year in Power*, Bloomsbury, London, 1998, is a balanced if rather early assessment of its subject. Norman Lamont and Ken Clarke remain largely unsullied.

Apart from these full biographies and essays, there is of course Edmund Dell's agenda-setting book *The Chancellors: a History of the Chancellors of the Exchequer 1945–90*, HarperCollins, London, 1996. It would be hard not to learn a great deal about the conduct of economic policy in the period, as well as about the characters of the men who held the post of Chancellor, by reading this book; whether its overall judgements are right is another matter, however.

Biographical and autobiographical works relating to other politicians

To understand the Chancellors we also need to understand the men and women with whom they worked. Clement Attlee, although often weak in his handling of ministers, was just about Britain's most successful post-war Prime Minister, eclipsed only and controversially by his apogee, Margaret Thatcher. Unfortunately, as a private and undemonstrative man, Attlee has not generated a biography that fully equals him in stature. Nevertheless, Francis Beckett's *Clem Attlee*, Richard Cohen, London, 1997, is a recent, well-written and convincing portrait of a difficult subject.

By comparison (and not without justification) there is an entire Churchill industry, within which Paul Addison's *Churchill on the Home Front, 1900–1955*, Jonathan Cape, London, 1993, provides material on Churchill's rather limited interest in economic policy-making in the fifties. There is not a lot to be said about Anthony Eden's interest in economic policy-making, and so David Dutton quite reasonably does not say a lot in his *Anthony Eden, a Life and Reputation*, Arnold, London, 1997; more questionable is Dutton's acceptance of Eden's Europhobia. Alec Douglas-Home also played only a small role in the story of Britain's post-war Chancellors. But D. R. Thorpe's biography, *Alec Douglas-Home*, Sinclair-Stevenson, London, 1997, does at least take Home seriously as a politician, and not as a figure of fun – although acknowledging that he was that too.

Harold Wilson produced his own accounts of his premierships, but they are not particularly revealing (perhaps he was modelling himself too closely on the other Harold). However, if treated with caution, the diaries and memoirs of some of his Cabinet colleagues can provide a few insights. Tony Benn, *Out of the Wilderness, Diaries 1963–67*, and his *Office Without Power, Diaries 1968–72*, Hutchinson, London, 1987 and 1988, shows just how little real understanding there was within the Cabinet about what was going on, but also inadvertently gives the lie to suggestions that most Cabinet ministers were told nothing and allowed to say nothing about Treasury policy. Much the same can be said of Barbara Castle's diaries, *The Castle Diaries, 1964–70,* Weidenfeld & Nicolson, London, 1984. Castle's diaries are, incidentally, less interesting then her autobiography, *Fighting All the Way*, Macmillan, London, 1993, which shows how the attitudes and policies of many sixties Labour ministers such as herself were rooted in the ambitions and experiences of the Attlee government.

Richard Crossman's diaries are notoriously unreliable, although insiders say that on economic policy issues he was less tendentious than normal. The most manageable version is that edited in a single volume by Anthony Howard and published as *The Diaries of a Cabinet Minister 1961–70*, Mandarin, London, 1991.

However, none of these stands comparison with Ben Pimlott's *Harold Wilson*, HarperCollins, London, 1992 which will interest anybody interested in post-war British politics.

Despite its unpleasant subject it is worth taking a look at Robert Shepherd's *Enoch Powell: a Biography*, Hutchinson, London, 1996, for what it tells us about the Conservative Party in the era of Edward Heath. John Campbell provides a balanced portrait of the Tory leader himself in *Edward Heath,* Jonathan Cape, London, 1993, and gets about as close to a very private politician as one could have realistically expected him to get (not very). Heath's autobiography *The Course of My Life*, Hodder & Stoughton, London, 1998, is of interest, if at all, for what it omits.

Margaret Thatcher's biography, *The Downing Street Years,* HarperCollins, London, 1993, provides the Thatcher view of events, and naturally takes no prisoners and allows for no doubts. Unfortunately for Mrs Thatcher, she has ranged against her not only the memoirs of her three Chancellors, but also Hugo Young's *One of Us, A Biography of Margaret Thatcher*, Macmillan, London, 1989, which is not only far more readable but also rather better reasoned.

Of the memoirs of Mrs Thatcher's colleagues, Peter Walker's, *Staying Power*, Bloomsbury, London, 1991, are amongst the more convincing. The memoirs of Mr Blair's colleagues have yet to appear.

Economic advisers

Apart from books by and about politicians, works by or about official advisers provide important reading. The first major figure here is Keynes: unfortunately, Robert Skidelsky's *John Maynard Keynes: Fighting for Britain 1937–1946*, Macmillan, London, 2000, appeared too late for its contribution to be reflected in this book. After Keynes's death, the senior expert government adviser was for many years Robert Hall, whose diaries, *The Robert Hall Diaries, 1947–53*, Unwin Hyman, London, 1992, are a mine of information on how the economic predicament appeared to those on the inside of government. Hall's diaries were edited by Alec Cairncross, who succeeded him as the Government's chief economic adviser, and who kept his own diaries. Cairncross has produced *Years of Recovery, British Economic Policy 1945–51*, Methuen, London, 1985, and *Managing the British Economy in the 1960s – a Treasury Perspective*, Macmillan, London, 1996. However, Cairncross's *The Wilson Years, a Treasury Diary 1964–1966*, the Historians' Press, London, 1997, is particularly helpful.

Alec Cairncross was succeeded in turn by Donald MacDougall, whose *Don and Mandarin: Memoirs of an Economist*, John Murray, London, 1987, is less magisterial but covers the full period from the Second World War, when MacDougall worked as Cherwell's assistant, onwards. It complements other studies such as Lord Birkenhead's book on Cherwell, *The Prof in Two Worlds*, Collins, London, 1961, or Edwin Plowden's *An Industrialist in the Treasury: The Postwar Years*, André Deutsch, London, 1989.

Historical accounts

Peter Hennessy and Anthony Seldon (eds.), *Ruling Performance: British Governments from Attlee to Thatcher*, Oxford University Press, Oxford, 1987, is a much respected account of successive administrations. However, amongst more general historical works, Peter Clarke's *Hope and Glory Britain 1900–1990*, Penguin, London, 1996, sets the standard as a description of Britain's post-war social, political and economic history.

Where shorter periods are concerned, the reconstruction period is particularly well served, not least by Paul Addison, *The Road to 1945 – British Politics and the Second World War*, Jonathan Cape, London, 1975, which sets the scene, and then by Peter Hennessy's *Never Again, Britain 1945–51*, Jonathan Cape, London, 1972. The period also features strongly in Nicholas Timmins's account of the founding and growth of the welfare state, *The Five Giants: a Biography of the Welfare State*, HarperCollins, London, 1995. Michael Sissons and Philip French (eds.), *Age of Austerity*, already mentioned, also contains evocative essays.

However, periods have generally received less scrupulous attention in the literature than have themes. For example, a longer perspective on the welfare state than that of Timmins is contained in a small but rather good book: David Gladstone's *The Twentieth Century Welfare State*, Macmillan, London, 1999. There are also several useful works on the main political parties. For example, Ian Gilmour and Mark Garnett, *Whatever Happened to the Tories: the Conservatives since 1945*, Fourth Estate, London, 1997, answers the question in its title pretty persuasively, although A.J. Davies *We, the Nation: the Conservative Party and the Pursuit of Power*, Little, Brown, London, 1995, is less opinionated.

It is hard to choose between that and other books on the Conservatives, such as Brendan Evans and Andrew Taylor's serviceable *From Salisbury to Major: Continuity and Change in Conservative Politics*, Manchester University Press, Manchester, 1996. There are also useful articles in Anthony Seldon and Stuart Ball (eds.), *Conservative Century*, and in Anthony Seldon (ed.), *How Tory Governments Fall: the Tory Party in Power Since 1783*, Fontana Press, London, 1996.

There may be fewer even-handed books on the Labour Party, but

A.J. Davies, *To Build a New Jerusalem: the British Labour Party from Keir Hardy to Tony Blair*, Abacus, London, 1996, sits nicely alongside his book on the Tories. Edmund Dell's *A Strange Eventual History, Democratic Socialism in Britain*, HarperCollins, London, 2000, bears the heavy weight of disenchantment, and most readers will probably stick with Henry Pelling's *A Short History of the Labour Party*, Macmillan, London, 1994.

Finally, a book that straddles this category and the one below is Peter Hennessy's *The Prime Minister: the Office and its Holder Since 1945*, Allen Lane the Penguin Press, London, 2000. If one is heading for a desert island and allowed only one Hennessy, then this (or perhaps *Never Again*) is the one to take.

The machinery of government

The relationship between the offices of the Chancellor and of other ministers, as opposed to the relationship between the individuals concerned, is a specialised subject, well served by the likes of Peter Hennessy, although Dennis Kavanagh and Anthony Seldon, *The Powers Behind the Prime Minister – the hidden influence of number ten*, HarperCollins, London, 1999, is also a good place to start. There is also an excellent essay by Anthony Seldon, 'Policy Making and the Cabinet', in Dennis Kavanagh and Anthony Seldon (eds.), *The Major Effect*, Papermac, London, 1994; several of the other essays in that volume are also well worth the time, as are those in R.A.W. Rhodes and Patrick Dunleavy (eds.), *Prime Minister, Cabinet and Core Executive*, Macmillan, London, 1995, while Simon James, *British Cabinet Government*, Routledge, London, 1992, is good on the advice given to British governments.

On the Treasury itself, Edward Bridges, *The Treasury*, 2nd edition, George Allen & Unwin, London, 1966, sets out the view of the insiders' insider. Joel Barnett, *Inside the Treasury*, André Deutsch, London, 1982, is a good politician's account, but Colin Thain and Maurice Wright, *The Treasury and Whitehall – the Planning and Control of Public Expenditure, 1976–1993*, Clarendon Press, Oxford, 1995, is more up to date and far more monumental. Dan Corry (ed.), *Public Expenditure: Effective Management and Control*, The Dryden Press, London, 1997, contains a wealth of broadly New

Labour essays. David Lipsey, *The Secret Treasury – how Britain's economy is really run*, Viking, London, 2000, delivers a much less sceptical verdict than its title leads us to expect.

Specific governments

Kenneth Morgan, *Labour in Power 1945–51*, Oxford University Press, Oxford, 1985, is a strong account of the Attlee government, but to really understand that administration, it is more important than normal to look at the wider social and political context, and some relevant texts have already been mentioned.

Moving on, the first years of the Conservative administration are covered in Anthony Seldon, *Churchill's Indian Summer*, Hodder & Stoughton, London, 1981, and in Paul Addison's *Churchill on the Home Front*. The story is taken further in Vernon Bogdanor and Robert Skidelsky (eds.), *The Age of Affluence 1951–64*, Macmillan, London, 1970, and in Andrew Boxer's slim volume *The Conservative Governments 1951–1964*, Longman, London, 1996, which is more recent and which provides a wealth of references.

More broadly, Samuel Brittan, *Steering the Economy*, Penguin Books, London, 1971, helps us to see the economic problems and policies of the fifties and sixties from a contemporaneous perspective, while Wilfred Beckerman (ed.), *The Labour Government's Economic Record, 1964–1970*, Duckworth, London, 1972, is useful in helping to understand how sceptical insiders saw the first Wilson government's economic policy decisions.

There are also several good books about the Heath government. Stuart Ball and Anthony Seldon (eds.), *The Heath Government 1970–74*, Longman, London, 1996, contains excellent essays on various aspects of its subject matter. Martin Holmes, *The Failure of the Heath Government*, Macmillan, London, 1997, is less balanced in its views. Douglas Hurd, *An End to Promises: Sketch of a Government*, Collins, London, 1979, is an insider's account.

On the Callaghan administration, Bernard Donoughue, *Prime Minister: the Conduct of Policy Under Wilson and Callaghan*, Jonathan Cape, London, 1987, contains some helpful material, while Edmund Dell, *A Hard Pounding: Politics and Economic Crisis 1974–76*, Oxford University Press, Oxford, 1991, is a clear statement of a clear view, from a Cabinet minister at the time. Kathleen Burk and Alec Cairncross, '*Goodbye Great Britain*', *The 1976 IMF Crisis*, Yale University Press, London and New Haven, 1992, provides a broader but not dissimilar perspective.

Moving on once more, Peter Riddell, *The Thatcher Government*, Martin Robertson, Oxford, 1983, shows how the Conservative Government initially looked. William Keegan was a powerful critic of the Thatcher government's economic policies: he set out his critique in *Mrs Thatcher's Economic Experiment*, Penguin, London, 1985, and later in *Mr Lawson's Gamble*, Hodder & Stoughton, London, 1989, both of which stand up reasonably well today.

It is a little too soon to expect much by way of serious analysis of the last two governments, but in the meantime, Sarah Hogg and Jonathan Hill, *Too Close to Call: Power and Politics – John Major in No 10*, Little, Brown, London, 1995, is another insiders' account, whereas *The Major Effect*, edited by Dennis Kavanagh and Anthony Seldon, Macmillan, London, 1994, provides the views of academics and journalists. A thorough and well-regarded book on the origins and early days of the Blair government is *Safety First: the Making of New Labour*, by Paul Anderson and Nyta Mann, Granta, London, 1997. The story is brought up to date in Andrew Rawnsley's scurrilous and entertaining *Servants of the People – the Inside Story of New Labour*, Hamish Hamilton, London, 2000.

Economics and economic history

All of these accounts need to be given some economic background. In the last ten years a lot of the best works on the economic history of modern Britain seem to have been written or edited by Nick Crafts. In particular, N.F.R. Crafts and Nicholas Woodward (eds.), *The British Economy Since 1945*, Oxford University Press, Oxford, 1991, is standing up well, to be supplemented by the relevant essays in Nicholas Crafts and Gianni Toniolo, *Economic Growth in Europe Since 1945*, Cambridge University Press, Cambridge, 1996, especially the article by Crafts and Charles Bean, 'British economic growth since 1945: relative economic decline ... and renaissance?'

In addition, a standard and very valuable set of papers is contained in Roderick Floud and Donald McCloskey (eds.), *The*

Economic History of Britain Since 1700, Volume 3: 1939–92, 3rd edition, Cambridge University Press, Cambridge, 1994. But the most succinct account of the evolution of economic policies, and their relationship to economic performance, is Roger Middleton's *The British Economy Since 1945*, Macmillan, London, 2000.

From an earlier generation, the writings of Alec Cairncross are required reading. This means the texts already cited, but in particular *The British Economy since 1945: Economic Policy and Performance, 1945–1990*, Blackwell for the Institute of Contemporary British History, Oxford and London, 1992.

In addition, a number of other books contain commentary on the post-war evolution of the British economy, and the older texts can be as helpful to read as the newer ones, since they give more insight into how policy issues were seen when they were written. (They also tend to be rather less technical.) Accordingly, G.D.N. Worwick and P.H. Ady (eds.), *The Britsh Economy in the 1950s*, Oxford University Press, Oxford, 1962, and Christopher Dow's *The Management of the British Economy, 1945–60*, Cambridge University Press, Cambridge, 1964, can be set alongside Derek Morris (ed.), *The Economic System in the UK*, 3rd edition, Oxford University Press, Oxford, 1985, and Andrew Britton's *Macroeconomic Policy in Britain, 1974–87*, Cambridge University Press, Cambridge, 1991.

A more modern variant, less concerned with macroeconomic policies and more with industrial competitiveness, as is the way nowadays, is the volume edited by Tony Buxton, Paul Chapman and Paul Temple: *Britain's Economic Performance*, 2nd edition, Routledge, London, 1998.

Britain, Europe and the international economy

Where international economic policies are concerned, Europe should have mattered most but seldom has. Brief summaries of Britain's tortuous relationship with the rest of Europe are provided by Stephen George, *Britain and European Integration since 1945*, Blackwell, Oxford, 1991, for the Institute of Contemporary British History, and John Young's excellent *Britain and European Unity, 1945–1999*, 2nd edition, Macmillan, London, 2000.

Much less brief, but well worth the time, is Hugo Young's *This*

Blessed Plot – Britain and Europe from Churchill to Blair, Macmillan, 1998. Young clearly believes in the great European enterprise, and is perhaps less sceptical than Alan Milward, who has articulated the view that European integration, although desirable, has come about because it served the interests of the nation-state and not as a result of the romantic ambitions of any great European heroes. Milward's books on the subject are *The Reconstruction of Western Europe 1945–51*, Methuen, London, 1984, and *The European Rescue of the Nation-State*, Routledge, London, 1992.

On European trade and monetary policies, Barry Eichengreen, *Reconstructing Europe's Trade and Payments – the European Payments Union*, Manchester University Press, Manchester 1993, is an account of the early days by a leading international economist. On recent policies, an enormous amount has been written on the Exchange Rate Mechanism and on the Euro: Richard Layard has edited *The Case for the Euro*, a set of papers setting out arguments for Euro membership and published in London in 2000 by the Britain in Europe Campaign.

On the sterling exchange rate, Alec Cairncross and Barry Eichengreen, *Sterling in decline: the devaluations of 1931, 1949 and 1967*, Blackwell, Oxford, 1983, while Kathleen Burk and Alec Cairncross, '*Goodbye Great Britain', The 1976 IMF Crisis*, already mentioned, continues the theme, which is picked up again by Philip Stephens in his *Politics and the Pound, the Conservatives' Struggle with Sterling*, Macmillan, London, 1996.

If one wants to go deeper behind all of this, then P. J. Cain and A.G. Hopkins, *British Imperialism Crisis and Deconstruction 1914–1990*, Longman, London, 1993, sets out a compelling explanation of the role of 'gentlemanly capitalism' in explaining Britain's economic history.

Economic ideas

No single comprehensive yet reliable account of the emergence of modern macroeconomics currently exists. There are, however, a couple of strong books on the emergence of Keynesian economics (apart from the various volumes of the Skidelsky biography, already mentioned). Peter Clarke, *The Keynesian Revolution in the Making*,

1924–1936, Clarendon Press, Oxford, 1990, is one; G. C. Peden's *Keynes, the Treasury and British Economic Policy*, Macmillan Education for the Economic History Society, London, 1988, is another: a slim but authoritative account of the rise of Keynesian policies, before and during the Second World War.

On the evolution of Labour Party thinking, Noel Thompson, *Political Economy and the Labour Party*, UCL Press, London, 1996, is useful, if sometimes a little too close to its subject. Kenneth Morgan's essay 'The Planners' in his *Labour People* says a great deal in a short space. For the Conservatives there are no simple references, but much of the flavour of the evolution of post-war policies, up until the late seventies, is captured in some of the essays and (especially perhaps) the discussions in Frances Cairncross (ed.), *Changing Perceptions of Economic Policy*, Methuen, London, 1981. The same is true of a book edited by both Cairncrosses, father and daughter, and dealing with just the sixties: *The Legacy of the Golden Age: the 1960s and Their Economic Consequences*, Routledge, London, 1992.

Notes

Chapter 1 **Managing the domestic economy**

1 Hugh Dalton, *High Tide and After: Memoirs, 1945–1960*, Frederick Muller, London, 1962, pp. 5 and 193–4; Ben Pimlott, *Hugh Dalton*, Jonathan Cape, London 1985, pp. 480–81.
2 Anthony Howard, *RAB, The Life of R.A. Butler*, Jonathan Cape, London, 1987, p. 94.
3 Roy Jenkins, *A Life at the Centre*, p. 43.
4 Denis Healey, *The Time of My Life*, Michael Joseph, London, 1989, p. 385.
5 Edmund Dell, *The Chancellors: A History of the Chancellors of the Exchequer, 1945–90*, HarperCollins, London 1996, p. 111.
6 Jenkins, *A Life at the Centre*, p. 231.
7 Nigel Lawson, *The View from No. 11: Memoirs of a Tory Radical*, Corgi Books, London, 1993, p. 320.
8 ibid., p. 274.
9 Jenkins, *A Life at the Centre*, pp. 244–5.
10 Lawson, *The View from No. 11*, p. 274.
11 Alec Cairncross, *Managing the British Economy in the 1960s*, p. 97.
12 Healey, *The Time of My Life*, p. 379.
13 S. N. Broadberry, 'Why was unemployment in postwar Britain so low?', *Bulletin of Economic Research*, 46 (1994), pp. 241–61.
14 Cairncross, *Managing the British Economy in the 1960s*, p. 41.
15 Healey, *The Time of my Life*, p. 386.
16 Lawson, *The View from No. 11*, p. 273.
17 Colin Thain and Maurice Wright, *The Treasury and Whitehall – the Planning and Control of Public Expenditure, 1976–1993*, Clarendon Press, Oxford, 1995, pp. 33–4.
18 ibid., p. 42.

19 Young, *One of Us*, p. 240; Geoffrey Howe, *Conflict of Loyalty*, Macmillan, London, 1994, pp. 187–8.
20 Howe, *Conflict of Loyalty*, p144.
21 Norman Lamont, *In Office*, Little, Brown, London, 1999, p. 304.
22 Andrew Rawnsley, *Servants of the People – the Inside Story of New Labour*, Hamish Hamilton, London, 2000, p. 160.
23 James Callaghan, *Time and Chance*, Collins, London, 1987, p. 519.

Chapter 2 International policy-making

1 Dell, *The Chancellors*, p. 116.
2 Howe, *Conflict of Loyalty*, p. 597.
3 Margaret Thatcher, *The Downing Street Years*, HarperCollins, London 1993, p. 309.
4 Jenkins, *Life at the Centre*, p. 302.
5 Lawson, *The View from No. 11*, p. 274.
6 Healey, *The Time of My Life*, p. 419.
7 Pimlott, *Hugh Dalton*, p. 429.
8 ibid., pp. 429–30.
9 ibid., p. 434.
10 Barbara Castle, *Fighting All the Way*, autobiography.
11 Dalton, *High Tide and After*, p. 254.
12 Wendy Carlin, 'West German Growth and Institutions, 1945–90' in Nicholas Crafts and Gianni Toniolo, *Economic Growth in Europe Since 1945*.
13 Kenneth Morgan, *Labour People: Leaders and Lieutenants Hardie to Kinnock*, Oxford University Press, Oxford, 1987, pp. 159–60.
14 D. Cameron Watt, *Succeeding John Bull-America in Britain's Place 1900–1975*, Cambridge University Press, Cambridge, 1984, p. 127.
15 Young, *This Blessed Plot*, pp. 44–5.
16 Pimlott, *Hugh Dalton*, p. 387.
17 Dell, *The Chancellors*, pp. 304–5.
18 Ian Gilmore and Mark Garnett, *Whatever Happened to the Tories: the Conservatives Since 1945*, Fourth Estate, London,

1997, p. 69.
19 ibid., p. 66.
20 Young, *This Blessed Plot*, p. 117.
21 ibid., p. 118.
22 John Campbell, *Edward Heath*, Jonathan Cape, London, 1993, p. 236.
23 Alan Milward, *The European Rescue of the Nation-State*, Routledge, London, 1992, p. 351.
24 Reginald Maudling, *Memoirs*, Sidgwick & Jackson, London, 1978, p. 232.
25 Gore Allen, *The Reluctant Politician: Derick Heathcoat Amory*, Christopher Johnson, London, 1958, p. 40.
26 ibid., p. 42.
27 Donald MacDougall, *The World Dollar Problem*, Macmillan, London, 1957; Robert Triffin, *Europe and the Money Muddle*, Yale University Press, Yale, 1957.
28 Maudling, *Memoirs*, p 104.
29 Healey, *The Time of My Life*, pp. 438–9.
30 Lawson, *The View from No. 11*, pp. 472–5.
31 Christopher Allsopp and David Vine, 'Macroeconomic Policy after EMU', *Oxford Review of Economic Policy*, Vol. 14, No. 3, Autumn 1998, pp. 1–23.
32 Rawnsley, *Servants of the People*, p. 88.

Chapter 3 **What sort of person does the job demand?**

1 Dalton, *High Tide and After,* p.4.
2 Robert Shepherd, *Ian Macleod*, Hutchinson, London, 1994, pp. 528–9.
3 Lawson, *The View from No. 11*, p. 248.
4 Howe, *Conflict of Loyalty*, p. 121.
5 Jenkins, *A Life at the Centre*, p. 215.
6 ibid., p. 216.
7 ibid., p. 221.
8 Dell, *The Chancellors*, p. 163.
9 Jenkins, *A Life at the Centre*, p. 222.
10 Alec Cairncross, *Managing the British Economy in the 1960s – a Treasury Perspective*, Macmillan, London, 1996, p. 92.

11 Shepherd, *Ian Macleod*, p. 528.
12 Thatcher, *The Downing Street Years*, p. 308.
13 ibid.
14 Brian Brivati, *Hugh Gaitskell*, Richard Cohen, London, 1996, pp. 37 and 41.
15 Campbell, *Edward Heath*, p. 178.
16 Pimlott, *Harold Wilson*, HarperCollins, London, 1992, p. 255.
17 ibid., p. 257.
18 Richard Davenport-Hines, *The Macmillans*, Heinemann, London, 1992, p. 286.
19 Lawson, *The View from No. 11*, p. 711.
20 ibid., p. 719.
21 Thatcher, *The Downing Street Years*, pp. 757–8.
22 ibid., pp. 758 and 717.
23 D.R. Thorpe, *Selwyn Lloyd*, Jonathan Cape, London, 1989, p. 310.
24 Lawson, *The View from No. 11*, pp. 727–8.
25 Pimlott, *Harold Wilson*, p. 66.
26 Philip Williams (ed.), *The Diary of Hugh Gaitskell, 1945–1956*, p. 216.
27 Pimlott, *Harold Wilson*, p. 157.
28 Hugo Young, *This Blessed Plot – Britain and Europe from Churchill to Blair*, Macmillan, London, 1998, p. 72.

Chapter 4 Cabinet government: relations with colleagues

1 Howe, *Conflict of Loyalty*, p. 144.
2 Pimlott, *Hugh Dalton*, pp. 441–3; Barbara Castle, *Fighting All the Way*, p. 151.
3 Jenkins, *A Life at the Centre*, p. 83.
4 Brivati, *Hugh Gaitskell*, p. 115
5 ibid., p. 108.
6 ibid., p. 117.
7 Philip Williams, *Hugh Gaitskell, a Political Biography*, Jonathan Cape, London, 1979, p. 248.
8 Donald MacDougall, *Don and Mandarin: Memoirs of an Economist*, John Murray, London, 1987, p. 90.
9 R.A.B. Butler, *The Art of the Possible, The Memoirs of Lord*

Butler, Hamish Hamilton, London, 1971, p. 159.
10 ibid., p160.
11 Edward Pearce, *The Lost Leaders*, Little, Brown, London, 1997, p. 33.
12 Davenport-Hines, *The Macmillans*, p. 269.
13 Dell, *The Chancellors*, p. 224.
14 Anthony Howard (ed.), *The Diaries of a Cabinet Minister 1961–70*, Mandarin, London, 1991, p.53.
15 ibid., p. 56.
16 ibid., p. 77.
17 ibid., p. 186.
18 Jenkins, *A Life At The Centre*, p. 224.
19 ibid., pp. 249–50.
20 ibid., p. 277.
21 Howard (ed.), *The Diaries of a Cabinet Minister*, p. 689.
22 ibid.
23 Howe, *Conflict of Loyalty*, p. 78.
24 ibid., p. 175.
25 ibid., p. 147.
26 ibid., p. 186.
27 Jim Prior, *A Balance of Power*, Hamish Hamilton, London, 1984, p. 140.
28 Hugo Young, *One of Us*, p. 219.
29 Howe, *Conflict of Loyalty*, p. 233.
30 ibid., p.234.
31 ibid., p. 240.
32 Thatcher, *The Downing Street Years*, pp. 701–3.

Chapter 5 Economic philosphies: the Tory chancellors

1 Davenport-Hines, *The Macmillans*, pp. 292–3.
2 Alistair Horne, *Macmillan, Vol. I, 1894–1956*, Macmillan, London, 1988, p. 243.
3 ibid., p. 74.
4 ibid., p. 84.
5 ibid., p. 103.
6 Howard, *RAB, The Life of R.A. Butler*, p. 156.
7 Horne, *Macmillan*, p. 93.

8 Pearce, *The Lost Leaders*, p. 9.
9 ibid., p. 76.
10 Alec Cairncross, *The British Economy Since 1945: Economic Policy and Performance, 1945–1990*, Blackwell for the Institute of Contemporary British History, Oxford and London, 1992, p. 95.
11 Roger Middleton, *The British Economy since 1945*, Macmillan, London, 2000.
12 Shepherd, *Enoch Powell*, p. 164.
13 Milton Friedman, 'The Quantity Theory of Money: A Restatement', in M. Friedman (ed.), *Studies in the Quantity Theory of Money*, Chicago University Press, Chicago, 1966.
14 Maudling, *Memoirs*, p. 28.
15 ibid., p. 237.
16 Campbell, *Edward Heath*, pp. 233–4.
17 Pearce, *The Lost Leaders*.
18 Robert Shepherd, *Enoch Powell: a Biography*, Hutchinson, London, 1996, p. 422.
19 Edward Heath, *The Course of My Life*, Hodder & Stoughton, London, 1998, p. 520.
20 Hugo Young, *One of Us, A Biography of Margaret Thatcher*, Macmillan, London, 1989, p. 107.

Chapter 6 Economic philosophies: Labour chancellors

1 Pimlott, *Hugh Dalton*, p. 56.
2 Morgan, *Callaghan: A Life*, p. 175.
3 ibid., pp. 220 and 238.
4 Pimlott, *Harold Wilson*, p. 603.
5 Jenkins, *A Life at the Centre*, p. 364.
6 Brivati, *Hugh Gaitskell*, p. 83.
7 ibid., p 98.
8 Healey, *The Time of My Life*, p. 378.
9 ibid.
10 ibid., pp. 379–80.
11 Pearce, *The Lost Leaders*, p. 220
12 Frank Field, *The State of Dependency – Welfare Under Labour*, The Social Market Foundation, London, 2000, p. 145.

13 The policy has been set out in many Treasury documents, such as 'Steering a stable course for lasting prosperity', the November 1998 Pre-Budget Report.
14 Eddie George, 'The New Lady of Threadneedle Street' in *Bank of England Quarterly Bulletin*, Vol. 38, No. 2, May 1998, pp. 173–7.
15 A. Alesina and L.H. Summers 'Central Bank Independence and Macroeconomic Performance', *Journal of Money Credit and Banking*, Vol. 25, May 1993, pp. 151–62.

Chapter 7 What happened to the economy

1 Nicholas Crafts and Charles Bean, 'British Economic Growth since 1945: relative economic decline ... and renaissance?', in Crafts and Toniolo, *Economic Growth in Europe Since 1945*, p. 133.
2 Peter Hennessy, *Never Again, Britain 1945–51*, Jonathan Cape, London, 1972, p. 130.
3 Michael Foot, *Aneurin Bevan: a biography*, Vol. II 1945–60, Davis Poynter, 1973, p. 35.
4 Pimlott, *Hugh Dalton*, p. 457.
5 Dell, *The Chancellors*, p. 61.
6 Dalton, *HighTide and After*, p. 4.
7 See Crafts and Bean, 'British Economic Growth since 1945', for a summary.
8 John Cole, *As It Seemed to Me*, Phoenix, London, 1996, p. 83.
9 Cairncross, *Managing the British Economy in the 1960s*, p. 69.
10 Douglas Jay, *Change and Fortune: a Political Record*, Hutchinson, London, 1980.
11 Cairncross, *Managing the British Economy in the 1960s*, p. 65.
12 ibid.
13 Pearce, *The Lost Leaders*, p. 351.
14 Dell, *The Chancellors*, p. 381.
15 R. Bacon and W.A. Eltis, *Britain's Economic Problem: too Few Producers*, Macmillan, London, 1970.
16 K. Brunner and A.H. Meltzer, 'Government, the Private Sector and "Crowding Out"', *The Banker*, 126 (1976), pp. 765–9.
17 Crafts, 'Economic Growth' in N.F.R. Crafts and Nicholas

Woodward (eds.), *The British Economy Since 1945*, Oxford University Press, Oxford, 1991.

18 Richard Layard and Stephen Nickell, 'Unemployed in Britain', *Economica*, 53 (1986), pp. 5121–69.

19 Broadberry, 'Why was unemployment in postwar Britain so low?', pp. 241–61.

20 S. J. Prais, *Productivity and Industrial Structure*, Cambridge University Press, Cambridge, 1981.

21 Jonathan Haskel, 'Imperfect Competition, work practices and productivity growth', *Oxford Bulletin of Economics and Statistics*, 53, (1991), pp. 265–79.

22 P. A. Grout, 'Investment and Wages in the absence of binding contracts: a Nash bargaining approach', *Econometrica*, 52, (1984), pp. 449–60.

Chapter 8 How they dealt with crises

1 Philip Stephens, *Politics and the Pound, the Conservatives' Struggle with Sterling*, Macmillan, London, 1996, p. 229.

2 Lamont, *In Office*, p. 236.

3 ibid., p. 242.

4 ibid., p. 267.

5 Howard (ed.), *The Diaries of a Cabinet Minister*, p. 411.

6 Callaghan, *Time and Chance*, p. 198.

7 ibid., p. 426.

8 Healey, *The Time of My Life*, p. 429.

9 ibid.

10 Dell, *The Chancellors*, p. 434.

11 Young, *One of Us*, p. 215.

12 Howe, *Conflict of Loyalty*, pp. 225 and 233.

13 ibid., p. 244.

Chapter 9 Resignations and reputations

1 Lamont, *In Office*, p. 374.

2 ibid., p. 400.

3 Gilmour and Garnett, *Whatever Happened to the Tories*, p. 84.

4 Butler, *The Art of the Possible*, pp. 160–61.

5 Dell, *The Chancellors*, pp. 202–3.

6 Pimlott, *Hugh Dalton*, p. 534.

7 Dalton, *High Tide and After*, p. 278.

8 Thatcher, *The Downing Street Years*, p. 716.

9 Lawson, *The View from No. 11*, p. 961; Thatcher, *The Downing Street Years*, p. 716.

10 Thatcher, *The Downing Street Years*, p. 718.

11 Lawson, *The View from No. 11*, p. 958.

12 Thatcher, *The Downing Street Years*, p. 703.

13 Lawson, *The View from No. 11*, p. 957.

14 Shepherd, *Enoch Powell*, p. 178.

15 Jenkins, *A Life at the Centre*, p. 303.

16 ibid.

17 ibid.

18 Healey, *The Time of My Life*, p. 466.

19 Simon Burgess, *Stafford Cripps: a Political Life*, Victor Gollancz, London, 1999, p. 312.

20 Morgan, *Labour in Power, 1945–51*, p. 175; David Marquand, in Michael Sissons and Philip French (eds.), *Age of Austerity*, Hodder & Stoughton, London, 1963, p. 167.

21 Burgess, *Stafford Cripps*, p. 313.

22 Lawson, *The View from No. 11*, p. 271.

23 Butler, *The Art of the Possible*, p. 154.

24 Jenkins, *A Life at the Centre*, p. 218.

25 Healey, *The Time of My Life*, p. 372.

26 Lamont, *In Office*, pp. 35 and 36.

27 Healey, *The Time of My Life*, pp. 253 and 373.

28 John Major, *John Major: the Autobiography*, HarperCollins, London, 1999, p. 135.

29 Jenkins, *A Life at the Centre*, p. 220.

Chapter 10 Perspective

1 Dell, *The Chancellors*, pp. 552–3.

2 Millward, *The European Rescue of the Nation-State*, p. 433; Peter Clarke, *Hope and Glory: Britain 1900–1990*, Penguin, London, 1996, p. 404.

Index